CW00735638

Investment Planning 2011/12

Investment Planning 2011/12
The Adviser's Guide

Second edition

Chris Gilchrist, Editor

Danby Bloch, Series Editor

taxbriefs
financial publishing

© 2011 Copyright Taxbriefs Limited

All rights reserved. No part of this work covered by the publisher's copyright may be reproduced or copied in any form or by any means (graphic, electronic or mechanical, including photocopying, recording, taping, or information storage and retrieval systems) without the written prior permission of the publishers or a licence permitting restricted copying in the United Kingdom issued by the Copyright Licencing Agency Ltd, 90 Tottenham Court Road, London W1T 4LP.

Every effort has been made to ensure that the information in this book is correct. No liability can be accepted for any loss incurred in any way whatsoever by any person relying solely on the information contained in this publication.

Taxbriefs Limited
Centaur Media plc
St Giles House
50 Poland Street
London W1F 7AX

Telephone 020 7970 6471
Facsimile 020 7970 6485
info@taxbriefs.co.uk
www.taxbriefs.co.uk

ISBN 978-1-905482-47-4

Printed and bound by CPI Group (UK) Ltd, Croydon, CR0 4YY

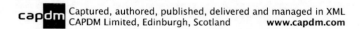

Captured, authored, published, delivered and managed in XML
CAPDM Limited, Edinburgh, Scotland   www.capdm.com

About the Authors

Chris Gilchrist

Chris is a director of a firm of IFAs specialising in investment. His 35-year career includes financial journalism and authorship as well as roles in financial services businesses. He is the author of five financial books including *Unit Trusts — what every investor should know* and *The Sunday Times Guide to Tax-Free Savings*, and a contributor to *Managing Collective Investment Funds*, the definitive guide for operators and regulators of collective funds. He edits a monthly investment newsletter, *The IRS Report*.

Kevin Rothwell

Kevin has spent over 30 years in the financial services industry and has practical hands-on experience of private client investment management, investment administration and dealing, settlement and custody. Kevin also has a high degree of specialist knowledge in areas such as financial planning, estate and tax planning, probates, trusts and managing unquoted assets such as property, land and business assets. Kevin operates his own consultancy and training company and provides training on specialised investment subjects and on a range of UK and international investment examinations offered by the Securities & Investment Institute. He is a fellow of the Securities & Investment Institute and writes a number of UK and international investment exam workbooks.

Jane Vessey

Jane's career spans hands-on experience of investment analysis and fund management with competencies in executive training and as a university lecturer. She graduated in Mathematics from Oxford University and is a CFA® Charterholder. She has some 18 years' experience working in the investment industry, starting out as an equity analyst before becoming an investment manager. She was based in London and Tokyo and took responsibility for managing equity portfolios invested in the Japanese and other Asian markets. In 1990 Jane moved to Indonesia and established and ran an investment management operation on behalf of MeesPierson. She took responsibility for all areas of the business, including investment, operations, marketing and administration. Whilst in Asia, Jane was involved in providing training to capital market participants, state officials and teaching at courses provided by local universities. She has been a visiting lecturer at Cass, the City University Business School, teaching classes in asset management and valuation, and is a visiting lecturer at Cranfield Business School. She also teaches a CFA revision course at a number of business schools including Cass and Said Business School, Oxford. She has written and published notes for students taking the

CFA examinations. Jane is an associate at BPP Professional Education where she teaches courses covering investment management and related topics. Jane has just completed a three year term as a director of the CFA Society of the UK and co-chair of the CFA UK Professional Development Committee.

Contents

Part 1: Investments and markets

Introduction

Economic theory makes general statements about the role of savings and investment, but the way saving and investing operates is heavily conditioned by national laws, cultures and regulatory systems. In chapter 1, we note that the UK's retail saving and investing markets were until recently dominated by occupational pension schemes and life assurers. Their decline and that of the systems they developed to smooth investment returns make it harder for individuals to invest 'safely'.

In chapter 2, we look at the history of UK regulation, explaining why 'light touch' was policymakers' preferred option until 2000. The 'single powerful regulator' model pioneered by the UK in the form of the FSA has not been as effective as advocates had hoped. But the FSA's proposals for the regulation of advice promise a bright future for highly-qualified independent advisers.

Economic and business cycles (though in reality irregular enough that their cyclicality remains disputed) form the basis of everyday experience. As we show in chapter 3, the credit crunch and ensuing crisis have caused a wholesale revision of economic developments since the 1980s. Few people are now likely to place the confidence in economic models that was common until 2007.

Chapter 4 addresses the issue of the different types of investment. Practitioners differ in their categorisation of assets, but at a fundamental level, investments are securities (shares or bonds), physical (eg property) or derivatives.

Over a century's worth of data on investment returns is now available (chapter 5), but a key issue remains what level of returns investors can reasonably expect from the different asset classes, and how much benefit they can expect to gain from diversification. Reinvestment of income and regular saving are proven methods of enhancing returns.

Chapter 1
Investment and investing

The forms in which individuals encounter finance in their everyday lives — such as car and home insurance, mortgages, short-term deposits and credit cards — enable them to live within a comfort zone of relative ignorance. You do not need to know how insurers rate cars and their drivers, or how banks price mortgages or credit score credit card applicants, in order to be able to use these products sensibly and to your personal advantage. Investment is different. You cannot simply trust a 'brand name' and buy investments over a high street counter — or rather, you are unwise to do so, and most people intuitively understand this. People realise that they need to know about different types of investment in order to make sensible decisions, but few people have enough knowledge to make such decisions with confidence. So most people rely on investment advisers, who must not only have technical knowledge of many different types of investment, but must also have an understanding of the role of investment within the economy.

The various types of investments available — ranging from shares in companies to cash deposits — reconcile the different needs of savers and the requirements of business, governments and other organisations that need finance. A developed economy is one in which surplus capital is used to finance the production of goods and services that people want (as measured by whether they are prepared to pay for them). The way surplus capital has been collected and allocated in Western economies has changed substantially over time within a broadly liberal-democratic framework that has given an increasingly important role to markets. As in many other fields, periods of stability have alternated with bursts of rapid change.

The change of most significance for individual savers and investors since 1945 has been the progressive separation of the ownership of publicly listed companies from the management of them. In the 19th century and up to 1945, most public companies had dominant shareholders, usually the families of their founders, who also acted as directors and managers. Today, this is an exceptional case. Most large public companies are managed by professional managers and are owned (primarily) by financial institutions. Particularly in the US and the UK, institutional shareholders have been, in general, passive and have permitted professional managers to secure a steadily larger share of the returns from the business in the form of remuneration, bonuses and share options. The dangers of this system were shown in the excessive risks run by banks in 2004–07, which were a rational response by the managers to a situation where there was enormous potential for personal gain from success and extremely limited potential for personal loss in the event of failure.

But this is only one particularly outstanding example. The lack of co-ordination of the interests of managers and shareholders is endemic in the management of public companies, and measures to mitigate this problem (one that has a long history in the literature of economics) are among the most important probable developments in capital markets over the next decade. The more astute among the financial regulators understand that if the incentives to take excessive risk are strong enough, no formal system of regulation is likely to control them. Thus significant reforms to 'corporate governance', an area that has often been derided for worthy statements of intent and politically correct box-ticking, are almost certain to be proposed, affecting the control of, and incentives permitted to, managers. To the extent that they protect shareholders, such moves will represent a natural extension of the long-term trend in the governance of capital markets over the past century.

1 The economic role of savings and investment

The supply of capital

In a market economy, individuals' buying and selling decisions convey information to providers of goods and services in the form of prices. The fact that higher or lower prices are achievable for specific goods encourages providers to produce more goods or discourages them from producing more. If they are encouraged to produce more, they need to finance an increase in production, and in most cases this requires capital. Traditionally, economics has viewed production as needing two forms of finance:

- Working capital, which bridges the gap between producing goods and being paid for them.
- Investment capital, required for the creation of new production facilities.

Working capital is regarded as a function of the credit markets and is supplied by commercial banks through overdrafts or other short-term borrowing facilities such as letters of credit and trade bills. Investment capital, to the extent that it exceeds the net profits generated by the business that are available for reinvestment, is supplied by investors in the form of long-term loans or equity.

While this model has broadly applied in Western economies for some 200 years, the methods, institutions and intermediaries have altered over time. Working capital used to be provided on a personal basis by merchants and small local banks, then by regional banks, then by national banks and now by multinational commercial banks. Investment capital used to be provided by wealthy individuals as equity, then by a wider network of wealthy individuals as long-term loans and from the 20th century onwards as equity or loans tradable on exchanges, which became progressively more heavily regulated.

Economists defined the primary role of these exchanges as the raising of new capital and their secondary role as the trading of existing loans and equity. Critics of markets and their often wild gyrations have used this distinction to characterise markets as casinos that fail to serve their primary role, but this misses the point. It is only because investors know they are capable of selling a long-term investment if they need to that they are prepared to commit capital to it in the first place. The tradability of capital is a key development in Western economies in facilitating the flow of capital, and an important measure of the progress of emerging economies is their ability to replace the foreign capital they typically use in the first phase of development with mechanisms for converting their own domestic savings into investment. Almost always this requires the creation and regulation of capital markets and of institutions that convert individual savings into long-term investments.

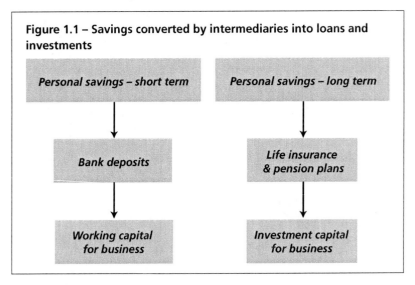

Figure 1.1 – Savings converted by intermediaries into loans and investments

Personal savings – short term

Personal savings – long term

Bank deposits

Life insurance & pension plans

Working capital for business

Investment capital for business

Why people save

Economists use simple models of saving and investment at a macroeconomic level. In fact, saving and investment must simply balance in most accepted models. But mainstream neoclassical economics has struggled to provide convincing models to explain individual savings behaviour. The principal problem with the neoclassical model is that it assumes rationality and the possession of far more information than most people ever do in fact have, so theories that assume that individuals assess their potential lifetime income in making current spending and saving decisions have always seemed rather remote from reality. The concept of 'bounded rationality' was introduced to justify the contention that even with incomplete rationality and incomplete information people would still tend to produce the outcomes predicted by theory. But the 'expected utility theory' of savings behaviour falls far short of being a useful model for real life applications.

Writers on behavioural finance have criticised mainstream economic theory and generated their own variations of expected utility theory, in which they claim to incorporate more of the irrationality that is observed in real life. 'Prospect theory' and the 'behavioural life cycle hypothesis' suggest that people do make judgments about their overall requirements for income over their expected lifetime and adjust saving and spending behaviour accordingly, but with biases that contradict the rationality assumptions in the mainstream neoclassical model. These theories have few practical applications. At a macro level, high rates of personal saving in developing economies are common and are usually explained by the absence of welfare or state pension systems, but low rates of saving in developed economies are less easy to explain on the basis of current economic theories.

The biggest gap between mainstream neoclassical theory and behavioural finance is in the field of risk. Neoclassical theory assumes symmetrical risk preferences, but behavioural finance has established that in most fields where risk is involved, including investment, our desire to avoid loss is approximately twice as strong as our desire for gain. The powerful bias this imparts to behaviour (and almost certainly to market trends) is an acknowledged fact, but is not yet adequately described by any theoretical model. Nevertheless, it is probably the most important issue facing the investment adviser and is dealt with in this chapter and in part 4.

The actual amount of saving is another key economic issue. Investment is financed from saving, and it is ultimately the savings of the personal sector that are recycled into business investment. The UK's domestic net savings have been low for many years, so if private sector investment is greater than these savings, it has to be financed by capital inflows from abroad. While an excess of domestic savings can result in too much investment – China is often cited in this regard – a deficit of savings means there is a possibility that too little investment will occur.

One reason why the UK savings rate is so low is that a disproportionately large fraction of the net disposable income of the personal sector has been devoted to residential property (by payment of rent or mortgage repayments). But the consequent increase in the value of residential property does not result in any increase in national wealth. The view that the undesirable consequences of long-term real appreciation of residential property values outweigh any benefits is becoming part of an economic consensus. Given a political reluctance to force people to save more, the UK's savings deficit cannot easily be altered except by enabling people to spend less on property. A reversal or attenuation of policies giving fiscal benefits for home ownership may therefore at some point be accompanied by policies that encourage saving that is recycled into productive investment.

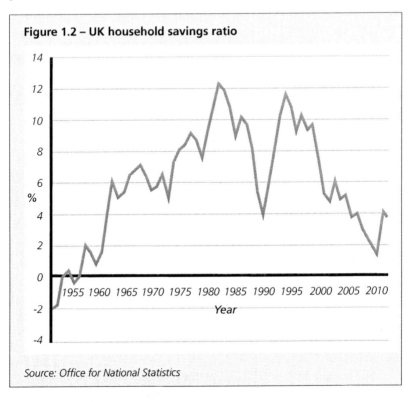

Figure 1.2 – UK household savings ratio

Source: Office for National Statistics

The role of intermediation

Financial intermediation enables the small savings of individuals to be aggregated and used for investment.

Commercial banks serve as aggregators for deposits, which are made available as loans to businesses needing working capital. Banks can also provide capital to businesses in the form of longer-term loans. However, given that most depositors have the right to withdraw their cash at relatively short notice, such a mismatch of liabilities and assets involves risk to the bank, which requires that it hold more capital in relation to longer-term loans. In recent years, commercial banks have disintermediated from longer-term financing, through the 'originate-and-distribute' model involving securitisation of loans which are then purchased by longer-term investors. Such disintermediation is a global trend, though it has gone further in the US than in continental Europe. The difficulties for the originate-and-distribute model revealed by the 2007–09 credit crunch resulted in more companies bypassing banks altogether and sourcing loan finance through the issue of long-term loans to investors.

In Europe, banks have often provided equity finance as well as longer-term loan finance, but this form of financing has come under increasing pressure and the increased risk-weighted capital requirements for banks imposed by regulators following the credit crunch are likely to discourage banks from this type of activity. In the UK, commercial banks have rarely provided equity finance to business. That role has been filled primarily by long-term investors such as pension funds and life assurers, whose practice was to buy shares and hold them for years if not decades. From the 1960s onwards, collective investment funds have played a larger role, and in the past two decades various forms of venture capital fund have become a significant source of capital for smaller companies. Venture capital funds display a characteristic feature of financial intermediation: the chains tend to become longer than in other business sectors. Many venture capital funds are financed by investment from pension funds, and such investment can be at one remove: for example, the pension fund invests in a pooled fund managed by an external manager, who in turn allocates some capital to a venture capital fund run by a different manager.

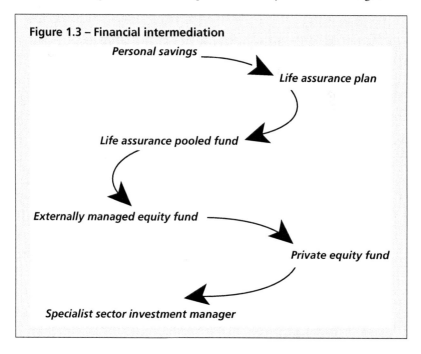

Figure 1.3 – Financial intermediation

Personal savings

Life assurance plan

Life assurance pooled fund

Externally managed equity fund

Private equity fund

Specialist sector investment manager

Long chains of intermediation are usually regarded by economists as inefficient; often they are the result of regulations preventing incomers from breaking existing chains. In financial markets, they are sometimes partly the result of regulation but more often they arise from the ability of highly specialised firms to capture a portion of transaction charges or management fees. One factor is that rapid changes in financial markets have made it less attractive to institutions to build capabilities that may quickly become obsolete, leaving many available niches for intermediaries. Another explanation for longer than normal chains of intermediation is that the purchasers of investments are not price sensitive, partly because of the opacity of charges but also because of the inability of most investors to accurately assess the value of the services provided – an endemic problem in investment management that is explored in part 2 and part 3.

Investing institutions

The promises made by most businesses to their customers are of a relatively short-term nature, and regulation in the interests of consumer protection has tended to focus on safety standards and accurate descriptions. Finance, and investment in particular, presents special challenges because the promises are of such a long-term nature, and the potentially catastrophic consequences of large-scale fraud or mismanagement – not just for many thousands of people and their families but also for the system as a whole – are such that both banks and long-term investing institutions are subject to special laws or regulatory regimes (see chapter 2).

Hence in most countries, in addition to banks, there are special categories of institution that play a major role in long-term savings. In the UK, the most important have been life assurance companies and pension funds, both being subject to specific law and regulation that both protected the public and created barriers to entry. For most of the 20th century these institutions dominated the investment markets because of their large cash inflows and steadily increasing pools of assets.

Today, both types of institution could be seen as dinosaurs destined for extinction. While UK life assurance funds still hold in excess of £1,400bn in assets, they are experiencing larger annual redemptions and maturities than new premiums. Companies specialising in managing 'run-off' have acquired many mature life funds, and only a minority of the funds that existed 20 years ago are still open to new business. Occupational defined-benefit pension schemes likewise hold over £800bn in assets, but because the vast majority is closed to new entrants and existing members retire and eventually die, these pools too are certain to shrink at an increasingly rapid rate in coming decades.

From modest beginnings in the 1930s, collective investment funds have grown to form a larger part of the investment market, accounting for £500bn in assets in 2009. The two varieties subject to most regulation, unit trusts and open-ended investment companies, account for over 90% of total collective investment fund capital. However, their annual inflows have, in many years, been modest compared with the historic inflows to pension funds.

If timescales announced in 2009 are adhered to, the proposed new national occupational pension scheme, National Employment Savings Trust (NEST), will by 2015 have annual cash inflows of in excess of several billion pounds a year and over the next 50 years this scheme could effectively become the UK's largest single investing institution. The format of the scheme is likely to set the agenda for other defined-contribution pension schemes and, if the experience of the US is a guide, could generate considerable popular interest in the management of retirement savings accounts.

Table 1.1 – Regular premiums paid on UK life insurance policies

Year	£ millions	Year	£ millions
1983	3,685	1996	12,098
1984	4,349	1997	12,352
1985	4,748	1998	12,856
1986	5,474	1999	12,965
1987	6,322	2000	13,157
1988	7,378	2001	12,273
1989	8,169	2002	11,863
1990	9,094	2003	12,724
1991	10,043	2004	10,985
1992	10,856	2005	9,908
1993	11,065	2006	9,944
1994	11,476	2007	9,829
1995	12,493	2008	8,247

Source: Association of British Insurers

2 The returns on investment

From an economic perspective, the returns achieved on investments pay for higher standards of living through enhanced productivity, higher wages and higher dividend payments to shareholders. It was the negative return on much of the investment mandated by the state in the Soviet Union that led to its collapse: the system generated no surplus to pay for the better standard of living that people had been led to expect.

However, given the perceived risks involved, businesses and individuals usually require a return on investment far in excess of the 'risk-free' rate, which economists often assume is equivalent to the return on long-term index-linked government bonds. While neoclassical economic theory posits an equilibrium state at which all desirable investment occurs, behavioural finance suggests that risk aversion on the part of the investor biases the required returns upwards so that in general a less than optimal amount of investment may occur.

In recent years, economists have researched links between investment and demographics. In general it appears that countries in which the proportion of the population entering the workforce is growing much faster than the proportion leaving the workforce achieve higher rates of growth in gross domestic product, creating more opportunities for profitable investment. Hence emerging economies such as India and Brazil offer greater investment opportunities than mature economies such as Britain, France or Germany.

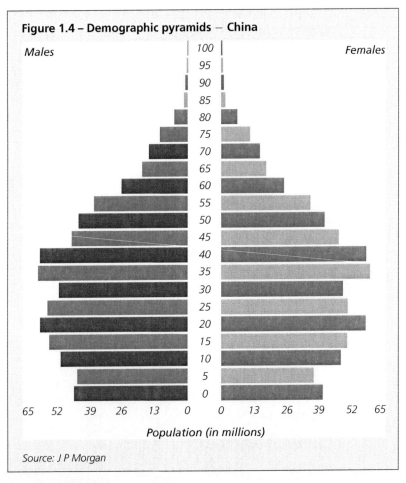

Figure 1.4 – Demographic pyramids – China

Population (in millions)

Source: J P Morgan

The individual perspective

From the individual's perspective, the desire for a high rate of return is tempered by the more powerful wish to avoid loss. In reality, very few

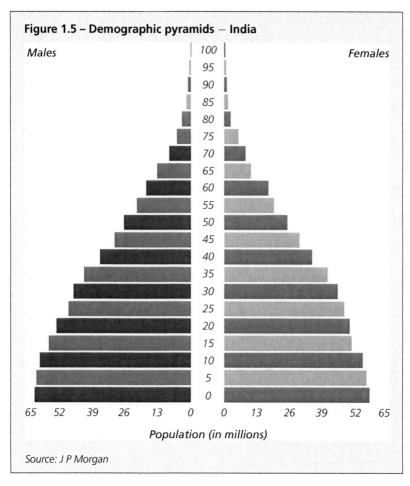

Figure 1.5 – Demographic pyramids – India

Males

Females

100
95
90
85
80
75
70
65
60
55
50
45
40
35
30
25
20
15
10
5
0

| 65 | 52 | 39 | 26 | 13 | 0 | 0 | 13 | 26 | 39 | 52 | 65 |

Population (in millions)

Source: J P Morgan

individuals can achieve their aims if they only achieve the risk-free rate of return. Hence a key issue in investing is the extent and nature of the risk involved in obtaining the required rate of return. While most people can quickly and intuitively grasp that there is such a relationship, quantifying it and clearly explaining its implications, as well as methods of lowering and managing the risk, are among the most important challenges facing any adviser.

While finance theory over the past 50 years has emphasised total return (all that the investor receives by way of income and capital gain) as the correct comparative measure, individual investors still tend to view capital and income returns separately and indeed differently, and they are broadly right to do so. Total return is a useful measure for comparing one investment or portfolio with another, but it is not so useful in designing portfolios, especially where there are specific requirements for income. Because of the volatility of market prices, it is dangerous to assume that gains will be accumulated in a steady fashion and will therefore be available to be encashed and spent: both real life experience and academic studies show there is a real risk of using up all one's capital. However, in the very long run, most investors do spend some of their capital — so how the capital and income components of return are secured and spent is a key issue in investment planning (see part 2 and part 4).

3 The role of markets

We have already referred to the distinction between the primary and secondary role of markets, defined as the raising of capital and the trading of capital. These activities are subject to two different regimes and involve different institutions.

Primary capital markets

Raising capital on behalf of businesses is the role of investment banks, many of which are now part of large multi-function banking groups that include personal and business banking. In the past, investment banks had ongoing relationships with companies and advised them on the majority of their financial transactions. Today, though, the bulk of capital raising for larger businesses is performed as a one-off activity. A company may put its proposal on a capital-raising exercise to two or three banks and choose the one that offers the best terms. The bank is then responsible for formulating the offer and its documentation and finding the buyers for the securities that are offered, a task it will often share with a stockbroker.

The rules governing listings on stock exchanges have, in general, become steadily more demanding over the past century. A listing is a passport to raising capital, and to the use of shares to purchase other businesses, so an important part of the listing process is testing the bona fides of firms seeking a listing. Individuals with a criminal record, for instance, may not serve as directors of companies applying for a listing on the London Stock Exchange. The bank managing an issue is responsible for a company's compliance with the listing rules and for the preparation of audited financial information contained in a prospectus on which investors can rely. In the UK, the London Stock Exchange itself used to be responsible for the rules, but these are now the responsibility of the UK Listing Authority, part of the Financial Services Authority.

In the UK, a business 'going public' by obtaining a listing on the London Stock Exchange used to make an 'offer for sale', when a prospectus was issued and advertised directly to the public. This was the method used in almost all the UK's privatisations, such as BT and British Gas, and demutualisations like Halifax and Standard Life. It is, however, both costly and cumbersome, and today the majority of businesses obtaining a listing on the London Stock

Exchange issue shares through placings. Here the investment bank obtains commitments from a number of investment managers to subscribe for shares at a set price. Some of them and/or the bank itself also subscribe for some shares that they then make available to other buyers once trading commences. Most individuals cannot buy shares directly from the bank but do so through the market once trading begins. In many cases, the bank makes some shares available to one or more stockbrokers, which in turn select the clients to whom such shares are offered. Some stockbrokers are known for their regular participation in such placings, which in good times offer their clients quick and easy profits, since if the bank has done its job well there will be enough demand to cause the share price to rise above the placing price when trading commences.

Where banks are involved in raising new loan capital through the issue of bonds, they solicit subscriptions direct from investment managers. Though individual investors can buy bonds through the London Stock Exchange, most transactions are conducted directly between dealers and institutional investors.

The amount of new capital raised through equity and bond issues varies substantially from year to year, tending to follow a 'feast-and-famine' pattern. During the Great Moderation – see section 3 – finance theorists promoted the substitution of debt for equity in the interest of 'balance sheet efficiency'. Highly leveraged private equity (with debt-to-equity ratios as high as 8 to 1) was the extreme example of this trend. Following the credit crunch of 2007–09, however, many businesses were forced by the non-availability of credit to issue new equity in order to pay off debt.

Table 1.2 – Value of companies listed on the UK stock market

| | LSE | | AIM | |
Date	No of companies	Amount raised (£bn)	No of companies	Amount raised (£m)
UK and Irish				
1981	2,485	100	N/A	N/A
1982	2,357	122	"	"
1983	2,295	157	"	"
1984	2,248	206	"	"
1985	2,188	247	"	"
1986	2,173	324	"	"
1987	2,135	366	"	"
1988	2,054	398	"	"
1989	2,015	515	"	"
1990	2,006	451	"	"
1991	1,915	536	"	"
1992	1,678	624	"	"
1993	1,927	810	"	"
1994	2,070	775	"	"
UK only				
1995	2,078	900	121	2
1996	2,171	1,012	252	5
1997	2,157	1,251	308	6
1998	2,087	1,422	312	4
1999	1,945	1,820	347	13
2000	1,904	1,797	524	15
2001	1,809	1,524	629	12
2002	1,701	1,148	704	10
2003	1,557	1,356	754	18
2004	1,465	1,481	1,021	32
2005	1,214	1,781	1,399	57
2006	1,146	1,932	1,634	91
2007	1,239	1,932	1,694	97
2008	1,080	1,288	1,546	38
2009	1,026	1,731	1,293	57
2010	1,004	1,952	1,194	79

Source: London Stock Exchange

Secondary capital markets

The trading of existing capital in the form of bonds and shares takes place on stock exchanges, which create trading and settlement systems to eliminate, as far as possible, the risk of non-payment or non-delivery, usually referred to as counterparty risk. These mechanisms can play an important role: in Wall Street's great crash in 1929, one reason for the spreading panic was that the reporting of transactions lagged so far behind actual trading that investors did not know whether they had sold or at what price. Paper-based ownership systems create huge difficulties for clearing and settlement, and the electronic registration and transfer of share ownership has largely eliminated delays that were endemic in the old system.

Like other stock exchanges, London long ago abandoned face-to-face dealing on trading floors and its sophisticated electronic trading platform, SETS, handles around £140bn of equity transactions each month. Market makers take on the obligation of quoting prices at which they will buy and sell shares (for each security these bid and ask prices are good up to a certain value of shares, the 'normal market size'). Stockbrokers can see the different market makers' quotes but can also let the system allocate purchases and sales automatically to the market maker offering the best price. Individual investors can access much of this information themselves by subscribing to 'level 2' price services, which are now used by day traders who effectively act as an additional source of market liquidity.

Property markets

Commercial property does not constitute a market in the same way as shares and bonds do, since there is no central trading or clearing system. However, a larger proportion of UK commercial property is leased, as opposed to owner-occupied, than in most other European nations. This results in an active market in transactions in offices, shops and industrial property. Standardised forms of lease make it easier to compare and value such properties. The UK also has a number of large and active property investment and management companies, now mostly in the form of real estate investment trusts (REITs).

The bulk of commercial property is owned by the long-term investing institutions — life assurance companies and pension funds. But collective investment funds investing in commercial property have grown in number, size and specialisation in the past decade, making this asset class easily accessible by individual investors (see part 3).

The same is not true for residential property, where personal ownership of properties remains almost the only way for individuals to participate. Institutional ownership of residential property on a large scale is common in continental Europe but was prevented by UK tax law and other laws that favoured tenants over landlords for most of the postwar period. The assured shorthold tenancy system introduced in 1988 has balanced the interests of landlord and tenant, but tax issues have remained an obstacle to the establishment of real estate investment trusts (REITs) investing in residential property. It is likely that such vehicles will be established in coming years and make this asset class accessible to individual investors.

The development of investment markets

While the number of individuals directly owning shares in exchange-listed companies has increased substantially since the 1950s in the UK – though to a far lesser extent than in the US – the bulk of personal long-term savings in the UK and in other European countries is intermediated by pension funds, life assurers and many varieties of pooled or collective fund.

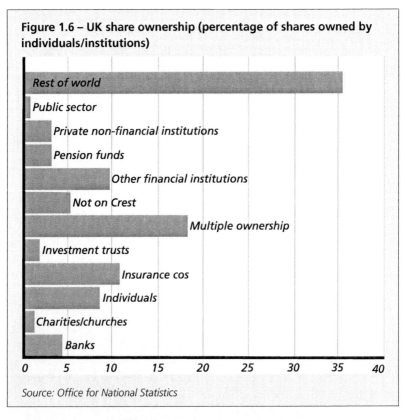

Figure 1.6 – UK share ownership (percentage of shares owned by individuals/institutions)

Source: Office for National Statistics

Just as the commercial banks drew on a widening pool of deposits from individuals to finance working capital loans during the 20th century, so institutions took shape to channel the modest longer-term savings of individuals into investments in industry. In the UK, the most important institutions of the first half of the 20th century were life assurance companies and friendly societies, followed by occupational pension funds from the 1950s and by collective investment funds from the 1970s.

Table 1.3 – Assets controlled by pension funds and life assurers from 1981

	Market value of pension funds (net assets) £	Insurance: combined: balance sheet (total investments) £
1981	63,435	67,669
1982	84,198	88,634
1983	110,970	106,061
1984	139,290	124,874
1985	168,059	142,563
1986	211,201	174,058
1987	227,552	187,457
1988	267,445	213,696
1989	338,950	264,338
1990	302,715	242,061
1991	343,634	286,973
1992	381,997	337,618
1993	480,547	453,052
1994	443,467	424,769
1995	508,581	515,075
1996	543,879	567349
1997	656,874	687,631
1998	699,191	789,727
1999	812,228	930,175
2000	765,199	923,424
2001	711,572	896,374
2002	610,441	832,453
2003	692,694	882,904
2004	761,066	959,971
2005	9149,55	1,107,989
2006	1,010,794	1,200,840
2007	1,023,979	1,262,844
2008	864,606	1,109,546
2009	1,124,262	1,210,785

As of 8/12/2010. Figures not seasonally adjusted.
Source: Office of National Statistics

There was an important distinction between the intermediation role played by the commercial banks and that played by life assurers and pension funds. In the case of deposits, capital security and the rate of interest obtainable are the key concerns of the depositor, and these are matched by the concerns of the borrower regarding availability of funds and the interest rate payable. The interest rate paid by the borrower and the rate received by the depositor usually move up and down in tandem, with the banks' lending margin remaining roughly constant. But the life assurers and pension funds placed capital in loans and equities whose prices fluctuated in often dramatic fashion on the exchanges. Rather than transmitting these fluctuations to their savers, these institutions instead used smoothing mechanisms to convert the volatile returns from investments into steady returns for savers. Foremost among these mechanisms were the with-profits system for life assurers and the 'final salary' or defined-benefit pension plan.

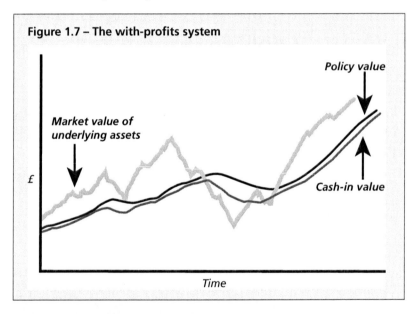

Figure 1.7 – The with-profits system

Members of a final salary pension scheme operating on the basis of one-sixtieth of salary for each year of pensionable service could be confident of a retirement income after a normal lifetime of work of two-thirds of pre-retirement earnings. Their personal annual contributions towards the scheme were typically of the order of 5%–10% of salary. They did not need to make additional retirement savings to provide an adequate retirement income.

Those with less generous pension schemes could contribute on a monthly basis to a with-profits endowment policy maturing at their intended retirement date. Between 1960 and the late 1990s these policies usually delivered annual returns well in excess of inflation, often as high as 10% a year in real terms, and capital could normally be invested to produce an adequate income. Though both pensions and life assurance had their problems, they delivered largely satisfactory results to a significant minority of the population.

Both life assurance and pensions products assumed that over the long term the average rates of return from major asset classes – principally shares, commercial property and bonds – would correspond to historical experience. A rate of return lower than the average return expected from the chosen portfolio of assets was allocated to savers, leaving a safety buffer of surplus capital which was reflected in a growing sum of unallocated capital for with-profit assurers (the 'inherited estate') or a surplus over liabilities for the pension fund. This surplus was assumed to be sufficient to cope with any short-term decline in returns.

The end of smoothing

The systems of life assurance and pensions worked well in UK until the late 1980s but over the next two decades they went into what was probably terminal decline as a result of two major trends. In both cases, a major problem was that the historical success of the system led to more optimistic assumptions regarding the rate of return that would be achieved in future, thus reducing the safety margin. Life assurers raised reversionary bonuses, which were added yearly to policy values and could not thereafter be withdrawn, and also terminal bonuses, so that pay-outs at maturity represented annualised historical returns for policyholders of up to 15%. But when interest rates started to fall as a result of the 'Great Moderation' (see section 3), assurers were too slow to cut their bonus rates and quickly used up most of the surplus capital they had accumulated over previous decades.

Occupational pension funds, too, were subject to pressures that led to the erosion of the surpluses that were a necessary part of the system. Companies whose pension funds were in surplus could choose to take contribution 'holidays' which increased the returns to their shareholders. This trend was exacerbated by the misguided application of rules by the tax authorities, so that pension fund surpluses above a certain level generated additional corporation tax bills for the sponsors.

The second major problem was that both life assurers and pension funds in the UK had allocated progressively larger proportions of their capital to equities, on the basis of sound historical evidence that equities generated higher returns for long-term investors (see chapter 5). However, most modelling of portfolio returns consistently underestimated the volatility of equities and thus made insufficient allowance for sharp declines in values.

Regulators began to appreciate the danger of potential capital shortfalls for pension funds and life assurers and both became subject to more stringent regulation, in the case of pension funds from the mid-1990s and for life assurers from 2001. Traditionally neither type of institution needed to report on their investment performance primarily on the basis of actual market valuations (marking to market); they could value their assets on the basis of their long term projected performance. In both cases, the adoption of 'mark to market' valuation rules reduced theoretical surpluses derived from the projection of returns. But the 2001–03 bear market generated many more and far larger deficits for occupational pension funds than anyone had anticipated, while several life assurers had to slash bonus rates to derisory levels in order to remain solvent under new rules with more onerous capital requirements. As a result, pay-outs from long-term life assurance policies have been in decline since 2001, and the number of new with-profits policies initiated each year has shrunk to a small fraction of former levels. Meanwhile a majority of corporate sponsors have closed defined-benefit plans to new members and replaced them with defined-contribution schemes, where the investment risk is transferred from the sponsor to the individual.

So by the first decade of the 21st century, the mechanisms that had been designed to encourage people to save by providing them with steady smoothed returns were in terminal decline. The role of intermediating between savings and investment was now left to collective investment funds, the vast majority of which do not smooth returns and thus expose holders to unwelcome volatility. This gap between the desire of savers for smoothed returns and the volatile unsmoothed returns delivered by most available investments creates both hazard and opportunity for investment advisers.

The demographic framework

Saving and investing take place within a demographic framework that changes slowly and predictably. Like many other Western nations, the UK faces the problem that in coming decades there will be a smaller number of workers and a larger number of pensioners. Increased life expectancy means a larger amount of government spending will have to be used for state pensions and other public services for the retired, notably healthcare. Because the current savings of those in the workforce are insufficient to provide for their own retirement, they need not only to raise the proportion of their earnings that they save but also to pay more (either in tax or in interest on government debt) to support a growing cohort of retirees. This poses hard policy choices which have not been adequately addressed, but which have important implications both for those planning for retirement and those trying to use their capital to support them through a longer than expected retirement.

Saving takes place during employment or self-employment, usually rising from low levels to a peak at ages 40–60. It is common for at least some of the capital accumulated before retirement to be used up during retirement, a

Table 1.4 – Number of members of occupational pension schemes – by membership type and sector[1], 1991–2008[2,3,4]

United Kingdom	*Millions*								
	1991	**1995**	**2000**	**2004**	**2005**	**2006**	**2007**	**2008**	**2009**
Active members	10.7	10.3	10.1	9.8	—	9.2	8.8	9.0	8.7
Private sector	6.5	6.2	5.7	4.8	4.7	4.0	3.6	3.6	3.3
Public sector	4.2	4.1	4.4	5.0	—	5.1	5.2	5.4	5.4
Pensions in payment	7.0	8.5	8.2	9.0	—	8.2	8.5	8.8	9.0
Private sector	3.8	5.0	5.2	5.6	5.3	4.6	4.8	5.0	5.1
Public sector	3.2	3.5	3.0	3.4	—	3.5	3.7	3.9	3.9
Preserved pension entitlements	4.5	7.0	6.7	9.3	—	9.4	9.4	9.9	10.1
Private sector	3.3	5.2	5.2	7.1	6.4	6.5	6.3	6.7	6.6
Public sector	1.2	1.8	1.5	2.2	—	2.9	3.1	3.2	3.5
Total	22.2	25.8	25.0	28.1	—	26.7	26.7	27.7	27.7
Private sector	13.6	16.4	16.1	17.5	16.4	15.2	14.7	15.3	15.0
Public sector	8.6	9.4	8.9	10.6	—	11.5	12.0	12.4	12.7

1. *The 2005 survey did not cover the public sector and total figure is therefore not available.*

2. *Due to changes in the definition of the private and public sectors, estimates for 2000 onwards differ from earlier years. From 2000, organizations such as the Post Office and BBC were reclassified from the public to private sector.*

3. *Changes to methodology for 2006 onwards mean that comparison with 2005 and earlier should be treated with caution.*

4. *Changes to the part of the questionnaire used to estimate pension in payment and preserved pension entitlements in 2008 mean that comparisons with 2007 and earlier should be treated with caution.*

Source: Occupational Pension Schemes Survey

period that has grown longer and longer in proportion to the normal period of employment. In the 1960s many people entered the workforce at age 16 and left it at 65. Today most graduates do not enter the workforce until age 21–22 and though state pension age is being progressively raised to 67 or more, the period of work has grown shorter while the average UK life expectancy of a 65-year-old man has increased from 14 years in 1981 to 20.8 years in 2008.

Yet in the UK, the state pension remains at a subsistence level. Only a minority of workers are members of defined-benefit pension schemes. Most defined-contribution schemes have contribution rates too low to produce more than a fraction of the capital that workers will need to secure the equivalent of a final salary pension. Even if the proposed NEST operates as planned, it will

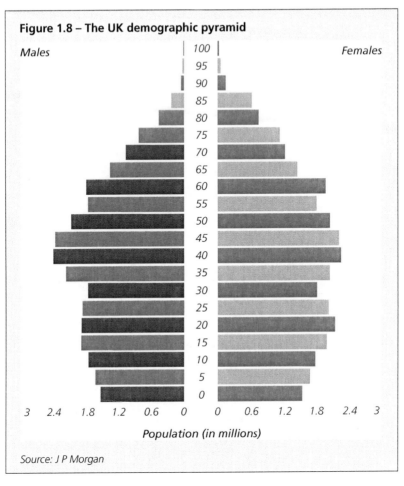

Figure 1.8 – The UK demographic pyramid

Males — Females

Population (in millions)

Source: J P Morgan

be 2060 before its first members retire with entitlements sufficient to provide a retirement income close to the financial planners' conventional target of two-thirds of pre-retirement income.

The fact that the UK's pension system is 'broken' is generally acknowledged by pension experts and by a growing number of politicians, but the remedies proposed so far are insufficient. Raising state pension age more quickly than had been proposed will give people more time to save, but if they do not do so the inadequacy of the state pension will still condemn them to poverty in retirement. The NEST will in time deliver increments to the state pension, roughly commensurate with the former state earnings-related pension (SERPS) or state second pension (S2P), but only for people starting work in 2016 or later. Reducing the number of years' payment of national insurance contributions required to qualify for a full pension will give many more women entitlement to a full state pension, but this will still not be enough to live on. It is therefore predictable that further changes to the UK's retirement savings system will occur in coming years, and because of their scale these changes are likely to have both short- and long-term effects on investment markets.

While it is natural for advisers, like investors, to focus on the current economic climate and market trends, these large demographic and policy issues are likely to play a dominant role in investment markets. When a large cohort of retirees needs to draw on capital to support their standard of living, there may well be periods in which there are more UK sellers of investments than buyers, with the result that price levels may increasingly be set by foreign buyers – an effect that may be seen as part of a general trend towards globalisation but is conceptually quite distinct.

4 The types of investment

Investment is, at least in popular parlance, a quite loose concept, and in recent years the desire of politicians to claim that the public money they are spending is 'investment' has made it even fuzzier. From a political point of view, training more teachers may be called a national 'investment', but since nobody has quantified the return to the nation – which is clearly impossible – nor compared it with the cost, this is at best a metaphorical use of the term.

Likewise, to say that you are investing in yourself by obtaining a higher qualification, though in theory justified by neoclassical economic thinking, is also metaphorical because in practice the return will never be sufficiently quantifiable to establish what return you have achieved.

Investment and speculation

This goes to the heart of what investment must mean it if is to be at all useful as a concept: that both cost and return are quantifiable, and with a reasonable degree of precision. While the boundary between investment and speculation is fuzzy, it is the degree of certainty about the anticipated return that makes something an investment and the degree of uncertainty about the return that makes something a speculation. Thus, nobody will argue with the proposition that gilt-edged securities are an investment since they have explicit guarantees over both the income and capital elements of the return, both of which are precisely quantifiable. A purchase of Unilever shares is an investment because the company's business and finances are long-established and fully audited and all the information you may require about the business and the dividends payable to shareholders is in the public domain. By way of contrast, a purchase of shares in an oil exploration company which has exploration rights over unexplored acreage in a politically unstable region of Africa, and which would need to raise substantial fresh capital if it is to be capable of drilling any wells, exposes you to uncertainty both over the cost (you may have to put up more capital to maintain your shareholding) and return, and is therefore a speculation.

A recurrent feature of investment markets is that in bull markets and periods of optimism, more and more investors define as investments securities that are clearly speculative. In 2005–06, for example, British 'investors' flocked to put down deposits for the purchase 'off plan' of city centre flats, then being built in large numbers. These flats were described as investments, and if purchasers intended to hold them as buy-to-lets for the long-term they could have been. In practice, however, most buyers were only speculating. They paid a deposit and planned to sell their flats using bridging loans as soon as they were built, without ever living in them or renting them out. Because most buyers were speculating, and many did not have the money to proceed with their purchases, there were many more sellers than buyers in 2007–08. Prices for many city centre flats crashed by 40%–50%, far in excess of the national decline in residential property prices.

As this example shows, it is not just the nature of the item but the individual's behaviour that makes something an investment or a speculation. Buying BP shares because you have heard a rumour that the company has found a giant new oil field is speculating. Buying BP shares to hold as part of a long-term income-generating portfolio is an investment.

Investments can be divided into two broad categories: physical and financial.

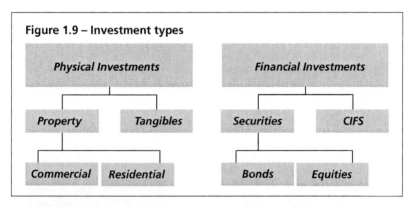

Figure 1.9 – Investment types

Physical investment

Most people consider residential property, and in particular their own home, as an investment. The primary return is the rent that could be obtained by letting, or that is not paid by virtue of ownership. This return (net of insurance and maintenance costs) has often been a relatively low percentage of the current capital value. Over the long term the larger part of the return from residential property has come in the form of capital gain. Because gains on a UK resident's primary personal residence are free of tax, home ownership is exceptionally privileged in tax terms and given the long-term uptrend in values it is not surprising that most people with the ability to do so own their own home.

Owning additional properties as buy-to-lets has become popular following the reform of UK tenancy law that gave landlords effective control of their properties through the use of shorthold tenancies. Around one in ten residential properties is now rented from private landlords. However, many amateur landlords suffered losses in 2005–08 because they bought new-build flats at such high prices that they could not earn a sufficient rental return to meet their financing costs. As with other investments, it is only by owning a portfolio of properties that private landlords can reasonably hope to obtain a consistent return.

Purchase of overseas property for a combination of personal use and holiday letting has also become more popular in the past decade. Traditional retirement areas like Florida have been joined by more exotic destinations such as Turkey and Croatia. Given the wide variations in national property laws, a considerable amount of research may be required to ensure the purchaser has good title and is fully appraised of any potential tax liabilities, in particular capital gains taxes and inheritance taxes, which in some countries are levied on sales of physical property regardless of the nationality or domicile of the owner.

Fractional ownership schemes for holiday properties require smaller capital commitments, but attention must be paid to the resale terms.

In the UK, three types of commercial property are recognized as distinct sub-asset classes:

- Offices, the most valuable but also the most volatile, since both demand and supply are most heavily influenced by business cycles.

- Retail, comprising principally high street shops and shopping malls.

- Industrial, including factories, warehousing and business parks.

New property may be built with leases to tenants agreed beforehand, or speculatively. The latter category has often been substantial during booms, but has diminished to very small proportions since 2007 since bank finance is now extremely difficult to obtain for speculative developments.

The UK is unusual in that a high proportion of commercial property is owned by investing institutions and not by the companies that occupy it. Pension funds and life assurance companies have been the principal owners of commercial property, and the more recent open-ended investment companies and unit trusts investing in the sector account for a small fraction of the amounts held by life and pension funds.

It is possible that following adaptations to the REIT legislation (see below) residential property may become a viable asset class for institutional investment.

This is a common pattern in Continental Europe. Already, much new UK student accommodation is built and leased by private companies.

Property returns and values

The return from commercial property is primarily the rental income, though in times of high inflation and/or economic booms and falling interest rates capital values can rise sharply.

The capital value of property is very sensitive to interest rates, since the conventional basis of valuation is to calculate the rent over a long period, assuming increases at rent reviews, and discount this to a present value using a yield somewhat higher than the relevant gilt yield. A sharp rise in long-term interest rates both raises the initial yield required from property and reduces the present value of the rental income stream.

Initial income yields are highest for industrial property. In this sector, large companies still tend to own their own premises, so the quality of tenant is usually lower than in other sectors. Moreover, firms that rent industrial property more often need to move than do retailers or office users.

Retail property, especially large shopping centres, has become progressively more highly valued in the past three decades, but the rise of internet shopping and an extended squeeze on UK consumer spending have at least temporarily halted this trend. Some supermarkets have undertaken sale-and-leaseback deals for their supermarket sites, obtaining long-term finance on more attractive terms than they could obtain in the bond markets.

The largest renter of office property is the UK government, in the form of its departments and agencies. In the City of London, the largest office market, the international banks are also regarded as triple-A tenants.

Quality of tenant is a major factor in determining the value of a lease. If a tenant were to default in the middle of a slump, the landlord would have difficulty in finding another tenant on similar terms, so property owners prefer the highest quality tenants. Often, developers of office properties will grant an initial triple-A tenant a period of several years at heavily discounted rents in return for their commitment to a long lease of 20 years with 5-yearly rent reviews.

'Prime' properties are those with excellent locations, which can be expected to be easily let in most market conditions, and therefore command a premium price.

Institutional owners of property attempt to balance their portfolios in terms of lease expiries and rent reviews. If rent reviews are evenly spread over a 5-year period, a gradual rise in income can be expected, whereas if they are all bunched in one year, a large rise in income may be followed by a period of no growth for several years. The effect of a decline in rental levels, as seen in 2009–10, will be very minor on a well-spread portfolio since it will affect only a small proportion of leases.

Over the long term institutional investors expect a return from commercial property somewhat higher than that from long-term gilts, the major difference being the expectation of a rise in the income.

Transactions and valuations

Buying and selling commercial property is costly. The biggest item is stamp duty at 4% on transactions of over £500,000 – schemes for avoiding this are the ground for an ongoing battle between the industry and HMR&C. Agents' and valuation fees may add another 1–2% to purchase costs.

There is no centralised market: the terms of ownership, leases and so on are unique to each case; each deal is separately negotiated. This means that taxes, valuation and transaction fees can often amount to 5% of the purchase price. In addition, the ongoing costs of managing commercial property can be substantial. Insurance, maintenance and lease negotiations are the main expenses.

This is part of the reason why Real Estate Investment Trusts (REITs) have become more popular in recent years. They are a special category of investment company that only owns property and are, for the most part, tax-transparent. Because their shares are usually listed on a stock exchange, investors find it easier to trade in and out of than physical property. The result, however, is that the prices of REITs are far more volatile than the value of their underlying assets.

As with residential property, the costs of maintenance can appear low over the short term but are substantial over the life of a building. Some of the 1960s office blocks in the City have been demolished and replaced, so effectively their entire building costs had to be recovered in rents over a period of less than 50 years. Many 1980s office buildings require costly refits to accommodate modern communications and meet environmental standards. The quality of facilities and, increasingly, the running costs for tenants, are a major factor in determining rental levels.

Commercial property owners often employ a rolling valuation model where one-twelfth of the portfolio is valued each month throughout the year. In times of rapid change, they may undertake wider valuations, as in autumn 2008, when several open-ended property funds suspended dealings, not because they did not have the cash to pay investors (they all hold lines of credit for this purpose) but because they were unable to establish a net asset value at which to undertake transactions.

The benchmarks used most often for UK commercial property are those created by the IPD (Investment Property Databank Ltd), whose All Property index is generally used as the widest representative measure of returns.

Many other physical items have been categorised as investments and are referred to in broad terms as 'tangibles'. They include gemstones (especially diamonds), art, antiques, stamps, coins and fine wines. Though some dealers and auction houses have created indices to measure returns, these are far less representative of average experience than are share or bond indices, and need to be treated with caution. From time to time one or other of these tangibles will attract publicity, but the key fact about them all is that the transaction costs are extremely high (often 20%–30%) compared with those in financial investments.

Gold and silver are special cases given their former role in monetary systems. Gold can be purchased as bars or coins, such as the British sovereign or the South African krugerrand. It can also be purchased in the form of certificates (entitling the owner to a portion of physical gold held by a bank) and exchange-traded funds, collective investment funds that issue shares backed by physical gold bars. Silver and gold coinage usually trades at a small premium over the current open market price for the metal.

Financial investment

Financial investment falls into two main categories:

- Securities traded on recognised stock exchanges and collective funds investing in such securities.
- Financial products based on derivatives.

There are two reasons why the definition of securities is limited to those traded on a stock exchange. The first is that the terms of private ownership may be unilaterally changed to the disadvantage of the owner. For example, existing shareholders in a private business may have their ownership diluted by the company's issue of more shares, and a majority shareholder may use their voting power to undertake transactions that benefit them while harming other shareholders. Securities traded on a stock exchange, in contrast, are subject not just to company law but to the rules of the listing authority and/or the exchange, and these provide considerable protection for investors. The second reason is that with securities listed on a stock exchange there is a commitment to enable owners of securities to sell them. Stock exchanges create liquidity, the ability to buy and sell, and just as important they create mechanisms that encourage competitive price creation, which drives down bid-ask spreads (the difference between buying and selling prices) to the benefit of buyers and sellers.

These are among the reasons why shares in private companies are universally regarded as a far riskier form of investment than publicly listed securities.

The principal types of security are bonds (loans) and shares.

Government bonds are a large category of bonds and account for a high proportion of all the listed debt in issue, also includes bonds issued by organisations such as the World Bank, which are considered to have the equivalent of government backing. In the UK, government debt or gilts are issued both in nominal and index-linked forms. 'Linkers' have both the interest payable and the redemption values adjusted with reference to the retail prices index. Gilts are divided into three categories:

- Shorts (where redemption is within five years).

- Mediums (redemption in five to 15 years).

- Longs (redemption after more than 15 years).

Corporate bonds (bonds issued by companies) are graded by rating agencies on scales running from AAA ('triple A') at the top to C– at the bottom. By convention, bonds rated BBB or higher are 'investment grade' and those below this (BB or lower) are 'sub-investment grade', or, colloquially, as 'junk'. The policies of many institutional investors commit them to holding only investment grade bonds. To achieve a rating of AA or above, a company must have sound finances and a business clearly capable of withstanding difficult economic conditions.

A few UK companies still have debentures. These are loans secured against specific assets of the company, usually property. Historically they ranked as the most secure form of corporate loan since, if the company went bust, the proceeds from the relevant assets had to be used to pay off the debenture holders.

Most corporate loans are unsecured, but the terms of the loan (the 'covenant') define the priority of the loan holders in the schedule of debt repayment. Loans defined as 'senior' entitle owners to a higher priority than holders of 'junior' debt.

Convertible loans, in addition to paying a rate of interest and having a redemption date, entitle owners to convert their holdings into ordinary shares in a given ratio (Y shares for £X of stock), usually on specific dates.

As in some other countries, the UK trades government bonds traded through a stock exchange, but most corporate bonds are traded by banks acting as market-makers. In the UK, a small range of corporate bonds is now traded on the London Stock Exchange, making them available to retail investors.

Government bonds in developed countries are a large and very liquid asset class, with extremely small bid-ask spreads and the ability to deal in large size. Bid-ask spreads can be as low as 0.1% and dealing costs even lower.

There is a range of FTSE indices for gilts. For corporate bonds, indices are created by banks and market-makers.

There are conceptual differences between equity and fixed-interest indices. The capitalisation-weighted methodology of equity indices does not necessarily create a representative index in fixed interest, since it can result in the securities of the largest borrowers dominating an index. Since it is typical for financial firms to borrow more than industrial firms, corporate bond indices will often have heavy weightings in the financial sector.

Shares or 'equities' are also called 'ordinary shares' in the UK, and are equivalent to the US term 'common stock'. Companies may have different classes of share, each of which has different entitlements and voting rights. Such structures were commonplace 50 years ago in UK-listed companies but are disliked by institutional shareholders and have also been discouraged by regulators. A few dual-domicile companies such as Shell still have two categories of share, but the vast majority of UK-listed companies have only one class of share and voting rights are almost universally 'one share, one vote'.

UK-listed companies must adhere to many rules. Among the most important are as follows:

- Financial results must be published on, at least, a semi-annual and annual basis.

- All price-sensitive information must be published through the London Stock Exchange Regulatory News Service, so that it is available to all investors at the same time.

- Listed companies must post all their financial information on their own website.

- If the directors become aware that the company's next financial results are anticipated to differ significantly from what is expected, they are obliged to make an announcement explaining this.

- The City Code on Takeovers and Mergers has its own set of rules governing takeover bids and is administered by the Takeover Panel. Its overriding aim is that shareholders should receive equal treatment.

- Shareholders' prior consent must be obtained for any significant new issue of shares.

The majority of companies listed on the London Stock Exchange are UK domiciled, though many multinational companies now maintain share listings in London as well as on their domestic stock exchange. In particular, the Alternative Investment Market, established with less onerous listing requirements for the benefit of smaller companies, has attracted many resource businesses that are domiciled elsewhere.

Table 1.5 – Capital raised by companies on UK stock markets

Date	LSE (New companies) Number of new equity issues	Market value (£m)	AIM (New issues of equity) Market value (£m)
UK and Irish			
1982	59	1,169	N/A
1983	79	1,592	"
1984	87	5,950	"
1985	80	1,462	"
1986	136	8,874	"
1987	155	5,002	"
1988	129	3,790	"
1989	110	7,578	"
1990	120	7,095	"
1991	101	7,474	"
1992	82	2,937	"
1993	180	5,966	"
1994	256	11,519	"
UK only			
1995	190	2,962	95
1996	230	10,607	816
1997	135	7,100	695
1998	124	4,196	558
1999	106	5,353	933
2000	172	11,399	3,074
2001	113	6,922	1,128
2002	59	5,082	976
2003	32	2,445	2,095
2004	58	3,610	4,656
2005	84	5,966	8,942
2006	77	8,415	15,678
2007	52	7,613	16,183
2008	23	3,110	4,312
2009	7	354	5,511
2010	40	7,059	6,957

Note: Figures for the LSE are for domestic UK companies only. Figures for AIM include international companies.
Source: London Stock Exchange

In the UK, the London Stock Exchange (LSE) is the primary exchange where shares are traded, though several smaller exchanges also handle trades for institutional investors. On the LSE, market-makers have obligations to quote bid and offer prices and, at those prices, to deal in 'normal market size' a quantity of shares that can be varied as conditions change. Individual investors transact through stockbrokers (which may be part of the same financial group as market-makers).

Bid-ask spreads on the LSE can be as low as 0.05% for the largest blue chips, but for companies capitalized at under £50m spreads can be as much as 10%. The maximum quantity of shares that can be traded at the quoted price may be as large as £10m for a blue chip, and as small as £1,000 for a small-cap stock.

Dealing costs for individual investors using execution-only online brokers start from a flat £10 per trade, but a more typical rate is £15. Institutions negotiate dealing commissions with brokers.

Most developed markets have a range of indices measuring the performance of groups of shares. The FTSE All Share Index is the widest generally used measure in the UK, and based on some 700 share prices. The FTSE100 Index, based on the largest 100 companies by market capitalisation listed on the LSE, includes many companies with very small fractions of their turnover derived from the UK, so it is not at all representative of UK PLC. FTSE calculates a wide range of indices, including those for sectors of the UK market.

Most indices of share prices are based on market capitalization, which means that a few very large companies often account for as much as half the index. A growing minority of professional investors favour alternative methods of index construction, such as indices based on equal weighting of constituents or on the use of fundamental factors (such as the FTSE RAFI series).

Collective investment funds have been in existence in the UK since the 1870s. The earliest funds invested in loans to foreign governments, but these 'investment trusts' gradually moved into equities and in the 1930s new laws created in response to the investment scandals of the 1920s enabled the creation of unit trusts investing in shares. The extremely robust investor protection built into the structure of unit trusts eliminated fraud and misappropriation of funds from the list of risks that investors faced, and allowed individual investors to obtain a professionally managed spread of investments at low cost. Unit trusts became much more popular in the 1970s and they and their successor open-ended investment companies (OEICs) remain the principal types of collective fund marketed in the UK.

From the 1960s onwards, life assurance companies created their own 'unit funds', so that savers could, as an alternative to the traditional with-profits system, choose to link the value of their savings directly to the performance of one or more funds investing in different types of security.

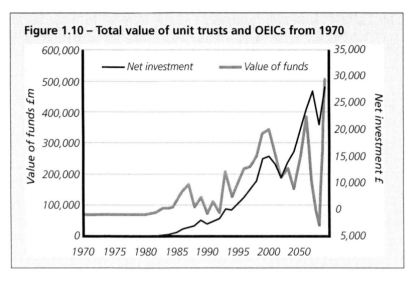

Figure 1.10 – Total value of unit trusts and OEICs from 1970

Most collective funds invest solely in securities. But since the 1990s, a different variety of investment product has offered investment returns by using derivatives. Derivatives are second-order financial instruments, the returns from which depend on the performance of one or more securities, commodities or indices; they include options, futures and swaps (see chapter 4). 'Structured products' such as guaranteed equity bonds, often have a term of three to six years and use derivatives to deliver a proportion of the return from a basket of securities while also providing guarantees of minimum capital values at maturity.

The many varieties of collective investment fund available to UK investors are discussed in detail in part 3, chapter 13.

Valuing companies

The conventional model for valuing companies is called the 'discounted cash flow model'. In principle, the aim is to estimate all the future flows of cash the investor will receive, discount these to a present-day value, convert this to a value per share and compare this figure with the market price of the share.

The model presents a number of huge challenges, and the range of valuations that can be derived can incur substantial variation with even small changes in the assumptions. Among the problems are:

- **Cash flows from dividends.** Current dividends can be taken as a base, but the rate at which dividends are assumed to grow can have a large effect on the total cash generated.

- **The discount rate.** Conventionally, the cost of capital for the company is the rate at which future cash flows should be discounted, but this is itself affected by the financial structure of the company, which can change.

- **Future capital value.** In principle, the model aims to capture all future cash flows, but normally the cash flows after an arbitrary date (usually 10−15 years later) are converted into one capital sum, which is then discounted to a present value. The calculation of such future cash flows and the way in which they are converted into a capital value give scope for wide variations in estimates.

Stockbrokers and banks have their own models and regularly publish estimates of discounted cash flow for companies they analyse.

In practice, most investors pay more attention to three valuation measures which can be used to estimate the comparative value of companies. We look at these below.

Dividend yield

The dividend yield is the income yield on the company's shares. Expressed as a percentage, it is equal to:

$$\frac{\text{Annual dividend payment per share}}{\text{Current share price}} \times 100$$

The highest yields are usually found in businesses regarded as mature and with limited prospects for profit growth in the future, such as utilities or oil 'majors'.

The dividend yield is a function of the dividend pay-out ratio and the share price. The pay-out ratio is the proportion of the company's annual net earnings attributable to shareholders that is paid as dividends. Mature businesses tend to pay out a larger proportion of their profits, often half to two-thirds, while faster-growing businesses, which can deploy retained earnings to earn higher returns, typically have lower pay-out ratios. This is expressed by the 'dividend cover' as the extent to which net earnings exceed dividend payments. A dividend cover of 1.5 means that net earnings are 50% greater than the amount paid out as dividends.

Price-earnings ratio

The price-earnings ratio (PER) is defined as:

$$\frac{\text{Current share price}}{\text{Earnings per share}}$$

Analysts will usually use a measure of earnings per share ('normalised earnings') that excludes one-off capital profits.

One way of describing the PER is as the number of years for which you have to own a share before the earnings attributable to that share equal the purchase price.

In general, PERs are highest for businesses expected to achieve the fastest rates of growth in future profits and lowest for those expected to achieve the lowest rates. 'Growth stocks' are those where high growth rates are generally anticipated by analysts.

In recent years, large fluctuations in profits have led analysts to return to a measure first proposed by Ben Graham, author of the most influential book ever published on investment, *The Intelligent Investor*. Graham advocated use of the cyclically adjusted price-earnings ratio, now usually referred to as 'CAPE'. This takes the average of the last ten years' earnings per share as the basis for calculation of the PER. This is then compared to the average CAPE for a very long run of years for the industry sector or market as a whole to assess whether a share is cheap or dear.

Net asset value

For certain types of business, the net asset value (NAV) is used as a measure of value. The NAV per share is calculated as:

$$\frac{\text{Total assets attributable to shareholders} \ - \ \text{Debts}}{\text{Number of shares in issue}}$$

The NAV may be calculated using a company's stated book values for its assets, or analysts may make their own estimates. In relation to intangible assets such as intellectual copyright, patents and exploration rights, such estimates may vary widely.

The NAV is more precise for businesses investing primarily in tangible assets such as real estate investment trusts and public house or hotel owners.

Valuing bonds

Listed fixed-rate bonds are valued using three principal measures: income yield, redemption yield and duration.

Income yield

The income yield, also referred to as the 'interest yield', 'flat yield' or 'running yield', is usually calculated on interest payments before deduction of tax. Expressed as a percentage it is equal to:

$$\frac{\text{Nominal annual interest}}{\text{Current price}} \times 100$$

The yield should be calculated on the 'clean price', which is the price of the bond excluding any accrued interest. Most bonds accrue interest, so that a purchaser becomes entitled to the next interest payment. Part of the purchase price therefore represents the value of the impending interest payment. The vast majority of bonds distribute interest at six-month intervals.

Where a bond is trading at above par (100), part of the income yield will represent payments of capital to compensate for the capital loss that will occur if the bond is held to maturity.

Redemption yield

The redemption yield, also referred to as the 'yield to maturity' (YTM), is the average annual return investors will receive if they buy a bond at the current price and hold it to maturity. Since the redemption yield includes the value of all future interest payments, an assumption has to be made about the rate at which those payments themselves are assumed to earn interest. It is assumed that the payments earn interest at the same rate as the redemption yield. This makes calculation of redemption yields impossible without a programmable calculator.

With conventional bonds, the maturity value is 'par' or 100. At maturity, there will therefore be a capital gain (if the current price is under 100) or loss (if the current price is over 100), and this has to be added to or deducted from the interest payments to determine the overall average yield.

The redemption yield is conventionally calculated on gross interest payments. Because of this it is often referred to as the 'gross redemption yield' (GRY).

Duration

Duration is a complex comparative measure of bond values. It measures the sensitivity of a bond to changes in the level of interest rates. It is dealt with in depth in chapter 7.

Summary

- Savings and investments in the economy must balance, so if the personal sector's savings are lower than the amounts invested, the difference must come from capital inflows to the country.

- In the UK, final salary pensions and with-profits life assurance provided smoothing mechanisms that reduced fluctuations in the value of investments; the decline of these schemes forces individuals to find other ways of managing risk.

- Investment is distinguished from speculation by the relative certainty of returns; bubbles, followed by crashes and panics, arise when the majority of investors become speculators.

- Physical property, securities and derivatives are the three main classes of investment.

Chapter 2
Regulation

Developed countries have generally established their systems for regulating financial services on a largely piecemeal basis, mostly as a reaction to scandals and other financial turbulence. Few countries directly regulate financial products or explicitly make providers liable for product defects — in stark contrast to the regulation of their manufacturing industries which are subject to the legal enforcement of rules about product quality and safety.

In the UK and several other countries, regulation has concerned itself mainly with capital adequacy and process and has been accompanied by consumer compensation schemes financed by product levies. Such regulation avoids many problematic issues involved in product regulation, but it can create perverse incentives, and in the UK at least, some providers have marketed what could be described as 'toxic' products (such as precipice bonds), yet have incurred penalties far below the commercial benefits they have gained.

1 A brief history of UK investment regulation

It is very helpful to know a little of the history of the development of financial regulation in UK to understand how we have arrived at the current position in terms of both the institutions and successive governments' attitude to regulation.

During the 1920s the UK's existing law governing securities and investments failed to prevent major scandals, several involving the then popular investment trusts. The Prevention of Fraud (Investments) Act of 1939 was the first serious attempt to provide a prescriptive framework with real consumer protection. The legal form of the unit trust was created by this Act and the fact that it has survived largely unchanged, and that no investor in a unit trust has ever suffered a loss from fraud (all potential losses having been made good by either the trustee or the management company), is a testament to the success of this piece of legislation.

Company law places few restrictions on what company directors can do, and rather than make company law too onerous, UK legislators have progressively restricted the ability of private companies to solicit investment from the public. Listed companies enjoy the privilege of being able to raise capital in this way, and pay for it through the more onerous requirements of the UK Listing Authority. These requirements and shareholders' exercise of their rights cannot prevent all cases of abuse, but such instances have been relatively rare in the UK. Unsurprisingly, the majority of cases where directors and promoters have been guilty of outright expropriation or fraud have been small companies lacking the establishment links (the reputable firms of stockbrokers, auditors and legal advisers) that provide another line of defence for investors.

The City Panel on Takeovers and Mergers

A notable development that set the tone for financial regulation in the UK was the establishment of the City Panel on Takeovers and Mergers in 1968. Several hotly contested takeover battles had led to widespread accusations of unfair and improper practices, and a Labour government threatened legislation. In response, the panel was constituted with the backing of the City establishment and the aim of ensuring equal treatment for all shareholders. Its first chairman, Lord Shawcross, was an eminent and formidable lawyer and City grandee, and rapidly made the panel's writ effective (and very rarely challenged, as it could be, by an appeal to the courts), and a secondment to the panel – a self-regulatory body with, initially, no statutory backing – regarded as a career-enhancing move for merchant bankers.

It was the success of the panel that made self-regulation the policymakers' preferred option in financial markets. In its favour were the saving of parliamentary time and the difficulty of creating organisations with remits that were sufficiently flexible to deal with fast-changing markets. The panel's rules were in fact in a state of constant evolution for its first decade and are still subject to change today. In addition, the field in which financial regulation was required in the 1970s did not seem large. Life assurance was already subject to a regime that ostensibly gave the Department of Trade and Industry and the Government Actuary's Department a considerable oversight role; occupational pension funds were not only subject to a body of existing trust law but to a large extent were controlled by actuaries; the London Stock Exchange regulated its own members; and both accountants and solicitors were regulated by their professional bodies.

Margaret Thatcher's Conservative governments had an agenda of deregulation that started with the privatisation of state-owned companies such as BT but also extended to financial services.

The Financial Services Act 1986

The Financial Services Act of 1986 separated the membership and ownership of the Stock Exchange, abolished fixed commissions on share transactions and opened up the issuance and underwriting of securities to foreign firms. This opening up of previously closed and oligopolistic City markets in the 'Big Bang' resulted in the purchase of most of the UK merchant banks by US companies within a few years, the merger or takeover of many stock broking firms and an outburst of innovation in the City. Its effects on retail financial services, though, were initially limited.

The 1986 Act gave the newly established Securities and Investments Board delegated powers to recognise self-regulatory organisations, which policed investment management, derivatives, life assurance and financial advisers. Initially this system seemed to work, but over the next decade these self-regulatory organisations experienced scandals that exposed a lack of diligence in supervising and regulating. Several member firms of the Investment Management Regulatory Organisation were involved in the management of the pension funds looted by Robert Maxwell prior to his death in 1991. The Financial Intermediaries, Managers and Brokers Association (FIMBRA) went through a number of frauds and scandals, the largest being Barlow Clowes, a fraudulent gilt management scheme that lost UK investors over £100m in 1988. The Life Assurance and Unit Trust Regulatory Authority (LAUTRO) created rules for life assurance projections that forced life assurers to assume lower charges than in fact applied to their policies in making maturity projections and failed to prevent life assurers projecting bonus rates that turned out to be overly optimistic. This contributed to the endowment shortfall scandal where hundreds of thousands of mortgage borrowers' policies produced maturity values lower than those required to pay-off their loans.

Equally damaging was the pensions misselling scandal that followed the creation of a new regime of personal pensions in 1988. Providers and salesmen encouraged hundreds of thousands of people to transfer from secure defined-benefit schemes to risky personal pensions, with the result that many suffered substantial losses in their pension entitlements. In both cases, large-scale investigations and restitutions were required. Both FIMBRA and LAUTRO were absorbed into the Personal Investment Authority in 1994, but it did not win the confidence of consumers or politicians.

The Financial Services and Markets Act 2000

The cumulative effect of these failures of self-regulation to prevent extensive damage to the financial situation of ordinary people led to the Labour government's creation of a new and powerful regulator, the Financial Services Authority (FSA). The Financial Services and Markets Act 2000 created a new regulatory framework in which the FSA (which took over from the Securities and Investments Board) absorbed all the former regulators and used its statutory powers to create unified rule books backed by visits, investigations, public reprimands and fines. The Act also transferred the responsibility for banking supervision from the Bank of England to the FSA, but it was not until the credit crunch of 2007–08 that the FSA realised that its supervision in this area was inadequate. It had focused a large part of its efforts on financial advisers, who were perceived as the group most likely to cause harm to consumers.

This large-scale failure to exercise effective regulation where it was most needed badly damaged the credibility of the FSA, which also came under fire from consumer groups for its perceived slowness to respond to the misselling of loan payment protection insurance by the banks. This was despite the convincing evidence of an Office of Fair Trading reference of the sector to the Competition

Commission. The fact that the Competition Commission, rather than the FSA, proposed remedies to avoid consumer detriment in this sector appeared to validate critics' claims that the FSA was behind the curve.

The FSA had, however, made attempts between 2001 and 2007 to alter corporate behaviour by imposing unprecedentedly large fines on banks and life assurers for breaching its rules. Several firms were fined in excess of £1m for such rule breaches, even though some of these were not directly linked to customer losses. The FSA's view seemed to be that adherence to its rule book would ensure that consumers did not incur losses, but it appeared to change this stance when it adopted 'treating customers fairly' as an overriding policy in 2007. While at one level this simply repeated common-sense injunctions about business practice, it also made the point that treating customers fairly was not just about slavish box ticking or rule following but required management at the highest levels to engage in these issues.

Between 2007 and 2009 the FSA formulated a new policy framework for consumer advice in its Retail Distribution Review (RDR), discussed below and in other sections of this book.

In 2009, the Conservative Party committed itself to abolishing the FSA, declaring its intention to transfer the regulator's responsibilities for banking supervision to the Bank of England and to establish a new agency with the sole aim of regulating retail financial services for the protection of consumers.

2 The FSA's remit

In the retail financial sector, the FSA is responsible for regulating bank deposits, shares, unit trusts and open-ended investment companies (OEICs), gilts, futures, mortgages (from 2004) and general insurance (from 2005). In these areas its rules cover dealing, arranging, managing and giving advice – effectively every aspect of businesses engaged in these activities. The FSA has powers to:

- Grant, vary and cancel authorisations to engage in these activities.
- Approve individuals for 'controlled' functions.
- Make specific rules for conduct of business, handling client money, financial promotions and money laundering.
- Take disciplinary action.
- Authorise unit trusts and OEICs.
- Recognise overseas stock exchanges.
- Recognise collective investment schemes operated from jurisdictions outside the UK.

The FSA has four statutory objectives:

- Market confidence.
- Public awareness.
- Protection of consumers.
- Reduction in financial crime.

The FSA is also responsible for implementing many EU directives affecting financial services, most recently the Markets in Financial Services Directive (MiFID), in November 2007. The aim of MiFID is to increase competition and consumer protection in the EU member states. Under new EU procedures, the scope for 'gold plating' (adding domestic content to EU directives) has been limited in order to prevent member states from using these additions to protect domestic firms or practices. The principal measures in MiFID affect wholesale rather than retail markets.

3 The FOS and FSCS

The consumer protection role of the FSA is backed up by the Financial Ombudsman Service (FOS) and the Financial Services Compensation Scheme (FSCS).

The FOS incorporates several pre-existing ombudsman schemes and provides a complaints process for all retail financial products apart from personal pensions, covered by the Pensions Regulator. If customers are dissatisfied with the response of a company to their complaint, they may bring it to the FOS, who will investigate and adjudicate. If an FOS decision is accepted by the complainant, it is binding on the company concerned, but the complainant is not bound by the decision and may refuse to accept it and can resort to the courts. The maximum award is £100,000.

The FSCS is a consumer compensation scheme financed by levies on banks, insurers, investment managers and advisers. The limits on compensation are set by the FSA. They are a maximum of £50,000 for deposits and investments (£100,000 for joint accounts) and 90% of eligible insurance claims. The FSCS pays compensation when an authorised firm goes into liquidation or other circumstances prevent consumers' legitimate claims from being met.

4 The FSA's principles for businesses and individuals

The FSA sets out six principles for regulated business and individuals:

- Integrity.
- The use of skill and diligence.

- The exercise of management and control, especially in relation to risk.

- Financial prudence and the possession of adequate resources.

- Protection of customers' interests.

- The management of conflicts of interest.

The protection of customers' interests is governed by the 'treating customers fairly' initiative introduced in 2007, in which the FSA identified six key outcomes it wished to achieve:

- Treating customers fairly is central to corporate culture.

- Retail products and services are aimed at targeted identified groups of consumers.

- Clear information is given pre-sale, at sale and post-sale.

- Advice is suitable and takes account of individual circumstances.

- Products and services perform in line with expectations.

- There are no post-sale barriers to switching or complaining.

5 The regulation of advice

Until 2004, the FSA operated a 'polarisation' regime that defined advisers as 'tied' or 'independent'. From 2005, a depolarised regime replaced this, in which advisers may be single-tied, multi-tied or whole of market. Single-tied advisers may advise on the products of only one company, for which they act as agents. Multi-tied advisers may tie to different companies for different products (for example company A for life assurance, company B for personal pensions). Whole of market advisers may select products from any company in the market; if they also offer the client the option to pay fees instead of commissions, they may describe themselves as independent financial advisers (IFAs).

Depolarisation was an unsatisfactory compromise between the desire of bancassurers for more freedom in creating viable business models for mass market financial advice and of independent advisers for continued exclusive possession of the IFA label. In its RDR in 2008–09, the FSA made more radical proposals to take effect in 2012. The key elements are:

- A ban on the payment of commission by product providers to advisers.

- A requirement that advisers agree remuneration in advance with clients ('client agreed remuneration').

- A requirement that advisers attain qualifications equal to the Qualifications and Curriculum Development Agency's level 4 (diploma level on the Chartered Insurance Institute classification) by the end of 2012.

Advice will be categorised as 'basic advice', 'sales advice' (or 'restricted advice') and 'independent advice'. Only advisers charging fees and advising over the full range of retail products (whole of market) will be permitted to describe themselves as IFAs. Advisers formerly tied and multi-tied will both be defined as giving sales advice. Basic advice may govern a limited advice process linked to the stakeholder suite of products. 'Generic advice' is restricted to analysis of needs and since it involves no recommendations of products or services it is not covered by FSA rules.

The proposals in the RDR are expected to lead to 'factory gate pricing', in which financial products are made available without any loading for the cost of advice. Advisers may, with the agreement of clients, draw specified fees or commission from products. This generally avoids the need to levy VAT on fees and is expected to become normal practice among IFAs. Client agreements will have to specify precisely what services are being provided in exchange for fees. Fees can be based on the value of the transaction or they can be time related or they may be fixed. But they must be agreed in advance. Ongoing or trail commissions for lump sum investments will have to be justified in relation to the services provided.

The RDR is covered in more detail in chapter 18.

6 Risk-based regulation

The FSA claims to use a risk-based approach, in which the intensity of supervision is related to the perceived risk of consumer detriment. In addition to analysing the periodic returns that firms must file with the regulator, the FSA sends out questionnaires on specific subjects and also engages in mystery shopping exercises. When it sends staff to visit firms, it is likely they will be following up one or more of these.

The FSA's 'enhanced strategy for small firms', initiated in 2008, envisages that 25% of relevant firms will have been visited by the time the exercise concludes in 2011.

7 Enforcement

The Financial Services and Markets Act gives the FSA a considerable range of responses to what it perceives as misconduct or rule breaches:

- It can 'name and shame' and has begin to do so in relation to the number of complaints dealt with by the FOS in relation to major firms.
- It can levy fines for breaches of its rules.
- It can set conditions for the continuance of certain classes of business by regulated firms.

- It can ban individuals from engaging in advising, managing or other controlled functions.

- It can withdraw a firm's authorisation, thus in effect barring it from business altogether.

- It can seek injunctions from the courts against individuals or firms.

The decisions of the FSA can be appealed to the Financial Services and Markets Tribunal.

8 Conduct of business

The meat of the FSA rules is in COBS, its manual of conduct of business rules. As far as advisers are concerned, the most important elements are:

- Definition of two types of client.

- Status disclosure.

- Client money.

- Know your customer.

- Suitability.

- Duty of care.

Two types of client

Customers are either retail or professional.

'**Retail**' clients are all those at that are not professional and are given significantly higher levels of consumer protection.

'**Professional**' essentially means large companies or FSA-authorised firms, but individuals can be classified as 'elective professional clients', which puts them in the same category. Professional clients are assumed to know more and to have more experience of investments, and therefore benefit from a lesser degree of protection.

In order to classify clients as professional, a firm must assess their expertise and knowledge, their experience and their understanding of investment risk. This should be related as closely as possible to the areas in which the firm expects to advise them. Expertise in the area of foreign exchange, for example, could be of little relevance to limited property partnerships.

Some firms deliberately restrict the availability of more complex or risky products such as single strategy hedge funds and geared forms of property investment to clients who have been classified as professional and have signed the requisite forms of consent to the reduction in protection that follows from this.

Status disclosure

Advisers must disclose their precise status at the first meeting with a potential client. The required information is usually contained in the 'services and costs disclosure document' (SCDD), which replaced the 'initial disclosure document' and the 'menu' in November 2007.

The SCDD may be a separate document or may be incorporated into the firm's client agreement.

Client money

If a firm is authorised to handle client money, it must maintain a separate client account for this purpose.

The majority of advisers are not authorised to handle client money, in which case they are barred from ever receiving any money direct from the client except in settlement of fees. All other payments must go to providers of products or services.

The protection created by preventing advisers from handling client money without having the necessary authorisation (which requires greater capital resources) does create disadvantages from the client's point of view. The main drawback is the inconvenience of having to write many cheques or arrange many transfers to different product providers. The increasing use of 'wraps', however, removes this inconvenience, as they usually contain the equivalent of a cash deposit account.

Know your customer

An essential requirement for giving suitable advice is a full knowledge of the client's circumstances. What information is mandatory is defined by the money laundering rules; beyond that, it is the adviser's responsibility to gather any information that may be relevant before giving any advice.

This subject is dealt with in part 4, 'Advising the client'.

Suitability

The suitability of advice must be related to clients' stated needs and their circumstances. Since advice may later be questioned or a complaint made, the reasons the adviser gives for the recommendations made should be clear and unambiguous.

In many cases, advisers will give comprehensive advice, but where a client wishes to be advised only on a specific issue ('limited advice'), this fact must be clearly stated at the outset. But merely stating the advice is limited may not be sufficient and it may be desirable to draw the client's attention to the risk involved in not being advised on other issues — as would be relevant, for example, in the case of an individual in poor health who had declined to be advised on life assurance.

The duty of care

IFAs act on the client's behalf and always owe the client the duty of care. Their obligations in relation to clients are greater than those of a tied agent and correspond to the duties of other professional advisers such as accountants and solicitors.

9 Financial promotions

Most advisers give investment advice in the form of written reports. Often these are preceded and followed by client meetings, and what is said at these meetings can be important, but it is on the quality of written and personalised recommendations that an adviser will normally be judged against the suitability criteria.

In contrast, communications to many people, whether by mail, newspaper advertisements or advertising on TV, radio or the internet, are 'financial promotions' subject to a different set of FSA rules. In the past, fraudulent promotion has been the cause of many large-scale financial losses, so the FSA requires financial promotions to be signed off by an individual specifically authorised within the firm to do this. Since such an individual will also be responsible to more senior managers, the process effectively forces senior management to accept responsibility for all promotions of their firm's financial products and services. The failure to exercise this control effectively can itself be the cause of FSA disciplinary action against a firm.

Any general mailing to clients or prospects can be a financial promotion if it recommends a specific product or a course of action that involves buying a specific product.

The prime requirement for financial promotions is that they must be 'clear, fair and not misleading'. This places the onus clearly on the firm, and there is plenty of evidence of the good practice required from cases that have been adjudicated by the FOS and where the FSA has levied fines and other penalties.

Failures that have led to compensation awards, fines and other penalties include:

- Making claims for which the firm had no or insufficient evidence.

- Emphasising positive outcomes and downplaying risks.

- Positioning negative information where it was less likely to be seen or read.

- Selecting information to exclude data that would have reduced the attractions of the proposition in the promotion.

In large firms, the creation of financial promotions is undertaken by marketing and compliance specialists. Small firms without these resources need to ensure that other people check their promotions. Preferably they should be people who are not involved in the creation of the promotion and who can read it as if they were the recipients. Use of external consultants familiar with the financial promotion rules is also advisable.

Records of the approval of financial promotions must be retained for at least five years.

10 Key features

Advisers recommending specific products must provide documents produced by the product providers containing the key features of these products. These documents must include information about all the relevant contractual terms, charges, costs and encashment penalties and projections of returns using a range of figures set by the FSA.

11 Adviser qualifications

As part of its RDR, the FSA has proposed higher minimum qualifications for advisers effective from 31 December 2012. However, since the attainment of these qualifications will require many advisers to pass several examinations, it has urged advisers to start on this process immediately.

The Financial Services Skills Council is the body charged with defining 'appropriate' examinations. As noted above, the minimum level qualification will correspond to the Qualifications and Curriculum Development Agency's level 4, which is very broadly equivalent to the standard required in the first year of a university undergraduate course.

This level 4 qualification will require up to approximately 370 hours of study and is considerably more demanding than former minimum standards as represented by the Certificate in Financial Planning. The Financial Services Skills Council has defined the framework as one in which certain examinations which validate 'core competency' will be mandatory, and advisers will have to take additional modules depending on their roles.

The core areas will include investment principles and risk, personal taxation and financial services, regulation and risk and IFAs and others who advice on packaged products will need to pass units in pensions and financial protection as well as the practical application of planning.

12 Individual authorisation

The FSA rules require individuals who exercise 'controlled functions' to be designated as 'fit and proper', for which the requirements are honesty, integrity and reputation. They should be competent, capable and financially sound. Firms should use these criteria in assessing employees.

Controlled functions include any activities where the individual has significant influence on dealing with customers in relation to regulated investments, and handling customers' property in regulated investments.

Relevant controlled functions within adviser firms are:

CF1 Director

CF2 Non-executive director

CF3 Chief executive

CF4 Partner

CF Apportionment and oversight (exercising management responsibility over advisers and other employees, for example managing the training and competence process)

CF10 Compliance (responsibility for a firm's adherence to FSA rules)

CF11 Money laundering (the money laundering reporting officer is responsible for the firm's adherence to the money laundering rules)

CF29 Significant management (responsibility for a business unit or function)

CF30 Adviser

The FSA Handbook defines the responsibility of individuals in each of these categories.

13 Training and competence

The FSA rules require firms to demonstrate that advisers are competent and that they receive ongoing training relevant to the areas in which they advise.

Firms must assess advisers and certify them as competent to give advice before they start advising clients. The FSCS publishes lists of the qualifications advisers need to obtain before advising in specific areas, such as pension transfers and equity release.

Firms must maintain training and competence files for each adviser recording their training and their periodic assessments.

14 Non-regulated investments

The major category of investment that is not regulated by the FSA is real property. Collective funds investing in real property (whether in the UK or overseas) require authorisation in order to be capable of being marketed to the public, but physical investment is not covered by FSA rules.

A number of companies that have offered land banking and other property investment schemes have been judged by the FSA to have been operating unauthorised collective investment schemes. Though operating such schemes is not illegal, their promotion is severely restricted and any public advertising, especially to normal (not elective professional) investors, is likely to be in breach of FSA rules.

Other tangible investments such as stamps, gems, coins and wine are also unregulated, though any firm that creates a collective fund investing in these assets will have to conform to FSA rules.

Though Unregulated Collective Investment Schemes (UCIS) are not authorised or regulated by the FSA, their marketing and promotion does fall within FSA regulation. Advisers also have to follow the 'know your client' rules carefully and ensure:

- They fully disclose all relevant risk factors.
- They assess the client's risk capacity before making any recommendation.

15 International factors

The FSA has the power to 'recognise' overseas stock exchanges. Any investment listed on a recognised exchange may be included within UK-authorised funds. Investments listed on non-recognised exchanges count as unlisted, and may therefore be ineligible for some funds or subject to restrictions when held by others.

EU law requires that funds conforming to the Undertaking for Collective Investments in Transferable Securities (UCITS) laws may be marketed anywhere within the EU subject only to domestic marketing rules. In practice, the only funds marketed in this way are those located in tax havens such as Luxembourg, since nationally authorised funds tend to create unwelcome tax complications when owned by foreign nationals.

The FSA has the power to approve the investor protection arrangements of a non-EU jurisdiction as being equivalent to the minimum required under EU law, in which case any fund within that jurisdiction may be marketed in the UK without specific authorisation. In the case of overseas-based funds, advisers should always ascertain the exact protection and compensation that applies. The inclusion of savings accounts with Icelandic banks in some offshore life bonds led to substantial losses for investors when these banks failed in 2008, since these accounts were not covered by the compensation arrangements made by the UK Treasury for domestic UK accounts.

Summary

- The UK regulatory system does not directly regulate financial products but instead regulates processes, firms and individuals.
- The success of a self-regulatory model with the Takeover Panel in the 1970s led to more widespread deregulation after 'Big Bang' in 1988. The failure of

the Self Regulatory Organisations set up after the Big Bang reforms led to the 2000 legislation establishing the Financial Services Authority.

- The FSA has far greater powers than former regulators and has used them to impose heavy fines, but it failed to prevent major scandals with retail financial products as well as the banking excesses that caused the credit crunch.

- The FSA regulates all financial services and investments except tangible investments that include property. It formulates the UK application of relevant EU legislation.

- The regulatory system consists of the FSA, the Financial Ombudsman Scheme for adjudicating consumer complaints and the Financial Services Compensation Scheme.

- The FSA's rules for advisers are contained in its Conduct of Business Rules (COBs).

- The FSA's regulation of investment advice changed from polarisation to depolarisation and in 2012 will sharply differentiate independent fee-based advice from 'restricted advice'.

- The FSA will become the Financial Conduct Authority in 2011 but most of its rules will remain unchanged.

Chapter 3
Economic and investment cycles

Until the events of 2007–09, the two principal economic schools, which had offered differing but similar views of the process of economic growth, had been on a gently converging path. The neoclassical school, based on the central axiom of 'rational expectations', provided the theoretical framework on which policymakers came increasingly to rely from the 1980s onwards and generally does not favour governmental economic intervention. But its foundations were shaky: hard evidence that people did not operate on the basis required by theory, often acting 'irrationally', accumulated steadily and led to the emergence of 'behavioural finance' as a separate field of enquiry, generating extensive evidence of 'irrationality' and casting doubt on the central neoclassical axioms.

This has so far had little influence on the complex macroeconomic models used by almost all governments, central banks and independent forecasters, which remain largely based on Keynesian elements. The more pragmatic Keynesian view, which unlike the neoclassical system legitimises government intervention in the fields of both fiscal and monetary policy, focuses on demand management through a combination of fiscal and monetary policy. Though this appeared less necessary during the 'Great Moderation' (see below), this proved a narrow Western perspective, since developing economies continued to display the same boom and bust cycles that previous generations of economists had struggled to explain.

The credit crunch of 2007–09 resulted in widespread resort to traditional Keynesian measures in the US, the UK and Europe, with one crucial difference. In the past, the fiscal and monetary authorities had never had to step beyond the functions of lender of last resort in guaranteeing the stability of the financial system. In contrast, with unprecedented interventions involving state support of commercial and investment banks, the guaranteeing of private sector liabilities such as mortgages and, most significantly, the adoption of 'purchaser of last resort' functions by finance ministries and central banks and of quantitative easing monetary policies, the governments of developed countries in 2007–09 stepped into regions where economic theories had never been tested before.

1 Theories downgraded

Of particular significance for the theories is the fact that, by acting as buyers of last resort, and using public money to buy securities (as quantitative easing does), governments blur the line between monetary and fiscal policy. This conforms to Keynesian theory, which sees monetary and fiscal policy as tools to be used in pursuit of policy objectives, but is in conflict with classical/neoclassical theory, which broadly argues for independent central banks to follow inflation targets and act independently of government and fiscal policy.

One result of the crunch was that policymakers had to view with suspicion the economic models that had so notably failed to forecast not just the credit crunch as an event but most of its major components. The reaction of some economists that even bigger and more complex models are needed has understandably been met with widespread scepticism. At the same time, central banks, finance ministries and others cannot admit in public that these models have comprehensively failed. Behind the scenes, new and more radical economic views are receiving more attention and a considerable reshaping of mainstream economics is likely to result over the next decade.

In the meantime, the lack of any generally accepted theoretical model is a fact that may distress officials and academics but may have few practical implications for macroeconomic management, where the pragmatism of politicians can often be relied upon to override theoretical considerations. In the field of finance theory, in contrast, the effects of model failure are certain to be profound, and in particular the modelling of risk seems likely to change significantly, an issue of great importance for investment advisers that is covered in chapter 9.

2 The business cycle

The idea of more or less regular oscillations in business activity goes back to the economist Clement Juglar in the 1860s. But his proposed cycle of seven to 11 years, often referred to as the 'business cycle', is in fact a cycle relating to fixed capital investment. Joseph Schumpeter and other Austrian economists devoted more attention to cycles in the mid-20th century. In practice, what is more often referred to as the business cycle today is the inventory cycle, identified by Kitchin and with a typical periodicity of three to five years. Two other possible cycles are the Kuznets cycle for infrastructure investment, with a periodicity of 15 to 25 years, and the Kondratieff cycle of 45 to 60 years.

Neoclassical economic theory gives little space for cycles of any kind – neoclassical economists tend to refer to 'fluctuations' rather than cycles – and the notion of more or less regular waves receives only limited support from historical data. Nevertheless, there clearly are fluctuations in inventories, for example, which have a cyclical nature even if the variations do not always conform to an ideal pattern. In broad terms, businesses tend to build their physical stocks of goods in boom times and then run them down in recession. At the top of the boom, businesses typically find themselves holding excessive amounts of stock and the first stage of the down turn is marked by businesses deciding to make fewer goods and reduce their inventories. Likewise, at the bottom of the cycle, businesses may find themselves holding too little stock, and the green shoots of recovery may become apparent when businesses initiate orders for goods and rebuild their stock levels.

Neoclassical theory

Classical and neoclassical economic models posit an equilibrium or stable state for the economy. When this is disturbed by exogenous shocks of any kind, for example such external changes as commodity price rises, the system diverges from equilibrium – upwards in a boom, downwards in a recession – and then gradually and naturally returns to equilibrium. Neoclassical theory mainly focuses on the most efficient allocation of scarce resources, rather than issues of overall supply and demand within an economy.

This model, with its implication that government action generally does not help and may even hinder the equilibrium-seeking tendency of the system, was that of the Austrian economists (Schumpeter and Hayek) and of the US school of monetarists led by Milton Friedman. This approach was influential throughout the 1980s and 1990s, when exclusively market-based solutions were at their most modish.

Keynesian theory

Keynesian economics has a different view. It suggests that economies can end up in non-equilibrium states as a result of endogenous factors, such as the 'paradox of thrift' (a policy of higher savings makes sense for an individual concerned about an economic downturn, but it will create an even bigger downturn if the policy is adopted collectively). The multiplier that amplifies the effects of government-led fiscal stimulus, on the other hand, can lead to a state of excess demand with a tendency to generate inflation.

Nobel prizewinner Paul Samuelson formulated an 'oscillator' Keynesian model incorporating these endogenous factors. The Keynesian model, with its justification of government action to manage demand, appeared to be validated by the recovery from the Great Depression of the 1930s, but seemed to fail when a succession of stop-go phases in Western economies ended in stagflation in the 1970s.

Financial instability

A model which has received more attention in recent years is the financial instability hypothesis of Hyman Minsky. In this, it is a credit cycle that is responsible for a gradual increase in business investment, leading eventually to over-investment (and often a bubble) and then to a recession. This is based in part on the Austrian economist's contention that the setting of interest rates by a central bank, as opposed to allowing the free market to set rates, inevitably results in interest rates being too high or too low and thus encourages too much or too little investment. The hypothesis appears to offer a more convincing explanation of the credit binge of 2004–06 and its collapse in 2007–09 than either the neoclassical or Keynesian schools.

These hypotheses about the business cycle demonstrate that there is no generally accepted model to explain the tendency of economic activity to rise and fall. But the acceptance and use of a particular model by politicians and central bankers at any particular time can have profound effects on economic activity.

3 The Great Moderation

The effects of accepting a particular economic model were crucial in what has been termed the 'Great Moderation', a period lasting from 1982 through to about 2006. For much of this period, economic fluctuations – in rates of growth of gross domestic product (GDP), interest rates and inflation – were much lower than in the two preceding decades, a phenomenon attributed by many economists to the use of a different model of economic management.

The challenge of inflation

The 1970s had witnessed a steady rise in rates of inflation in the US and Europe. One factor – held by some economists to be the decisive one – was that politicians used Keynesian methods to deal with recessions, regularly expanding demand through both fiscal and monetary measures. This was particularly the case with the 1973 oil shock, when an embargo by Middle Eastern oil producers in an attempt to counter US support for Israel resulted in a quadrupling of the price of oil to $12 a barrel by 1974.

Central bankers largely accommodated this extraordinary economic shock with increases in the money supply, and the simultaneous breakdown of the post-World War II Bretton Woods system for managing exchange rates, the end of US dollar convertibility into gold and the effective devaluation of the US dollar created exceptionally turbulent conditions. A severe stock market crash in 1973–74 (larger than that of 2008–09 in inflation-adjusted terms) was followed by a recovery. But by 1979, inflation rates reached record levels in the UK and US.

The monetarist solution

Paul Volcker was appointed chairman of the US Federal Reserve in 1979 and applied strict monetary measures, heavily influenced by the monetarist school of economics, to drive out inflation. Interest rates were raised to extraordinary levels – 20% in 1981 – and the result was the worst recession since the 1930s, with record levels of unemployment and business failure. Volcker was much criticised, but the policy worked and inflation fell from over 13% in 1981 to just over 3% in 1983.

Over the same period in the UK, Margaret Thatcher's Conservative government also applied tight monetary and fiscal policies, in contrast to the accommodative Keynesianism of previous years. Again, high interest rates and record levels of unemployment resulted. These were exacerbated by a substantial rise in the sterling exchange rate that led to the permanent closure of the significant part of UK manufacturing industry that was heavily dependent on exports. But inflation fell from 18% in 1980 to 4.6% in 1983, and in both the US and UK the remainder of the 1980s saw lower rates of inflation and less volatility in the economy generally.

Complacency

For the US and much of Europe, the great moderation continued through the 1990s, though the UK suffered the consequences of a failed attempt to enter the precursor of the Eurozone in 1991−92 and its economy suffered from the high interest rates used to defend the currency. However, in both the US and the UK the monetarist/classical recipe of light-touch regulation and − at least in theory − balanced budgets was taken to be responsible for the abolition of stop-go or, as one UK politician unwisely said, "No return to boom and bust".

The rapid economic recovery from the technology bubble and crash of 1999−2001 was taken as further evidence that the light touch regulatory regime and appropriate monetary policies (independently managed in the UK by the Bank of England from 1997) could be relied upon to steer the economy.

History revised

The credit crunch of 2007−09 put an end to this view of recent history. The largest financial crisis for a century involved: the near-meltdown of the world financial system, the need for governments to inject hundreds of billions into the recapitalisation of banks, the extension of state guarantees to further hundreds of billions of private liabilities such as mortgages and the adoption in the US, the UK and Europe of exceptional monetary policies to counter a spiral of deflation.

Subsequent to the initial shock, sovereign states' assumption of liabilities arising from bank failures has added another dimension, creating tensions within the eurozone between nations that had used cheap credit to permit asset booms and loss of competitiveness (principally Greece, Ireland and Spain), and those (Germany in particular) which had constrained credit and wages. New methods of underwriting the finances of weaker states have been created to prevent sovereign defaults, but the fiscal rules enshrined in European treaties have failed and have yet to be replaced with credible new arrangements.

4 Boom and bust

Politicians in Western democracies have known for over a century that winning elections depends on delivering steady increases in prosperity, if not for the majority then at least for a significant minority of the population. In the attempt to achieve this, they have reached for whatever tools the technicians (increasingly informed by highly abstract economic theories) have provided them with. Given the lack of incontrovertible evidence about cause and effect relationships – economics is not a hard science and, according to some detractors, barely even qualifies as a social science – it is not surprising that a wide variety of tools have been employed.

Who benefits?

Only now is a more anthropological-sociological strand of economics emerging that asks questions to which it is possible to give more certain answers. Among them are what might be considered classic economic questions about incentives, such as, in a given period, who were the main beneficiaries of the methods and models employed to manage the economy? Such questions are given point by the credit crunch, where light-touch regulation played a role – possibly even a major one – in facilitating disaster. The laissez-faire approach to regulating markets was justified by an economic theory that largely lacked empirical foundations. It may have contributed substantially to the creation of an unsustainable credit boom and a fragile financial system, whose major beneficiaries were the banks and bankers with the greatest lobbying power.

An awareness that the generally accepted theory of the day usually serves the most powerful interest groups of the day may prove a useful corrective to the groupthink that allowed regulators and central bankers to stand by while the financial system headed to the verge of the abyss.

Bubbles throughout history

The 'herding' that applied in the period leading up to the credit crunch is only one example of a phenomenon that has been observed in financial markets for almost three centuries, the earliest examples being tulip mania in Holland in 1637 and the South Sea Bubble in England in 1720. Such bubbles are a universal feature of financial markets across time and across the globe.

The pattern is that an asset's price rises steadily for some time, and then begins to accelerate, with a huge expansion in the number of participants, until it rises to levels far in excess of any rational estimation of the asset's economic value. It may stay at a high level for some time, but when the collapse comes, it is precipitous, with price gaps denying owners any opportunity to sell except at far below the previous day's or hour's price. Since a majority of participants buy at or near the peak, collective losses are enormous and have effects across the whole economy.

The dotcom boom

A notable recent example, the 'dotcom' boom and bust of 1999–2000, saw a wave of enthusiasm about the transformative business potential of the internet. More and more investors bought shares in internet and telecom businesses that were expected to benefit. Hundreds of companies with plans for dotcom business floated shares on stock exchanges at increasingly high valuations. Yet on the first day of dealings, the share prices of many of these new issues rose by 50%–100%. Share prices rose by up to 1,000% over a year, often for businesses that had no or negligible revenues and that were incurring substantial losses. In 2000–01, the majority of dotcom shares crashed, with losses of 90%–99% not unusual.

Greater fool theory

A popular explanation of bubbles is the 'greater fool' theory. The investor knows he is a fool to buy at a high price but believes he will be able to sell to a greater fool at an even higher price. Behavioural finance experiments, though, have so far failed to identify a convincing explanation of bubbles, although Kahneman, the father of behavioural finance, did identify over-confidence as perhaps behavioural finance's most robust finding. Excessive optimism was almost certainly a large component in bankers' and investors' behaviour.

Some commentators have also claimed that the concept of 'bounded rationality' can explain bubbles. This is a concept of neoclassical theory that permits individuals to have less than perfect information and to analyse it less than perfectly while still producing collective behaviour conforming to rational expectations. In other words we do the best we can or at least well enough with limited resources. But while these claims seem to be obviously true in general terms, behavioural economists and others have questioned their practical impact.

Bounded rationality and behavioural finance agree that in many situations humans substitute heuristics – rules of thumb – for proper rational analysis, and while this use of heuristics can certainly produce errors (see part 2 and part 4), it seems inadequate to explain bubbles on its own.

The role of leverage

The most convincing account so far is one based on a combination of herding and leverage. Over many decades a minority of bankers have contended that credit which is too easily available plays a major role in the generation of bubbles. However much someone may want to buy a dotcom share, if they have no cash and neither their banker nor their broker will lend them the cash, they cannot do so. Hence a general lack of credit places a limit on the possible extent of a bubble.

Easily available credit, on the other hand, enables someone to borrow to buy an asset and then to use that asset as collateral for further loans when its price rises – a feature of individual behaviour in most bubbles and a major contributor to the US housing bust of 2006–09. Moreover, high leverage ratios ensure that a bust will be precipitous, because holders will be forced to liquidate at any price to meet their debts, whereas unleveraged investors can choose to hold on for a recovery.

Networks and crowds

Recent research suggests that network effects may be partly responsible not just for bubbles but for much of the daily variation in market prices. Individuals linked in common networks – those who read the latest report on oil price trends from the same major bank, for instance – are likely to respond in similar ways, buying and selling the same securities.

This effect is already known in other areas: someone is far more likely to give up smoking if a friend gives up than if they hear about someone they do not know who has given up, and they are even more likely to give up if several of their friends quit. It would not be surprising if research established similar effects in purchases and sales of investments. The larger social networks facilitated by the internet may, therefore, prove to have some dangerous implications for financial markets. This effect was anticipated almost 100 years ago by Gustav le Bon when he asserted that people did not have to be physically together to behave like a crowd.

Contrarianism

Contrarianism, the investment policy of betting against the crowd, is certainly a prophylactic against the infectious power of bubbles. It can, however, prove difficult and painful to implement. Between 1997 and 2000, for example, 'value' stocks underperformed the UK market average, putting pressure on investment managers who held those stocks to sell them and buy fashionable high-growth technology shares instead. One of the UK's most prominent 'value' managers, who steadfastly refused to do this, was sacked by his employers just before the bubble burst in 2000.

Again in 2009–11, 'value' stocks languished while shares in highly-leveraged enterprises (including banks) soared, so that many 'value' managers significantly underperformed the market average.

5 Bull and bear markets

The origin of the designation of rising prices as a bull market and falling prices as a bear market is disputed. The most convincing suggestion lies in the bull-baiting and bear-baiting rings on the disreputable south bank of the River Thames in the 17th century. In their first usage, a 'bull' and a 'bear' were wagers that the price of government bonds would rise or fall. The first precise definition was that of Charles Dow (of Dow Jones fame), who largely invented technical analysis in the 1920s and set out rules for determining when bull and bear markets began and ended. Though many people dispute the validity of technical analysis itself, his definition of market phases is still very widely used.

Market cycles

While the terms 'bull' and 'bear' are applied to financial markets such as bonds and property, their primary use is in stock markets, where the belief remains prevalent that market cycles are loosely aligned with business cycles. As the charts of the US and UK stock markets show, bull markets usually last longer than bear markets.

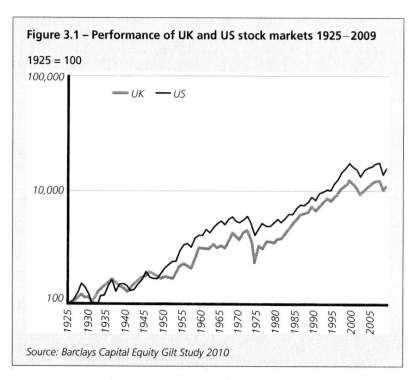

Figure 3.1 – Performance of UK and US stock markets 1925–2009

Source: Barclays Capital Equity Gilt Study 2010

In popular usage, a bull market runs from the low point of the preceding bear market to the next all-time peak, after which a bear market proceeds until the lowest point is reached. Dow theory provides a means of assessing whether any particular low or high is the lowest or highest of its sequence, and therefore represents the end of a bull or bear phase.

One of the key functions of stock markets is to put a price today on tomorrow's expected cash flows. They are therefore forward looking and share prices usually start to recover well before an economy moves out of recession. Likewise, bull markets often end before an economy enters a recession. But the timing gap in both cases is unpredictable, and all attempts to come up with simple rules that link the behaviour of share prices with major economic variables, such as interest rates, money supply, inflation or GDP growth, have failed.

Each bull and bear market has its own particular characteristics. The 1998–2000 bull market was the 'TMT' boom (technology, media and telecoms) – before it ended as a dotcom bubble. The 2003–06 bull market was the resources boom. In both cases, there were valid reasons to be optimistic about the relevant groups of stocks, but as in previous cases, optimism became over-enthusiasm and eventually speculation.

Identifying excess

Given this historical pattern of excessive optimism and pessimism, a valid question is whether it is possible to identify periods when shares are clearly overvalued or undervalued. Recent research suggests that variations in 'Tobin's Q' help to identify periods when shares are valued significantly above or below their long-term averages. Tobin's Q (named after the American economist who also proposed the so-called Tobin tax on financial transactions) is a ratio comparing the market value of companies with the replacement cost of their assets based on their accounts. The approach can be used for sectors of listed companies or whole markets – although the data is only strong enough in US markets. Shares are cheap when the ratio is less than 1 – meaning the value of assets is greater than the share price.

An alternative approach for US markets is to use an average of corporate earnings over a ten-year period to generate a price/earnings ratio rather than the latest reported or predicted earnings (the 'cyclically adjusted PE', or CAPE). Shares are regarded as cheap when CAPE is significantly below its long-term average.

In other markets, where the data is not as good, a cruder but broadly comparable approach is can be used. Prolonged periods of good returns are, in general, followed by periods of poor returns for investors. Analysts compare medium term returns over ten to 30-year periods with long-term returns over the past 100 years to determine the likelihood of good or poor returns over the following five to ten years.

However, this approach must be tempered by the effects of the big variations in economic conditions (economic volatility, interest rates, inflation) that have occurred in the past three decades and which may have made these measures less effective yardsticks.

6 Globalisation

The term 'globalisation' has at least three levels of meaning:

- A process in which regional societies and cultures have become integrated through a globe-spanning network of communication and transactions.

- The integration of national economies into the international economy through trade, foreign direct investment, the spread of technology and flows of capital.

- The integration of national and regional financial markets into one global market system.

Companies go international

The last two meanings are specifically relevant to finance and investment. They are significant for investment advisers because more and more listed firms generate revenues in a wide range of national markets and are less and less dependent on their home market.

The UK may be at the leading edge of this trend, since it is home to a significant number of multinational firms that generate a very small proportion of their revenues in the UK (the phenomenon also applies in Europe and the Far East, though less so in the US). In addition, the UK's relatively open economy has encouraged its entrepreneurs to operate on a global scale, with the result that the country is also home to many medium-sized and smaller companies that are, nevertheless, among the world leaders in their industry sectors.

Accordingly, the distinction between investing in the UK and investing abroad is less and less meaningful. An investment in stocks such as BP (oil), BAT (tobacco), HSBC (banking), GlaxoSmithKline (pharmaceuticals), Rio Tinto (mining), Vodafone (telecoms) and Diageo (alcoholic beverages), all of which are domiciled in the UK, is in no meaningful sense an investment in the UK, because none of these companies derives more than 15% of its revenue from the UK.

Sectors and themes

Today, investment managers increasingly tend to view the world economy in terms of sectors or themes. A theme such as the ageing of populations in Japan and Europe leads to focus on stocks that should benefit, such as those in health care and sheltered housing. Many of those stocks will be companies that operate in many national markets. A single sector, such as telecoms, is increasingly composed of large firms operating in many national markets under similar constraints of costs and competition.

While most investment managers recognise these effects of globalisation, the definition and naming of funds still mostly conforms to an older reality, with the vast majority of investors' money going into geographically based funds.

Currency factors

Given the higher growth rates that are likely to persist in the major emerging economies over the next decade, a geographical focus remains a valid way whereby investors in slower-growing developed economies can capture the benefits of faster economic growth. However, advisers will increasingly have to adapt their portfolio construction models to take account of thematic investing that is not subject to domicile-based geographical constraints. This is already evident in the equity income sector, which until a few years ago consisted only of funds investing in higher-yielding UK shares. Now most major management groups offer global equity income funds that apply the same discipline and methodology to a much wider universe of stocks.

An argument that used to be applied to overseas investing was that UK investors should keep the bulk of their capital in UK investments denominated in sterling, since this was the currency of their liabilities, especially their day-to-day living expenses. As regards equity investment, this too is a historical relic of a previous era and is no longer valid. If a UK company generates 90% of its revenues abroad, then the dividends it pays to UK shareholders will largely or entirely consist of the translation of these revenues from foreign currencies into sterling. The sterling value of its assets overseas will likewise be affected. So while it is possible to match some income-generating assets with currency liability – for example with fixed interest and commercial property – it is possible to do this in equity markets only by investing mainly in smaller companies focusing in the main on their domestic markets.

However, purchase of shares or bonds denominated in other currencies does create an added degree of exposure to the effects of exchange rate changes.

7 Economic indicators

A variety of measures are used to assess the state of the economy. This section covers most of the widely used indicators. The charts include long data series because most people and media reports tend to focus almost exclusively on recent data, and advisers need to be able to put recent developments in context for their clients.

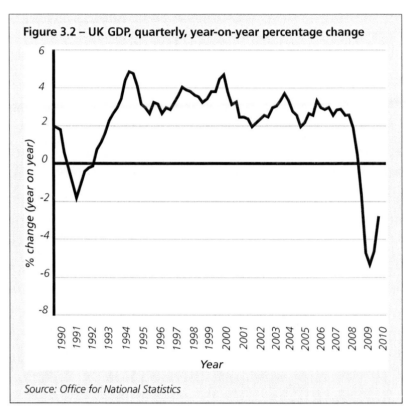

Figure 3.2 – UK GDP, quarterly, year-on-year percentage change

Source: Office for National Statistics

Gross domestic product (GDP) is widely viewed as the best measure of 'the economy' and changes in this number also define recessions (two consecutive quarters of decline). The trend rate of GDP growth consistent with steady inflation is regularly estimated by the Bank of England in its Inflation Reports. GDP growth at above this trend rate is likely to result in rising inflation and/or interest rates.

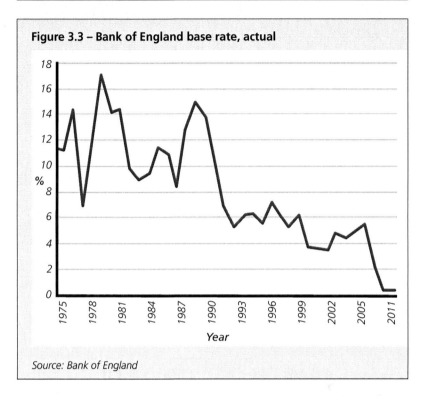

Figure 3.3 – Bank of England base rate, actual

Year

Source: Bank of England

The Bank of England's base rate is the rate at which it will lend to banks in sterling. This sets short-term sterling rates throughout the financial system. The lower the base rate is, the looser monetary policy is. In a fractional reserve banking system, the lower the interest rate, the easier it is to create new credit. High interest rates deter new investment. The interest rate trend is a key factor in the economic outlook. Rising interest rates suggest strong GDP growth and/or rising inflation, and vice versa.

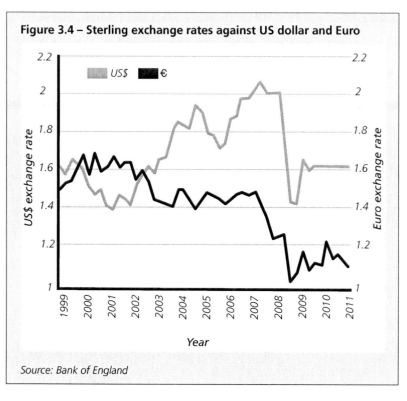

Figure 3.4 – Sterling exchange rates against US dollar and Euro

Source: Bank of England

The sterling exchange rate has major effects on the domestic economy. A lower exchange rate boost exports, and should, after a time lag, result in a lower trade deficit. It also boosts the sterling value of UK companies' overseas profits, which account for over 75% of the top 100 UK companies' earnings. But a lower exchange rate also raises UK import costs, which contributes to a higher rate of inflation, so a falling exchange rate can be an early warning indicator for higher short-term interest rates.

The London interbank offered rate (LIBOR) is the rate at which one bank will lend to another. Rates are quoted in sterling, US dollars, euros and other currencies. For sterling LIBOR, the key factor is the premium banks are willing to pay above the Bank of England base rate to obtain deposits from another bank. In normal conditions, the gap is very small; in crisis conditions it widens, and in extreme conditions, such as late 2008, it soars. Many currency and interest rate swaps use LIBOR.

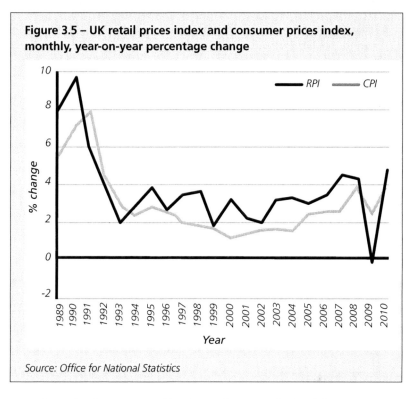

Figure 3.5 – UK retail prices index and consumer prices index, monthly, year-on-year percentage change

Source: Office for National Statistics

UK inflation has been measured by the retail prices index (RPI) for 50 years. But this index includes housing costs in the form of imputed rents and mortgage interest rates. It is therefore out of step with Europe's harmonised index of consumer prices, which excludes housing costs. The UK's consumer prices index (CPI) conforms to the European norm and has generally shown a lower rate of inflation than the RPI. However, state benefits have been linked to changes in RPI, as are index-linked gilts. If UK inflation is significantly higher than European and US rates this suggests domestic overheating. The Bank of England's target for CPI inflation is 2%.

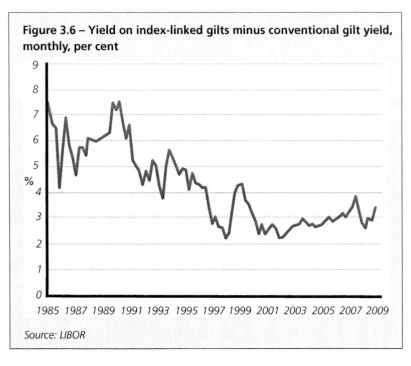

Figure 3.6 – Yield on index-linked gilts minus conventional gilt yield, monthly, per cent

Source: LIBOR

The best forecast of future inflation rates is to be found in the yield gap between conventional gilts, where both interest and final redemption values are fixed in nominal terms, and index-linked gilts (where both the interest payment and the final redemption value are indexed to the RPI). Since these are long-dated securities, the gap is investors' best guess about the likely long-term average inflation rate.

Figure 3.7 – UK retail sales, monthly, year-on-year percentage change

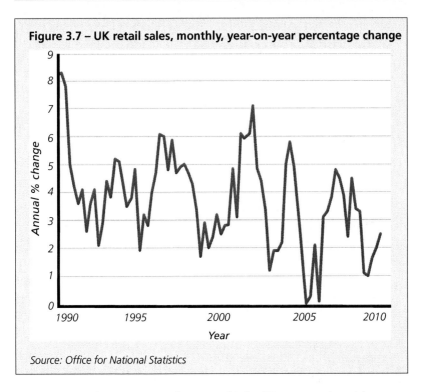

Source: Office for National Statistics

Consumer spending represents about two-thirds of UK economic activity, so the trend in retail sales is closely watched. Analysts look particularly at non-food spending. Sometimes trends are clear but there are also periods when rises and falls alternate, making assessment of a trend difficult.

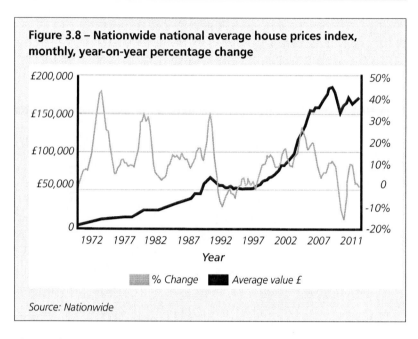

Figure 3.8 – Nationwide national average house prices index, monthly, year-on-year percentage change

Source: Nationwide

The trend in house prices is important for several reasons. Rising house prices are associated with a 'wealth effect' because they make people more optimistic and inclined to spend. They are usually accompanied by rising disposable incomes and falling unemployment.

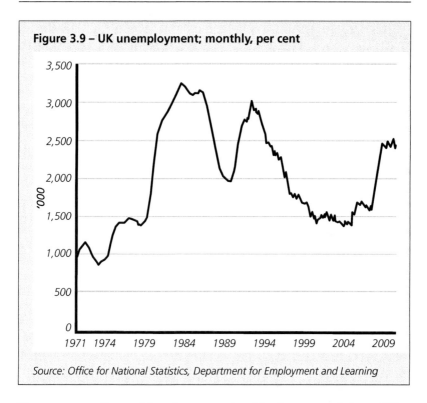

Figure 3.9 – UK unemployment; monthly, per cent

Source: Office for National Statistics, Department for Employment and Learning

The percentage of potential workers unemployed is a key economic factor. UK unemployment benefits are well below the net income from work (though the net difference between employment and unemployment can be small for low-income workers entitled to a range of state benefits). So the higher the rate of unemployment, the lower the total net income available for spending. Unemployment has tended to peak several months after the trough of a recession.

The percentage of net disposable income that households save tends to rise when unemployment rises and people feel less secure, and fall during periods of relatively full employment. As an aggregate, it may not reflect significant trends, such as the large increase in overpayments that were made by homeowners on their mortgages as interest rates fell in 2008. Trends are likely to persist for years.

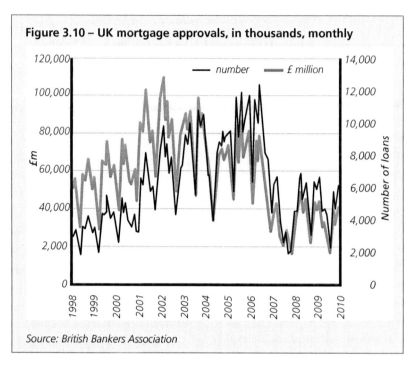

Figure 3.10 – UK mortgage approvals, in thousands, monthly

Source: British Bankers Association

A good indicator of likely trends in house prices is the number of mortgage approvals, which typically precede purchase by one to three months. The vast majority of first-time buyers use mortgage finance, so a rise in this number usually means greater optimism about the future trend in house prices.

A trade or current account deficit means the UK is paying more for imports than it receives for exports. This has to be financed by inflows of capital from overseas. Deficit rates of over 5% of GDP used to be regarded as unsustainable.

Summary

- The 2008 credit crunch has led to widespread questioning of both neoclassical and Keynesian economic models, and has ended a period of 'free market' dominance in economic thinking.

- Neoclassical theory, with its emphasis on deregulation and free markets, was the dominant model from the mid-1980s until 2008. Government responses to the crisis have been more Keynesian.

- Business normally operates in a cycle of 3–5 years driven mainly by variations in inventories, usually referred to as 'the business cycle', even though it is far from regular.

- Bubbles like those seen in the US and UK property markets from 2000 to 2007 have been frequent throughout history. Overconfidence (behavioural finance) and over-easy credit (Austrian economists) explain them better than conventional economic theories.

- Bull and bear markets follow an irregular pattern. Comparison of current with long-term measures of value using Tobin's Q and the cyclically adjusted PE may identify periods of excessively high or low stock market values.

- Economic data series (house prices, retail sales, interest rates, inflation, etc.) cannot predict market behaviour, but changes can be suggestive.

Chapter 4
Diversification, asset classes and risk

The oldest and simplest investment adage is: 'Don't put all your eggs in one basket.' As Warren Buffett of Berkshire Hathaway, rated by many as the world's greatest investor, has noted, this is a defensive strategy: "Diversification may protect wealth, but concentration builds wealth." Since those who have accumulated capital – often through concentrating their energies and capital – are usually more concerned with protecting it than augmenting it, finding effective methods of diversification and thus reducing the risk of loss is a key concern for advisers.

1 Asset allocation and investment planning

Portfolio theory says that by holding a set of assets whose returns are uncorrelated, an investor can secure a higher rate of return for a given level of volatility or they can achieve a lower level of volatility for a given rate of return. The details are explored in part 2. Here we focus on the implications for investment planning of these key propositions from portfolio theory.

'Asset allocation' is the generic name for a methodology used to divide capital between different asset types to design portfolios. Increasingly, the term is used to refer to methods that use the mathematical tools derived from portfolio theory to construct and manage portfolios. It is possible to apply asset allocation methods pragmatically, without using the mathematical tools described in part 2. However, since the benefits of diversification depend crucially on the degree to which asset returns are correlated with each other, even pragmatists who distrust portfolio theory need to consider past returns and their variability. Most will therefore end up using at least some of the tools of portfolio theory, even if they do not use its modelling techniques.

The basis for asset allocation lies in the wealth of academic studies that have clearly identified decisions on the allocation of capital to asset classes as the major determinant of investment returns (see chapter 10).

The importance of asset allocation can be exaggerated from these findings, which typically say that 90% or more of variations in returns derive from choices on asset allocation rather than from the choice of individual investments. The experience of many investment clients diverges from this. Many will have derived their wealth from a concentration of capital in one investment (their own business), which has returned many hundred times the return they could have achieved in conventional equity investments. They could not have achieved the same results by investing in a set of other, similar private businesses instead. Only by investing in their own business and personally taking on the attendant risks, both operational and financial, could they achieve exceptional returns.

It is clear from this that the choice of specific investments can and does contribute enormously to the returns investors achieve. But asset allocation methodology and decisions properly apply to free capital where there are constraints on the level of risk the investor is prepared to accept.

It is worth emphasising that asset allocation methodology is essentially a defensive strategy where the prime motivation is to protect capital. While portfolio theory provides tools an investor can apply to generate more return for the same level of risk, in reality investors unconcerned with risk and focused solely on the maximum growth of capital are unlikely to use them.

2 Defining asset classes

The broad aim of diversification can be pursued in two different ways:

- By pragmatically looking for assets whose returns have consistently followed different patterns in the past.

- By deriving from economic theory asset classes whose behaviour should, according to economic principles, be consistently different.

In practice, almost all textbooks on asset allocation methods combine these approaches to a greater or lesser extent.

It is possible to derive from theory between four and seven major asset classes. The primary four are cash, bonds, property and shares. For each there are economic drivers that will result in predictable changes in returns on the basis of a change in one major economic variable. It can be argued that government (or sovereign) bonds and corporate bonds are distinct asset classes, and that index-linked government bonds (where typically both interest payments and capital at redemption are linked to an index of retail prices) are a different asset class from conventional bonds. It can also be argued that residential and commercial property constitute separate asset classes. In all these cases, historical data also shows a significant divergence in the pattern of returns.

Index-linked and conventional bonds

Index-linked and conventional bonds offer a good illustration of the economic foundations of asset class definition:

- Conventional government bonds, where both interest and capital at redemption are fixed in nominal terms, are vulnerable to inflation. The longer the term of such a bond, the more the current price is likely to rise or fall in response to a fall or rise in estimates of future rates of inflation. This predictable pattern of returns is borne out in practice for the bulk of the data available.

- Index-linked government bonds, on the other hand, assure the investor that both interest and capital will be regularly adjusted to keep them at the same real, inflation-adjusted level (though this ignores deflation, which was not an issue when the formulae for such bonds were invented).

Hence a rise in the projected rate of inflation, which causes a fall in the price of conventional bonds, should cause a rise in the price of inflation-linked bonds, because investors will be prepared to pay more to obtain protection from its effects. Again, this theoretical prediction is borne out in most of the data.

The result is that any individual member of one of these two asset classes can be expected to react in different and predictable ways as compared to a member of the other asset class in response to one of the major economic variables of concern to investors.

Disputed asset classes

Many other potential asset classes are, however, the subject of ongoing debate among theoreticians and practitioners. Commodities, for example, are often referred to as an asset class, but only a few (the precious metals) are investable in physical form. The rest, such as zinc, coffee, oil, sugar and wheat, can be bought only in the form of futures contracts or by using other derivatives (see below) or funds based on derivatives. For technical reasons, the purchase of derivatives will not produce a return equivalent to the price change in the commodity.

Private equity is a leveraged form of equity investment, and in theory at least, its returns should link in a predictable pattern with those of listed equities, yet some practitioners consider it a separate asset class.

3 Asset subclasses

US practitioners have tended in recent years to expand the number of asset subclasses used in creating portfolios. Much of this is based on long-term studies by commentators such as Ibbotson Associates.

The small cap effect

Small cap shares seem to have produced higher long term returns for investors than the shares in larger companies (a conclusion reached by studies both for the UK and the US). The variation in a long run of historical returns led analysts to hypothesise about why these higher returns had persisted, in an apparent contradiction of portfolio theory, and why they could be expected to persist. The definition of small cap is rather elastic and relative rather than absolute; in the US a widely agreed definition is companies with a market capitalisation of $300m to $2b — levels that at the top end are nudging the lower end of the FTSE 100. In UK the term is generally used to cover companies that are outside the FTSE Actuaries 350 Index. The FTSE SmallCap index tracks the shares of about 315 companies representing about 2% of the market by value.

Portfolio theory offers no convincing rationale for historically proven higher returns from the small cap effect – or indeed from momentum effect. Several hypotheses have been advanced to explain the small cap effect. One of the more convincing is that investors with large capital sums cannot deploy sufficient capital in small cap stocks to obtain meaningful rewards in relation to the effort they must expend to select such stocks, and therefore ignore or 'underweight' such investments. Once a small cap stock has attained a certain size, though, it is more widely bought by institutions. This phenomenon essentially leaves arbitrage profits available, but they have been far larger than is consistent with portfolio theory. The use of small cap as a separate asset subclass is therefore entirely pragmatic.

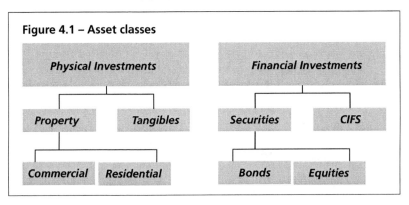

Figure 4.1 – Asset classes

The characteristics of the major asset classes are covered in chapter 5, and the risk factors in part 4, chapter 19.

For most investors, the key concept is that the risk of a catastrophic loss is reduced by dividing capital among asset classes. But while this is true for the major asset classes, it does not necessarily apply to asset subclasses.

4 Asset class correlation

The use of a large number of asset classes and subclasses to allocate capital is now common in the US, where practitioners have often used 15 or more classes. However, in the extreme market conditions of 2008–09, correlation between these assets increased substantially (as it had done in previous crises). As a result, their use proved ineffective in diversifying risk at exactly the point when risk was highest and such diversification would have had the greatest value (see part 2, chapter 10).

While many commentators have remarked on the higher correlation between bonds and equities in 2008–09, this was true only of corporate bonds. The crisis conditions reminded investors of the equity-like features of corporate bonds, with the result that lower-quality bond prices saw dramatic falls. Government bonds, on the other hand, remained uncorrelated with equities.

This reinforces the point that some correlations are certain, while others are variable. Cash must remain uncorrelated with equities (the only exception is in hyperinflation situations, when interest rates could reach astronomical levels). Because there are links between short- and long-term interest rates, the correlation between cash and government bonds can be high, at least for short periods, and on average can be expected to be higher than that between cash and equities. Degrees of correlation between the subclasses of equities (domestic, international, emerging market, large cap, small cap, etc.) have varied in the past but correlation has always increased in crisis conditions.

Correlation and risk

Advisers must therefore be realistic about the limited value of diversification in asset classes other than cash and government bonds for the purpose of reducing capital risk during crises. As discussed in section 2, most models built on portfolio theory systematically underestimate risk because uncertainty and 'black swans' cannot, by definition, be modelled. That being so, advisers need to ensure that clients understand this and accept that one-off events like credit crunches may result in abrupt reductions in the market value of their capital, or they need to ensure that clients set lower tolerances for risk, implemented by adjusting the model inputs.

Since most clients are more concerned with protection of capital than increasing return, the adviser should focus efforts primarily on ensuring that realistic risk tolerances are agreed and are implemented with reference to history rather than models.

Allocation and returns

The allocation of capital across subclasses, particularly of equities, is concerned not primarily with limitation of risk but with the augmentation of return. Given that subclasses share all the economic features of the asset class, there cannot be large diversification benefits. This approach is validated by portfolio theory and by much historical data, but in practice it is the strategy where judgment is most required.

Today, for example, conventional wisdom dictates that only by allocating significant capital to equities in fast-growing emerging economies can residents of mature developed economies secure high rates of capital growth. This is a forward-looking judgment typical of what is required to construct a portfolio and has a number of significant implications, since historic data shows emerging market equities to have higher volatility than developed market equities.

Whether they design their own model portfolios or use portfolio-modelling tools, it is hard for advisers to escape making such judgments. Setting procedures for making and implementing such judgments is essential if an adviser is to deliver an ongoing service that can be effectively managed for a group of clients and remain consistent.

5 Securities and portfolios

A key concept of portfolio theory is that risk is a feature of the portfolio as a whole. Adding a risky security to a portfolio does not necessarily increase the overall risk; provided the risky asset is uncorrelated with the other investments in the portfolio, it can even reduce risk.

Views of risk

This concept is at odds with how many people think about investments. The normal way of thinking about investments and risk is additive/subtractive. You have a low-risk layer of investments, and add a slightly higher-risk one, and then an even higher-risk one, until you have a pyramid shape. The proportion of your capital that you hold in the different layers determines how much risk you incur. To reduce risk, you subtract capital from the riskiest layer and add it to the layer with least risk.

The way portfolio theory looks at risk is multiplicative/divisive. Multiplying and dividing returns and risks for a set of securities requires the mathematics of algebra and standard deviation, but it generates a reading for the portfolio as a whole. You can only assess the effect of adding or subtracting one security on likely returns and risk by repeating the calculations for the whole portfolio.

Graphic representations such as the classic zigzag (or 'two stock') portfolio can help to explain this. They are, however, impractical for large groups of securities.

6 Multi-asset funds

Most individual investors (other than the extremely wealthy) use collective funds for the bulk of their capital, for reasons of cost, containment of risk and convenience (see part 3). The vast majority of traditional funds invest in a single asset class. They are therefore easy to accommodate within portfolios based on asset classes.

Allocation of multi-asset funds

Funds that invest in several asset classes do not fit so easily into an asset allocation framework. Some funds containing several different asset classes can be dealt with by looking at their actual holdings. Distribution funds, for example, will normally hold equities and bonds, and the relevant proportion can be allocated to each asset class.

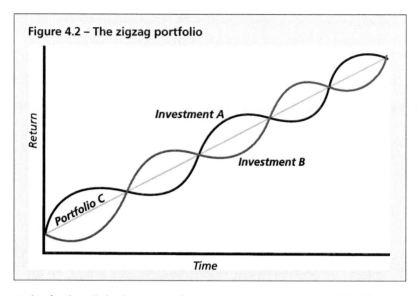

Figure 4.2 – The zigzag portfolio

Return

Investment A

Investment B

Portfolio C

Time

Hedge funds and absolute return funds, however, do not necessarily hold conventional assets, or, if they do, the proportions within the fund may change. These and other funds, such as those investing in timber or agricultural land, are often defined as 'alternatives', constituting a separate category of investments. Some practitioners treat absolute return funds as a separate asset class. The key issue is the historic correlation of returns with other asset classes, the variability of such correlations and the amount of historic data available.

The main difference between conventional funds on the one hand and hedge funds and absolute return funds on the other hand is the hedge funds' and absolute return funds' use of derivatives.

7 Investments and derivatives

We have already defined investments as either physical or securities. A derivative is an instrument derived from a security, currency, commodity or index, the price of the derivative varying in a direct relationship with this underlying asset. Derivatives are not investments nor are they an asset class, but they may be used in the construction of investments like structured products and in the management of collective investment funds.

In response to the extreme volatility of financial markets in 2008–09, advisers are under pressure to find ways of mitigating the volatility of clients' portfolios and this is leading to greater use of techniques, funds and other products that employ derivatives.

Types of derivative

The main categories of derivative are as follows:

- **Futures.** These have been used in agricultural markets for centuries; they enable producers to sell their products forward (with a future delivery date) and manufacturers to fix key input costs. A futures contract carries the obligation to acquire or deliver the relevant quantity of the commodity on the settlement date, and its terms are set and policed by the exchange on which it trades.

- **Options.** An option confers the right but not the obligation to buy (a 'call') or sell (a 'put') a set quantity of shares, bonds, gold, oil etc at a specified price for a given term.

- **Swaps.** A swap is a contract whereby one set of cash flows is exchanged for another (currency and interest rate swaps) or a set of cash flows is exchanged for a capital sum (credit default swaps).

Many futures and option contracts relate to physical commodities and to securities or indices based on securities, but by far the greatest growth in recent years has been in financial derivatives. Until recently, the vast majority of these have been over-the-counter products traded between banks, which has created opacity in pricing and potential problems in counterparty risk and in settlement – i.e. the risk that one of the parties to a transaction defaults because it cannot meet its obligations. The most dramatic illustration of this was the aftermath Lehman Brothers' bankruptcy in September 2008.

As of 2011, regulators are attempting to convert large sections of financial derivatives trading to exchanges with common contract terms and central clearing systems in order to reduce counterparty risk.

Using derivatives

Hedge funds were the first collective investment funds to use derivatives to reduce the level of volatility in portfolios. With shares, this can be done in two main ways:

- **Cash and call**, where a fund holds cash but also buys call options which will generate profits if share prices rise.

- **Stock and put**, whereby a fund holds shares but also buys put options enabling it to limit its losses if share prices fall.

Vastly more sophisticated strategies using a variety of derivatives are now employed by offshore hedge funds and increasingly by UK-based collective investment funds seeking absolute returns (see chapter 13).

Structured products (see chapter 16) use derivatives to provide investors with specific guaranteed levels of income or capital return or both. Usually they require commitment of capital for three to six years, but the latest trend is for these products to be created in the form of tradable notes or funds so that investors can exit early if they wish, though usually at 'mark to model' prices derived from the product creator's pricing model. Guaranteed equity bonds, which provide explicit guarantees of no loss of capital, have been the principal form of structured product promoted by product providers in the UK.

Derivatives may be used by many authorised funds, and advisers need to understand the extent of their use and any potential problems that may arise. Counterparty risk remains problematic: the failures of AIG and Lehman caused losses for many structured products and created valuation problems for some exchange-traded commodities.

8 Gearing and leverage

The uses and implications of leverage gearing (the terms are interchangeable) in clients' portfolios are dealt with in part 4, chapter 19. Here we cover its role in the financial system at large and in financial products.

As mentioned in chapter 3, the easy availability of credit encourages investors to borrow more and to 'gear up' or 'leverage' their position ('leverage' being the US term gaining currency in the UK). This certainly contributes, to some extent, to the formation of bubbles and their eventual collapse.

Leverage in housing

In one area of finance, the use of leverage is now taken for granted: housing. Until the 20th century the majority of homeowners owned their homes outright without resort to borrowing. Mortgage finance only became a mass market phenomenon in the UK after 1945, but it is now universally accepted that at some stage young people get on the housing ladder by obtaining a mortgage. The principal reason for the popularity of housing as an investment is the effects of gearing on the original capital employed.

During a boom such as that of 2000–07, during which many UK house prices doubled, someone buying a £100,000 home with a £75,000 mortgage would have seen their capital or 'equity' increase fivefold. Yet most homeowners fail to recognise the role leverage has played in generating capital, and consider housing as more attractive than any form of financial investment.

Since UK residents benefit from valuable tax concessions on home ownership, there are sound reasons to own residential property and possibly to use mortgage finance in order to own a larger property than would otherwise be possible. But it is important to help clients distinguish the tax-incentivised merits of personal home ownership from the merits of residential property as an investment in itself. As tens of thousands of buy-to-let investors discovered from 2006–09, gearing works both ways. It is inevitable that gearing increases risk as well as potential return.

In this context, it is worth noting that many of the largest multinational companies tend to have levels of gearing of under 30%, and that blue-chip status in developed equity markets depends not just on the size of a business but on the soundness of its finances.

Operational and financial gearing

In the analysis of listed companies, a distinction is often made between operational gearing and financial gearing.

- **Operational gearing or leverage** arises from having fixed costs that are a high proportion of the sales price of goods or services produced. A small increase in sales then results in a much larger percentage increase in profits.

- **Financial gearing or leverage** is a feature of the company's financial structure, in particular the proportions of its total capital that are supplied by equity and debt. The higher the leverage (the ratio of debt to total capital), the greater the return on shareholders' capital, but the greater the vulnerability of the company to a downturn in revenues. Private equity firms used very high levels of leverage in 2004–07, with the result that many of the businesses they financed experienced serious problems after the 2008–09 credit crunch.

Many collective investment schemes create the equivalent of operational gearing by selecting investments with risk-return ratios well above the average for the relevant sector. For example, small oil exploration companies have much higher risk-return ratios than the oil majors.

Financial leverage, however, remains forbidden to most mainstream classes of open-ended fund and it has been used only by a minority of closed-ended funds.

Among collective investment funds that use leverage are some of the oldest, namely investment trusts, and some of the newest – recently listed investment companies. In the case of investment trusts, gearing levels have been modest and rarely exceed 20%.

However, some schemes available only to professional investors, such as property investment partnerships, employ significant levels of leverage. Advisers need to pay particular attention to funds or schemes that employ gearing since the terms of their loan agreements may impose heavy penalties on equity holders if certain ratios of loans to asset values are breached, or if interest payments are not met.

9 Limiting losses

Portfolio theory provides a framework for limiting risk through asset allocation methods. But since almost all asset prices fall in a crisis, often steeply, the benefits of diversification can only truly be said to be reliable during 'normal' periods in the financial markets. If this were not the case, there would be no need for hedge and other funds that seek 'absolute returns' and adopt a variety of strategies to limit the potential for capital losses.

Insuring portfolios

Some very large financial institutions have offered portfolio insurance to clients. In the UK, this has been in the form of investment bonds, where a 'ratchet' mechanism has been used to guarantee a minimum capital level for a portfolio, with an automatic reset of the guaranteed base if market values rise more than a certain percentage above previous levels. The cost of this insurance has been about 1%–1.5% a year, though the insurance only applies to portfolios meeting the provider's specifications. Usually this limits the amount that may be invested in equity funds and also precludes investment in the riskier forms of equity funds. Providers may also require a minimum holding period.

An alternative insurance offered on some investment bonds provides a death benefit equal to the original investment, which can provide a useful measure of protection for older clients.

Since individuals can in effect construct their own portfolio insurance by purchasing futures and options, it is logical to expect that such insurance will be offered more widely in future, and may provide a simpler way of meeting the requirements of risk-averse investors.

Likewise, structured products that provide specific guarantees of minimum capital returns can provide the security some investors need, though careful analysis of both charges and opportunity costs is required.

Summary

- Diversification is primarily a method of protecting capital. Asset allocation is a means of applying diversification, which can be done using all the mathematical tools of portfolio theory or in a more pragmatic way.

- Membership of asset classes can be determined by economic theory or on the basis of historical evidence; preferably they should coincide.

- The correlation of returns of asset classes varies over time, and may diverge substantially from long-term averages during crisis conditions, as happened in 2008–09.

- Asset allocation must be based at least in part on forward-looking judgments based on assessments of uncertain outcomes rather than those that can be probabilistically measured.

- Portfolio theory's view of risk is based on multiplication and division of returns and contradicts the 'addition-subtraction' method used by most people.

- 'Alternative' investments such as commodities conventionally form a separate asset class, but it is the actual content/strategies of funds that will determine their returns, which may or may not correlate with other assets.

- Gearing or leverage always generates an increase in the level of risk, even in residential property, the area where it is taken for granted.

Chapter 5
Asset classes and investment returns

In order to construct portfolios, we need to estimate what future returns and volatility are likely to be. The most logical approach is to do this for each of the major asset classes, which is the primary focus of research and analysis. A secondary question will be how much returns vary within a particular asset class, depending on the nature of the investment and especially its implicit gearing.

Clearly we cannot simply project forward any recent data on returns or volatility for any asset class, since we have no grounds for expecting these to persist. However, there is evidence for reversion to the mean in investment returns; so that a period of exceptionally good or poor returns is likely to be followed by the opposite trend bringing back long term performance to the average rate. We could therefore project forward more confidently *historic* long-term average rates of return. But it is important to remember that the investor is likely to obtain such average rates of return only over long periods: over short periods (in practice, up to a decade), returns may vary significantly from the long-term averages.

When it comes to volatility, the situation is more difficult, because it is not so much the *volatility* of asset classes that concerns us but their correlation, and here we have no grounds for using long-run historic data and have no choice but to use largely subjective estimates.

1 Historic returns

Financial markets have existed in their modern form for some 150 years and data on investment returns is available for some developed markets for over 100 years. More recently analysts have created databases that permit detailed analysis of returns, volatility and correlation. In the US, Ibbotson Associates has pioneered this work, while in the UK the *Equity Gilt Study* from Barclays Capital and the Credit Suisse *Global Investment Returns Yearbook* (formerly from ABN AMRO), both produced annually, provide the key data used in asset allocation planning.

The long-term returns from the major asset classes as shown in the Barclays Capital study are detailed in Table 5.1.

Table 5.1 – Returns by asset class — annual average real returns before tax to December 2010

Asset class	Annual returns over			
	10 years	20 years	50 years	110 years
Cash	1.1%	2.6%	1.7%	1.0%
Government bonds	2.4%	5.8%	2.5%	1.2%
Corporate bonds	2.1%	—	—	—
Equities	0.6%	6.0%	5.4%	5.1%

Source: Barclays Capital, Equity Gilt Study 2011

Long-run data is available only for three asset classes, cash, equities and government bonds:

- Cash returns are measured by the returns on treasury bills, which reflect short-term wholesale money market interest rates.

- Equity returns are calculated from indices of share prices dating from the 1930s, supplemented by back-calculation using similar methods.

- Government bonds can easily be combined to provide representative indices of performance.

Table 5.1 shows that equities displayed exceptionally poor returns in the most recent decade, while government bonds showed exceptionally good returns over the past 20 years. Studies of the variation in returns over time show a strong tendency to reversion to the mean, so there is little likelihood of either asset class delivering similar performance over the next decade.

Long-run data is also available on some specific assets, such as some of the industrial metals, the precious metals and agricultural commodities such as wheat and corn. But long-run data is not available on many of the equity subclasses, nor on equities in many recently developed economies. Only about 25 years' worth of data is available on corporate bonds and commercial property.

The Barclays Capital study inflation-adjusts all figures to make comparisons easier. Over the long term, real annual returns of about 5% on shares, 1.2% on bonds and 1% on cash represent the average experience of investors. However, there have been substantial variations over time. Annual returns in equities have been as high as 12% in the best decades and as low as −3.8% in the worst.

2 Variations in returns

Substantial variations in returns from decade to decade mask a more consistent longer-term effect. As Figure 5.1 shows, the average annual returns from the three major asset classes have been very wide over the short term, but over

Table 5.2 – Real investment returns (% pa)

	Equities	Gilts	Index-Linked	Cash
1899–1909	4.9	−0.2	N/A	1.6
1909–19	−3.8	−78.6	N/A	−4.9
1919–29	7.8	8.1	N/A	7.4
1929–39	4.3	5.8	N/A	0.9
1939–49	3.8	0.5	N/A	−2.0
1949–59	12.9	−3.2	N/A	−1.2
1959–69	4.4	−1.9	N/A	1.9
1969–79	−2.3	−4.1	N/A	−3.3
1979–89	15.6	6.9	N/A	4.8
1989–99	10.7	8.3	5.7	4.5
1999–2009	−1.2	2.6	1.9	1.8

Source: Barclays Capital

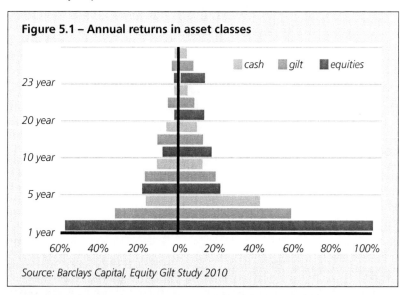

Figure 5.1 – Annual returns in asset classes

Source: Barclays Capital, Equity Gilt Study 2010

the long term the gap between the minimum and maximum returns has been much lower.

This analysis is based on rolling returns, which means that in a ten-year period, nine of the returns are the same as in the next ten-year period. While this analysis is a fair representation of the average returns investors have earned, it cannot on its own be used as evidence of mean reversion of returns.

The variations in returns are widest for equities, smaller for gilts and smaller still for cash.

This narrowing of the gap between minimum and maximum returns over time cannot simply be described as a reduction in risk, because it ignores the volatility of investments within those timescales.

3 Reversion to the mean

There is evidence of a general reversion of returns towards the mean – that theory that investment returns vary in the short term but eventually return to the average. This is demonstrated by the analysis of the Barclays Capital data shown in Table 5.3, which compares the returns from equities in a series of poor decades to those in the immediately following decades.

Table 5.3 – Analysis of Barclays Capital data

Average annual returns in the ten years to	%	Average annual returns in the ten years immediately afterwards	%
1915	−0.2	1916−25	3.9
1916	−3.7	1917−26	6.5
1917	−3.8	1918−27	9.1
1918	−3.5	1919−28	10.3
1919	−3.8	1920−29	7.8
1920	−7.9	1921−30	12.8
1921	−5.1	1922−31	7.6
1922	−1.9	1923−32	7.5
1923	−1.3	1924−33	9.6
1974	−6.0	1975−84	17.4
1976	−0.3	1977−86	14.6
1977	−0.2	1978−87	12.0
1978	−3.5	1979−88	12.4
1979	−2.3	1980−89	15.6
1981	−2.4	1982−91	13.2
1982	−1.2	1983−92	12.7
2008	−1.5	2009−18	?
Average	**−2.85882%**	**Average**	**10.8125%**

Annual returns are adjusted for inflation.
Source: Fidelity International

In the decade following a decade of poor returns, investors have on average earned almost twice the long-term annual average return from equities.

4 Dispersion of equity returns

The most commonly encountered view of shares among individual investors is that they are very risky. The wide range of short-term returns is responsible for this view.

However, if we look at long series of data the picture is somewhat different, as is shown in Figure 5.2. In the vast majority of calendar years over the past century, annual returns fall within a range of −10% and +20%. Much higher or lower returns are experienced in only a small minority of years.

Most of the relevant data is summarised in Table 5.4, which shows both nominal and real returns and the 'premiums' or excess returns earned by equity and bond investors.

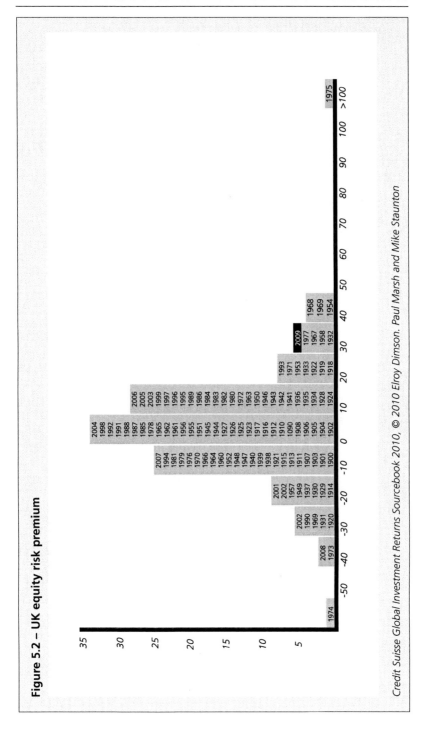

Figure 5.2 – UK equity risk premium

Credit Suisse Global Investment Returns Sourcebook 2010, © 2010 Elroy Dimson. Paul Marsh and Mike Staunton

Table 5.4 – Returns on asset classes

Return	Asset	Mean returns % p.a					Annual returns %				Ten-year returns % p.a.				Current year rank
		GM	AM	SE	SD	SC	Lowest		Highest		Lowest		Highest		
Nominal	Equities	9.4	11.3	2.1	21.8	-0.08	-48.8	1974	145.6	1975	1.1	2008	31.5	1984	13
	Bonds	5.3	5.9	1.1	11.9	0.06	-17.4	1974	53.1	1982	-2.5	1956	18.7	1984	91
	Bills	5.0	5.1	0.4	3.8	0.91	0.5	1946	17.2	1980	0.7	1951	12.1	1989	99
	Inflation	3.9	4.2	0.6	6.6	0.51	26.0	1921	24.9	1975	-5.4	1930	14.1	1981	58
Real	Equities	5.3	7.2	1.9	20.1	-0.07	-57.1	1974	96.7	1975	-5.6	1920	17.6	1984	11
	Bonds	1.3	2.2	1.3	13.7	0.14	-30.7	1974	59.0	1921	-11.2	1920	9.8	1930	83
	Bills	1.0	1.2	0.6	6.3	0.37	-15.4	1915	42.4	1921	-6.0	1920	9.8	1930	88
	Exchange rate	-0.1	0.6	1.1	11.8	-0.04	-36.7	1946	52.6	1933	-8.6	1947	5.3	1980	12
Premium	Equities vs bills	4.2	6.0	1.9	20.0	-0.13	-54.6	1974	121.8	1975	-4.9	1974	17.7	1984	8
	Equities vs bonds	3.9	5.2	1.6	17.1	-0.10	-38.4	2008	80.8	1975	-3.9	2008	16.4	1959	7
	Bonds vs. bills	0.3	0.8	1.0	10.7	-0.03	-26.6	1974	36.7	1932	-6.9	1974	6.6	1941	67

GM = geometric mean; AM = arithmetic mean; SE =standard error of mean; SD = standard deviation; SC = serial correlation; Ten-year returns to end of given year

Source: Elroy Dimson, Paul Marsh and Mike Staunton, Triumph of the Optimists, 101 Years of Global Investment Returns, Princeton University Press, 2002, and subsequent research.

5 The equity risk premium

While very long-run average returns tell us what investors have achieved in the past, this can only be a general guide to the future. But exactly how good a guide they are depends partly on whether there are good theoretical grounds for expecting returns at any specific level.

This explains theorists' concern, over the past two decades, at the 'equity risk premium', the return earned by equity investors over and above the risk-free rate. The most convincing exposition on this topic is that by Dimson, Marsh and Staunton in *The Triumph of the Optimists*, a definitive guide to a century of stock market returns for 17 countries. They update this survey in the annual Credit Suisse *Global Investment Returns Yearbook*.

Dimson, Marsh and Staunton 'decompose' or split the historic equity risk premium into five components, of which the most important are:

- **The growth rate for real dividends.** The authors show that despite many more positive assertions, the average real growth in dividends over the past century has been just under 1% annually. While some growth in real dividends can be expected in future, projections at above 1% would be regarded as optimistic.

- **The change in the price/dividend ratio** (the rate at which dividends are valued by the market). On average, over the past century, the ratio expanded by 0.6% annually. But indefinite expansion is not possible, so a zero rate of change is a realistic projection.

- **The average dividend yield.** The authors argue that this is the best guide to the future. The historic country average over the past century was 4.5%, with a geometric average for the world (17 countries) of 4.2%.

The other two components of the equity risk premium are the real interest rate and exchange rate effects, which the authors argue must sum to zero over the long term.

On this basis they argue for a future equity risk premium roughly equivalent to the current market yield of 3% to 3.5%, which is lower than the historical average. Bearing in mind that this is a real, inflation-adjusted figure, it is still an adequate reward for the risk involved in equities on a long-term basis. But both theorists and practitioners can question whether it is sufficient compensation for the short-term volatility experienced in equities, or for the possibility of periods as long as a decade in which returns are below the average.

Theorists continue to debate the significance of investor expectations in generating the equity risk premium, and that attempts to link it to economic theory have been largely unsuccessful. So there is still considerable scope for disagreement about the 'right' level of the equity risk premium.

6 Strategic returns

Many studies of the stock markets have focused on the issue of whether there are any reliable strategies equity investors can adopt to secure superior returns.

The most obvious, selling before a fall and buying before a rise, has been comprehensively discredited by academic studies. This strategy requires investors' judgment, not only of the effect (the fall or rise) but also of its timing and its extent, to be far better than any individual or organisation can hope to achieve with any consistency. This explains why virtually no conventional fund managers now claim to use market timing as a significant element in their investment strategies, and why even more speculative funds like hedge funds use derivatives and options strategies to protect capital rather than selling outright.

However, analysts have identified three strategies that do appear to have worked in the past.

- **Value.** Using methods outlined by Ben Graham in The Intelligent Investor, value investors buy stocks in companies with sound finances, low operational risks and substantial assets. Often, high dividend pay-outs are used as a criterion. Over the long term, filters using such 'value' criteria have generated portfolios that have outperformed the general market indices. Some equity income funds use such methods.

- **Small cap.** Over the long term, in both the US and UK markets, smaller capitalisation stocks have generated higher returns than large capitalisation stocks. Theorists debate the reasons, but one factor may be that institutional investors dislike stocks with poor liquidity, which is a typical characteristic of small cap stocks, and may therefore systematically underweight them in their portfolios. Some theorists argue that the risks involved in small caps are larger than conventional measures suggest, so that the higher returns are simply a reward for higher risks.

- **Momentum.** Contrary to expectations based on portfolio theory, the evidence suggests that investors who have applied momentum strategies over the past century have been more successful than average. Using these strategies, investors buy the stocks that had shown the best recent returns (and, in a long-short version, short sell those with the worst recent returns). Dimson, Marsh and Staunton provide evidence that this has broadly worked over the past century. Theory would suggest that the availability of profits from this strategy should ensure that sufficient capital was allocated to them to eliminate the profits. But Dimson, Marsh and Staunton note that very frequent transactions are necessary to implement the strategy, and other analysts have suggested that in practice the transaction costs, especially in small cap stocks, might eliminate the additional returns.

7 Returns and volatility

As noted above, the real average long-term annual return from equities from 1900 to 2007 as recorded by Dimson, Marsh and Staunton was 5.5%, and the volatility, as measured by standard deviation, was 19.8%. Bonds returned 1.3% with a standard deviation of 13.8 and cash returned 1% with a standard deviation of 6.4. The relationship between the asset classes has remained consistent: equities are about 1.5 times more volatile than bonds, which in turn are twice as volatile as cash (where the short-term interest rate measures cash volatility). But actual levels of volatility have varied substantially over five- and ten-year periods, with equities often twice as volatile as bonds.

In broad terms, the historic returns and volatilities provide grounds for traditional portfolio construction, where fixed interest provides low, secure returns, commercial property somewhat higher returns and equities the highest returns but with much higher volatility.

The issues involved in the assessment of risk in constructing portfolios are dealt with in chapters 7 to 9.

8 Correlation of returns

To achieve maximum diversification benefits, asset returns should be non-correlated or show low correlation. Correlation is measured on a scale of −1 to +1. Perfect correlation (+1) arises when the returns from two assets move exactly in step; perfect non-correlation (−1) is when the returns from two assets move exactly in opposite directions.

If you could find two assets with the same annualised rates of return and perfect non-correlation, you could invest 50% of your capital in each and have a portfolio that showed no volatility whatever. While this is not possible in practice, even a moderate degree of non-correlation can significantly reduce the volatility of a portfolio that includes non-correlated assets. Hence the degree of correlation, and the probability of its persistence, are important factors in portfolio design.

9 Correlation matrices

Practitioners in asset allocation use asset matrices to show the degrees of correlation between asset classes. An example is shown in Figure 5.3. Usually, these use no more than three to four years' worth of data.

The problem with correlations is that they can vary significantly over time. Table 5.5 shows rising correlation over time between world equity markets.

During the period 1969–75, the highest correlation was between the US and the UK. But the low degree of correlation between other markets meant that

Figure 5.3 – Asset class correlation

Historical correlation*: January 2004–December 2008

	A	B	C	D	E	F	G	H	I	J	K	L
A	1.00											
B	(0.05)	1.00										
C	(0.04)	0.02	1.00									
D	(0.38)	(0.07)	(0.37)	1.00								
E	0.04	0.18	0.60	(0.49)	1.00							
F	(0.20)	0.09	0.45	(0.58)	0.87	1.00						
G	0.12	0.12	0.52	(0.48)	0.95	0.92	1.00					
H	(0.23)	0.00	0.21	0.15	(0.02)	(0.22)	0.01	1.00				
I	0.27	(0.03)	0.17	(0.44)	(0.48)	0.63	0.46	(0.36)	1.00			
J	0.12	0.12	0.32	(0.37)	0.77	0.89	0.79	(0.33)	0.75	1.00		
K	(0.20)	0.19	0.53	(0.17)	0.73	0.50	0.71	0.28	0.01	0.36	1.00	
L	0.16	0.11	0.42	(0.50)	0.86	0.98	0.89	(0.27)	0.70	0.96	0.47	1.00

			Positive	**Negative**
A	Bonds			
B	Cash	High	0.7–1.0	**(0.7)–(1.0)**
C	Commodities	Moderate	0.4–0.7	**(0.4)–(0.7)**
D	Currency	Low	0.0–0.4	(0.0)–(0.4)
E	Hedge Funds			
F	International Equity			
G	Long/Short			
H	Managed Futures			
I	REITs			
J	S&P 500			
K	Market Neutral			
L	Global			

* Correlation is a measurement between -1 and 1, which indicates the linear relationship between two variables. If there is no relationship between two variables, the correlation coefficient is 0. If there is a perfect relationship, the correlation is 1. And if there is a perfect inverse relationship, the correlation is -1.

Source: Calculated by Rydex/SGI using data from Bloomberg.com, Barclays.com and Standardandpoors.com.

Table 5.5 – Correlations between equities, 1969–75

	France	Germany	Japan	UK	US
France	1.00	0.41	0.46	0.58	0.57
Germany	0.41	1.00	0.41	0.63	0.43
Japan	0.46	0.41	1.00	0.38	0.49
UK	0.58	0.63	0.38	1.00	0.75
US	0.57	0.43	0.49	0.75	1.00

Correlations are based on annual returns in home currencies.
Source: Andrew Smithers, Wall Street Revalued

during this period an investor spreading capital across these markets would have achieved useful diversification benefits.

But in the most recent decade, these benefits have largely disappeared, as shown by Table 5.6.

Table 5.6 – Correlations between equities, 1999–2008

	France	Germany	Japan	UK	US
France	1.00	0.97	0.89	0.98	0.92
Germany	0.97	1.00	0.85	0.97	0.93
Japan	0.89	0.85	1.00	0.87	0.84
UK	0.98	0.97	0.87	1.00	0.93
US	0.92	0.93	0.84	0.93	1.00

Correlations are based on annual returns in home currencies.
Source: Andrew Smithers, Wall Street Revalued

Between 1999 and 2008, an investor gained virtually no diversification benefit from spreading capital across these markets, with one exception – a minor benefit in the case of Japan.

The long-run average correlations between these markets up to 1999 were far lower than in 1999–2008 and would also have proved a poor guide to portfolio construction for the latest decade.

10 Crisis correlations

The most extreme case of correlation occurred in autumn 2008, when the prices of all financial assets with the sole major exception of government bonds fell at the same time and correlation between returns from most asset classes reached exceptional levels. However, similar correlation during crisis had been noted in 1998, in 1987 and in 1973–74, so this is a persistent and predictable feature of financial markets and one that advisers cannot ignore. During such crisis conditions, the only assets that can be expected to withstand a general plunge in prices are cash and, to a lesser extent, short-dated government bonds from developed markets.

Given the evidence for mean reversion, the use of long-run returns as the basis for projecting the returns investors can expect from each of the asset classes is soundly based. Some degree of mean reversion can be assumed, as in the example for UK equities cited above, so that after decade-long periods of low returns, a higher annual rate could be projected, and vice versa.

On the other hand, it does not necessarily make sense to use long-run correlation data − and nor can using short-run correlation data be justified. Here, there are no good grounds for expecting reversion to the mean. On the contrary, if the globalisation of financial markets continues, a further increase in correlations is more likely in the future.

With models that simply use recent data discredited by the market meltdown experience of 2008−09, users of portfolio modelling tools need to pay particular attention to the assumptions being used for correlation.

11 Correlations in theory

Given that actual correlations have varied over time, what grounds can we have for expecting any particular degree of correlation to persist in future? To answer this question we have to look at the economic characteristics of an asset class and consider its 'normal' response to specific economic factors such as rising or falling interest rates, rising or falling inflation and rising or falling economic growth.

Three of these factors are summarised in Table 5.7 for five asset classes.

While these 'normal' responses can be expected to occur, they may not do so when expected. Investors tend to anticipate events, hence equities often rise or fall nine to twelve months before changes in economic trends. Moreover, the delays or advances in these responses may result in returns becoming correlated even for assets that should be uncorrelated. For example, a fall in interest rates should be good for conventional bonds, but if investors fear it will result in overheating and rising inflation, it may lead to bond prices falling instead of rising.

However, these are merely timing effects, and in the long run we can be certain that cash and equities will remain uncorrelated, as will cash and property, and that bonds and equities will show only moderate correlation. These admittedly broad brush conclusions are the only really solid ground we have in designing portfolios. Any pattern observed in correlations over short periods is likely to prove temporary and theory provides no grounds for expecting it to repeat.

As previously observed, the increasing integration of world capital markets implies a trend to higher correlations in returns from listed assets.

Table 5.7 – Asset class behaviour

Asset class	Inflation	Response to Interest rates	Economic growth
Cash deposits	+ Interest rates rise in response to rising inflation − Capital value eroded by inflation	+ Rising interest rates bring higher returns − Falling interest rates bring lower returns	+ Faster growth prompts a rise in interest rates − Faster growth makes rising inflation more likely
Government bonds (conventional)	+ Low inflation means good returns − Rising inflation erodes both interest and capital	+ Falling interest rates result in higher capital values − Rising interest rates result in falling capital values	+ Low/stable growth means low risk of inflation − Rapid growth threatens a rise in inflation
Index-linked bonds	+ Rising inflation generates higher returns − Stable/falling inflation generates low returns	+ Falling interest rates make index-linked more attractive − Rising nominal rates can lower index-linked returns	+ Rapid growth often means rising inflation − Low/stable growth means low risk of inflation
Commercial property	+ Rising inflation is reflected in higher rents − Deflation results in falling rents	+ Falling interest rates result in higher capital values − Rising interest rates result in lower capital values	+ Rapid growth means a rise in rents − Low growth means stable or falling rents
Equities	+ Profits and dividends usually follow rising inflation − Deflation puts pressure on profits and dividends	+ Falling interest rates stimulate investment − Rising interest rates divert capital away from equities	+ Rapid growth rates mean rising profits and dividends − Negative/low growth threatens profits and dividends

12 Reinvestment of income

Studies have shown that the reinvestment of income is the dominant contributor to returns from equities.

Table 5.8 – The effect of equity income reinvestment

Value as at December 2009 of £100 invested in 1899

	Nominal	Real
Without reinvestment of dividends	£11,407	£170
With reinvestment of dividends	£1,486,860	£22,150

Source: Barclays Capital, Equity Gilt Study 2010

The principal reason for this effect, which is far stronger than most people expect, is that the reinvestment of dividends uses cost-averaging principles (see below). In particular, dividends buy more shares when prices are low.

The implications for portfolio construction are significant. For long-term investors, the more equity yield that is secured and reinvested, the greater the proportion of total equity returns that is predictable. The equity income strategy is a reliable foundation for the equity element of portfolios.

13 Nominal and real returns

The data presented so far in this chapter has been mainly in real terms. Inflation – the change in monetary values – is 'noise' that obscures what is of real interest to investors: what their money will buy, now or in the future.

Product providers are required by the rules of the Financial Services Authority to produce tables showing projected returns at officially mandated nominal rates, and tables showing the effect of inflation on the purchasing power of money.

This is far from being an ideal way of presenting information to people who are, in most cases, not naturally numerate. Advisers should, in general, aim to illustrate returns from asset allocations and portfolios in real terms, especially for terms of ten years or more.

Though thinking 'in real terms' does not come naturally, if advisers explain the concept clients will find it easier to relate projected returns to their current situation and their expected situation in the future. 'Money illusion' (see part 4, chapter 20) is a handicap in making sound investment decisions.

14 Cost averaging

The principle of cost averaging is potentially of great advantage to investors. This is simply the principle that if you spend a fixed sum of money at regular intervals on an item whose price varies, the average price per unit that you end up paying for all your purchases will be lower than the average unit price. This is because you have bought more units at lower than at higher prices.

Table 5.9 – Cost averaging for a £100 savings plan

Period	Unit price	Number of units bought
1	100p	100
2	90p	111
3	80p	125
4	70p	143
5	60p	167
6	65p	154
7	75p	133
8	80p	125
9	85p	117
10	90p	111
11	95p	105
12	100p	100
Total units bought		1491
Average price	82.5p	
Average cost price		80.5p

The advantage gained is greatest with more volatile investments. This can be illustrated by taking two investments whose starting and finishing prices are the same – so that their average annualised returns are also the same – but whose volatility varies.

In this (admittedly extreme and artificial) case, the more volatile fund delivered more than three times the benefit of the less volatile fund. In reality, a benefit at around the 3% level would be a more realistic expectation, since even normally volatile funds usually undergo periods when they cease to be volatile.

Over the long term, cost averaging in volatile funds that also have above-average rates of return is a profitable strategy for investors. Given the risks inherent in such funds, spreading a monthly investment across several different funds can mitigate these risks and potentially provide a further benefit in that the funds are likely to hit peaks in returns at different times.

15 Compounding and discounting

The phenomenon of compound interest is far from intuitive. Its exponential quality means that most people will underestimate the final value of a lump sum or regular saving at a given rate of return.

Table 5.10 – Cost averaging for a £100 savings plan — effects of volatility

Period	More volatile fund Unit price	More volatile fund Number of units bought	Less volatile fund Unit price	Less volatile fund Number of units bought
1	100p	100	100p	100
2	70p	143	90p	111
3	50p	200	80p	125
4	70p	143	70p	143
5	100p	100	60p	167
6	125p	80	65p	154
7	150p	67	75p	133
8	130p	77	80p	125
9	100p	100	85p	117
10	80p	125	90p	111
11	70p	143	95p	105
12	100p	100	100p	100
Total units bought		1,378		1,491
Average price	95.4p		82.5p	
Average cost price		87.1p		80.5p
Discount from average price		8.7%		2.4%

Since the effect of compounding is in essence what most investors want, investment advisers need to ensure that their clients understand it. Advisers themselves will benefit from having ready access to a set of compound interest tables.

The non-intuitive nature of compounding is best seen in extreme examples. Assume someone saves £100 a month in an equity fund. At the end of ten years, the value will be £16,300 if the return is a steady 6% a year, while at 12% a year it will be £22,400. But if we extend the period to 30 years, the final values will be £97,900 and £308,000 respectively. Over ten years, a 12% return delivered a payout 37% higher than a 6% return, but over 30 years the difference is 214%. And the difference will continue to grow over time.

Behavioural finance (see chapters 11 and 20) has shown that most people over-emphasise the short term, in part because the future is hard to imagine. If they focus on the short term, the small difference in outcome from obtaining a higher rate of return can seem insignificant. For this reason, advisers usually need to emphasise the long-term benefits of higher returns. They also need to be aware of how sensitive the outcomes can be to changes in the rate of return achieved. The use of cash flow modeling in financial plans (see chapter 19) can make this sensitivity more obvious.

For institutional investors, discount rates are just as important as rates of return. The rate at which a future liability is discounted to a present value plays a large part in the formulation of investment strategy for pension funds and life assurance companies. It is rare to apply this method with individuals; most people would struggle with the idea that the discounted present value of their £100,000 interest-only mortgage is £75,000 at an interest rate of 5%, but £82,000 at 4%.

In general, discounting is only applied with individuals in showing the effects of inflation. Here, a typical statement is that if inflation averages 3% over ten years, the purchasing power of £1 at the end of that period will be 74.4p. Such examples are useful in reminding clients (who again tend to focus on the short term) of how, over the long-term, inflation can cause erosion to the real value of capital.

It is possible to project investment returns in nominal form and then adjust for inflation, but this can be confusing. Especially for long-term plans, it is often better to make assumptions about the real rates of return so that outcomes can be projected in terms of today's purchasing power. Table 5.1 shows the historic long-term real returns from cash, gilts and equities in the UK.

16 Income and capital returns

Portfolio theory uses total returns. The presumption is that investors earn total returns and choose what proportion of them to spend. However, capital values are far more volatile than income streams. To avoid the effects of capital volatility, many investors, especially income investors, prefer to secure streams of income with low volatility.

In fact, both theory and practice show that if investors attempt to draw too large an income from capital invested in equities, they can suffer permanent and irrecoverable losses of capital. If the amount withdrawn is specified as a monetary amount, then the percentage of the actual market value of the investments that has to be encashed to provide the income rises as market prices fall. A downward spiral ensues and after a few years, the value of the portfolio can be so diminished that only extraordinarily high rates of return could ever return it to its former values.

Since most clients will end up drawing on some of their capital during the 'decumulation' period (see part 4, chapter 21), advisers need to take care over the actual rates of capital withdrawal from portfolios and to ensure that clients are aware of the implications of rates of withdrawal above 3% annually.

In Table 5.11, drawing a total of £20,000 from a £100,000 portfolio results in the situation that a doubling in the value is required to restore initial capital, while another four similar withdrawals would reduce the capital value to just over a third of its starting level.

Table 5.11 – The danger of capital withdrawal

| | Capital value | | | |
Period	Before withdrawal	After withdrawal	Amount withdrawn	% of capital value
1	£100,000	£96,000	£4,000	4%
2	£85,000	£81,000	£4,000	4.7%
3	£75,000	£71,000	£4,000	5.3%
4	£65,000	£61,000	£4,000	6.1%
5	£55,000	£51,000	£4,000	7.2%

17 Absolute and relative returns

The returns from investments are what they earn. Returns can be measured in two distinct ways:

- **Absolute returns** measure what has been achieved in money terms, and possibly in real (inflation-adjusted) terms.

- **Relative returns** compare what has been achieved with a representative index (such as the FTSE All-Share index).

There are arguments for both approaches, more fully discussed in part 2, chapter 6.

In principle, advisers adopting asset allocation methods should be determining risk preferences and creating portfolios appropriate to these, with defined asset mixes. A suitable benchmark for relative purposes would then be an index which allocates the relevant proportions of capital to a representative index in each asset class. In practice, less precise measures are often adequate.

However, the absolute or money returns achieved are also of interest to the investor. The more cautious the individual, the larger the part money returns are likely to play in the way they think about their investments.

The absolute return measures the progress made towards the client's objectives, which (see chapter 21) have to be expressed in terms of future cash flow needs to serve as guides to portfolio construction. The absolute return has to be put in the context of both long-term and short-term financial market trends.

A negative return resulting from a fall in the stock market may not represent a failure to progress towards the client's objectives if the fall is within the range expected for the portfolio.

Provided an appropriate benchmark is used, the relative return measures the success or otherwise of the selection of investments within the asset allocation framework, or of the investment manager's buying and selling decisions within a fund.

18 Indices and benchmarks

Issues involved in benchmarking are covered in chapter 7. For individual investors, indices that are familiar may be preferable to others that may be more representative but are not familiar or easily accessible. The FTSE index series, for example, is easily accessible by UK investors and widely used by UK media.

However, indices may be widely used as representative of a specific market but at the same time diverge from what advisers are attempting to achieve in portfolio construction. The FTSE 100 index, for example, being capitalisation weighted, is heavily invested in a small number of 'mega cap' stocks, several of which have in recent times constituted over 10% of the index, and has at times had an overall exposure to financials of over 35%. The argument that the index *is* effectively the market and is therefore the appropriate yardstick, is as much a part of portfolio theory as the efficient frontier, and requires if not scepticism then at least an openness to alternative measures.

The Dow Jones index, the FT30 index and other share indices have used methods other than capitalisation weighting to represent market returns. Fundamental-weighted, equal-weighted and dividend-weighted indices are among recent developments that may provide more useful benchmarks for some categories of investor.

19 The difficulties of thinking about probabilities

The basis of portfolio theory is probabilistic. While certain of its concepts are intuitively obvious, such as the advantages of non-correlation, the actual methods and mathematical techniques used will be beyond the grasp of anyone without advanced mathematical understanding (equivalent to at least GCSE A-level in the case of much of the theory discussed in part 2 of this book). Hence a large majority of the population will, in practice, be unable to grasp the details of portfolio theory or the techniques being used.

Deterministic thinking ('If A, then B'), being based on inductive logic, is much easier to grasp and is still used much of the time by financial market participants.

Numerous studies have shown that not only ordinary people but also many professionals with higher degrees are poor at probabilistic reasoning. Add this to the behavioural biases discussed in chapter 11 and chapter 20, and we can see how difficult it is to ensure clients clearly understand what is possible in investment, and what the adviser is actually trying to achieve for them.

However, in the process of designing a portfolio, the adviser must investigate the client's wants and needs, and help the client to prioritise these on the basis of probabilities — the client's own assessment of the likelihood of certain life and other events (see chapter 21). Most people will comfortably address these issues when faced with a question along the lines of 'Is this more or less probable?' but will become uncomfortable if asked, 'Would you assign a 30% or 50% probability to that?'.

Probabilistic thinking is multifactorial, and most people do it intuitively without using mathematical processes (it is likely that successful traders are more adept at this than average). But they are aware that they are assessing different factors when making such judgments. Advisers can use this as an analogy for the processes involved in portfolio design, for it is important that clients understand that investment is almost never a matter of certainties and that assessing probabilities is an essential feature of a disciplined investment process.

Summary

- Over a century's worth of data tell us that shares earn the highest returns, followed by commercial property, bonds and cash. But these are long-term averages and returns can be below-average for as long as a decade. The data, especially for shares, show reversion to the mean, so that returns in the decade that follows a poor decade are likely to be higher than the long-term average.

- Economic theory does not provide a full explanation for equity investors' reward for risk, the Equity Risk Premium, so economists' suggestions that it will be lower than the historical average in future can be taken with a pinch of salt.

- Consistently successful equity management strategies over the past 100 years have been value, smallcap and momentum.

- Asset class characteristics determine their long-term correlations, but in crises correlations usually increase, and globalisation appears to have raised correlations between many assets over the past three decades.

- Reinvestment of income and securing the benefits of cost averaging through regular investment are two reliable ways of enhancing equity returns.

- Too high a rate of income withdrawal incurs significant risks of capital erosion.

Part 2: Managing risk and return — the theory

Introduction

Modern portfolio theory has come under heavy criticism following the crisis of 2007–08, with the main principles being widely challenged. Many of the key conclusions and applications of the theory have proved to be flawed. Firstly, buying risky assets has not generated superior returns; for example, over the ten years to end-2010 holding equities generated a negative equity risk premium since equities delivered lower returns than gilts. Secondly, portfolio diversification was largely ineffective at protecting portfolios against losses in the 2007–08 collapse of markets: equities, corporate bonds, commodities (with the exception of gold), commercial property and hedge funds all fell more or less in tandem. Thirdly, extreme events, or what would have been extreme events in the past, became commonplace as market volatility multiplied.

Despite the distrust of modern portfolio theory and the models it has created, it is important for advisers to understand the concepts, many of which can best be regarded as 'illuminating but not true'. They are widely used in finance and will remain the starting point for constructing portfolios until a more complete theory is developed. It is important to remember that modern portfolio theory is a theory and in extreme markets all economic theories have largely failed to predict or explain market behaviour.

In chapter 6, we start by defining risk and return. The mathematically determinable measure of risk used in theory must diverge from the dictionary definition and understanding the distinction is vital. Chapter 7 covers the measurement of risk using the techniques of standard deviation and other measures. Understanding the types of risk that affect investments and how they do so is key to creating portfolios that aim to control risk (chapter 8).

Once we create portfolios containing different types of investment, we have to consider how to model the risks involved (chapter 9), which leads us to look at correlation, optimisation and the notion of the efficient frontier. This leads on to the methods most widely used to manage risk in chapter 10, especially the use of derivatives to separate the market-related return (beta) from specific (or skill-related) return (alpha).

In chapter 11 we consider the significance of the biases identified by behavioural finance on the behaviour of investors and markets (chapter 20 in Part 4 revisits this issue in relation to advising clients).

Appendix 1 takes a closer look at the Efficient Market Hypothesis and its role in portfolio theory.

Chapter 6
Defining risk and return

1 Introduction

The theory of investment has been built up around the relationship between risk and return and how an optimal trade-off between the two can be achieved. In this chapter we will consider the major definitions of risk and return, and then in chapter 7 we will look in more detail at the various risk measures and how returns are adjusted for risk.

2 Return

There are two main types of return, total return and relative return, and which of these is applicable will depend on client objectives. For example, has the client asked to obtain positive returns over any 12-month period, or a return of 5% a year? These are absolute or total return objectives, since the client wishes to achieve these returns regardless of whether markets are rising or falling. Or has the client asked that his or her investments outperform a benchmark or market index and is he or she willing to accept a decline in the value of investments if the underlying market falls? This is a relative return objective.

Total return

The total return is the capital gain and income over a period; this can be the return for an individual security or a portfolio of securities and is sometimes referred to as 'holding period return' or 'absolute return'. Usually the return is expressed as a percentage of the initial value. The formula for total return (R) is

$$R = \frac{EV - BV + C}{BV}$$

where:

- EV is the end value.
- BV is the beginning value.
- C stands for the cash outflows paid to the client.

Note that the total return calculated using this equation will have the following characteristics:

- It will reflect the performance of the underlying markets.
- It can be calculated over any period, although clients are usually presented with annual returns.

Example 6.1: Calculation of total return

A portfolio has an initial value of £100m, one year later the portfolio has increased in value to £110m and over the year payments of £5m were made to the client from the portfolio. The total return is:

$$R = \frac{EV - BV + C}{BV} = \frac{110 - 100 + 5}{100} = 15\%$$

The portfolio generated a total return of 15%.

Relative return

The relative return is the return from an investment or portfolio measured against the return from a benchmark such as the FTSE All-Share index. This isolates how well the investments have done from the return of the market and measures whether a fund manager has added value over and above the index return. The formula for relative return (R_{REL}) is

$$R_{REL} = R - R_B$$

where:

- R is the total return.

- R_B is the benchmark return.

Example 6.2: Calculation of relative return

A portfolio has generated a return of 15% over the last year, and the benchmark index rose by 12% over the same period. The relative return is:

$$R_{REL} = R - R_B = 15\% - 12\% = 3\%$$

The portfolio outperformed the benchmark by 3%.

Other returns

Some of the other terms used for returns are described below.

Real return

Real returns are returns after inflation, as opposed to nominal returns, which include inflation. Most investors are concerned about the increase in purchasing power of their portfolio so the real return is an important measure, particularly in periods of high inflation. The real return is approximately the total return minus the inflation rate, but more accurately it is calculated as the total return discounted by the inflation rate.

The formula for real return (R_{REAL}) is

$$R_{REAL} = \frac{(1 + R)}{(1 + R_{INF})} - 1$$

where:

- R is the total return.

- R_{INF} is the inflation rate.

Example 6.3: Calculation of real return

A portfolio has generated a return of 15% over the last year, and the inflation rate was 2% over the same period. The real return is:

$$R_{REAL} = \frac{(1 + R)}{(1 + R_{INF})} - 1 = \frac{1.15}{1.02} - 1 = 12.74\%$$

The portfolio generated a real return of 12.74%.

Excess return

The term 'excess return' is often used to mean the same as relative return, namely the difference between the return on an investment and the benchmark return. More strictly, excess return is the return over and above the risk-free rate. The risk-free rate is commonly set as the 90-day Treasury bill rate, although there are arguments in favour of using a long-term gilt yield as the risk-free rate, or a long-term index-linked bond yield as the real risk-free rate.

Gross/net return

The net return is the return after all the costs have been taken from the portfolio. These costs will include:

- Transaction costs, including commission and stamp duty.

- Annual charges, including investment management fees, fund administration costs and custody fees.

- Taxes.

The total return should also be net of transaction costs (according to Global Investment Performance Standards or GIPS, the international standard for performance presentation), and is usually after tax. The main difference between gross and net returns is the annual charges, of which the largest portion is usually the investment management fees.

Measuring returns over multiple periods

When returns are quoted as an average return over multiple periods there are two main methods for computing the number, the first a time-weighted return and the second a money-weighted return. The time-weighted rate of return is the most commonly used since it is not affected by the timing of cash inflows and outflows from a portfolio, which are usually deemed to be outside the investment manager's control. But for private equity portfolios, for example, where the fund manager is making the decision to invest more money, use of the money-weighted rate of return is more appropriate.

Time-weighted return

The time-weighted rate of return is the compound rate of growth of £1 initially invested in the portfolio or fund. The time-weighted return over N periods (R_N) is given by

$$R_N = [(1 + r_1)(1 + r_2) \ldots \ldots (1 + r_N)] - 1$$

where r_I is the return in period I.

The average time-weighted return (R_{Nave}) is given by:

$$R_{Nave} = [(1 + r_1)(1 + r_2) \ldots \ldots (1 + r_N)]^{1/N} - 1$$

In example 6.4 the cash flow came in at the end of the quarter. If there is a significant cash flow in the middle of a period then the portfolio should be revalued at the time of the cash flow. What is considered 'significant' will depend on the size of the cash flow relative to the size of the portfolio and the volatility of the underlying markets.

Example 6.4: Calculation of time-weighted return

A portfolio starts with a value of £100m. After the first quarter the value falls to £90m and the client then adds £20m to this portfolio at the end of this quarter (increasing the value to £110m after the inflow). In the second quarter the value of the portfolio has risen to £130m.

The return generated by the portfolio in the first quarter is calculated as follows:

$$r_1 = \frac{EV - BV + C}{BV} = \frac{90 - 100}{100} = -10\%$$

In the second quarter the return is calculated as:

$$r_2 = \frac{EV - BV + C}{BV} = \frac{130 - 110}{110} = 18.18\%$$

The time-weighted return is calculated as:

$$R_N = [(1 + r_1)(1 + r_2) \ldots \ldots (1 + r_N)] - 1 = [(0.90)(1.18)] - 1 = 6.20\%$$

The portfolio generated a return of 6.2% over the year.

The average quarterly return is calculated as:

$$R_N = [(1 + r_1)(1 + r_2) \ldots \ldots (1 + r_N)]^{1/N} - 1 = [(0.90)(1.18)]^{1/2} - 1 = 3.05\%$$

The average quarterly return was 3.05%.

Money-weighted return

The money-weighted rate of return is the internal rate of return (IRR) or average growth rate for all money invested in the portfolio or fund. The IRR is best found using a calculator and in example 6.4 it is 4.45%.

This is higher than the time-weighted return since the cash inflow occurred before a rise in value of the portfolio. If the cash inflow had occurred before a decline, the opposite would have happened and the time-weighted return would be more than the money-weighted return.

3 Risk

Risk measurement has become even more important in the light of the 40% to 50% falls in equity markets in both 2000–02 and 2008. If managers wish to generate returns they have to take on risk, so risk in itself is not bad as long as it is generating returns to compensate. Of course the risk taken must be at levels that are acceptable to clients.

Standard deviation of returns

The standard deviation (SD) of total returns is the most commonly used risk measure for investment funds. It measures the volatility or dispersion of individual returns around the average return of the fund. It is important to note that SD is not directly a measure of risk: more accurately, it measures variations in returns around an average.

Definition

Standard deviation is the square root of variance, and is often denoted by sigma (σ). Variance is the average of the squared deviations around the mean, based on past performance.

The formula for variance is

$$\sigma^2 = \frac{\sum\limits_{I=1}^{n}(x_I - \overline{x})^2}{(n-1)}$$

where:

- x_I is the return in period I.
- $\bar{x}$ is the average return.
- n is the number of periods.

This is *ex-post* or historic variance as opposed to *ex-ante* or predicted variance. We will apply this formula in the next chapter.

Interpretation

Figure 6.1 illustrates the difference between high and low standard deviation funds.

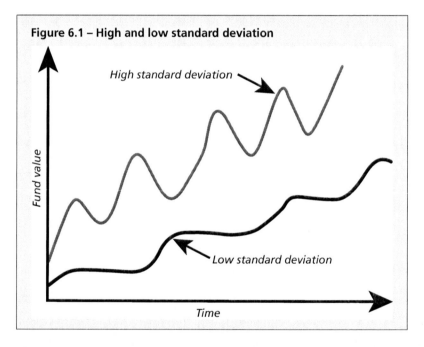

Figure 6.1 – High and low standard deviation

The conventional way of describing this is to say that the higher the standard deviation, the riskier the investment or fund.

This is the risk of total, not relative, returns so it incorporates the risk of the underlying market or benchmark as well as the risk the fund manager took against the benchmark. Therefore, for equity funds, an annual standard deviation of anywhere from 10% to 25% for mature markets, or above 25% for emerging markets, is common. For bond funds the standard deviation is usually lower and often less than 10%.

In the credit crunch the S&P 500 VIX Index (an index of volatility based on equity option prices) rose to over 70, indicating that the implied volatility of the US equity market was over 70%. Subsequently volatility numbers have dropped back and, with the exception of mid-2010, have stayed in the 20% to 30% range, which is still higher than the long-term historic averages.

Figure 6.2 – CBOE SPX market Volatility Index, 5 years to April 2011

Source: Chicago Board Options Exchange (CBOE)

To get an indication of whether the fund manager has been adopting a risky strategy it is also helpful to know the tracking error (the risk against the benchmark) or the standard deviation of the benchmark and the standard deviation of funds with similar objectives.

Tracking error

Tracking error is an appropriate risk measure for clients whose objective is a relative, as opposed to a total, return objective.

Definition

Tracking error is usually defined as the standard deviation of returns relative to the benchmark. (Relative return is the fund's return minus the benchmark return.) The formula is

$$TE^2 = \frac{\sum_{I=1}^{n} \left(R_I - \overline{R}\right)^2}{(n-1)}$$

where:

- R_I is the relative return in period I.
- $\overline{R}$ is the average relative return.
- n is the number of periods.

This is *ex-post* or historic tracking error as opposed to *ex-ante* or predicted tracking error.

Interpretation

Figure 6.3 illustrates the difference between high and low tracking error.

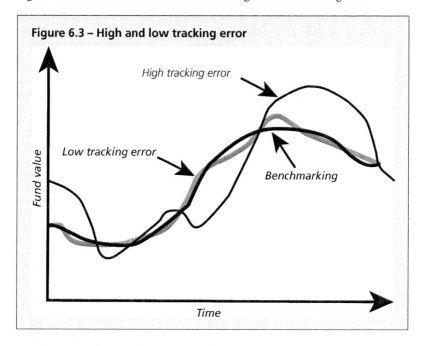

Figure 6.3 – High and low tracking error

The higher the tracking error, the more risk the fund manager has taken against the benchmark.

If tracking error is low, say less than 0.5%, the fund is effectively a tracker or index fund and the manager has been taking almost no risk against the index.

For active equity funds tracking error is usually between 2% and 6%. For bond funds it is often lower, say 1% to 4%. In order to generate outperformance of the benchmark a manager will have to take on risk relative to the benchmark. If tracking error is very low investors are probably getting poor value for money if they are paying an active manager a high level of fees. With a passive index tracker fund you can gain index exposure at a very low cost (see chapter 15).

A very high tracking error would lead one to question whether the benchmark is appropriate for the fund.

We will return to standard deviation and tracking error in the next chapter.

Portfolio risk

The method of calculating portfolio returns is intuitive; it is simply the weighted-average return of assets in the portfolio. So if an investor owns two shares and both make up 50% of the portfolio, and one rises by 10% and the other by 20%, the return is simply 15%. The calculation for portfolio risk is more complex, since portfolio risk takes into account the covariance or correlation between each pair of assets.

The formula for portfolio risk (σ_{Port}) provided by Markowitz looks complicated:

$$\sigma^2_{\text{Port}} = \sum_{I=1}^{n} w_I^2 \sigma_I^2 + \sum_{I=1}^{n} \sum_{\substack{j=1 \\ I \neq j}}^{n} w_I w_j \text{cov}_{ij}$$

where:

- w_I is the weighting in security I.
- σ_I is the standard deviation of security.
- cov_{ij} is the covariance between securities I and j and measures how closely two assets move together.

Without attempting to apply the formula we can see there are two ways we can minimise risk in portfolios. The first is to buy low-risk (low σ) assets, but low-risk assets tend to have low long-term returns so this not an attractive option. The second way is to buy risky assets that have attractive long-term returns, but to choose assets with low, or even negative, covariance. This will reduce (or theoretically eliminate if we are hedging) the portfolio risk. In this context this is referred to as 'diversification'.

Covariance and correlation

Covariance and correlation between assets is critical to portfolio construction so we will now look at them in more detail.

The covariance measures how closely two assets move together relative to their mean values. Covariance is 'standardised' to give the correlation coefficient, which lies between −1 and +1. The correlation coefficient r_{xy} between two variables x and y is given by:

$$r_{xy} = \frac{\text{cov}_{xy}}{\sigma_x \sigma_y}$$

where:

- cov_{xy} is the covariance between the returns of x and y.
- σ_x is the standard deviation of returns of x.
- σ_y is the standard deviation of returns of y.

If r_{xy} is +1, this is perfect positive correlation. It means that there is a perfect linear relationship between the returns from the two assets. The stocks move in the same direction, although one stock may make more exaggerated moves than the other.

If r_{xy} is 0, the returns are not linearly correlated.

If r_{xy} is −1, this is perfect negative correlation. If one return is above its mean then the other will be below the mean by a comparable amount.

In Example 6.5 we simplify the equation for portfolio risk when we apply it to a two-asset portfolio. Thus:

$$\sigma^2_{\text{Port}} = \sum_{I=1}^{n} w_I^2 \sigma_I^2 + \sum_{I=1}^{n} \sum_{\substack{j=1 \\ I \neq j}}^{n} w_I w_j \text{cov}_{ij}$$

simplifies to

$$\sigma^2_{\text{Port}} = w_1^2 \sigma_1^2 + w_2^2 \sigma_2^2 + 2r_{12} w_1 w_2 \sigma_1 \sigma 2$$

Example 6.5: Portfolio risk

The standard deviations of the returns of two securities are 5% and 10%, with expected returns of 8% and 12% respectively. A portfolio is invested with 40% in the first security and 60% in the second security. Looking at the three cases where the correlation coefficient between the returns of the assets are (1) 1.0, (2) 0 and (3) −1.0, the expected return and standard deviation of the combined portfolio are calculated as follows.

1. The expected return is:

$$E\left(R_{\text{Port}}\right) = w_1 E\left(R_1\right) + w_2 E\left(R_2\right)$$
$$= (0.40 \times 8\%) + (0.60 \times 12\%)$$
$$= 10.4\%$$

The portfolio risk, when the correlation is 1.0, is:

$$\sigma^2_{\text{Port}} = w_1^2 \sigma_1^2 + w_2^2 \sigma_2^2 + 2w_1 w_2 \sigma_1 \sigma_2$$
$$\sigma_{\text{Port}} = w_1 \sigma_1 + w_2 \sigma_2 = (0.40 \times 5\%) + (0.60 \times 10\%) = 8.0\%$$

When the correlation is 1.0, the expected return is 10.4% and the standard deviation of returns is 8.0%.

2. As before, the expected return is 10.4%. The portfolio risk, when the correlation is 0, is calculated as follows:

$$\sigma^2_{\text{Port}} = w_1^2\sigma_1^2 + w_2^2\sigma_2^2 = 0.0004 + 0.0036 = 0.004$$

$$\sigma_{\text{Port}} = 6.3\%$$

When the correlation is 0, the expected return is 10.4% and the standard deviation of returns is 6.3%.

3. As before, the expected return is 10.4% and the portfolio risk, when the correlation is −1.0, is calculated as follows:

$$\sigma^2_{\text{Port}} = w_1^2\sigma_1^2 + w_2^2\sigma_2^2 - 2w_1w_2\sigma_1\sigma_2$$

$$\sigma_{\text{Port}} = |w_1\sigma_1 - w_2\sigma_2| = |(0.40 \times 5\%) - (0.60 \times 10\%)| = 4.0\%$$

When the correlation is −1, the expected return is 10.4% and the standard deviation of returns is 4.0%.

We can see that when the correlation is 1.0, the risk is simply the weighted-average risk of the two assets. There are no diversification benefits since the two assets always move in the same direction relative to their mean return. When the correlation is 0 we start to see the benefits of diversification and risk drops to 6.3%. With correlation of −1, portfolio risk falls even further, to 4.0%.

With correlation of −1 we could have eliminated risk altogether if we had weighted the assets differently, putting two-thirds in the first asset and the remaining third in the second asset.

In chapter 9 we will look at the actual correlation between asset classes and discuss the stability of correlation numbers.

Other risks

Up to now we have focused on the commonly used measures of portfolio or market risk, and ignored other risks which have shown to be destructive to portfolio value. These risks include credit or counterparty risk and liquidity risk, both of which have been primary considerations in the credit crisis. We will look at these risks in chapter 8.

Summary

This chapter has set the foundation for an analysis of portfolios in terms of the main risk and return measures used in investment. Investment returns can be defined and measured in several ways. Absolute return and relative return are valid and useful measures in different contexts.

- Standard deviation is the generally used measure of risk and measures the extent of deviations from the asset's average return

- Portfolio returns are the average of the returns of assets in the portfolio, but the risk cannot be calculated in this way because of correlation.

- Greater or lower correlation between the returns of assets in the portfolio increases or reduces the overall risk of the portfolio.

In the next chapter we will move on to a more detailed explanation of how risk is measured and look at the interpretation of the numbers as well as the limitations of each measure.

Chapter 7
Measuring risk

1 Introduction

In this chapter we will look at the standard deviation of returns and tracking error in more detail before looking at other risk measures widely used for analysing equity and bond portfolios. Finally we will examine the main methods for computing risk-adjusted returns and discuss when it is appropriate to use them.

2 Standard deviation

We will first of all return to the main statistic used to measure the risk of funds, portfolios, assets and securities. Throughout this chapter we will commonly use examples of fund or portfolio performance but the analysis can equally be applied to assets or individual securities.

Calculation

In the previous chapter we looked at the definitions of variance and standard deviation. The formula we used for variance (which is standard deviation squared) was

$$\sigma^2 = \frac{\sum_{I=1}^{n} (x_I - \overline{x})^2}{(n-1)}$$

where:

- σ is the standard deviation.
- x_I is the return in period I.
- $\overline{x}$ is the average return.
- n is the number of periods.

If all of the returns from a portfolio or fund are being measured, the $(n-1)$ in the denominator is replaced by n, but if it is only a sample of the returns $(n-1)$ is used instead. Typically the calculation uses monthly returns over the last three years, or a similar number of returns, in which case using n or $(n-1)$ will not make a significant difference. If too few returns are used then the standard deviation number will not be statistically meaningful.

It is important to check whether a standard deviation number is monthly or annualised, since both versions are quoted in different publications. If a monthly standard deviation number is given it can be annualised by multiplying by $\sqrt{12}$, and a quarterly one can be annualised by multiplying by 2 (which is $\sqrt{4}$) and so on.

In example 7.1 we will compute the standard deviation of a portfolio when we are given the monthly returns for three years, 2008–10.

Example 7.1: Calculating the standard deviation of a portfolio

The returns for each month are given in the second column and we calculate the average monthly return, $\overline{x}$, which is simply the sum of the returns divided by the 36 months. The average is 0.1% a month. We then calculate, in the third column, month by month, the difference between the return and the average of 0.1%, $(x_I - \overline{x})$. In the fourth column we square each number and then take the average, which is 0.05%. This is the variance of the returns and the standard deviation is the square root, which is 2.31%. This is the monthly standard deviation and the annual standard deviation is $2.31\% \times \sqrt{12} = 8.00\%$.

Month	Return (x_I)	Difference $(x_I - \overline{x})$	Variance $(x_I - \overline{x})^2$
January 2008	−1.2%	−1.3%	0.02%
February 2008	1.9%	1.8%	0.03%
March 2008	0.2%	0.1%	0.00%
April 2008	3.4%	3.3%	0.11%
May 2008	−2.4%	−2.5%	0.06%
June 2008	1.9%	1.8%	0.03%
July 2008	2.8%	2.7%	0.07%
August 2008	−0.9%	−1.0%	0.01%
September 2008	−3.6%	−3.7%	0.14%
October 2008	0.7%	0.6%	0.00%
November 2008	−2.1%	−2.2%	0.05%
December 2008	0.5%	0.4%	0.00%
January 2009	−4.1%	−4.2%	0.18%
February 2009	−2.3%	−2.4%	0.06%
March 2009	1.5%	1.4%	0.02%
April 2009	−2.6%	−2.7%	0.07%
May 2009	4.2%	4.1%	0.17%
June 2009	3.1%	3.0%	0.09%
July 2009	−0.8%	−0.9%	0.01%
August 2009	1.1%	1.0%	0.01%
September 2009	−5.3%	−5.4%	0.29%

October 2009	−1.7%	−1.8%	0.03%
November 2009	2.4%	2.3%	0.05%
December 2009	2.5%	2.4%	0.06%
January 2010	0.3%	0.2%	0.00%
February 2010	−0.9%	−1.0%	0.01%
March 2010	−1.9%	−2.0%	0.04%
April 2010	0.7%	0.6%	0.00%
May 2010	1.6%	1.5%	0.02%
June 2010	0.6%	0.5%	0.00%
July 2010	2.5%	2.4%	0.06%
August 2010	−2.1%	−2.2%	0.05%
September 2010	1.9%	1.8%	0.03%
October 2010	0.8%	0.7%	0.00%
November 2010	2.5%	2.4%	0.06%
December 2010	−1.6%	−1.7%	0.03%
Total	**3.6%**	**0.0%**	**1.87%**
Average	0.1%		0.05%
Standard deviation	$\bar{x}$	−	2.31%

Interpretation

The risk number calculated in example 7.1 needs to be interpreted. Clearly the higher the number the higher the risk, so we can use the number to compare the risk of different assets, portfolios or funds or to monitor a fund over time.

If we assume that the returns from a fund are normally distributed we can draw some more conclusions. A normal distribution means that if we plotted the number of times a return or observation occurs on the y-axis and the actual return on the x-axis then we would get a bell-shaped curve which peaks at the average return and with most of the observations clustering around the mean.

The bell shape will be flatter if the standard deviation is high and the returns are more dispersed. If the returns are more tightly clustered the fund will have a lower standard deviation.

For any normal distribution:

- 68.3% of returns lie between the mean return ± 1 standard deviation.
- 95.5% of returns lie between the mean return ± 2 standard deviations.
- 99.7% of returns lie between the mean return ± 3 standard deviations.

This is illustrated in Figure 7.1, which shows a bell-shaped normal distribution and the proportion of observations or returns in each range.

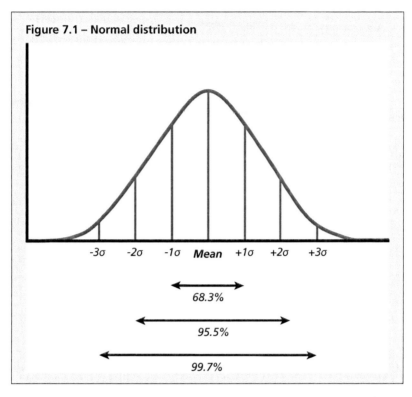

Figure 7.1 – Normal distribution

Returning to example 7.1, where we calculated that the average monthly return was 0.1% and the standard deviation of returns was 2.31%, we can conclude that if the returns were normally distributed then 68.3% (often approximated to two-thirds) of the monthly returns have been between 0.1% ± 2.31%, that is, between −2.21% and 2.41%. Similarly we can say 95.5% of the returns have been between −4.52% and 4.72%, and 99.7% have been between −6.83% and 7.03%.

If returns remain as they have been in the past, we can predict that future returns will fall in a similar pattern. Standard deviation can also give an indication of the likelihood of a loss in any one period. In example 7.1 approximately half of the monthly returns will be below the average of 0.1% and in one in six periods they will be below −2.21%, if the return and standard deviation of the fund continue at the same level.

Kurtosis

This type of analysis, although commonly covered in textbooks, is misleading, because although security returns may be *approximately* normally distributed, they almost always have fat tails, which means there are more extreme events than predicted by a normal distribution. These fat tails occur when there is positive excess kurtosis, which is called a leptokurtic distribution; see Figure 7.1

for a comparison between a normal distribution and one with positive excess kurtosis.

In security markets the occurrence of extreme events is far more common than it would be if returns were normally distributed, which continues to surprise market commentators. The extent of the difference between 'normal' and actual distribution is sometimes described in terms of sigma. A '5-sigma event' is one that would occur only on one day in every 6,700 years if distribution was normal. Many events in the credit crunch were described as '7-sigma events', which would occur on only one day in every 1,553 million years in a normal distribution.

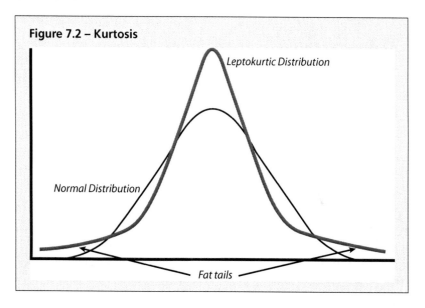

Figure 7.2 – Kurtosis

Leptokurtic Distribution

Normal Distribution

Fat tails

Skew

The other main concern in the calculation of standard deviation is that it treats returns below the mean and returns above the mean as equally important, since we are squaring the deviations and losing any minus signs. So we are treating downside risk and upside risk as the same. If returns are symmetric this is not a problem, but if they are skewed we could underestimate downside risk.

If a distribution of portfolio returns is positively skewed this indicates that poor returns occur frequently but losses are small, whereas very high returns occur less frequently but are more extreme (see Figure 7.3).

Skewness is calculated using the cubes of the deviations, which preserves the 'direction' of the deviations, that is, whether the observations are above or below the mean. When interpreting investment returns, positive skewness is usually considered attractive since it indicates that there is a greater probability of very high returns.

Positive skew combined with kurtosis, indicating that surprises will be on the upside, is far preferable to negative skew and kurtosis, which indicates that the surprises will be on the downside.

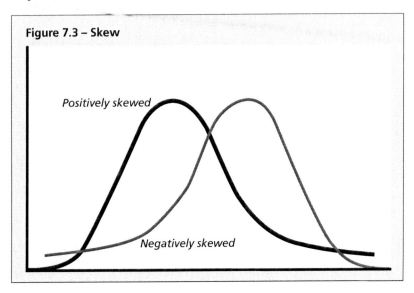

Figure 7.3 – Skew

Positively skewed

Negatively skewed

When there are skewed distributions, an alternative risk measure to variance is semi-variance. The square root of semi-variance is downside deviation, which measures downside risk. The calculations are similar to those shown in example 7.1 but to calculate downside risk only the returns below the mean, or a specified minimum return, are included in the calculation. This avoids 'penalising' the manager for strong positive performance.

Limitations

To summarise, the key limitations of standard deviation are as follows:

- Being based on monthly returns, standard deviation is a measure of the short-term volatility of an asset or portfolio: for an investor with a long time horizon this may not be a relevant measure of risk.

- When standard deviation is reported for portfolios it is a backward-looking risk measure: it tells you what the risk of the portfolio was in the past. If the market environment or the strategy of the fund manager changes, the risk profile of the fund will change.

- It is only an appropriate measure of risk when a portfolio's returns are normally, or approximately normally, distributed. If there is kurtosis or skew it will not be picked up by the standard deviation calculation.

- The standard deviation number will reflect the standard deviation of the underlying market, so further analysis is needed to evaluate the risk taken by the fund manager against the market. One way to do this is to look at tracking error.

3 Tracking error

For clients or funds with relative return objectives, tracking error is an appropriate risk measure, rather than measuring the standard deviation of total returns.

Calculation

Tracking error (TE) is relative risk and the formula we used in chapter 6 is

$$TE^2 = \frac{\sum_{I=1}^{n} \left(R_I - \overline{R}\right)^2}{(n-1)}$$

where:

- R_I is the relative return in period I.
- $\overline{R}$ is the average relative return.
- n is the number of periods.

This is a standard deviation calculation, but this time for relative returns. So as before, if all of the relative returns from a portfolio or fund are being measured the $(n-1)$ in the denominator is replaced by n, but if a sample only is being measured $(n-1)$ is used. Often the calculation uses monthly returns over the last three years; again if too few returns are used then the standard deviation number will not be statistically meaningful.

The usefulness of a tracking error calculation will only be as good as the benchmark used; an incorrect benchmark will lead to higher tracking error than if the correct benchmark is used.

In example 7.2 we compute the tracking error of the portfolio used in example 7.1. The data for the fund return is the same as in example 7.1, but in this case we also need to know the benchmark returns for each period so we can calculate the relative returns.

Example 7.2: Calculating tracking error

In the fourth column we calculate the relative return for each month (portfolio return minus benchmark return) and then compute the average of all the relative returns. In this case the average is zero, so overall the fund has performed in line with the benchmark. We need to compute the standard deviation of these relative returns and in the final column we square the relative return (minus the mean relative return of zero), add the numbers and divide by 35 and then take the square root to get the monthly tracking error of 0.59%.

Month	Return	Benchmark return	Relative return	
	(x_I)			
January 2008	−1.2%	−1.1%	−0.1%	0.0001%
February 2008	1.9%	2.0%	−0.1%	0.0001%
March 2008	0.2%	0.5%	−0.3%	0.0009%
April 2008	3.4%	−0.6%	4.0%	0.0036%
May 2008	−2.4%	−3.0%	0.6%	0.0036%
June 2008	1.9%	2.2%	−0.3%	0.0009%
July 2008	2.8%	2.7%	0.1%	0.0001%
August 2008	−0.9%	−1.5%	0.6%	0.0036%
September 2008	−3.6%	−3.8%	0.2%	0.0004%
October 2008	0.7%	0.1%	0.6%	0.0036%
November 2008	−2.1%	−2.4%	0.3%	0.0009%
December 2008	0.5%	0.3%	0.2%	0.0004%
January 2009	−4.1%	−5.0%	0.9%	0.0081%
February 2009	−2.3%	−2.0%	−0.3%	0.0009%
March 2009	1.5%	1.8%	−0.3%	0.0009%
April 2009	−2.6%	−3.1%	0.5%	0.0025%
May 2009	4.2%	4.1%	0.1%	0.0001%
June 2009	3.1%	2.2%	0.9%	0.0081%
July 2009	−0.8%	0.9%	−1.7%	0.0289%
August 2009	1.1%	0.2%	0.9%	0.0081%
September 2009	−5.3%	−6.3%	1.0%	0.0100%
October 2009	−1.7%	−2.3%	0.6%	0.0036%
November 2009	2.4%	2.2%	0.2%	0.0004%
December 2009	2.5%	2.8%	−0.3%	0.0009%

January 2010	0.3%	0.5%	−0.2%	0.0004%
February 2010	−0.9%	−1.2%	0.3%	0.0009%
March 2010	−1.9%	−2.3%	0.4%	0.0016%
April 2010	0.7%	0.9%	−0.2%	0.0004%
May 2010	1.6%	2.5%	−0.9%	0.0081%
June 2010	0.6%	1.0%	−0.4%	0.0016%
July 2010	2.5%	3.4%	−0.9%	0.0081%
August 2010	−2.1%	−1.4%	−0.7%	0.0049%
September 2010	1.9%	2.2%	−0.3%	0.0009%
October 2010	0.8%	1.1%	−0.3%	0.0009%
November 2010	2.5%	2.9%	−0.4%	0.0016%
December 2010	−1.6%	−1.5%	−0.1%	0.0001%
Total	**3.6%**	**3.6%**	**0.0%**	**0.1202%**
Average			0.0%	0.0034%
Tracking error				0.59%

Interpretation

The tracking error calculated in example 7.2 can be interpreted in a similar way to the standard deviation of total returns since this is simply a standard deviation of relative returns. Again, the higher the number the higher the risk taken against the benchmark, and we can use the number to compare the relative risk of different assets, portfolios or funds or to check for changes in the risk over time.

If returns are normally distributed we can say that:

- 68.3% of relative returns lie between the mean relative return ± 1 tracking error.

- 95.5% of relative returns lie between the mean relative return ± 2 tracking errors.

- 99.7% of relative returns lie between the mean relative return ± 3 tracking errors.

In example 7.2 the mean or average relative return is zero.

If we assume that the relative returns from a fund are normally distributed, then 68.3% of the monthly relative returns will be within 0.59% of the average of zero, that is, the fund will be within 0.59% of the benchmark 68.3% of the time, within 1.18% of the benchmark 95.5% of the time and within 1.77% of the benchmark 99.7% of the time.

We can see that tracking error is giving us a clear indication of how closely the fund has been following the benchmark index.

Limitations

Many of the limitations of using tracking error are similar to those for standard deviation of total returns:

- Tracking error, calculated using monthly data, is a measure of the short-term volatility of a portfolio against a benchmark: for clients with long holding periods this may not be a relevant measure of risk.

- Tracking error is usually reported based on historic returns: if the strategy of the fund manager changes future tracking error could be quite different.

- The choice of benchmark is critical; an inappropriate benchmark will usually lead to tracking error being overstated.

- It is only an accurate measure of risk when a portfolio's relative returns are normally distributed: if there is kurtosis or skew it will not be picked up by the calculation.

- The tracking error does not incorporate the risk of the underlying benchmark market, so a portfolio could have low tracking error (for example an index fund) but be very risky because it is tracking a volatile market. Also a fund could have high tracking error because it is very defensively invested relative to the market so the overall risk is less than the market itself.

4 Other risk measures

We have examined standard deviation and tracking error and touched on semi-variance and downside deviation. Before we break down total risk into different components we will look at value at risk.

Value at risk

Value at risk (VaR) has long been used by proprietary trading desks, company treasurers and regulators as an internal measure of risk. It has also become more widely used by investment managers, especially in the hedge fund industry. VaR is a statistical measure of possible portfolio losses that combines all the market risks affecting a portfolio to give a single measure which indicates the portfolio's exposure to risk.

A general VaR statement would be something along the lines of 'With a probability of x% and a holding period of t days, the VaR is £y million.' VaR is the loss that is expected to be exceeded in x% of the t-day holding periods. If x is 5% (or typically 1% or 10%), and t is ten days we might quote 95% VaR as £100m. This means that the probability of losing £100m or more is 5%, and the probability of not losing as much as £100m is 95%. VaR is often quoted as a percentage of the portfolio value.

There are three mains methods for calculating VaR:

- **Historical simulation.** Past returns are analysed to find how much was lost in the worst x% of cases.

- **Variance/covariance or a delta-normal approach.** This assumes that the distributions of the assets in a portfolio are normal.

- **Monte Carlo simulation.** This gives greater flexibility in the assumptions used and allows 'what if' analysis.

Comparing the VaR of different funds, given that the VaR has been calculated using the same methods and assumptions, is useful. VaR can also be used to track a fund over time to pick up a change in the risk taken by the manager.

There are some disadvantages in using VaR:

- VaR was widely criticised for underestimating the possible losses in the recent credit crunch. This problem partly resulted from many models assuming that assets had normal distributions, not incorporating fat tails, so they did not capture the risk of extreme events. Also, risk and correlation numbers were unstable.

- For an outside observer, unless the method used to calculate the VaR number is known, it will be of little help.

- VaR doesn't on its own tell you how big the losses could be, it simply indicates the probability of losing a certain amount, or more than this amount.

- It gives no information on the upside potential from a fund.

To estimate how big the expected loss will be, conditional VaR is used. This is the expected tail loss, or the expected loss in the worst x% of cases.

Market risk

Beta (β) is a measure of market risk and is most frequently used for individual equities or equity portfolios, but can be used for other assets such as bond portfolios. It is the sensitivity of a stock or portfolio to the underlying benchmark market. Before we look at beta, we need to go back to theory and look at the breakdown of total risk (σ) into its different components, and then we will consider the capital asset pricing model, which links betas to returns.

Systematic and unsystematic risk

If we consider a portfolio invested within a single market and look at how many securities are needed to diversify the portfolio, it has been shown that investing in only a relatively small number of securities has a dramatic effect on reducing variance. Investment in 12 to 18 randomly selected stocks is sufficient to achieve 90% of the maximum benefits of diversification. Eventually, if you add enough stocks volatility will be reduced to the volatility of the whole market. So, for example, if you are investing in UK equities and picking stocks at random, you cannot reduce variance below that of the UK equity market itself. As you add more and more stocks you will end up buying an index portfolio. The market risk that you cannot diversify away is called 'systematic' risk.

This is illustrated in Figure 7.4.

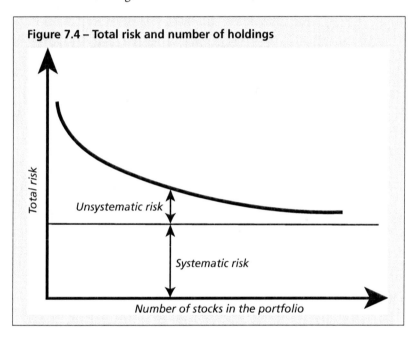

Figure 7.4 – Total risk and number of holdings

Total risk

Unsystematic risk

Systematic risk

Number of stocks in the portfolio

Variance is equal to systematic variance plus unsystematic variance, where:

- Systematic variance or systematic risk is market risk and cannot be diversified away. Systematic risk is measured by beta.

- Unsystematic risk is specific risk which can be eliminated by diversification. Sometimes it is called 'specific' or 'diversifiable' risk.

The theory says that investors should not expect a higher return for taking on unsystematic risk because this is their choice; they could add more holdings to diversify it away. Therefore an investor should expect a return which is dependent on the market risk of an asset or portfolio. We will now consider beta, which is a measure of market risk, in more detail.

Beta

Beta is the measure of a security's volatility in terms of market risk. It is a standardised measure of risk since it compares the covariance of a stock to the variance of the market. For a stock x and market M, beta is given by:

$$\beta_x = \frac{\text{cov}_{x,M}}{\text{var}_M} = \frac{\sigma_x \sigma_M r_{x,M}}{\sigma_M^2} = \frac{\sigma_x}{\sigma_M} r_{x,M}$$

where:

- σ_x is the standard deviation of x.

- σ_M is the standard deviation of M.

- $r_{x,M}$ is the correlation between x and M.

Beta can be estimated using regression analysis to plot the characteristic line. This is the line of best fit through a scatter plot of points with the y-axis being the return from the security and the x-axis the return from the market. The slope of the line is the beta. There is no single correct time period to use for the regression; there is a trade-off between using a long time period with a large number of observations, giving a more stable beta, and using a short time period, which gives a more current beta.

The beta of the market is always one. If an asset has higher systematic risk than the market itself, the beta will be greater than one, if lower than the market it will be less than one. The beta of the risk-free asset, which has zero correlation with the market, is zero.

In the UK market companies such as utilities which are defensive tend to have low betas; for example, United Utilities has a beta of 0.55 and Imperial Tobacco has a beta of 0.47. On the other hand, companies whose business or assets are linked to the stock market will usually have higher than average betas; for example, Man Group's beta is 1.53 and Prudential's is 1.21.

Portfolio beta is simply the weighted average of the betas of the stocks in the portfolio.

The capital asset pricing model

The capital asset pricing model (CAPM) links return to the beta or market risk of a stock or portfolio. Since unsystematic or specific risk can be diversified away, investors cannot expect an additional return for taking on unsystematic risk. CAPM expresses the expected return of asset I, $E(R_M)$ as:

$$E(R_I) = R_f + \beta_I [E(R_M) - R_f]$$

where:

- R_f is the risk-free rate.
- $E(R_M) - R_f$ is the market return less the risk-free rate, which is the market risk premium.
- β_I is the beta of asset I.

Another way to think of CAPM is to consider the general rule for any asset:

$$E(R) = R_f + \text{ Risk premium}$$

In the case of bonds the risk premium could partly come from credit risk; for unlisted equities it could be partly an illiquidity premium and so on. In the case of equities, CAPM is saying that the risk premium is the overall market risk premium adjusted for the sensitivity of the investment to the market. So if you buy a share with a higher than average beta (above 1), you expect to be compensated for the extra risk by collecting a higher than average equity market risk premium, and if you buy a defensive stock with a low beta you cannot expect to receive the average equity risk premium.

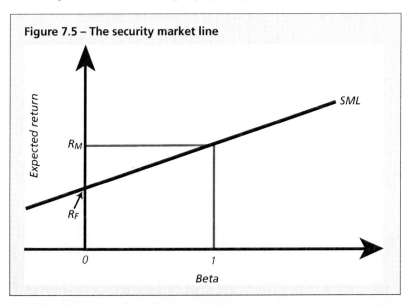

Figure 7.5 – The security market line

CAPM's great advantage is that it is easy to apply and is widely used in finance, but there are some major issues:

- There is scant evidence that it works. Fama and French's research in the 1990s found that size and price to book value ratios were stronger explanatory factors for stock price performance than market beta. Their three-factor model explained over 90% of the returns of the diversified portfolios.

- CAPM makes demanding assumptions:
  - Investors are motivated by risk and return.
  - The expected return and risk of assets are consistent among investors.
  - Unlimited money can be borrowed or lent at a risk-free rate (the same for all investors).
  - There are no transaction costs or taxes.

Example 7.3: The capital asset pricing model

The return for the market portfolio is expected to be 15% and the risk-free rate 6%. If a stock ABC has a beta of 1.5 then the expected return from the stock (or the required rate of return) is:

$$E\left(R\right) = R_f + \beta\left[E\left(R_M\right) - R_f\right] = 6\% + 1.5\left(15\% - 6\%\right) = 19.5\%$$

Because the beta is greater than the market average we expect a return above the market return, assuming the market rises by more than the risk-free rate.

An analyst estimates that the return from the same stock is 20% (including capital gain and dividend). Plotting the stock against the SML we can see that the estimated return is higher than the required return, so it is above the SML. Assuming that the analyst is correct then the stock is undervalued.

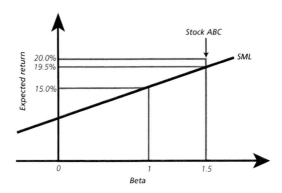

The analyst is forecasting an alpha of 0.5% (alpha is the difference between an actual return – historic or forecast – and the return expected using CAPM). We shall return to alpha later in the chapter.

Using CAPM we can plot the security market line (SML), which relates the expected return on a stock to the risk-free rate (R_f), the market premium and the beta of the stock.

All stocks should be in equilibrium and lie on the SML, but in the short term they may be incorrectly priced and lie above or below the line. This provides an opportunity to identify mispriced stocks.

Interpretation

The beta of a portfolio indicates the manager's market exposure. While we would expect a tracker fund to have a beta of one, a market timer or active portfolio manager could have a beta above or below one, although in many cases active managers with diversified portfolios end up having betas fairly close to one. A beta above one indicates a higher than average level of market exposure so presumably the manager is forecasting a rise in the benchmark index, and a beta below one indicates the manager is defensive and has bought low beta stocks or holds cash (with a beta of zero).

Different hedge fund strategies might have very different betas; market neutral strategies would generally have betas close to zero. Historically equity long/short strategies have had average betas around 0.4 and 0.5, meaning the funds tend to follow the direction of the equity market but dampen out the swings in the market.

Limitations

The limitations of this measure are as follows:

- The beta is dependent on the right choice of benchmark.

- Beta is only a measure of market risk, and it does not take into account the specific risk of a stock or portfolio.

- Beta is usually calculated using historic data and is dependent on the time period over which data is collected (for example, one-year versus three-year data). Betas are frequently unstable since market conditions change and companies alter their business mix.

Duration

There are two major risks that apply to bonds: interest rate risk and credit risk. In this section we will focus on duration, which measures the interest rate sensitivity of a bond or a portfolio of bonds and is widely quoted in bond fund reports. Portfolio duration is simply the weighted average of the duration of the bonds held in the portfolio.

Duration is useful as a measure of the sensitivity of a bond's market price to interest rate (yield) movements and so is a key driver of price volatility. It is approximately equal to the percentage change in price for a given change in yield. For example, for small interest rate changes, the duration is the approximate percentage by which the value of the bond will fall for a 1% a year increase in market interest rate. So a 15-year bond with a duration of 7 would fall approximately 7% in value if the interest rate increased by 1% a year.

Mathematically we can express the move in price of a bond as:

Percentage change in price $\approx$ − Duration × Percentage change in yields

In this case the duration is modified or effective duration. So, if a portfolio has a duration of 5, and if interest rates rise by 1%, as a first approximation the portfolio will fall by 5%. On the other hand, if interest rates fall by 1% the portfolio will rise by approximately 5%. Generally bond prices move in the opposite direction to interest rates, hence the minus sign in the equation. When we say 'interest rates move by 1%', we actually mean 'if the yield curve shifts upwards or downward by 1%', so gross redemption yields or yields to maturity on all bonds move by 1%.

Types of duration

We need to distinguish between the different types of duration:

- **Modified duration** and **Macaulay duration** assume no changes in the expected cash flows, that is, the cash flows are fixed at the time of issue so we are not considering bonds with embedded options or mortgage backed securities.

- **Effective duration** can be used for bonds which have embedded options or the flexibility to make early repayments of capital.

The relationship between the Macaulay duration and the modified duration is as follows:

$$\text{Modified duration} = \frac{\text{Macaulay duration}}{(1 + \text{Yield} / k)}$$

where:

- Yield is the yield to maturity or gross redemption yield of the bond.
- k is the number of coupon payments a year.

Macaulay duration is defined as the weighted-average time it takes to receive the cash flows, the weighting being the present values of the cash flows as a percentage of the bond's full price.

The Macaulay duration **is equal to**

$$\sum_{I=1}^{n} \frac{t \times PVCF_t}{\text{Price}}$$

where:

- n is the number of cash flows.
- t is the time in years until the cash flow is expected to be received.
- $PVCF_t$ is the present value of the cash flow in period t discounted at the yield to maturity.
- Price is the bond's price (total present values of all cash flows).

Example 7.4: Modified duration

A three-year bond has a par value of 100 and an annual coupon of 4%. The bond is issued at 100 and has a yield of 4%. In this case the cash flows will be made up of three coupon payments and one final maturity payment.

The Macaulay duration is:

$$\sum_{I=1}^{n} \frac{t \times PVCF}{k \times \text{Price}}$$

$$= \left[\left(1 \times \frac{4}{1.04}\right) + \left(2 \times \frac{4}{1.04^2}\right) + \left(3 \times \frac{104}{1.04^3}\right) \right] / 100$$

$$= 2.8860$$

So the Macaulay duration is 2.89 years.

The modified duration is 2.89/(1.04) = 2.78.

There are three factors which influence the duration of a bond:

- **Time to maturity.** The longer the time to maturity the longer the duration and vice versa. For a straight bond (one without embedded options) the duration will be between zero and the time to maturity. A zero coupon will have duration equal to the time to maturity.
- **Coupon rate.** The higher the coupon the shorter the duration and vice versa. A coupon bond will have a shorter duration than a zero-coupon bond with the same maturity.
- **Yields.** The higher the market yields, the shorter the duration of bonds. This is because in a high interest rate environment the present value of the cash flows which will be received first becomes relatively more important (remember, this is the present value of the cash flows, not the actual cash flows) and this shortens the average time until the present value of the cash

flows is received. This is important because market yields are constantly changing, so the average duration of the market is also changing (unlike beta, which is always 1).

Up to now we have considered straight bonds. However, if bonds have options or we wish to calculate the duration of certain derivative instruments such as an interest-only security we might have a duration measure of, say, −6. This implies that for a 1% increase in interest rates the price of the bond will *increase* by 6%. A calculation using a weighted average for the number of years cannot explain negative duration. We therefore need to consider effective duration.

The effective duration formula can be expressed as:

$$\text{Duration} = \frac{V_- - V_+}{2\,(V_0)\,(\Delta y)}$$

where:

- Δy is the change in yield in decimals, for example, 100 basis points is 0.01.
- V_0 is the initial price.
- V_- is the price if yields decline by Δy.
- V_+ is the price if yields increase by Δy.

Example 7.5: Effective duration

Consider the bond in example 7.4.

With yields at 4% the initial value of the bond is 100. If yields were to increase by 50 basis points (Δy is 0.005) we can use a calculator to compute the value of the bond to be 98.6255 (V_+). If yields fall by 50 basis points the value of the bond rises to 101.4008 (V_-).

Applying the duration formula we can see that effective duration is:

$$\frac{101.4008 - 98.6255}{2 \times 100 \times 0.005} = 2.7753$$

Effective duration is pricing along the gradient of the price yield curve of a bond. In Figure 7.6 we have sketched the price yield curve for a bond. If initial price is P_1 when yields are I_1, when yields move to I_2, using the effective duration formula we are estimating the price (P_{est}) based on the tangent, when the correct price is P_2.

We can see that for large yield changes effective duration does not give an accurate estimate of the price move since the tangent is moving away from the curve; we need to expand the formula for price change to incorporate convexity.

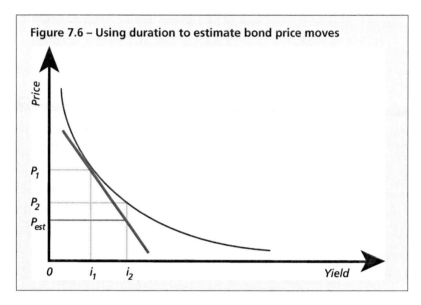

Figure 7.6 – Using duration to estimate bond price moves

Convexity measures the curvature of the curve, which is how rapidly the slope of the tangent changes. Convexity is beyond the scope of this book.

Interpretation

Looking at the duration of a bond portfolio tells us the interest rate risk taken by the manager. If the duration is above the duration of the benchmark, it indicates that the manager is taking more interest rate risk than average, so presumably is expecting yields to fall by more than the market as a whole expects them to and therefore is expecting bond markets to perform well. By lengthening duration managers can outperform the market if their forecast is correct. To lengthen duration they will buy long-dated bonds with, if anything, low coupons.

Similarly, if managers are defensive and concerned that rates are going to rise by more than expected they will shorten duration, by buying short-dated bonds or holding cash.

Limitations

The limitations of duration are as follows:

- The duration formula assumes that yields all move by the same amount, in other words, the yield curve makes a parallel shift. In reality, the yields of bonds in a portfolio do not always move in parallel. For example, the yield curve might steepen as yields fall.

- Duration is only a first approximation of the price move for a given change in yields. To get a more accurate estimate we need to extend the formula to incorporate the convexity or curvature of the price-yield curve.

5 Risk-adjusted returns

Risk and return go hand in hand and a key question for advisers is how much extra risk fund managers are incurring in order to earn extra returns. When investors measure the performance of funds or portfolios there are four main measures:

- Information ratios.
- Sharpe ratios.
- Alphas.
- Treynor ratios.

In all cases it is assumed that investors want the highest return with the least risk. We look at each of the measures in turn.

The information ratio

The information ratio (IR) is a risk-adjusted return measure used to evaluate fund managers' relative performance. It looks at the return of a fund relative to the benchmark divided by the risk taken by the manager against the benchmark.

Calculation

The information ratio is the relative return divided by the relative risk or tracking error. The formula is:

$$\text{Information ratio} = \frac{R_P - R_B}{\text{tracking error}}$$

where:

- R_P is the average annual portfolio return.
- R_B is the average annual benchmark return.

Tracking error is the standard deviation of relative returns.

Often the calculation uses monthly returns over the last three years and then the number is annualised. Occasionally IR is defined as alpha divided by the standard deviation of the alpha.

Example 7.6: The information ratio

	Fund A	Fund B
Average return	12%	11%
Benchmark return	10%	10%
Tracking error	8%	3%
Information ratio	(12 − 10)/8 = 0.25	(11 − 10)/3 = 0.33

Although fund A has a higher return than fund B, when we adjust for the risk taken to achieve these returns against the benchmark we can see from the IRs that B has generated a higher risk-adjusted return.

Interpretation

- The higher the positive IR the better the risk-adjusted return based on performance relative to the benchmark.

- The average active fund manager does not outperform benchmarks after costs, so when a fund has a positive IR it has almost certainly outperformed the average fund.

- An IR of above 0.5 would generally be considered very good, and the manager would be top quartile, if not top decile. An IR above 1.0 would be exceptionally good. A negative IR means an investor would have achieved a better result by matching the index using a passive index fund.

Limitations

The limitations of the information ratio are as follows:

- If the incorrect benchmark is selected the calculation will be meaningless.

- If a fund's returns are not normally distributed, using the IR can be misleading since the tracking error may not be an appropriate measure of risk.

- It does not incorporate the performance of the benchmark so a fund could have a high IR but generate a negative return because the underlying market has fallen.

- It is a measure of past performance, and there is evidence to suggest past IRs are not a good predictor of future IRs, at least for traditional funds.

The Sharpe ratio

The Sharpe ratio, sometimes called the Sharpe measure, is a risk-adjusted return measure used to evaluate fund managers' performance. It calculates excess return above the risk-free rate divided by the risk taken by the manager.

Calculation

The excess return of the fund above the risk-free rate is divided by the standard deviation of returns. The risk-free rate is usually defined as the rate on 90-day treasury bills in the relevant market.

The formula is:

$$\text{Sharpe ratio} = \frac{R_P - R_F}{\sigma}$$

where:

- R_P is the average annual portfolio return.
- R_F is the average annual risk-free rate.
- σ is the standard deviation of returns.

Often the calculation uses monthly returns over the last three years and then the number is annualised.

Example 7.7: The Sharpe ratio

	Fund A	Fund B
Average return	12%	10%
Risk-free rate	4%	4%
Standard deviation	10%	6%
Sharpe ratio	(12 − 4)/10 = 0.8	(10 − 4)/6 = 1.0

Although fund A has a higher return than fund B, when we adjust for the risk taken to achieve these returns we can see from the Sharpe ratio that B has generated a higher risk-adjusted return.

Interpretation

The higher the Sharpe ratio the higher the risk-adjusted return. The ratio measures the return the investor achieved over and above the return on cash in units of standard deviation.

It is important to note that the Sharpe ratio will take into account the risk-adjusted return of the underlying market or benchmark as well as the performance of the fund manager against the benchmark.

A negative Sharpe ratio means the manager did not achieve returns as high as could be generated on cash.

Sharpe ratios need to be considered in the context of the markets that a fund is invested in. For example, over the last ten years most global equities markets have generated negative Sharpe ratios (with the exception of emerging markets), whereas global bonds have generated a Sharpe ratio of 0.06. However, if we look at longer periods the Sharpe ratios for equities have been closer to 0.5, and for bonds 0.3. In bull markets for equities Sharpe ratios are often well above 1.

Sharpe ratios are most useful for comparing funds which have the same benchmark and provide performance data over the same time period.

If a fund's returns are not normally distributed the Sharpe ratio can be misleading, and a more appropriate measure is the Sortino ratio, which looks at returns in units of downside risk.

Limitations

The limitations of the Sharpe ratio are as follows:

- The Sharpe ratio will reflect the performance of the underlying market so further analysis is needed to evaluate the value added by the fund manager. One way to do this is to look at the information ratio.

- The Sharpe ratio is only an accurate measure of performance when a fund's returns are normally distributed.

- This is a measure of past performance. As with the information ratio there is little evidence to suggest that if a manager achieved high Sharpe ratios in the past they will be repeated.

Alpha

Alpha is a measure of return that is independent of the underlying market or benchmark performance. It is a measure of a manager's stock-picking skill.

Calculation

'Alpha' can simply indicate outperformance of an index but more accurately it is the return that is not explained by the capital asset pricing model (see above). This is sometimes called 'Jensen's alpha'.

The formula is:

$$\alpha = \text{Actual return} - [R_F + \beta (R_M - R_F)]$$

where:

- R_F is the average annual risk-free rate.
- R_M is the average annual market return.
- β is the beta of the portfolio or fund.

Often the calculation uses returns over the last three years.

Example 7.8: Alpha

	Fund A	**Fund B**
Average return	12%	10%
Risk-free rate	4%	4%
Market return	10%	10%
Beta	1.2	0.8
Alpha	12 − [4 + 1.2(10 − 4)] = 0.8%	(10 − [4 + 0.8(10 − 4)] = 1.2%

Although fund A outperformed fund B, B had a higher alpha. This shows that B's manager added more value through stock picking than A's manager − 1.2% a year rather than 0.8%.

Interpretation

For a fund the higher the alpha the better. The alpha indicates how much return the fund manager has generated that is independent of the market. This is often generated from stock picking, from buying stocks with positive alpha and possibly from shorting stocks with negative alpha. An alpha of 2% means the manager generated an additional 2% annual return from identifying mispriced securities. However, alpha is a historic number and, as with any performance number, could have been due to luck, not skill.

The alpha will be meaningless if the wrong benchmark market has been used. This will have led to the beta being misstated, and in a rising market if beta is understated it will look as if returns come from alpha rather than from taking beta risk.

Positive alpha is something that investors are usually prepared to pay for, whereas returns generated from taking beta risk could be achieved by buying a derivative or index fund very cheaply.

Limitations

Alpha has the following limitations:

- The beta and therefore the alpha are dependent on the right choice of benchmark.

- Alpha is the return independent of the benchmark performance so a fund could have a positive alpha but generate a negative return because the underlying market has fallen.

- Alpha is a measure of past performance: there is little evidence to suggest it is a good predictor of future performance.

The Treynor ratio

The Treynor ratio measures excess return above the risk-free rate, divided by the market risk, or beta risk, taken by the manager. It gives the same indication of performance as the alpha and is less commonly quoted.

Calculation

The Treynor ratio is the excess return divided by the beta of the fund. The risk-free rate is usually defined as the rate on 90-day treasury bills in the relevant market.

The formula is:

$$\text{Treynor ratio} = \frac{R_P - R_F}{\beta}$$

where:

- R_P is the average annual portfolio return.
- R_F is the average annual risk-free rate.
- β is the beta of the portfolio or fund.

Often the calculation uses returns over the last three years, annualising the number.

Example 7.9: The Treynor ratio

	Fund A	Fund B
Average return	12%	10%
Risk-free rate	4%	4%
Market return	10%	10%
Beta	1.2	0.8
Treynor	(12 − 4)/1.2 = 6.67	(10 − 4)/0.8 = 7.50

Although fund A outperformed fund B, B had a higher Treynor ratio. This shows that B's manager added more value relative to the market risk than A's manager. The market Treynor is (10 − 4)/1 = 6, so both funds had higher Treynor ratios than the market. We can see in example 7.8 that they both had positive alphas.

Interpretation

The higher the Treynor ratio the higher the market risk-adjusted return. The ratio measures the return the investor achieved over and above the return on cash in units of beta.

A Treynor ratio that is above the Treynor for the market (calculated using a beta of 1) indicates that the alpha is positive so the fund has added value through stock picking. Similarly a Treynor ratio below the market indicates that the manager has lost value through poor stock picking.

A negative Treynor ratio means the manager did not achieve returns as high as could be generated on cash.

Limitations

The Treynor ratio has the following limitations:

- The beta and therefore the alpha are dependent on the right choice of benchmark.

- Alpha is the return independent of the benchmark performance so a fund could have a positive alpha but generate a negative return because the underlying market has fallen.

- Alpha is a measure of past performance: there is little evidence to suggest it is a good predictor of future performance.

Which measure to use?

When reviewing the performance of a fund it is more common to look at the Sharpe ratio or the information ratio since these measure returns that are adjusted for total risk or risk taken against the benchmark.

Using alpha or the Treynor ratio will give return measured against the market or beta risk, so they are incomplete, but they do give an indication of a manager's stock-picking ability. Alphas and Treynor ratios are incomplete in the sense that they do not give information on the manager's skill in market timing (whether the manager had a high beta in a rising market or a low beta in a falling market) or the manager's skill in portfolio construction (for example, did the manager diversify sufficiently to reduce total risk relative to the total return). Alpha and Treynor give the same information so it is not necessary to use both. Alpha is more commonly used.

Note that if we are looking at the value added for an internationally diversified portfolio we would be concerned about the alpha generated by the manager in each geographic area, since the volatility of investments in any one country would be at least partially diversified away by investments in other countries.

Example 7.10: Evaluating investment performance

The following data is provided on the performance of fund managers X and Y over the previous year. Both managers were managing a country fund with the same objectives.

	Manager X	**Manager Y**
Return	11%	9%
Standard deviation	5.0%	4.0%
Beta	1.5	0.7

The benchmark market rose by 10% over the year and the risk-free rate was 6%.

If we calculate the Sharpe and Treynor ratios and the alphas for each fund we can then summarise each fund manager's strengths and weaknesses in managing the funds from a risk/reward viewpoint.

Adding the Sharpe, Treynor and alpha measures to the table gives the following:

	Manager X	**Manager Y**	**Market**
Return	11%	9%	10%
Standard deviation	5.0%	4.0%	
Beta	1.5	0.7	1.0
Sharpe	1.0	0.75	
Treynor	3.3	4.3	4.0
Alpha	(1.0%)	0.2%	0.0%

The Treynor ratio and alpha show that manager Y managed market or beta risk better than X. This manager did better than the market if we take into account the level of beta risk taken, whereas manager X took on too much beta risk for the excess return generated. Manager Y was a better stock picker.

However, if we look at total risk (standard deviation) we see that manager X's performance was better than Y's since X's Sharpe ratio is higher. So Y must have managed specific risk, as opposed to market risk, badly: the manager took on too much specific risk that could have been diversified away, and did not add sufficient extra return. This manager's return was also hit by the low beta of the portfolio in a rising market.

Skill versus luck

Work by many academics on investment performance stresses the difficulty of differentiating between skill and luck. For example, Richard Grinold and Ronald Kahn in their book *Active Portfolio Management* show that to be 95% confident that a manager is top quartile, which they define as having an information ratio of greater than 0.5, requires 16 years of monthly observations. Given that the average fund manager (for traditional funds) stays with a fund management company for just over three years we can see just how difficult it is to collect information that shows that a manager is skilful rather than just lucky. Good performance will always be claimed to be the result of skill and bad performance the result of bad luck! Ten per cent of managers without any skill can achieve information ratios over 0.7 over five years.

Remember that the average fund manager does not outperform benchmark indices after costs. In 2010, Standard & Poor's (S&P) published research based on returns from actively managed funds over the previous five years. The study, which used data from the Center for Research in Security Prices, found that over 60% of American equity funds failed to match the return of the S&P Composite 1500 index over the period. Similar studies show the same pattern for UK active managers: the majority of managers do not achieve the benchmark index returns over any five-year period.

The persistence of performance is also the subject of much academic debate. If a fund manager achieves good performance in one quarter, and is top quartile, what is the probability of the manager being top quartile in the next quarter? The academic results are mixed, but there is little evidence that performance is persistent for traditional long only managers, particularly when returns are adjusted for risk. On the other hand, other asset classes such as private equity do show evidence of persistence in manager performance.

Given the difficulty of isolating skill from luck and the evidence that past performance is not a reliable guide for the future, investors may question the point of analysing past performance data. While this view is understandable, past performance is still useful since it provides information on the past strategies employed by the fund manager, and the success of these strategies. It is a starting point for challenging the fund manager on what he or she has achieved and whether the promise of previous targets and strategies has been fulfilled.

Performance attribution analysis can identify what the fund manager has been good (or lucky) at doing: is it long-term asset allocation, market timing or stock selection? If a fund manager has achieved good performance in the past it is important to understand what the manager's competitive edge was and whether this is likely to lead to superior performance in the future.

Outperformance comes from adding value through superior information or research or superior processing of this information. If a fund manager has delivered good performance it is important to decide whether the manager can realistically claim to have a better source of information or a better way of processing this information. In reality, both are very difficult to achieve in mature markets where information is widely dispersed and models are widely used.

Using past performance data is always going to be imperfect and will rarely provide a definite answer to the question, has the manager achieved superior performance through luck or skill?

Understanding the investment process is key to deciding whether good performance is likely to be repeated in the future. This enables advisers to determine which of the decisions that resulted in improved returns were the result of a manager's skill and which simply had lucky outcomes. The adviser may well wish to obtain further information from the manager about:

- Sources of information.
- Research.
- How information is processed.
- Who makes decisions.
- Market and portfolio risk controls.
- Portfolio turnover, etc.

Summary

In this chapter we have considered the major measures of risk used for bond and equity portfolios, and looked at how returns are adjusted for the risk taken. These measures include the main ones reported by fund managers and they provide a starting point for evaluating whether a manager has met his or her objectives.

- Standard deviation gives accurate measures of risk in the normal distribution or 'bell curve'.
- In a normal distribution, 68.3% of returns will fall within 1 Standard deviation of the mean return.
- Extreme events occur more often in markets than in normal distribution. '5-sigma' events occurred repeatedly in the credit crunch.
- Market risk can be analysed into systematic risk (beta) and unsystematic risk (alpha).
- Duration, measuring the sensitivity of a bond to interest rate changes, is a key measure of risk in bonds and bond portfolios.
- The Sharpe ratio and the Information ratio are used to measure risk-adjusted returns and check whether fund managers are creating value.

Chapter 8
How risk affects investments

1 Introduction

Up to now we have considered risk as total risk, relative risk, beta (for equities) or duration (for bonds) and talked largely in terms of measuring risk for funds or portfolios of securities. In this chapter we will look at the drivers or components of these risks and their impact on individual securities and investments. We will consider first the major asset classes – cash, debt and equity investments – and then the alternative asset classes of property and commodities and the alternative strategies of hedge funds and structured products.

2 Cash

When we refer to cash in an investment context we usually mean money market instruments, which will become cash within a year. This includes time deposits, commercial paper, treasury bills and certificates of deposit. These assets are considered the safest but of course, as we have seen in the recent financial crisis, it depends on whom the investor has deposited with or lent money to. Liquidity is another advantage of holding cash, although clearly the ability to access deposits in the credit crunch depended on the deposit-taking institution.

We will now look at the major risks associated with holding cash: default or credit risk, interest rate risk, inflation risk and foreign exchange risk.

Default risk

Default risk is the risk that the bank or other deposit-taking institution does not repay the capital and/or interest. As we saw in 2008 this was a very real risk, since Northern Rock, HBOS, Royal Bank of Scotland, the Icelandic banks and many others were at risk of bankruptcy. Assessing the credit risk of financial institutions is complex and made worse by a lack of confidence in the quality of information provided by them.

The creditworthiness of an institution is indicated as follows:

- Credit default swap rates measure the premium to the risk-free interest rate (usually measured against gilts) that a bank has to pay, and indicate the market's view of how likely a financial institution is to default.

- If high interest rates, relative to the market average, are offered by an institution this often indicates higher risk.

- Another indicator is provided by the credit ratings issued by the big rating agencies on financial instruments issued by the banks. Major agencies are Standard & Poor's and Moody's. However, the ratings lost much of their credibility in the recent financial crisis.
- Tier one capital is a measure used by regulators. It is the ratio of a bank's core equity capital to its total risk-adjusted assets. The higher the ratio the higher the ability of the bank to cover future losses.

When considering default risk investors also need to take in account any deposit protection schemes. In the UK the Financial Services Compensation Scheme will pay compensation of up to £85,000 for each depositor at any authorised institution. It may take some time for any money to be repaid under the scheme.

Interest rate risk

Although money market instruments have a very short duration and are therefore not particularly sensitive to interest rates when compared to long-term bonds, changes in rates can still impact them:

- If an investor buys a one-year deposit at a fixed rate and then rates rise there has been an opportunity cost. The investor could have obtained a more attractive return by holding the money in an instant access account and investing the funds at a later date.
- Many accounts pay interest that is linked to the base rates. In this case falling interest rates will reduce returns.
- Linked to interest rate risk is reinvestment risk. This is the risk that rates will fall over the term of a deposit and the investor will receive a much lower rate of interest when the capital repaid is reinvested. This has been the experience of many investors over the last two years.

Inflation risk

The rate of inflation will impact on real returns from money market investments:

- If the rate of return is not linked to inflation, inflation will erode the value of both interest payments and the capital. In some cases, such as in the UK in the 1970s, the interest and capital repaid fell in real terms.

Some products are index linked, which means that the capital and interest paid are linked to inflation; in the UK they are usually pegged to the retail prices index (RPI). Until the end of 2009 we had a number of years of low inflation and even negative numbers for the RPI. However, the introduction of Quantitative Easing (QE, designed to make more money available), plus imported inflation from other countries and VAT rises have pushed up UK inflation to a rate of over 4% and 5% for the CPI and RPI respectively (see Figure 8.1).

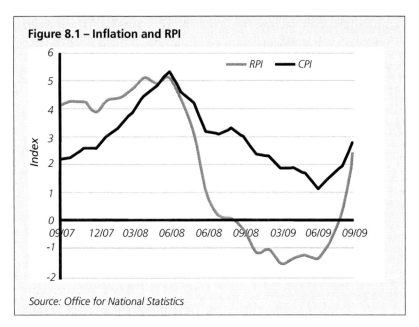

Figure 8.1 – Inflation and RPI

Source: Office for National Statistics

Foreign exchange/currency risk

Investing in instruments denominated in foreign currencies exposes the investor to foreign exchange risk. There are some important issues to consider here:

- If the foreign currency depreciates against the home currency, when the capital returned is converted back to the home currency a loss will be incurred.

- Buying foreign currencies adds risk without adding any automatic risk premium. For every investor who gains from a bet on foreign currencies there is an investor who loses: it is a zero-sum game.

- High interest rates on foreign currencies might offset any foreign exchange loss, but interest rate parity means that high interest rates signal a depreciating currency.

- If investors are making a deposit overseas there may be no deposit protection scheme in place.

Money market funds

Up to now we have spoken generally about deposits and other money market instruments but it is important to point out that some money market funds, though generally perceived as low risk, have actually been making investments with considerable credit risk. They invested in complex and risky instruments, such as credit derivatives or asset-backed securities. Where this is the case, an investor needs to identify and analyse the underlying investments.

3 Debt investments

We will now look at debt investments where the investor is lending money to the issuer of the debt, and depending on the terms, will usually expect to receive periodic interest payments and the principal back at maturity. We have already addressed duration in chapter 7; we will now explore the other risk factors:

- Interest rate risk.

- Yield curve risk.

- Reinvestment risk.

- Credit risk.

- Liquidity risk.

- Foreign exchange/currency risk.

- Inflation risk.

- Event risk.

- Sovereign risk.

Interest rate risk

Interest rate risk has been covered in chapter 7 in the section on duration. Duration measures the sensitivity of a bond or portfolio to a move in interest rates: the higher the duration, the greater the risk and vice versa. The drivers of interest rate moves are:

- **Capital supply and demand.** In a booming economy rates will tend to rise, in a recession rates will be lower.

- **Monetary and fiscal policy.** If the government is about to increase borrowing and is expected to issue bonds, this will have an upward impact on medium and longer-term rates. Quantitative easing has had the effect of reducing short-term rates.

- **Government monetary policy.** This is most effective at determining short-term rates; the market will usually determine longer-term rates.

- **Expected inflation.** Nominal rates will reflect real interest rates plus expected inflation. If inflation expectations rise, long-term rates will tend to rise even if short-term rates remain the same.

Yield curve risk

There are various interest rates in the market. Interest rates for fixed-income securities vary depending on the maturity and credit risk.

When these different interest rates and yields are plotted against their respective maturities, the result is called the 'yield curve'. In Figure 8.2 we show the UK yield curve.

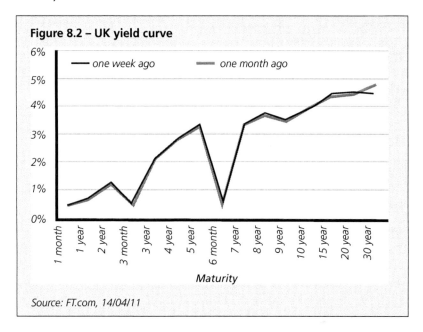

Figure 8.2 – UK yield curve

Source: FT.com, 14/04/11

The shape of the yield curve reflects a number of factors, including:

- **Interest rate and inflation expectations.** If interest rates are expected to rise, investors will tend to prefer to keep their money in short-dated bonds, hence the yield curve will tend to slope steeply upwards. Likewise, if inflation is expected to rise, investors will also expect a rise in interest rates and the yield curve will be steep. On the other hand, expectations of falling interest rates or inflation will lead to a flat or even inverted yield curve, where it slopes downwards to the right.

- **Liquidity preference.** Other things being equal, investors prefer to hold short-dated paper, which is more liquid and less risky, and avoid committing their money to long-term securities. In normal circumstances this leads to a slightly upward-sloping curve.

- **Supply and demand for bonds of different maturities.** There may be a shortage of bonds with certain maturities. In the past there have been insufficient long-dated bonds available to meet demand from pension funds, which has exerted a downward pressure on long-term yields.

- **Government monetary policy.** This often distorts the short end of the curve – very tight policy raising interest rates and very loose policy lowering

157

them. Also, if the government purchases long-dated bonds as part of QE this will tend to reduce long-term rates.

A change in the yield curve can be in the form of a parallel shift, where every interest rate in the yield curve changes by the same amount and in the same direction. In this case duration is adequate as a measure of interest rate risk. However, most of the time there are shifts which are not parallel, where the interest rates in the yield curve do not change by the same amount and/or in the same direction. The risk that affects a bond portfolio due to different changes in the various interest rates in the economy is called the 'yield curve risk'.

Reinvestment risk

Reinvestment risk arises when the investor does not know at what rate the interest received, or early repayment of capital, will itself earn when reinvested. This is true for all forms of bond except for zero-coupon bonds, where no actual interest is received. The computation of gross redemption yields assumes that reinvestment of the coupon payments is at the same rate, but if rates fall, the investor will obtain an actual yield lower than the original gross redemption yield.

Investors are exposed to reinvestment risk in the following situations:

- It arises when the yields of reinvestment opportunities are lower than the original yield.

- Pre-payable amortising securities such as mortgage-backed securities expose investors to greater reinvestment risks because it might only be possible to reinvest at a lower yield the proceeds of principal repayments and prepayments as well as coupons, particularly during an environment of declining interest rates.

- Callable bonds – that is, corporate bonds which the issuer has the right to repay early – are attractive for the issuer when interest rates have fallen, so they can refinance at a lower rate, but from the investor's viewpoint they are subject to considerable reinvestment or 'call' risk.

Credit risk

Credit risk is very important for bond portfolios. There are three types of credit risk: default risk, credit spread risk and downgrade risk.

Default risk

Default risk is the risk that an issuer will fail to meet the obligation of interest and principal payments. A single delay in an interest payment on the coupon payment date is considered a default. An investor does not necessarily lose the whole amount of the principal and accrued interest when a default occurs and the percentage amount recoverable in a case of default is called the 'recovery rate'.

Based on the historical data on default rates and recovery rates for outstanding bonds in the market, credit-rating agencies evaluate and classify the creditworthiness of the issuers or issues. The rating is a measure of the potential default risk for an issuer in respect of a particular bond issue. Investors use credit-ratings to get an idea of the ability of an issuer to meet the payment obligations associated with the bond.

The ratings issued by the three major ratings agencies are briefly described in Table 8.1.

Agencies regularly issue updates either upgrading or downgrading existing issues, or warning that an issuer's current rating is at risk. Of particular significance are downgrades that move an issue from investment grade to sub-investment grade. Since many investing institutions have mandates that forbid them from holding sub-investment grade bonds, a bond subject to such a downgrade is likely to see selling pressure and a significant price decline.

Credit spread risk

Credit spread risk is the risk of the yield spread of a particular issue or sector widening against the risk-free benchmark, causing the price of the bond to decline. The prices of fixed-rate bonds are determined by two factors which drive the yield:

- The yield of a risk-free bond with a similar maturity.
- The premium paid for the credit risk over and above the yield of the similar risk-free bond.

This premium is the compensation required by the investor for taking on an additional credit risk with regard to the risk-free bond. This premium can increase or decrease depending upon the market's perception of the credit risk.

Over the long term there is an inverse relationship between GDP growth and credit spreads. As confidence in the economy declines, default risk increases and investors require a higher yield to compensate for the greater risk. In a stable economic environment with low default risk, credit spreads decline, as the additional yield required by investors falls.

Downgrade risk

Downgrade risk is the risk that a rating agency decides the individual creditworthiness of a bond has deteriorated. The credit spread will widen due to the downgrade, or anticipated downgrade, which will lead the bond price to decline. The rating agencies' opinions on individual issues can be

Table 8.1 – Credit ratings for long-term obligations (original maturity one year or more)

Moody's	S&P	Fitch	Description
Investment grade – high creditworthiness			
Aaa	AAA	AAA	Prime, maximum quality
Aa1	AA+	AA+	
Aa2	AA	AA	High grade, high credit quality
Aa3	AA−	AA−	
A1	A+	A+	Upper-medium grade, economic
A2	A	A	environment will affect financial situation
A3	A−	A−	
Baa1	BBB+	BBB+	Medium grade, satisfactory at present
Baa2	BBB	BBB	but longer-term risk
Baa3	BBB−	BBB−	
Non-investment grade, speculative – lower creditworthiness			
Ba1	BB+	BB+	Lower grade, speculative, substantial
Ba2	BB	BB	credit risk
Ba3	BB−	BB−	
B1		B+	Highly speculative, financial situation
B2	B	B	volatile
B3		B−	
Predominantly speculative, substantial risk, or in default			
Caa	CCC+	CCC+	Substantial risk, in poor standing
	CCC	CCC	
Ca	CC	CC	Very speculative
			Extremely speculative, may be in
C	C	C	default or arrears but still paying some
			obligations
	CI		Income bonds – interest not being paid
		DDD	
	D	DD	Default, and expected to default on most
		D	or all obligations

very influential in the bond market, although in the financial crisis the independence of the rating agencies from the issuers was brought into question. Despite questions over the quality of ratings they are still important – if a bond is downgraded below investment grade status, for example, many bond funds which are only permitted to hold investment grade issues will be forced to sell their holdings.

Liquidity risk

Liquidity risk is faced by investors when they have to sell a bond at a price below its true value, possibly due to a temporary imbalance of supply and demand for the individual bond. Clearly liquidity became more important in the credit crunch, with bid-ask spreads in many bonds widening far beyond historic norms. The market liquidity of an issue is reflected in the size of the bid-ask spread quoted by dealers. The wider the bid-ask spread, the less liquid is the issue in the market. Market liquidity should not be confused with the financial liquidity of the issuer as a going concern.

Newly introduced fixed-income structures or instruments generally have wide bid-ask spreads because of the limited number of investors and market makers. As the new structures or instruments become more popular, the bid-ask spreads narrow as liquidity improves.

Often a market sector becomes unpopular and is avoided by investors and market makers. In such a case, the bid-ask spread may widen considerably. An example is residential mortgage-backed securities, an asset class that saw a steep decline in popularity in the wake of the sub-prime crisis.

Foreign exchange/currency risk

Foreign exchange or currency risk is the risk that the currency of the investment moves adversely against the home currency, causing the local currency value of coupon payments and of the principal repayment to decrease.

Inflation risk

Inflation risk was covered in section 2 above. High inflation erodes the purchasing power of the interest or capital from bonds that pay a fixed rate of interest. Index-linked bonds offer inflation protection, but if inflation levels are lower than expected will generate disappointing returns.

Event risk

Event risk arises very infrequently but with a serious impact on a bond issuer's ability to honour its debt obligation. There are three main risk factors:

- Natural catastrophe risk. This includes the risk of earthquakes, hurricanes, floods and industrial accidents. This type of event will lead to a downgrade but is normally confined to individual issuers.

- Corporate restructuring risk. For example, a leveraged buy-out may lead to investors demanding a much higher yield to compensate them for the risk.

- Regulatory risk – the risk of a change in the regulatory environment.

Sovereign risk

Sovereign risk is the risk that an investor assumes when investing in securities issued by foreign governments. Changes in political circumstances or in economic policies might affect the ability or the willingness of the issuer to pay the coupons or principal. In most cases foreign governments default on their obligations due to unfavourable economic conditions that adversely affect their ability to pay rather than because of a one-sided repudiation of the debts.

4 Equity investments

Equity investments are generally much riskier than bond investments, partly because the cash flows from bonds are fixed or more readily forecast than the cash flows from equities, given the greater uncertainty associated with equity returns. Bond returns are largely determined by the duration and credit risk associated with the bond (except for lower grade corporate bond issues). The returns from particular equities are not so easily explained by common factors and are more likely than bonds to be explained by stock-specific factors.

We will simplify the assessment of equity risk by assuming that the value of a company's shares is based on two factors: the earnings per share of the company and the price the market is willing to pay for those earnings. Both asset value and cash flows play a critical role in valuation, but the asset value reflects both paid-up capital and retained earnings, and cash flows over time reflect earnings, so we will simply look at earnings in this section.

Risks to earnings

First of all there are a number of macroeconomic factors that affect all companies, including changes in GDP, labour and raw material costs, tax rates and inflation.

GDP

Since GDP measures the aggregate output for an economy it is linked to aggregate corporate sales. A slowdown in GDP, or GDP that is below the consensus forecast, will feed through to a reduction in corporate sales. In turn this will lower capacity utilisation rates, which will tend to reduce profit margins.

The state of the economy is an important risk factor for equities. Equities have tended to underperform against other assets as an economy heads into recession and outperform as it moves towards recovery. Cyclical stocks will be hardest hit by a change in GDP whereas defensive stocks are less sensitive to change.

Resource costs, etc

The following factors will all have an impact on net profit margins, and therefore on earnings:

- Unit labour costs.
- Raw material costs.

- Depreciation.
- Amortisation.
- Interest rates.
- Tax rates.

The profitability of companies will be reduced by increases in resource costs, wage rates and related taxes that are not accompanied by increases in productivity, by high interest rates (for leveraged companies) and general increases in taxes. However, for investors who focus on earnings before interest, tax, depreciation and amortisation (EBITDA), unit labour and raw material costs are the major factors.

Inflation

The effect of inflation on equities is not straightforward since there are two possible causes of inflation. Demand-pull inflation indicates a strong economy, with the potential for companies to increase prices and therefore profit margins. Cost-push inflation means higher resource prices or wage costs for companies, which may be difficult to pass on in the short term, leading to lower profit margins.

Uncertainty about inflation levels is bad for decision makers as it hinders planning and tends to lead to companies being reluctant to make long-term commitments to expansion.

In the long term equity investment provides some protection against inflation since investors are buying real assets rather than a fixed income stream from a bond. Over time asset values and sales would be expected to rise in line with the rate of inflation.

Foreign exchange/currency risk

Equity investors face the risk of buying shares denominated in a foreign currency and then seeing depreciation in that currency against the home currency. But there are other currency risks:

- Depreciation of the domestic currency, increasing the costs of imports.
- Appreciation of the domestic currency, reducing international competitiveness.
- Sales in foreign currencies increasing or declining in value when converted back to the home currency.
- Similarly, assets held overseas will be vulnerable to currency fluctuations.

Company-specific risks

Company-specific risks potentially constitute a very long list, but some of the key risks are highlighted below:

- Unsuccessful diversification or expansion of business.

- Raw material costs, for example oil price volatility.

- Management issues.

- Regulatory risk, for example demands by the EU to break up the partially state-owned banks.

- Technological change.

- Financial leverage.

Risks to valuation multiples

There are two drivers of price/earnings ratios:

- The required return of investors, which depends on the perceived risk premium for a specific investment.

- The forecast growth rate for earnings and dividends.

We can see this if we look at the equation for the forward price/earnings ratio, where price is replaced by $D/(k-g)$ using the constant growth dividend discount model. This is:

$$P/E = \frac{(D_1/E_1)}{(k-g)}$$

where:

- D_1/E_1 is the expected dividend pay-out ratio.

- k is the required rate of return.

- g is the expected growth rate of dividends.

Looking at these in turn:

- The expected pay-out ratio will depend on the residual income a company has available to distribute and how many investment opportunities are available to the company as well as the decision by the management on pay-out ratios.

- The required rate of return for investors will depend on the equity market risk premium, adjusted for the risk premium for the specific company. The individual risk premium will depend on several factors, including:

- The business risk of the company, reflected in the volatility of sales and operating earnings.

- Financial risk, which is the risk arising from the capital structure of the company. High leverage increases financial risk and uncertainty over what earnings will be available to pay ordinary shareholders.

- Exchange rate risk – the sensitivity of the company's operations to a change in foreign exchange rates.

- Political risk – the sensitivity of the company to a change in regulation or the political environment.

- The **growth rate** for a company is dependent on its asset base and the return it can generate on these assets. Therefore a decline in the return on assets or a contraction of the asset base would present a risk for the growth rate and lead to a decline in the price/earnings multiple.

The price or value of an equity will be the earnings multiplied by the price/earnings multiple applied to these earnings. So now we have identified the risks attached to both factors we can conclude that the major risks for equity markets are as follows:

- Macro factors:

  - GDP growth.

  - Inflation.

  - Resource costs.

  - Foreign exchange.

- Equity risk premiums.

- The forecast growth rate for earnings.

Private equity

Many of the risks associated with equity apply also to private equity. We can see this in the correlation between private equity and global equity returns, which is now estimated as being over 0.80. The private equity market is now dominated by the expansion and buy-out market, rather than early stage venture capital, and the drivers of performance are:

- The availability and cost of credit.

- The business environment.

- Acquisition price which is based on the earnings multiple paid to purchase an investment).

- Exit price.

There are some additional risks that apply to private equity:

- **Leverage.** Most of the returns generated from buy-outs result from increased leverage when companies are taken into private ownership. Investments are very vulnerable to an increase in borrowing costs or a withdrawal of credit.

- **High specific risk.** Small companies often focus on a niche business and have a limited range of products, making them vulnerable to a change in the business environment.

- **Limited information.** Private equity investments require analysis and there may be little public information on relevant industry or activities. This also relates to the difficulty in valuing private equity given the absence of market price.

- **Liquidity risk.** Private equity is by definition not listed so there is not an efficient marketplace to dispose of holdings in. If investors cannot sell to other investors they will rely on an initial public offering or trade sale to provide an exit route.

5 Commercial property

Like equities, commercial property is sensitive to changes in the economic climate and returns are positively correlated with equities; but like bonds, income payments are more reliable than equity dividends. Historically, volatility has been lower than in equity markets and the UK system of leases where rents are only reviewable upwards has provided steady income at least partially protected from erosion by inflation.

Economic risks

The economic cycle

A strong growth in GDP indicates a strong corporate environment, which feeds through to a healthy demand for property, whether industrial, office or retail. On the other hand a recession diminishes the availability of tenants, pushing up vacancy rates, exerting downward pressure on rents and reducing selling prices. This was the situation in 2008 when UK commercial property prices fell by just over 22% before recovering by 3.5% and 15.1% in 2009 and 2010 respectively (based on the Investment Property Databank indices).

Inflation

Property has long been seen to offer protection against high inflation, partly because rental rates are frequently pegged to the retail prices index. Rental income makes up approximately half the returns generated by property investment and long-term capital values should increase in line with rental income. When inflation is expected to be low there is less reason to hold property.

Interest rates and the availability of finance

Many property purchases are leveraged, with a mortgage or borrowing used to finance the purchase. In a rising property market this will magnify positive returns, but in a falling market negative returns will also be amplified.

Rising interest rates can also hit property owners because their borrowing costs increase. The credit crunch wiped out many sources of finance with the result that investors looking to divest were unable to find buyers.

Other risks

Liquidity risk

Direct property is illiquid. In a declining market it can be very difficult to find a buyer, and even if a buyer if found, realising the sale proceeds is a lengthy process.

High management and transaction costs

Managing property and finding tenants is time consuming and using an agent involves additional expense. Transaction costs are also high, particularly if they are structured in a way that involves the purchaser paying stamp duty.

Supply of property

Whereas demand is led by economic environment as well as longer-term lifestyle changes, the supply of property is led by developers and investor demand. It can take time for supply to adjust and if the economic environment deteriorates there will be surpluses of property in certain sectors. A 'boom and bust' cycle affected the London office market in the 1970s, 1980s and 1990s.

Listed property companies and real estate investment trusts

For many smaller investors the way to access a diversified portfolio of property has been via a listed property company or a real estate investment trust (REIT).

Historically, listed UK property companies acted as both developers and owners, but under the REIT legislation the major companies have become principally owners, while property development is usually now undertaken (often on behalf of REITs) in one-off financing vehicles. This makes REITs a lower-risk proposition than companies heavily exposed to the risks of property development.

REIT rules permit qualifying companies to be 'tax transparent', so that no corporation tax is levied on rental income. Instead the equivalent of basic rate tax is deducted from all income (Property Income Distributions) distributed to shareholders. The rules also restrict the amount of development activity a REIT may undertake. Some property companies listed on the London Stock Exchange achieve similar results by being registered in the Channel Islands so that they are not subject to UK tax.

Changes to the REIT rules have been made which may prompt the creation of REITs investing in residential property. Historically, the pattern of behaviour of residential has been quite different from commercial property, so this may provide some diversification benefit for investors. The lower availability and higher cost of residential mortgages since 2008 have led commentators to predict that many more people will adopt renting a home as a norm. New-build blocks of city flats are the type of property most likely to be owned by REITs.

Unlike life or pension funds, REITs and other listed property companies use gearing, which accentuates the effect of a rise or fall in property prices. At the end of 2008 listed UK property funds were selling at discounts of more than 40% to their underlying net asset values, although discounts contracted over the next two years to a level of around 10%.

Open-ended commercial property funds

Pension and life assurance funds have been major owners of commercial property for over a century. From the 1970s onwards, life assurance companies have offered open-ended funds investing in commercial property. From the 1990s, unit trusts and OEICs joined them.

Life assurance property funds could rely on their parent companies to act as 'banks' in the event of investors wanting to sell and the fund not having enough cash. Unit trusts and OEICs required a change to the regulations whereby these funds have to secure lines of credit so that they can deal with redemptions without having to sell property before paying investors. Funds investing in direct property also have terms that permit the managers to suspend redemptions if they are unable to ascertain a net asset value or if their lines of credit are exhausted.

Life assurance, pension, unit trust and OEIC funds investing directly in property are forbidden from employing gearing. In this case, the IPD indices are appropriate benchmarks for UK property. However, some OEICs and unit trusts invest not in direct property but in 'property securities', principally REITs. The typical level of gearing of REITs worldwide is about 50%, so the performance of such security-investing funds should not be compared with an ungeared index and the indices produced by NAREIT (www.reit.com) are more appropriate benchmarks.

Inefficient markets

Property is not an efficient market, for several reasons:

- There are imperfect information flows.
- There is no central market place.
- No two properties are identical.

Inefficiency provides an opportunity to buy properties that are undervalued, but on the other hand other investors can end up overpaying for properties.

6 Residential property

Residential property shares many of the same risks as commercial property. It is vulnerable to changes in the economic climate, availability and the cost of finance, is illiquid and bears high management costs. Also, leases for residential property are typically shorter than for commercial property, increasing the potential time spent finding tenants.

For many private investors the route to investment has been through directly purchasing buy-to-let property. In 2007–08 many of these investments lost money, with the recession hitting demand and the availability of finance drying up, which has further reduced liquidity in the secondary market. Since then, there has been a recovery in the market but with significant geographical differences in property price performance.

Although REITs can invest in residential property, the rules make this inefficient, but at some point residential REITs may offer investors a more efficient way to access this asset class.

7 Commodities

The commodity sector covers a wide range of different commodities with different risk/return profiles. The major commodities are:

- Oil and gas.
- Industrial metals.
- Precious metals.
- Soft commodities:
  - Agriculture.
  - Livestock.

The attraction of investing in commodities is their low correlation with other assets. The historic correlation with global equities is 0.1 and the movement in commodity prices has been largely independent of other asset classes. However, in the financial crisis commodities fell alongside almost every other asset class (even gold fell at the end of the period) and correlation with equities jumped to 0.5.

The major risks associated with commodities are as follows.

Economic risks

The economic cycle

There is a strong link between demand for commodities and the economic or business cycle, creating a strong cyclicality in their returns. As economies expand, the demand for commodities increases, pushing up prices. Increasing the supply of commodities takes months or years: either mothballed facilities need to be brought back on stream or commodity producers need to increase capital expenditure and exploration budgets. So an increase in demand, or an anticipated increase in demand, can lead to dramatic jumps in prices. For example, the oil price (Brent crude) rose from just over $50 a barrel at the beginning of 2007 to over $140 a barrel in mid-2008 and then fell back to $40 a barrel at the end of 2008, before rising steadily to its current price of over $120 per barrel.

With strong growth in emerging markets leading demand for industrial metals, particularly in China and India, commodities are often seen as a way of gaining exposure to these and other industrialising economies.

Inflation

Industrial metals and oil and gas are often seen as inflation hedges, although studies using past data show that energy has been the commodity most strongly linked with inflation.

Exchange rates

Commodity prices are primarily quoted in US dollars. When the dollar depreciates commodity prices tend to rise and vice versa.

Other risks

Political risk

Political instability in the Middle East which threatens the oil supply can drive up prices. Political instability also impacts on the gold price, which is seen as a safe haven in times of uncertainty.

Central bank policy

In the 1990s central banks were major sellers of gold, which increased supply. Now, as governments lose faith in paper currencies, central banks in countries like China, India and Russia are increasing their holdings of gold.

Futures markets

Risks can also arise from futures markets. Exposure to commodities can be directly or via:

- Commodity derivatives.
- Commodity funds.
- Listed companies.
- Exchange-traded commodities.
- Exchange-traded funds.
- Structured notes.

Where exposure is gained through derivatives, typically futures or swaps, or through exchange-traded commodities or exchange-traded funds that are holding derivatives, there is a problem that the futures markets are in contango (futures prices higher than spot prices), rather than in backwardation (futures prices less than spot prices). This increases the cost of rolling over futures positions, and makes it hard for investors to achieve the gains seen in the spot prices.

8 Hedge funds

The boundaries between hedge funds and traditional onshore funds are blurring, with funds compliant with UCITS III able to make similar investments to many hedge funds. Many of the comments below also refer to absolute return onshore funds.

It is difficult to generalise about the investment risks associated with hedge funds because their managers use many different strategies, investing in a wide range of asset classes and derivatives. Some of the major risks are highlighted below.

Investment risks

Underlying assets

Hedge fund performance is linked to the performance of the assets held in each fund. The most popular hedge fund strategy is equity long/short, which has had a positive beta with respect to equity markets, so the funds follow the direction of equities but dampen the returns; that is, they fall by less in declining markets and rise by less in bull markets.

For an investor buying a diversified portfolio of hedge funds via a fund of hedge funds the performance has also followed the direction of world equity markets. At the end of 2007 the correlation between the HFRI funds of hedge funds index and the MSCI EAFE international stock market index was over 0.8, which partly explains the fall in the average hedge fund by over 20% in 2008. In the last collapse in equity markets, in 2000–2002, the correlation was much lower (0.6) and hedge funds held their value against large falls in equities, so for many investors their recent performance was a disappointment.

Other strategies in the fixed income sector and convertible arbitrage have been shown to be highly sensitive to events in their markets. Not only did we see massive movements in credit spreads and declines in equity-linked fixed-income products but liquidity in these markets dried up, so funds facing redemptions were forced to sell, if they could, at below fair value.

Some strategies such as managed futures, and to a lesser extent global macro, have shown a low correlation with equities and bonds and appear to offer genuine diversification benefits to investors.

Leverage

Certain strategies have been heavily leveraged. Fund managers using some arbitrage strategies are faced with the problem that arbitrage profits are generally very small, so they use leverage to magnify the profits. However, this also magnifies the losses. Leverage is achieved by:

- Borrowing external funds to invest, or selling short by more than the equity capital of the fund.

- Using derivatives that only require the posting of margins, rather than the outright purchase of the cash securities.

In the past leverage ratios have often been between 2:1 and 10:1 (gross investment value to net asset value) and there have been cases of much higher ratios: the Long-Term Capital Management hedge fund registered a ratio of over 40:1. It is now much harder to source financing, so gearing levels are much lower than historic levels. However, leverage is extremely dangerous: if a market falls by 20% a fund invested in the market with long exposure which is leveraged by 2:1 is likely to see a 40% loss on its investment. Additionally, if financing is withdrawn a hedge fund can be forced to liquidate positions in a falling market.

Liquidity risk

Liquidity risk can be very important for certain strategies, particularly those involving the purchase of asset-backed securities, convertibles and over-the-counter derivatives. When the market for these instruments all but disappeared, funds were faced with being unable to sell holdings. Liquidity risk becomes more important if hedge funds dominate a certain asset class; this is often referred to as 'concentration risk'.

Model risk

Model risk is the risk that a model fails. The quantitative strategies used by hedge funds are based on complex models using historic information to assess the fair value of securities or to identify trends in markets. If the wrong model is used, or it is incorrectly applied, or it relies on historic data which is inconsistent with current data, then the model will fail.

Operational risks

Liquidity risk

Liquidity risk is also an operational risk. Hedge funds which hold illiquid assets can be faced by client redemptions, as well as margin calls on derivative or broker-funded positions. The risk that a fund's creditors stop financing its activities can force it to liquidate positions in an adverse market, thereby pushing prices down further and forcing more sales, forcing prices into a downward spiral. This caused the final collapse of Long-Term Capital Management. From the client perspective the risk is that funds will often try to stop redemptions or use side pockets to segregate assets that are illiquid.

Credit risk

In addition to being an investment risk, counterparty credit risk is also an operational risk. Hedge funds will face this risk since they deal with brokers, dealers and other financial institutions when trading or buying on margin. When credit conditions are deteriorating a hedge fund will experience greater risk of default by its counterparties.

Manager risk

An investor in a hedge fund, particularly one which is lightly regulated, is putting an enormous amount of trust in the manager. Information from many hedge funds is sparse, so an investor may not be aware of a change in strategy or in the level of risk being taken. There are also risks relating to unauthorised trading and the risk of fraudulent activity.

Pricing risk

The general lack of transparency is particularly worrying with regard to the pricing of some hedge funds' holdings, especially holdings of over-the-counter and complex securities. When there is no market price the funds will rely on broker prices (shown to lack consistency from broker to broker) or model-driven prices (reliant on the assumptions input into the models). Given the strong motivation to hide bad news in times of market difficulty, due to both performance fees and the threat of redemptions, there will always be the temptation for funds to distort prices and therefore net asset values when times are hard.

Other risks

Regulatory risk

The pressure to strengthen the regulation of European hedge funds continues, and greater disclosure will be required with possible limits on leverage and short selling. UCITS III funds will need to comply with the European directive for open ended retail funds. They are only permitted to invest in eligible investments, must provide at least fortnightly liquidity for investors and leverage, which can only be achieved using derivatives, is limited to 200% gross exposure. The removal of flexibility from the way hedge funds manage investments will, for the hedge funds that decide to continue to be managed from the EU, reduce the potential to achieve superior performance.

Listed funds

Listed funds can move to a discount to the net asset value. Many investors have used funds of hedge funds to access a diversified portfolio of hedge funds, but the listed funds of hedge funds were badly hit in the recent market crash, with some of them moving to discounts of over 40% to their net asset value. For investors this compounded the falls seen in net asset values. Discounts have now contracted to around 10% to 20% of net asset values.

Complex strategies

Many hedge fund strategies, particularly those based on 'black box' models where the input and output can be seen but the internal workings of the model are difficult, if not impossible, for the average investor to understand and evaluate. There is now a move to using less complex strategies and buying less complex securities.

9 Structured products

Structured products are typically fixed-term products (often with terms of three or five years) that can be offered as an investment note, a fund or a bond. They have the following features:

- They usually guarantee the original capital invested plus a percentage of the upside of an index, for example the FTSE 100 index. Normally investors receive the capital return only and not the dividend income.

- Alternatively the product might offer income with 'soft protection', so the capital is guaranteed as long as there is not a fall in the market of more than a certain percentage, for example, 30%.

- The fund is usually invested in a combination of zero-coupon bonds and call options on the underlying index.

While these products can be attractive for investors who do not wish to take on the full risk of investing in the underlying market, and for whom capital protection is important, there are significant risks, as follows.

Performance of the underlying index

If the underlying index does not rise over the term of the product, at best the capital will be returned (without interest in most cases). At worst if there is a limited guarantee clause a capital loss might still be made.

Credit risk

It is important to check on the counterparty to the guarantee or issuer of the zero-coupon bond and any derivative transactions. Investors in structured products backed by Lehman Brothers found their funds were lost when Lehman collapsed.

Liquidity

These products are generally fixed term and cannot be cashed in early. If it is possible to cash in early there will usually be penalties and the capital guarantee may not apply. Some products are traded in the secondary market but the level of trading may be very limited.

Summary

In this chapter we have examined the risks that affect different asset classes. There are many common risks: inflation, GDP growth and currency exchange rates, as well as the trade-off between investing directly or through a pooled vehicle (which offers diversification but the potential to trade at a discount to net asset value). Specifically:

- The principal risks to cash deposits and money market funds are default risk and inflation.

- Bonds are vulnerable to default risk, reinvestment risk, and event risk; credit ratings are not always reliable.

- In addition to general economic factors, equity earnings are affected by many company-specific risks.

- Commercial property risks include the availability of finance as well as general economic factors, inflation and interest rates.

- Political and currency risk are more significant for commodities.

- Counterparty risk is the most important risk with structured products.

In the next chapter we will consider how managers can build models to incorporate the different risk factors.

Chapter 9
Modelling risk

1 Introduction

In this chapter we will examine how portfolio risk is modelled. First of all we will consider optimisation models, which are used to determine the best trade-off between risk and return in the construction of portfolios. Then we will look at multifactor models, which can be used to explain the major drivers of return and risk exposure.

2 Optimisation models

In chapter 6 we looked at how the risk and return of a portfolio containing different securities or asset classes is calculated. The return is simply the weighted average of returns of assets held in a portfolio, and the risk is determined by the weighting in each asset, the risk or standard deviation of each asset's return, and the correlation or covariance between each pair of assets' returns.

Using the formulae in chapter 6 we can calculate the risk and return of any multiple asset portfolio as long as we know, or can forecast:

- Return for each asset class.
- Risk for each asset class.
- The correlations between each pair of asset classes.

The efficient frontier

Continuing this analysis we can see that for a multiple asset portfolio, if all possible portfolios were plotted on a graph with expected returns measured against risk (standard deviation), the possible portfolios would fall on and under a curve. This curve is the 'efficient frontier'. This is the set of portfolios that offer the maximum rate of return for any given level of risk.

In Figure 9.1 portfolios A and C have the same level of expected return but A is lower risk; therefore portfolio A is more attractive then portfolio C. Similarly portfolios B and C have the same level of risk, but B offers a higher expected return; therefore portfolio B is more attractive. Portfolios A and B both lie on the efficient frontier; for their levels of risk they offer the highest return.

The curve will flatten as risk increases. This is because adding more risk leads to diminishing levels of additional return.

So for a low-risk client, based on the input data A might be the optimal portfolio, and for a client that can tolerate higher risk, B might be the optimal portfolio.

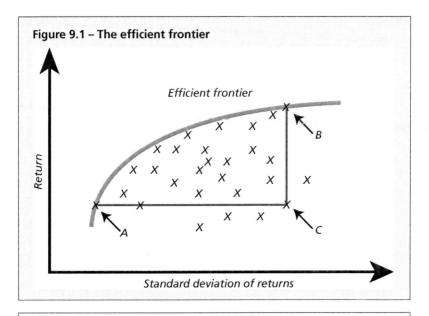

Figure 9.1 – The efficient frontier

Efficient frontier

Return

Standard deviation of returns

Example 9.1: Risk/return trade-offs

We will now consider a portfolio investing in three assets, UK equities, gilts and funds of hedge funds, all priced in sterling. We are provided with the following data:

	UK equities	Gilts	Funds of hedge funds
Expected return	12%	9%	8%
Expected standard deviation	18%	7%	6%
Expected correlation			
UK equity	1		
Gilts	0.1	1	
Funds of hedge funds	0.8	0.2	1

We can plot an infinite number of points that can be used to draw an efficient frontier, but we have calculated the risk and return for 12 portfolios below. In the first three columns we give the percentage weighting in each asset class, and we then calculate the expected returns and standard deviation of each portfolio in columns four and five respectively.

UK equities	Gilts	Funds of hedge funds	Expected return	Expected standard deviation
100%	0%	0%	12.00%	18.00%
70%	15%	15%	10.95%	13.48%
30%	35%	35%	9.55%	7.90%
0%	50%	50%	8.50%	5.04%
0%	100%	0%	9.00%	7.00%
15%	70%	15%	9.30%	6.36%
35	30%	35%	9.70%	8.61%
50%	0%	50%	10.00%	11.54%
0%	0%	100%	8.00%	6.00%
15%	15%	70%	8.75%	6.82%
35%	35%	30%	9.75%	8.48%
50%	50%	0%	10.50%	9.98%

These 12 portfolios can be plotted on a chart, as shown below:

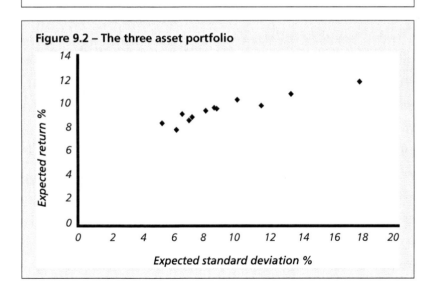

Figure 9.2 – The three asset portfolio

We can see from this chart that investing 100% in UK equity will generate the highest risk (18%) and the highest return (12%), so this point lies at one extreme on the efficient frontier. We can also see that some points are sub-optimal. For example, investing 100% in funds of hedge funds, which would have an expected risk of 6% combined with a return of 8%, is not as attractive as investing half in hedge funds and half in gilts, which has an expected risk of only 5.04% with an expected return of 8.5%. If the client can take on slightly more risk, investing 15% in equity with the remaining 70% in gilts and 15% in hedge funds, with a risk of 6.36%, generates a higher expected return of 9.30%.

For clients willing to take on greater risk, portfolios holding a higher percentage of equities have a higher return, whereas risk-averse clients will tend to hold a higher percentage in gilts and hedge funds. This assumes risk is defined as purely the standard deviation of returns and the input data is correct.

Applications

Optimisation models are widely used for asset allocation. Usually the returns for markets are forecast and historic numbers are used for risk and correlation. An optimisation model simply works out, given the inputs, which is the optimal mix of assets to hold from a risk/return view point.

Managers can then plot where a client's existing portfolio lies, and if it is significantly below the efficient frontier, they can adjust the asset classes held so the portfolio lies on the efficient frontier. In theory they will be able to increase the expected return for any given level of risk. Typically optimisation models are run ahead of each asset allocation meeting, often on a monthly basis, which can lead to the frequent rebalancing of portfolios.

The model may not be followed rigorously but it provides a starting point for making asset allocation decisions and at the very least raises questions if existing client portfolios lie below the efficient frontier.

However, there are many limitations to using optimisation models, most notably that they tend not to work in extreme market conditions, just when they are needed most. We will consider this problem in the next section.

Limitations

The theory used to build an efficient frontier makes many assumptions, and there are problems with the input data that severely limit the use that can be made of efficient frontiers to decide asset allocation. Some of these issues are as follows:

- Forecasts, if used, for risk, return and correlation may be incorrect. The output from these models will only be as good as the data input. Another problem is that errors in return forecasts will tend to be magnified by the model. For example, if two markets have been highly correlated with similar risk, but very different returns are forecast, the model will tend to suggest investing almost entirely, if not entirely, in the market with the higher return forecast rather than in the market with the lower return forecast.

- Confidence in forecasts is not incorporated into the model. It may be that the UK market forecasts have been arrived at after thorough analysis and wide discussion, but perhaps the forecasts for some of the emerging markets have been made on the basis of less rigorous analysis.

- Historical data, if used, for risk and return may be a poor indicator of future risk and return. This is particularly true in extreme conditions. In the recent credit crunch volatility of markets rose to four to five times their historic averages. The VIX Index chart in chapter 6 illustrates the changes in volatility numbers over the last few years.

- In extreme market conditions, correlations will often be quite different to those in more normal conditions. See Table 9.1, which compares the long-term average correlation and then the correlation in the market crash. We can see that asset classes that historically had moderate correlation with equities suddenly had strong correlation. Using optimisation models, investors may have thought they had diversified away risk by including commodities, corporate bonds and hedge funds but found that just when they needed diversification to reduce losses it didn't work.

- The asset classes are assumed to have normal distributions. This is rarely true. In the example above we have included funds of hedge funds, but individual hedge fund strategies will in many cases have returns which are skewed or exhibit kurtosis.

- The appropriate measure of risk is assumed to be standard deviation, not, for example, downside deviation. Other risks that we covered in chapter 8, such as liquidity risk and counterparty risk, are not included in the model.

- The objective is assumed to be to achieve absolute rather than relative returns. We would need to modify the model to incorporate relative returns and relative risk or tracking error.

Other practical difficulties in using an efficient frontier to decide asset allocation for clients include the following:

- Individual clients may have investment constraints that have not been incorporated into the model.

- If asset allocation is reviewed monthly clients may not be comfortable with the level of turnover needed to keep the portfolio lying on the efficient frontier.

- Individual portfolio managers construct portfolios in different markets, which can have quite different profiles to the indices that are used for inputs into the model (for example, they may buy portfolios with an average beta not equal to 1).

Table 9.1 – Correlation with global equities

	Dec 1993–Sept 2007	Oct 2007–Feb 2009
Emerging market debt	0.5	0.7
Emerging market equity	0.7	0.9
Commodities	0.1	0.5
High yield bonds	0.4	0.7
Hedge funds	0.6	0.8

The capital market line

We will now extend the theory and include the possibility of investing in a risk-free asset. We first of all define the risky asset as the point, M, where the line from the risk-free asset to M is tangential to the efficient frontier. The set of points representing portfolios investing in M and the risk-free asset is described by the equations below.

The expected return is simply the weighted average of the returns for the risk-free asset and M. This is calculated as

$$E\left(R_{\text{Port}}\right) = w_{RF}\left(R_{RF}\right) + \left(1 - w_{RF}\right) E\left(R_M\right)$$

where w_{RF} is the weighting in the risk-free asset.

We can simplify the equation for portfolio risk (σ_{Port}) for a two-asset portfolio. The equation we used in chapter 6 is:

$$\sigma_{\text{Port}}^2 = w_1^2\sigma_1^2 + w_2^2\sigma_2^2 + 2r_{12}w_1w_2\sigma_1\sigma_2$$

Since the standard deviation of the risk-free asset is zero and the correlation between M and the risk-free asset is zero then

$$\sigma_{\text{Port}} = \left(1 - w_{RF}\right)\sigma_M$$

A new set of optimal portfolios will lie on this line. The line is called the 'capital market line' or sometimes the 'capital allocation line', and the point, M, where the tangent touches the curve is the market portfolio. All portfolios on this line will be a combination of the risk-free asset (or borrowing the risk-free asset) and the market portfolio. Theoretically the market portfolio must consist of a completely diversified portfolio which includes all risky assets.

Note that the borrowing rate will be above the risk-free rate, so strictly speaking the capital market line would not be a straight line but would change slope at the point M.

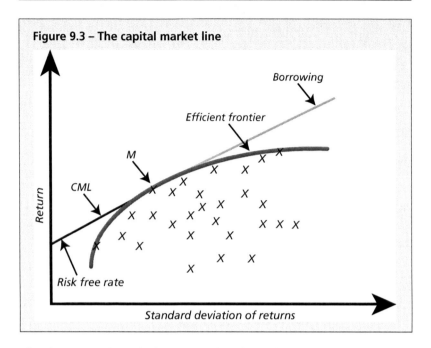

Figure 9.3 – The capital market line

This theory is rarely applied in practice, but the implications are:

- All optimal portfolios consist of the risk-free asset plus the combination of assets included in *M*. So all portfolios will have the same mix of risky assets in the invested portion, the mix that is included in *M*.

- Clients' risk objectives will be met by the level of cash or borrowing in their portfolio: a low-risk client will have a significant proportion held in cash, a high-risk client borrowing. It is possible to increase the expected return indefinitely by increasing the leverage.

Among the reasons why this is not used in practice is that most clients would be uncomfortable holding large levels of cash or leverage (and may not be willing to pay a fee for the cash portion).

3 Multifactor models

Multifactor models relate returns from securities or portfolios to a number of factors. Whereas the capital asset pricing model (CAPM) uses a single factor, and assumes that all returns are linked to the return of the market, a multifactor model recognises that returns might be linked to economic factors such as the oil price or inflation, or to fundamental factors, which for an equity might be the price/earnings ratio, earnings growth and so on. A multifactor model has potentially much greater explanatory power for security price moves than CAPM.

Fama and French created one of the first multifactor models to be applied to equities when they added two more factors, value and size, to CAPM. Value is measured by the book value divided by the market price of a company.

We can rearrange CAPM and add the effect of the two additional factors to get

$$E\left(R_I\right) - R_f = \beta_I\left(R_M - R_F\right) + \beta_{\text{HML}}\ \text{HML}\ + \beta_{\text{SMB}}\ \text{SMB}$$

where:

- R_f is the risk-free rate.

- $R_M - R_F$ is the market return less the risk-free rate, which is the market risk premium.

- β_I is the market beta of asset I.

- *HML* is 'high minus low', or high book to market price minus low book to market price factor premium. Factor premium means the additional return expected for having exposure to the factor.

- *SMB* is 'small minus big', or small market capitalisation minus big market capitalisation factor premium.

- β_{HML} and β_{SMB} are the sensitivities to the *HML* and *SMB* factors respectively.

Note:

- We are now considering the excess return of security I, which is $E\left(R_I\right) - R_f$. We have simply moved R_f to the left-hand side of the equation.

- The above formula is used to calculate the expected return; the actual return would include α and an error term.

- The market beta, β_I, has an average of one. Both β_{HML} and β_{SMB} have averages of zero. In a multifactor model all betas except the market beta would normally have an average of zero, and then the beta is the number of standard deviations the exposure is away from the average of zero. Technically this is called 'at standardised beta'.

- Betas are usually determined by regression analysis using historic returns.

Example 9.2: Multifactor models

Using Fama and French's three-factor model we will analyse two stocks. We are given the following information, which shows that stock A is a very small value stock (1.5 standard deviations above the mean), and B a large, growth stock.

Stock	Market beta	Sensitivity to *HML*	Sensitivity to *SMB*
A	0.8	0.8	1.5
B	1.1	−0.7	−0.5

If the factor premium forecast for *HML* is 2% and for *SML* is 1%, that is, value stocks and small stocks will outperform, and the equity market risk premium is 4%, then the expected excess return for stock A is:

$$\beta_I (R_M - R_F) + \beta_{\text{HML}} \text{ HML } + \beta_{\text{SMB}} \text{ SMB}$$

$$= 0.8\,(4\%) + 0.8\,(2\%) + 1.5\,(1\%) = 6.3\%$$

And for stock B it is:

$$\beta_I (R_M - R_F) + \beta_{\text{HML}} \text{ HML } + \beta_{\text{SMB}} \text{ SMB}$$

$$= 1.1\,(4\%) - 0.7\,(2\%) - 0.5\,(1\%) = 2.5\%$$

The average excess return for stocks in the market would be 4% (the equity risk premium times the average beta of one). We can see the negative effect on B's performance of its being a large growth company; it is expected to underperform by 1.9% due to the *HML* and *SMB* factor exposures. Its above average market beta partially offsets the negative impact and the overall expected return is 2.5%, compared to the market return of 4%. On the other hand A's return is helped by its being a small, value stock; these factors add 3.1% to the expected return, whereas the low beta leads to an expected loss of 0.8% versus the market average return.

Figure 9.4 shows that when we look at extended periods we can see that these factors have had a large influence on stock returns in UK markets. When we look at the effect of compounding returns we can see that small value stocks have dramatically outperformed large growth stocks. Some explanations have been proposed for this and its apparent contradiction of the theory proposed by CAPM: for example, that small cap and value stocks are riskier (and this risk is not captured by beta) and generate a higher return to compensate for this risk.

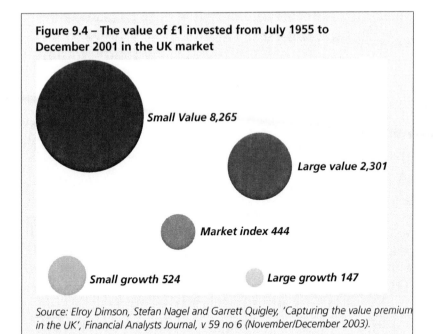

Figure 9.4 – The value of £1 invested from July 1955 to December 2001 in the UK market

Small Value 8,265

Large value 2,301

Market index 444

Small growth 524

Large growth 147

Source: Elroy Dimson, Stefan Nagel and Garrett Quigley, 'Capturing the value premium in the UK', Financial Analysts Journal, v 59 no 6 (November/December 2003).

Calculation

A factor is simply an element to which security returns are correlated. We can broaden the formula out from three factors to any number of factors. The expected excess return for k factors is given by

$$E\left(R_n\right) = \sum_{k=1}^{K} \beta_{n,k} m_k$$

where:

- $E\left(R_n\right)$ is the expected excess return from stock n.

- $\beta_{n,k}$ is exposure of stock n to factor k. This is often called an 'alternative beta'.

- m_k is the factor forecast for factor k.

To summarise, there are three steps in factor analysis:

- Specify a number of factors affecting historic data.

- Measure the beta of investment against each factor.

- Measure the risk premium for each factor.

Factors

Examples of typical factors used are in an equity factor model are:

- Macroeconomic:
  - Interest rates.
  - GDP growth.
  - Exchange rates.
  - Oil price, etc.
- Company – fundamental:
  - Earnings growth.
  - Financial leverage.
  - Asset turnover.
  - Net profit margins, etc.
- Company – market related:
  - Price/earnings ratio.
  - Price/book value.
  - Dividend yield.
  - Market capitalisation.
  - Price momentum, etc.

For fixed-income funds there are three major factors that are usually incorporated into models:

- Term structure of interest rates, that is, changes in yield curve.
- Changes in credit spreads for different grades of bonds.
- Currency.

Measuring betas

Betas are usually measured using regression analysis, so the historic returns for a stock or portfolio are compared to returns from the factor over a period to work out the sensitivity of the stock to that factor.

Measuring risk premiums

The historic risk premiums can be used for the different factors, for example the historic, very long-term, equity market risk premium in the UK is around 4%. However, depending on how the multifactor model is being used, estimated risk premiums can be applied.

Applications

Multifactor models allow for a greater level of analysis and are widely used in the investment world. The major applications are covered below.

Performance attribution analysis

Using multifactor models we can identify the source of an active fund manager's returns, isolating the portion that comes from 'skill' as opposed to exposure to a specific risk factor.

Style analysis commonly isolates the impact of a value or growth style, and compares big and small cap styles using a factor model. A small cap manager may appear to generate positive alpha when compared to a broad index such as the FTSE All-Share, but when the return is regressed against different styles it may become apparent that the attractive return has simply come from holding small cap stocks (not the manager's own decision) and when we include this factor it turns out that there is negative alpha. In this case an investor would have been better off investing in a small cap index fund.

Research into hedge fund returns is ongoing, using multifactor models to evaluate which portion of the returns has come from factors that can be cheaply replicated. Such factors include the MSCI World Index returns and the movement in credit spreads. The residual returns can be attributed to alpha.

Active management

Multifactor models allow an active manager to act on a particular view on what the drivers of returns will be in the market. If for example they expect high price/earnings stocks to outperform and price/earnings is a factor in the model used the manager can increase the exposure or beta with respect to this factor. On the other hand, if the manager is concerned that inflation is going to be higher than the consensus forecast he or she may wish to have a negative exposure to an inflation factor. These models allow a manager to reduce the number of decisions needed and focus on forecasting the factor premiums.

The models also highlight exposure to factors that a manager might have made inadvertently.

Constructing index or tracker funds

Rather than buying all the stocks in an index it is cheaper to buy a portfolio with fewer holdings which matches an index's exposure to the key factors. For example, in an index fund you would ensure that the market beta is one.

Enhanced index funds use factor models, as do many funds which are quantitatively run. These will often tilt a portfolio towards factors for which there is expected to be a positive return, for example from value or price momentum exposure, and then neutralise exposure to other factors. These models have historically been relatively successful, but they performed very badly in the credit crunch when the performance of particular sectors (such as the financials) was reversed, and momentum and value stocks underperformed.

Risk management

Multifactor models allow managers to decompose their risk exposures, using either total risk or more commonly tracking error. See example 9.3.

Example 9.3: Multifactor models used to decompose risk

Most models use variance rather than standard deviation because the variance of uncorrelated items is additive. In this example we will look at tracking error squared (TE^2) as the measure of risk. We can break down TE^2 into two components:

- Active factor risk – the part of risk explained by the factor exposures.
- Active specific risk – the residual risk not explained by the factors, generated by active security selection.

In the table below we consider two portfolios and their exposure to three independent risk factors. All numbers are in squared percentages.

Portfolio	Factor 1 risk squared	Factor 2 risk squared	Factor 3 risk squared	Active specific risk squared	TE^2
A	11.25	4.50	1.25	19	36
B	0.18	0.25	0.37	0.20	1

Portfolio A has a tracking error of 6%, which indicates that it is an actively managed portfolio, whereas the second portfolio has a tracking error of only 1%, so it is staying very close to the index.

Over half of the risk for portfolio A comes from specific risk (19/36), so active stock bets are being made. A high proportion of the factor risk comes from an active view being taken on exposure to factor 1 since it represents 11.25 out of 17 of the factor risk.

In portfolio B we have a different situation. Here specific risk is only 20% of the total risk and the factor risk accounts for the remainder.

A next step would be to calculate the marginal contribution of each factor to total risk, which would incorporate correlation between the factors. This is beyond the scope of this book.

A multifactor model allows the investor to decide which active exposures contributed most to risk and whether they are consistent with the investment objectives and returns achieved.

Limitations

Although factor models are an effective tool for managing portfolios and monitoring risk there are some adverse issues to consider:

- There is an enormous amount of work involved in developing and updating an accurate factor model.

- Choice of factors is critical. A good factor model will include factors so that:

  - The factors have high explanatory power for the returns of a large number of assets in a market.

  - The residual error term is minimised.

  - Factors are independent.

  - Factors are easily identified and measurable and, if this is required, can easily be forecast.

  - The error term is independent of the factors.

- Betas or sensitivities to different factors may be unstable.

CAPM versus multifactor models

Despite multifactor models offering a more rigorous approach to analysing risks and returns CAPM continues to be used widely in finance for performance analysis, calculating the cost of capital and so on. In comparing the two some considerations are:

- CAPM makes many assumptions (for example that investors hold diversified portfolios). Multifactor models, based on arbitrage pricing models, make few assumptions.

- CAPM is simple to apply; market betas are available from a multitude of sources.

- Multifactor models are complicated to apply; also it is difficult to forecast risk factors and premiums.

- If a company or a portfolio is sensitive to factors not well represented in the market index we should use a multifactor model. For example a small niche company will tend not to be highly sensitive to the market and will have a low beta, meaning that expected returns are low if we use CAPM. However, it will have significant specific risk, so CAPM-based forecast returns are understating investors' expected returns.

4 Models in extreme conditions

As John Authers pointed out in the *Financial Times* on 28 September 2009, models have failed to explain market behaviour:

> ... extreme events happen far more often than a "normal" distribution would imply. Benoit Mandelbrot, the mathematician who invented fractal geometry, proved this more than 40 years ago, when efficient markets theory was in its infancy, and has continued to criticise the established theory ever since.

> If stocks really followed a bell curve, he observed, then a swing of more than 7 per cent in a day for the Dow Jones industrial average should happen once every 300,000 years. In fact there were 48 such days during the 20th century. "Truly, a calamitous era that insists on flaunting all predictions. Or, perhaps, our assumptions are wrong," he concluded.

So what went wrong? The following can be asserted:

- Security returns don't follow a normal distribution. Models that depend on risk being defined as standard deviation, which would apply to most efficient frontier/optimisation models, have understated the risk of extreme outcomes. Kurtosis or fat tails are apparent in most if not all security markets.

- Risk numbers and correlations are assumed in both models to be stable, so historic numbers are used. In extreme conditions this is not true.

- Efficient market theory is based on an assumption that investors act rationally, Behavioural finance has shown otherwise. Behavioural biases are probably strongest in extreme market conditions.

Nassim Taleb in, his bestselling book *The Black Swan*, wrote about black swans as the events that have not been anticipated, because nothing in the past indicated they could happen. Yet these are events with extreme consequences. With the benefit of hindsight they are rationalised. As Taleb points out, the inability to predict 'outliers' negates the utility of models based on past events and behaviour; models focus on what is known rather than what is not known; and models miss the events which present the greatest opportunity.

John Kay also makes the distinction between risk and uncertainty: known unknowns and unknown unknowns. Uncertainty is not in a model and by definition cannot be, so the users of models need to know what has been included and analysed and what has not been included, and appreciate that models underestimate the true risks facing investors. One implication is that the investor or adviser should reduce the size of the bets implied by a model for any given level of client risk, or, to get a similar outcome, reduce the client's risk tolerance when applying a model.

Summary

We have addressed two key methods of modelling risk. The first method, using optimisation programmes, is widely used for making asset allocation decisions, and can also be used for security selection. The second method is the use of multifactor models to construct portfolios with specified exposure to certain factors and as a way to break down the risk arising from exposure to these factors.

Both types of model are in use today, although work is being done to improve their accuracy as a result of the poor performance of models in the recent market turmoil. It is essential to remember that in extreme market conditions models are likely to fail and when used for decision making they should always be combined with a measure of common sense.

- The efficient frontier gives a model for creating portfolios with higher return or lower risk.

- The greatest diversification benefits are gained by adding a new asset to a small group of assets. Very little is gained by adding one extra asset to a portfolio of twenty.

- Only three pieces of data: return, standard deviation and correlation, are needed to create efficient portfolios.

- Optimisation models aim to improve return or lower risk based on historic volatility and correlation.

- Multifactor models provide better explanations of returns than CAPM and are widely used by investment managers particularly for attribution analysis.

- Models do not work in crises, because returns to not follow normal distribution and extreme events are unpredictable and by definition cannot be included in models.

Chapter 10
Managing risk

1 Introduction

In chapter 9 we looked at the ways that risk is modelled, focusing on optimisation models and multifactor models. In this chapter we will consider how fund managers structure portfolios and what instruments are available to isolate and manage risk effectively. We will also consider some of the funds or products that use these strategies.

We focus first on asset allocation, which is the process of deciding how to divide an investor's assets between different countries and asset classes. The asset allocation decision is extremely important since it, rather than stock selection, has been the key factor in determining the performance of portfolios, and it is also a means of controlling risk.

2 Portfolio construction

The first and arguably most important step in constructing a portfolio is relating the objective to the market environment. Some managers apply a 'top down' discipline based on asset allocation, others a 'bottom up' stock selection approach. These approaches are explored further in chapter 14. Here we focus on the different methods fund managers use to apply asset allocation.

3 Asset allocation

Asset allocation is the process by which funds are allocated across different asset classes. Usually asset allocation includes a geographic decision, although some international equity portfolios are invested on a global industry or sector basis rather than using a country approach.

The importance of asset allocation

Several studies have assessed the importance of asset allocation and almost all agree that it is the key driver of returns. For example, using empirical data Roger Ibbotson and Paul Kaplan showed that long-term asset allocation policy accounts for about 90% of the performance of US funds. Using time series regression the R^2 between fund returns and target asset allocation returns was around 0.90, which means that on average 90% of the variation in a fund's returns is explained by the markets' returns. The remainder is explained by stock selection, market timing and other active decisions.

It is important to note that these studies are based on the historic performance of managers and reflect the problem that many managers are closet indexers and are taking few stock bets. Also, the relative importance of stock selection and asset allocation is partly a function of the market environment. When there is very low dispersion of returns for individual stocks, that is, they move very closely together, it is harder to add value through decisions on stock selection. But if we look at periods of market stability, say in the mid-1990s, asset allocation was relatively unimportant and stock selection played a larger role in returns.

Types of asset allocation

Asset allocation takes place at different points in the investment process. Unfortunately the terms used to describe different types of asset allocation have not been standardised, and what is 'strategic asset allocation' in one fund management company is 'tactical asset allocation' in another. Different types of asset allocation include:

- Selecting the benchmark or the policy portfolio.
- Strategic asset allocation.
- Tactical asset allocation.

The benchmark

The benchmark sets the long-term normal asset mix for a client. A benchmark is typically a recognised index such as the FTSE All-Share (for UK equities), S&P 500 (for US equities) or a combination of indices for different assets or markets. The objective when setting the benchmark is to meet client targets for risk and return at the lowest long-term cost, consistent with any other client constraints or preferences. In many cases the fund manager will recommend or set the benchmark but in other cases the client, especially if a sophisticated institutional client, will instruct the fund manager on which benchmark is to be used.

The characteristics of a benchmark include the following:

- Only major classes of asset are included.
- It is based on capital market forecasts over a long period.
- It is not affected by short-run changes in capital market conditions and includes the appropriate mix under normal conditions.

An example of the benchmarks provided by the Association of Private Client Investment Managers and Stockbrokers (APCIMS) is shown in Table 10.1.

In some cases the benchmark is the peer group, for example one of the Investment Management Association's fund sectors. Though there are arguments against using fund sectors as benchmarks, they are in practice

Table 10.1 – APCIMS benchmarks

	Income	Growth	Balanced
UK shares	40.0%	47.5%	42.5%
International shares	15.0%	32.5%	25.0%
UK bonds	35.0%	7.5%	20.0%
Cash	5.0%	2.5%	5.0%
Commercial property	2.5%	2.5%	2.5%
Hedge funds	2.5%	7.5%	5.0%
Total	100.0%	100.0%	100.0%

Source: FTSE

widely used by fund management groups in promoting their funds. Usually, they are not the primary benchmark used by fund managers themselves.

Strategic asset allocation

The purpose of both strategic and tactical asset allocation is to add value to the benchmark through active asset allocation. Most fund managers will not need to follow the benchmark exactly but will have some flexibility to overweight or underweight asset classes relative to the benchmark as their view of the markets changes. Strategic asset allocation involves:

- Taking advantage of inefficiencies in the pricing of asset classes. This process is often based on structural and cyclical factors and an intermediate time period (more than six months).

- Regular meetings, typically quarterly for private client managers and monthly for institutional managers. Members of the asset allocation committee will usually be the chief investment officer, senior fund managers, etc.

- Considering markets that are not included in benchmark allocation.

Factors that determine strategy will centre on valuation issues, the economic environment and business cycle, and technical factors.

Tactical asset allocation

Tactical asset allocation involves:

- Looking for inefficiencies in the pricing of asset classes on a shorter term — typically six months or less. Tactical asset allocation responds to changing economic and market conditions and is driven by changes in expected returns.

- Frequent meetings, on a daily or weekly basis. They are often attended by more people than the strategic asset allocation meetings and involve all the fund managers and relevant analysts.

- Adjusting the asset allocation of client portfolios on a daily or weekly basis.

Unless the fund manager can use derivatives, the frequent trading involved in tactical asset allocation may not be appropriate and will be expensive. Many managers carry out strategic allocation only.

4 Managing market risk

While models, including optimisation programmes, can be used to help decide the optimum asset allocation, there are some practical issues to consider. These include:

- Transaction costs for buying and selling individual securities. Even in low-cost markets such as the US these are over 0.25% for equities, and in the UK, where stamp duty has to be paid, average costs can approach 1% or more. Using optimisation models leads to portfolios requiring frequent rebalancing as forecasts change, which will drive up transaction costs.

- How quickly changes in asset allocation can be implemented. This is partly determined by how long fund managers take to decide which stocks to buy and sell, as well as delays in executing trades, particularly if limit orders are used (where the trade cannot be executed unless the security is above or below a limit price) and whether derivatives or ETFs can be used to implement asset allocation changes.

- The risk that individual fund managers buy portfolios with betas different to one, which negates the asset allocation decision.

Overlay strategies

One solution to some of these problems is to manage the asset allocation decision using an 'overlay strategy'. This means that the securities held in the underlying portfolio are left untouched and the market exposures are changed in an overlay portfolio. By 'market exposures' we generally mean beta for equities, duration for bonds and currency exposure. Using an overlay has the advantage that the underlying portfolio of individual securities does not need to be adjusted, which saves on transaction costs. It also allows the fund manager to focus on making the best long-term investment decisions rather than being distracted by the need to raise funds or invest new funds because of an asset allocation decision.

Overlay strategies are often based on the assumption that most equity or bond portfolio managers do not have expertise in predicting market or currency movements. This is a reasonable argument since security selection and asset allocation skills are very different and most managers are not expert at both types of decision making. In this case the market decisions are made by another manager – either within the same firm or an external manager if the overlay management is contracted out. In some cases a client using several fund managers can aggregate the portfolios and then pass on to an external manager the responsibility to manage market and currency exposures for the combined portfolio.

We will now consider how overlay strategies are managed using derivatives.

Using derivatives to change market exposure

The three main risks that are managed using derivatives are:

- Equity market risk (measured by beta).
- Interest rate risk (measured by duration).
- Currency risk.

We will look at three examples showing the use of derivatives to manage each of these risks. We will then consider the advantages of using futures, forwards, options or swaps.

Managing exposure using derivatives will involve dynamic positions in the sense that the market value of underlying portfolios and the beta and duration of underlying portfolios are constantly changing.

Example 10.1: Using futures to adjust equity exposure

A fund has £500m invested in the UK stock market and the benchmark is the FTSE 100 index. At the asset allocation meeting the committee discusses the outlook for the equity market and decides there is a strong possibility of a market setback in the short term. The committee decides to reduce the equity market exposure to £400m to reduce the losses if its forecast is correct. We will assume that the average beta of the UK equity holdings is one.

The level of the index today (the spot price) is 5068 and the price of the futures contract that expires in three months' time is 5075. Prices are quoted in index points and each index point is valued at £10. The return is based on the capital only index.

The asset allocation team decides to reduce its exposure to the FTSE 100 index using futures. The number of contracts it needs to sell (the team is going short since it wants to decrease exposure) is:

$$\frac{\text{Exposure}}{(\text{Pounds per index point} \times \text{Futures price})}$$

$$= \pounds100\text{m}/(5075 \times \pounds10)$$

$$= 1,970 \text{ contracts}$$

If the committee was correct and at the end of three months the value of the index has fallen by 10% to 4561 (5068 x 0.90) then the underlying portfolio of £100m in equities (out of the £500m total) will have lost around £10m (given the beta was one) and the futures position will make sufficient profit to offset the loss on the equities. The profit on the short futures position is:

$$\text{Number of contracts} \times (\text{End index} - \text{Price dealt at})$$

$$\times \text{ Pounds per index point}$$

$$= -1,970 \times (4561 - 5075) \times \pounds10$$

$$= \pounds10,125,800$$

We have not taken into account dividends that would be earned over the period from the £100m of equities still held in the portfolio.

The alternative would have been to sell £100m of shares and have earned interest on the proceeds. The two transactions, shorting futures and collecting dividends versus selling shares and collecting interest, should give the equivalent return if the futures were correctly priced.

The calculations have ignored transaction costs but costs for futures trading would be less than 0.1% (assuming the price impact cost is low).

Example 10.2: Using forwards to hedge currency risk

A UK portfolio manager has invested in US bonds and is concerned that the US dollar is going to depreciate against sterling. He decides that he will hedge out the currency risk associated with a US$100m position in the bonds using forwards. In this case, the manager needs to sell short dollars against pounds to benefit from a decline in the dollar. He looks at the spot rate, which is $/£= 1.6484, and then approaches an investment bank, which quotes a three-month forward rate of $/£= 1.6476. This means he can sell dollars at this rate in three months' time. He deals at this rate. The contract stipulates that the profit or loss can be settled in cash rather than the manager having to actually deliver the dollars.

Let's say that after three months the dollar has actually appreciated against sterling, so the manager's concerns on dollar depreciation were unfounded. If the dollar closed at 1.5835 against sterling he has made a loss on the forward contract of:

$$\$100\text{m} \times (1/1.6476 - 1/1.5835)$$
$$= £60,694,343 - £63,151,247$$
$$= £2,456,904$$

He sold the dollars forward to generate £60,694,343 but if he had waited he could have sold at the spot rate for £63,151,247, so he made a loss of £2,456,904 on the contract.

However, the purpose of the transaction was to hedge out risk, and the underlying portfolio will have increased due to the dollar appreciation, so the currency forward has removed the exposure to currency for £100m of the portfolio.

The difference between the forward rate and the spot rate is explained by the slightly higher interest rates in the UK. If you buy dollars forward and hold on to pounds, earning higher interest, you will receive less dollars per pound when the forward transaction settles.

The forward premium (or discount) to the spot rate is determined by the interest rate differential between two currencies, in this case the pound and dollar. The basis is the interest rate differential. 'Basis risk' relates to a change in the interest rate differential affecting the validity of the hedge, which is not so important for short-term contracts, where the price is dominated by the spot rate, but can affect long-term contracts.

Example 10.3: Using futures to manage duration

In chapter 7 we defined duration as the interest rate sensitivity of an individual bond or portfolio of bonds. For bond managers the duration of their portfolios will be a major determinant of performance.

In this case, a manager has invested $500m in the US bond market and calculates the duration of the portfolio to be 7.6. The manager sees a revised forecast for growth in gross domestic product and believes this will lead to an unanticipated jump in interest rates. She decides to reduce the duration of the portfolio to 5 using bond futures. She identifies a treasury bond futures contract that is priced at $76,500 and which has a duration of 6.4. We will assume that an interest rate change will affect the yield on the portfolio and the implied yield on the futures on an equivalent basis yield.

$$\frac{(\text{Target duration } - \text{ Current duration})}{\text{Futures duration}} \times \frac{\text{Portfolio value}}{\text{Futures price}}$$

$$= \frac{(5 - 7.6)}{6.4} \times \frac{\$500\text{m}}{\$76,500} = -2,655.23$$

The negative indicates she needs to take a short position, and since fractional contracts are not traded she will sell 2,655 contracts.

A month later yields have moved upwards by 50 basis points across the yield curve and the bond futures have fallen to $74,100. The profit on the short futures position is:

$$-2,655.23 \times (\$74,100 - \$76,500) = \$36,372,000$$

The manager sees that the portfolio of bonds has fallen to $481,372,550, representing a loss of $18,627,450. The net loss, after taking into account the profit on the futures position, is $12,255,450 or 2.45% of the original $500m portfolio.

We can check if the manager was successful in reducing the duration to 5 by calculating the ex-post duration of the portfolio. This can be calculated from the equation:

Percentage change in price $\approx -$ Duration $\times$ Percentage change in yields

$2.45 \approx -$ Duration $\times 0.50$

Duration ≈ 4.9

It would be good to see a precise answer of 5 for the duration in line with the manager's objective, but the result is unlikely to be exact because duration is not itself an exact measure and only approximately estimates the change in price of a bond or portfolio of bonds.

Futures versus forwards

The profit or loss calculation is the same for both futures and forwards. However, futures are dealt through an exchange whereas forwards are dealt outside an exchange, which creates some important differences between using futures and forwards:

- A forward transaction is customised whereas in a futures transaction all the terms (expiry, underlying asset etc) with the exception of the price are set by the exchange.

- Since futures contracts are standardised they can be traded more easily, making them potentially more liquid than forward contracts. However, the forward markets for currencies are highly liquid and are usually used for currency hedging.

- The clearing house of a futures exchange guarantees that trades settle, by acting as the counterparty to both sides of a futures transaction. In a forward transaction each party takes on the risk that the other party will default. In the current environment counterparty risk is still a major risk and parties may require margin or early partial settlement of forward transactions to protect their position.

- A futures contract is 'marked to market' (also referred to as 'daily settlement'), which means that gains and losses to each party's position are calculated daily and credited or debited to their account. When a party enters into a futures contract the exchange requires an initial margin deposit, and after this there will be daily settlement of gains or losses and margin calls if the position loses money.

- In most markets, futures contracts are regulated by the government.

- A forward transaction is a private transaction, whereas a futures transaction is reported to the futures exchange, the clearing house and often a regulatory authority. Some investors may not want traders in the futures market to know their position.

Using options

Options are completely different to futures and forwards because the holder has the right to receive (call) or deliver (put) an asset at a pre-specified price (the exercise or strike price). This is a right, not an obligation, and the option buyer pays the price, or option premium, for the right to choose. Traditional hedging with options involves the purchase of a put option on the underlying asset being hedged. If the asset price falls the holder can exercise the option to make a profit (assuming it falls to a price below the exercise price less the option premium), to offset the loss on the underlying asset. Options can certainly be used to hedge out risk but there are two main issues to consider:

- There is an initial payment to buy an option, whereas with forwards and futures there is no initial payment. (A margin payment can be thought of as a deposit against possible future losses that will be returned if the position makes a profit.) With an option, the initial payment or premium is similar to buying insurance; it is the maximum an option holder can lose.

- Using options allows the holder to benefit from a movement in the underlying asset in one direction. If the decision to hedge turns out to be incorrect the investor can still profit from a rise or fall in the underlying asset. So, if an investor holds shares and decides to hedge against a fall in the stock market by buying a put option on the stock market index, and the stock market rises, then the put option will expire worthless but the investor will still benefit from a rise in value of the share portfolio.

Using swaps

Currency forwards are sometimes referred to as 'currency swaps', but generally this term indicates an agreement between two parties to exchange a series of cash flows over a period of time; currency swaps are equivalent to a series of forward agreements. The cash flows of at least one party will be made up of variable payments. For example, in a plain vanilla interest rate swap, one party pays a fixed rate and the other a floating rate. There are a few issues concerning the use of swaps to manage risk:

- Swaps are unregulated over-the-counter instruments and each party takes on counterparty risk. Counterparty risk can be significant for longer-term agreements since the credit quality of parties can change dramatically over the tenor or life of the option.

- Swaps can run for years and can be used to gain or reduce long-term exposure to market factors. For example, buying an equity swap that pays the return on an equity index such as the FTSE 100 can be used to gain index exposure. Compare this to the use of futures, where the liquidity is in the short-term contracts and the contracts will probably need to be rolled over on a monthly basis.

- Credit default swaps (CDSs) have been a popular way to manage credit risk. With a CDS the protection buyer pays a fee (quoted as basis points of notional principal that is being protected) to a protection seller, who will make a contingent payment which follows a credit event for a reference entity. For example, a five-year default swap for company ABC is traded at 228 basis points a year, so a protection buyer would pay £22,800 each year to protect each £1m of ABC's debt. If managers are concerned they have too much credit risk in a portfolio of bonds they can purchase a CDS which will pay out in the event of default, and the CDS will increase in value if credit spreads widen.

Advantages of overlay strategies

The use of overlay strategies to manage market exposure has the following key advantages:

- It is less disruptive for the portfolio manager running the underlying fund.

- It is quick: derivatives markets are often more liquid that the underlying securities. While it could take weeks for one manager to sell securities in one market and another manager to invest the proceeds in a different market, the derivatives transaction can achieve the same objective in minutes.

- It is cheap: it has been estimated to be 95% cheaper to trade derivatives rather than the underlying securities.

- Performance attribution is made easier, because security selection is separated from market strategy. The added value of the asset allocator can be measured by the success of the overlay strategy.

Limitations of overlay strategies

Despite these benefits, overlay strategies have disadvantages:

- They are usually dependent on the use of derivatives to keep costs low, but some clients prohibit the use of derivatives for their portfolios.

- Liquid derivatives may not be available for all markets and for the futures market the liquidity is usually concentrated in the shorter-term contracts.

- Estimating betas and durations can be difficult and these are not stable, so using derivatives to hedge risk is not going to be perfectly accurate.

- Cash management will be tricky if derivates are used. Swaps may require quarterly payments and futures need daily margin payments.

5 Separating beta from alpha

The essence of an overlay is that it separates returns from beta (market exposure) from those from alpha (returns that are uncorrelated with the markets). This leads on to the next topic – 'portable alpha'.

Portable alpha

The term 'portable alpha' refers to the addition of returns from alpha (independent of market movements) to a portfolio which has the required market exposure. The portfolio which gives market exposure might be an index fund or an actively managed portfolio. In some cases a diversified portfolio of alpha-generating strategies is attached to a portfolio investing in different asset classes.

One practice is for an institutional investor to identify fund managers who generate positive alpha, from whichever asset class they specialise in, and to then invest funds with these managers in order to capture the alpha. The second step is to use an overlay portfolio to adjust beta exposures employing derivatives to achieve the required asset allocation.

For example, if a manager of Japanese equities exhibits skill in identifying alpha, this manager could be given money to manage and then the allocation to Japanese equities could be eliminated (or almost eliminated, given the values and betas of positions would need to be monitored) by shorting futures on the Tokyo Stock Price Index or the appropriate Japanese equity index.

It is usually assumed that emerging and inefficient markets offer more opportunity to generate alpha, so these opportunities can be exploited and the market risk reduced by hedging strategies.

Portable alpha strategies can be used for asset-liability management where liabilities are linked to inflation. For example, alpha can be captured from equity investment positions, but in the overlay equity exposure is reduced and exposure to index-linked bonds or inflation-linked derivatives (such as inflation swaps) increased.

Advantages of portable alpha strategies

Portable alpha strategies are targeted at enhancing returns while managing market risks. Some of the advantages are:

- Returns are increased, since the focus moves to identifying managers who can persistently generate returns that are independent of markets and who can therefore also generate attractive returns in falling markets.

- Investment is more flexible, since investors are not constrained to generating alpha in the asset classes they wish to be invested in.

- It can be cost effective if active fees are only paid for the alpha-generating portion of the fund and beta exposure is gained through low-cost tracker funds or derivatives.

- Alpha-generating portfolios often have low correlations, so combining these portfolios can lead to a well-diversified portfolio.

- Risk management is simplified by the segregation of market risk and specific risk.

Disadvantages of portable alpha strategies

Disadvantages are:

- Managers need the appropriate skills to identify alpha-generating managers or strategies, to develop overlays and to efficiently adjust market risk.

- Using derivatives to manage market exposure will never be completely accurate for several reasons: risk factors are not stable, derivative settlement dates may differ from the desired hedging period and so on.

Products targeting alpha

Over recent years products targeting alpha rather than beta have become more popular. The perception is that beta is cheap, since exposure to markets can be gained using derivatives or tracker funds such as exchange-traded funds. On the other hand, alpha is expensive, since identifying alpha requires skill and investors are prepared to pay for returns from alpha. This is probably somewhat oversimplified since market timing is also a skill. However, the evidence is that it is harder to generate consistent returns from decisions on market timing, that is, from switching exposures between different markets to generate returns over and above the return generated by the long-tem asset allocation strategy.

Where managers apply both alpha-generating and market-timing strategies, advisers will need to see attribution analysis before they can judge the success or otherwise of their alpha generation.

Hedge funds and other funds that use alpha-generating methods are reviewed in chapter 14.

6 Risk budgeting

The term 'risk budgeting' refers to the management of risk exposure by fund managers and the decisions made on the efficient allocation of risk across different investment opportunities. There are different ways that managers approach this:

- Multifactor models were discussed in chapter 9 and in example 9.3 we looked at how multifactor models can be used to break down risk, in this case tracking error, in a portfolio. Multifactor models can be used for 'what if' analysis, to work out the effect on tracking error of changing the exposure to an asset in the portfolio.

- On a proprietary trading desk traders are allocated capital and a daily permitted value at risk. The profits of a trader take into account the allocated capital and the acceptable level of risk. Capital and risk are being allocated between the different trading desks but the risk budget for the whole trading room will be less than the sum of the individual budgets because of diversification. Similar risk-budgeting strategies are used by some hedge funds and other fund managers.

- An investor considering allocating funds to different portfolio managers might use tracking error as the risk measure and compute the managers' information ratios to see if they are adding value. Again, correlation between asset classes will be considered when an assessment is made on whether a manager adds value, and to decide the optimal tracking error to allocate to each manager.

- Risk-budgeting programmes may also include the following:

  - Stop losses. When a portfolio or individual holding has lost a given amount in a period it is stopped from trading or the position is liquidated.

  - A scenario approach. Under this, managers have to invest portfolios that will not lose more than a certain amount under different scenarios (see below on stress testing).

  - Maximum limits on individual positions in terms of value.

- Limits on positions as a percentage of their daily trading volumes or the size of the free float, in order to reduce liquidity risk or prevent a large fund dominating the trading in a security.

- Limits on leverage.

7 Stress testing

Risk models usually measure potential losses in normal market circumstances. Stress testing looks at losses in extreme circumstances. There are two main approaches to this:

- **Scenario analysis.** This entails looking at the effects of large changes on the assets held in a portfolio. Such changes will include yield curve shifts, movements in currency rates and equity markets, volatility in equities or bonds and changes in market liquidity. Scenario analysis will also look at changes in the relationship between these variables. In some cases scenarios are based on hypothetical situations and in others they are based on past extreme events.

- **Applying shocks to market models.** This process looks at a range of possibilities rather than specific scenarios. In many cases it is assumed that all prices and risk factors move in an unfavourable direction.

Stress testing is essential if risk management is going to be effective in worst case scenarios. Inadequate stress testing has often been a factor in the collapse of financial institutions.

8 Comments on managing risk

Most of this chapter has been relatively technical in its approach to managing risk, but there are a few basic points that need to be emphasised:

- Managers need to take on risk if they are to generate returns. Even strategies which are supposedly arbitrage strategies are unlikely to be pure arbitrage and will not have hedged out all risks. If investors are paying an active fee they are paying for the possibility that the manager will outperform the benchmark return and so the manager will need to take on risk.

- Volatility provides an opportunity to buy assets that are mispriced and thus to increase returns.

- Volatility also indicates an active market. Some assets appear to have low volatility because they are priced by models or broker quotes (for example, property, private equity, with profits and some hedge funds). Prices are smoothed, which understates the true volatility of the underlying assets.

- The period over which correlations are measured is critical when you are calculating the benefits of diversification. Some assets may have correlations that are low based on monthly returns but higher when based on annual returns. For a long-term investor who is not switching actively between asset classes the long-term correlations may be more relevant.

- Simple mechanisms such as cost averaging can reduce risk. Investors who put the same amount into a portfolio each month will smooth out the effect of fluctuations in security prices. It is almost impossible to time the peaks and troughs in markets accurately and cost averaging avoids investors panicking at the bottom of markets and stopping investment, or being overconfident and increasing investment at market peaks.

- Reducing one risk often leads to increasing another: there is no free lunch. For example, investors might buy listed funds to gain liquidity (as opposed to making direct investments), but the volatility is greater as the funds can move from premiums to their net asset value to discounts and vice versa.

- As a general rule, if you have not clearly identified several risks for a particular investment, you have not looked at it hard enough.

Summary

- Asset allocation – the choice of asset classes – has accounted for 90% or more of variations in investment returns, and has therefore been the primary investment decision.

- Comparing portfolio returns against a benchmark enables managers and advisers to evaluate their performance.

- Investment managers use overlay strategies to enhance returns from selected asset classes.

- 'Portable alpha' strategies use derivatives to reduce the market-related (beta) element in investment returns.

- Investment managers use complex risk budgeting and stress testing systems to limit the risk in their chosen strategies.

Chapter 11
Risk and behavioural finance

Many investment management techniques are based on modern portfolio theory and the 'efficient market hypothesis'. These techniques make several assumptions, including that:

- Investors are looking to maximise return and minimise risk.

- The market price of a share is the best estimate of its value and any mispricing of shares is random and short lived.

- News is incorporated into share prices very rapidly.

- Investors are equally motivated by gain and loss.

Finance theory has, however, proved incapable of explaining market behaviour, in particular the phenomena of panics and bubbles. There are also well-researched anomalies in the efficient market hypothesis such as seasonal factors and the fact that small companies and value stocks perform better over the long term (these points are expanded on in the appendix to part 2). Dramatic swings in market or sector performance often occur on the basis of little new information.

1 Behavioural finance and finance theory

Behavioural finance is a discipline that has grown steadily in influence since the 1980s. It aims to explain market and investor behaviour by looking at the effects of individual psychology and emotional and perceptual biases. It shows that investors make mental shortcuts and systematically, rather than randomly, make errors.

Neoclassical economics provides the framework for finance theory and both of these disciplines depend upon 'rational expectations'. The demonstrations of irrationality provided by behavioural finance (see below) have led to defensive moves in neoclassical economics, such as the concept of 'bounded rationality', according to which outcomes can still conform to what theory predicts even if market participants lack perfect information and perfect rationality. However, for panics and bubbles finance theory offers no explanation – and as yet, nor does behavioural finance, which to date has focused on individual psychology and behaviour. The latest trend in behavioural finance is to research 'network' or crowd effects, already established in other fields, and obviously a key factor in crashes and bubbles where the 'madness of crowds' has been recognised for over 300 years.

2 Behavioural finance and psychology

Behavioural finance attempts to integrate classical economics and finance with psychology. The primary aim of behavioural finance is to identify the errors or mental shortcuts (heuristics or 'rules of thumb') that investors use and the persistent biases that influence behaviour.

It is very difficult to override mental shortcuts even when you are aware of them. As an illustration of this, look at the two pictures in Figure 11.1 and decide which of the vertical lines is longer. Most people say the right-hand one looks longer, although in fact the lines are the same length. This is explained by perspective: the brain is adjusting for its interpretation that the lines in the second picture are further away, hence the impression that the line is longer. But the important point is that even after you have been told that the lines are equal length, they still look different.

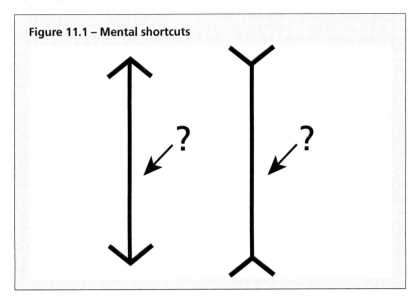

Figure 11.1 – Mental shortcuts

The same issues arise with investing, and even if you learn about heuristics, it is very difficult to override the biases and avoid making irrational decisions. Warren Buffett's long-term business partner at Berkshire Hathaway, Charlie Munger, has always insisted that the removal of perceptual biases is the single most difficult and important task facing the investor, since it is these biases that lead to potentially disastrous errors.

It is important that advisers help clients to make or accept decisions that meet their objectives, but advisers also need to be aware that clients may not see things rationally. They may be selective in the facts that they look at and find it difficult to accept particular investment decisions. The practical issues faced by advisers are dealt with in part 4 of this book.

3 The main cognitive errors

The main cognitive errors made by investors are:

- An aversion to realising losses.
- Poor calibration of probability.
- Optimism.
- Hindsight bias.
- Representativeness.
- The illusion of control.
- Familiarity.

Attitude to losses

Research strongly supports the view that investors weigh losses far more heavily than gains. Researchers have offered people a bet on the toss of a coin and told them that if they lose, they will lose $100. They have then asked: 'What is the minimum gain that would make this gamble acceptable?' The answers have averaged somewhere between $190 and $250. Most people weigh possible losses 2.5 times more heavily than possible gains. This and other experiments are usually interpreted to mean that investors experience the pain of a loss much more deeply than the happiness they experience when making a similar gain. The resulting asymmetry in risk preferences — loss aversion is much stronger than the desire for gain — contradicts both neoclassical economic theory and portfolio theory, and undoubtedly has profound effects on market behaviour.

Another well-researched area is the link between purchase price and the attitude to a fall in value of an investment. Let's say one investor bought shares at 100p per share and a second investor bought at 200p per share, and yesterday the shares were worth 150p. If today the share price drops to 120p, the second investor is more upset: a reduction in a gain is not as painful as an actual loss. So book value is an important consideration when making investment decisions and managing client expectations. This tendency to 'anchor' on a price can be mitigated by presenting ranges for prices or returns rather than single numbers.

There is a strong aversion to realising losses and a well-known tendency to sell winners before losers. This is probably because when a loss is realised, rather than remaining a paper loss, you are removing the opportunity for the investment to recover its value, thus creating more scope for regret. The worst instance of this is when you sell an investment at a loss only to see the price rise rapidly afterwards. Moreover, when you sell at a loss, you tend to self-critically judge the investment as a mistake rather than seeking to identify the causes of the loss.

Research suggests that although on average fund managers' buying decisions add value, their selling decisions destroy value. This is presumably partly because fund managers tend to focus on selecting winners and see selling as a way to raise cash. But their selling decisions are also influenced by loss aversion.

There are some other interesting issues with respect to losses and the feeling of regret:

- Regret is usually much stronger for something you do (making a loss) rather than something you omit to do (failure to make a gain). The exception to this is risk-tolerant investors who do regret opportunities missed.

- Regret is stronger if it is linked to your own decision or your fund manager's decision, weaker if it can be blamed on something which is beyond your control, for example the state of the economy.

- Regret is stronger if it results from an action that took you away from your traditional position or activity. For example, if an investor buys a hedge fund for the first time just before a fall in price, this will be more painful than making a similar loss on equities that they have held for a long period.

Attitude to risk

When researchers asked analysts which of the eight gambles shown in Table 11.1 would be most attractive to investors, the analysts ranked them in the order of preference shown. Note that all the gambles have the same expected payoff of $10,000. (The expected payoff is the outcome that will be achieved according to the laws of probability if the bet is repeated a sufficient number of times.)

The results show that investors prefer a high probability of a moderate gain combined with a small probability of a very large gain, that is, lots of hope and little fear. This helps to explain the popularity of structured products, where derivatives are used to protect investors' capital but there is upside potential from the underlying market, and also the lasting popularity of National Savings & Investments premium bonds, where overall returns are low, the chance of winning a large prize is extremely low but the chance of winning a small prize is relatively high.

Nassim Taleb has noted that many traders and short-term investors adopt a similar approach and take numerous small profits while also exposing themselves to the risk of a large loss (often the result of a 'black swan' or unpredicted and unpredictable event). This approach has been likened to

Table 11.1 – Preferred risk/return payoffs

Gamble	Payoff 1	Probability	Payoff 2	Probability
A	$5,000	95%	$105,000	5%
B	$5,000	50%	$15,000	50%
C	$1,000	10%	$11,000	90%
D	$1,000	90%	$91,000	10%
E	$2,000	50%	$18,000	50%
F	$0	50%	$20,000	50%
G	($2,000)	90%	$118,000	10%
H	($5,000)	50%	$25,000	50%

Source: Daniel Kahneman and Mark W Riepe, 'Aspects of investor psychology', Journal of Portfolio Management, v 24 no 4 (summer 1998)

picking up 10p pieces on a busy road: sooner or later you will be hit by a car. Really successful traders, on the other hand, accept many small losses in order to make occasional very large gains. This requires overriding the normal experiences of pain and regret induced by losses.

The impact of the past

Investors are influenced by the past in their appetite for risk. If people are offered the chance to toss a coin and win or lose £10, less than half will accept the bet. This is rational since it involves taking a risk without a positive expected return. However, if they have won £50 earlier in the day, over 50% of people will take the bet. It appears that when people make a gain they do not consider the winnings to be completely their own, which is referred to as the 'house money effect'.

On the other hand, the 'snake bite effect' leads investors to avoid risk after a loss – unless a 'double or nothing' bet is available. The biggest risk takers are people who have already made significant gains or losses.

This research has mainly involved gamblers, but is probably more widely applicable.

Poor forecasting

Investors typically lack skill at linking probability with forecasts and tend to forecast a very narrow range of outcomes. This, coupled with underestimating the kurtosis ('fat tails') in financial markets, means that investors are surprised by the range of actual outcomes. This is also linked to overconfidence: if investors are overconfident of an outcome being achieved they will tend to take more risk.

Another issue that behavioural finance has highlighted is the tendency to anchor estimates in the recent past and to ignore new information which contradicts your own view. This includes investors or advisers only reading research that supports their own investment decision, so if they have bought a security they prefer to read 'buy' research notes rather than 'sell' notes. This helps to explain long-term trends being established in sectors of the market; it takes a lot of information to make investors change their view of an investment.

Over-optimism

Investors show a tendency to be optimistic and this explains why people:

- Buy lottery tickets.
- Overpay for options.
- Underestimate the possibility of bad outcomes.

Hindsight bias

With hindsight bias, knowledge of an outcome leads to prior probabilities being reassessed as posterior probabilities. Hence we usually hear explanations after an event that makes it seem as if it was easily predictable. This can make communicating with clients difficult. If clients have seen a loss in their portfolio, with hindsight they may believe that the loss should have been avoided, and this, combined with regret, will make things even worse.

Representativeness

Representativeness is the tendency to pigeonhole people, investments etc on the basis of superficial information. This was evident in the technology boom, when any stock that had any technology or 'new economy' features was enthusiastically purchased by investors.

The illusion of control

Investors have a tendency to see patterns in random events. If a fund manager outperforms for four quarters, say, this is seen as evidence of skill, though in many cases it will be due to luck. This is another factor in explaining overconfidence: a trader has a good run of luck, believes it was due to skill and starts to make heavier and heavier bets.

Familiarity

Investors prefer to invest in familiar and known brand names. This is similar to home country bias, where investors overweight the allocation to their own market despite the arguments for diversification. It probably also partly accounts for individual investors' excessive enthusiasm for residential property investment.

4 The importance of behavioural finance

The 'irrational exuberance' of recent years, especially the huge increase in the financing of residential investment for sub-prime borrowers in the US and the UK, has again drawn attention to the importance of psychological factors in financial markets. For example, the vast majority of British investors probably felt wealthier and more optimistic as a result of the steady appreciation of house prices between 2000 and 2007. However, from a rational point of view, as many economic commentators have pointed out, rising house prices create no wealth for a nation. Hence any short-term increase in 'economic growth' based on the resulting optimism could only be a transfer of future spending to the present, as higher personal borrowing (to be repaid later) financed more current consumption. And the increase in borrowing ratios could not continue indefinitely.

While policymakers confront the issues of regulation and the incentives that encouraged individuals and institutions to take excessive risks, with the potential for 'black swan' wipe-outs such as those that created the credit crunch, advisers need to be aware that markets have moods and that being swept away by them can be far more damaging to wealth than making the wrong choice of an investment fund.

To avoid such trend effects, stock market analysts are increasingly resorting to much longer-term measures of value in assessing the cheapness or otherwise of stocks – in particular, long-term price to book and cyclically adjusted price/earnings ratios. Likewise, long-term ratios of house prices to income are a more consistent way of measuring the cheapness or dearness of property than short-term affordability measures. In both cases, the underlying assumption is a rational one: that reversion to the mean is an almost universal phenomenon, so that the further the price or the return moves from the mean, the more likely a change of trend. This view is a useful corrective to the groupthink that can lead you to take enormous risks without realising it by taking continuance of a long-term trend for granted.

The value of scepticism

Fund managers do not have the same incentives to avoid disaster as advisers and individual investors. Managers of most long only active funds are usually rewarded for relative performance, which is rational since management groups use relative performance to promote funds. So long as managers lose less than the average of their peer group, they will be judged successful. This means managers will tend to adopt the same strategy as their chief executive. Chuck Prince, the former chief executive of Citigroup, famously outlined for the firm a few months before meltdown in 2008: "So long as the music's playing, you have to get up and dance."

Fund managers will ride trends that are past their sell-by date and will in general, as J M Keynes recognised 70 years ago, tend to take a shorter-term view than is in the long-term investor's interests. Only absolute return fund managers are penalised for taking on risk.

While advisers have to recognise that fund managers possess great analytical skills and huge information resources, they must also be aware that incentives for fund managers do not align perfectly with the motivations of investors. Fund management firms are almost without exception publicly listed or privately owned businesses: a mutual model is virtually unknown in the UK, though there are several US examples. Fund management firms therefore aim to have large assets under management, on which they earn fees. History has shown that managers can achieve this and prosper without delivering good returns to investors.

In relation to fund managers, therefore, advisers should in general adopt a questioning if not sceptical stance, particularly as regards their enthusiasm for any well-established trend or novel approach.

Normality and crisis

Periods of 'normality' in financial markets have been punctuated by crises throughout history. Advisers cannot simply adopt the view that crises cannot be foreseen or planned for: if they occur so regularly, it must be part of the adviser's role to take account of the possibility of a crisis in the solutions put forward to clients. While advisers cannot hope to foresee such crises any better than fund managers, they can aim to identify periods when the mood of a market is excessively optimistic or pessimistic and use this to temper the advice they give.

Summary

- Finance theory makes several assumptions about individual behaviour which research has shown to be false. The 'rationality' assumed in the theory is not the rationality used by people or investors.

- Investors are not necessarily irrational because they share perceptual and cognitive biases, but these biases can lead to behaviour that appears irrational.

- Cognitive biases identified by behavioural finance researchers include loss aversion, optimism, and hindsight.

- Investors are on average twice as averse to losses as they are keen for profits. This is a powerful influence on investor behaviour.

- 'Reversion to the mean' is a well established phenomenon in financial markets and is a useful correction to over-optimism.

Appendix 1 The efficient market hypothesis

The concept of efficient markets in its broadest sense is based on the belief that markets are self-correcting. This has been almost completely discredited by the recent financial crisis. If government policy makers had had a little less faith in efficient markets they might not have adopted a 'light-touch' style of regulation and might have stepped in earlier to avert disaster.

There is growing support for the concept that market are disposed to form bubbles, and the efficient market hypothesis (EMH) is now seen at best to be incomplete and only the starting point in explaining market performance. Some are complete disbelievers. James Montier says:

> EMH should be consigned to the dustbin of history. We need to stop teaching it, and brainwashing the innocent. Rob Arnott tells a lovely story of a speech he was giving to some 200 finance professors. He asked how many of them taught EMH — pretty much everyone's hand was up. Then he asked how many of them believed it. Only two hands stayed up!

With this in mind we have assigned the EMH to this appendix to provide the background to the theory.

1 Definition

The efficiency of capital markets depends on whether all the information available about a security is already reflected in its price. An efficient market, or to be more precise an *informationally* efficient market, is a market where security prices adjust rapidly to the arrival of new information so that current security prices reflect all the information available about the relevant securities.

2 Assumptions

The assumptions behind the EMH are that the market is one with active participants reacting to new information. More specifically:

- A large number of competing, independent, profit-maximising participants are analysing and valuing securities.

- New information comes to the market in a random fashion: the timing of one announcement is generally independent of others, so after good news from a company the next piece of news could be good or bad.

- Investors attempt to adjust the security prices rapidly to reflect new information. Although price adjustments will not always be perfect they are unbiased.

If these assumptions hold then the expected security returns should only reflect the risk of the security. This means all stocks should lie on the market's security market line; their returns are consistent with their risk.

3 Forms of EMH

The EMH takes three forms, as follows:

- **Weak form EMH** says that stock prices reflect all security market information, for example price and volume data. The implication is that past rates of return should have no relation to future rates of return.

- **Semi-strong form EMH** says that stock prices adjust rapidly to all public information released. This includes non-market information such as earnings and dividend announcements, valuation measures and so on. This means that basing decisions on information already in the public domain will not consistently lead to outperformance on a risk-adjusted basis.

- **Strong form EMH** says that stock prices reflect all information from public and private sources. This means that no group of investors has sole access to a certain type of information and can consistently outperform on a risk-adjusted basis. Information has no cost and is available to all investors. The strong form includes the weak form and semi-strong form EMH.

4 Testing the EMH

The evidence on the EMH is mixed, and extensive work has been done to test the validity of the different forms of the hypothesis. Much of this is based on the US market but the research has been confirmed by work on the UK market.

Weak form

Tests for the weak form EMH can be broken down into two categories:

- **Testing the independence between rates of return.** Tests have indicated little correlation between stock returns over time. They have also found no evidence of patterns of movement (increases followed by decreases) that could not be explained by random movements.

- **Testing trading rules.** Tests have focused on relatively simple trading rules based on using past market data. There are problems applying rules: some trading rules use subjective interpretation of data and there are potentially unlimited trading rules. There are also high theoretical trading costs. Generally, but not in all cases, tests support the weak form hypothesis, that is, buying and selling securities based on trading rules does not outperform a buy-and-hold policy.

Semi-strong form

Tests for the semi-strong form of EMH can again be broken down into two categories:

- **Studies to predict future returns using public information.** This includes time series analysis using valuation measures. There is evidence from these studies that markets are not semi-strong form efficient because of anomalies (see below).

- **Event studies.** These tests examine how fast security prices react to public announcements, for example, announcements regarding stock splits and accounting changes, as well as economic news. Generally the findings support the hypothesis, although studies on stock price movement after an exchange listing indicate that there are some short-term opportunities to make an excess return.

Anomalies

The following anomalies provide evidence that the markets are not semi-strong form efficient (note that performance is being measured on a risk-adjusted basis relative to the market):

- Stock prices do not respond as rapidly as expected to earnings surprises. There is evidence of abnormal returns 13–26 weeks after an announcement.

- There is a 'January effect' in the US, whereby investors sell loss-making stocks in December and then reinvest in January, leading to a superior relative performance of security prices in January. This is possibly explained by tax year end dates in the US.

- Under the 'weekend effect' average relative returns between Friday's close and Monday's open are negative for large firms and during Monday's trading are negative for small firms.

- Stocks with a low price/earnings ratio perform better.

- Stocks with high book value to market value tend to outperform; these are generally classified as value stocks. Outperformance is particularly noted in periods of monetary expansion.

- Small company stocks perform better although the performance is not stable. The differential may be accounted for by higher transaction costs, and the risk of smaller companies may not be adequately explained by beta.

- Neglected company stocks perform better. 'Neglected' refers to stocks that are only followed by a small number of analysts.

Strong form

Tests for the strong form EMH have focused on investors with access to non-public information or an ability to react to new information before other investors:

- **Corporate insiders**, such as company directors, are required to report to the Securities and Exchange Commission transactions in the stock of the firms where they are insiders. Analysis indicates that insiders achieve above-average returns as a result of these transactions.

- **Stock exchange specialists or market makers** have access to information about 'unfilled limit orders' that is not available to other investors. It seems specialists can make money from selling shares at higher than the purchase price and also from trading in blocks of shares and after unexpected announcements.

- **Security analysts** may have access to special information and have special skills. Studies have compared the performance of shares given high and low rankings by Value Line, a well-known independent research and advisory firm in the US. These studies show that changes in a share's ranking are usually reflected very rapidly in the share price and it is not possible to obtain excess returns from investing on the basis of these rankings, after taking into account transaction costs. There is some evidence of the existence of superior analysts who are apparently accessing private information. They appear to have market timing and stock-picking skills.

- **Fund managers** have good access to information and the opportunity to interview the management of listed companies. Studies show that fund managers on average do not outperform a buy-and-hold strategy over longer periods.

The results from the four groups are mixed but much of the evidence supports the strong form of the hypothesis. The main exceptions are the results from corporate insiders and market makers. Fund managers have not consistently outperformed, so from the point of view of the majority of investors it can be argued that the hypothesis holds.

Conclusion

The markets appear to be efficient with regard to much of the information available but there are a number of instances where the markets are not semi-strong form or strong form efficient.

The evidence supports the hypothesis that the markets are weak form efficient, that technical analysis using historic market information will not lead to outperformance on a risk-adjusted basis, after transaction fees.

Fundamental analysts believe that market valuations and intrinsic valuations can be different, but eventually these differences will be corrected. The EMH suggests that using historic data will not help because prices adjust very quickly to news. However, analysts can add value by forecasting economic variables that lead to long-term market movements. Understanding how these variables affect security returns can lead to superior performance if estimates are correct and differ from the consensus. Also, it should be possible to achieve superior returns by exploiting the anomalies in the weak form of the EMH, for example by focusing analysis on neglected companies.

5 Implications for portfolio managers

If portfolio managers have access to analysts with forecasting ability they should use them for recommendations, taking into account the risk preferences and objectives of each client. Analysts should be asked to focus on mid-sized or small stocks, or stocks in emerging markets, that are not so widely followed so there is a greater chance of identifying undervalued stocks.

Portfolio managers who do not have analysts with forecasting ability, and in particular those managing large cap and well-researched stocks, should do the following:

- Construct a portfolio which has the appropriate risk profile and maintain this risk level on an ongoing basis.

- Diversify to eliminate any unsystematic risk.

- Minimise costs including taxes and transaction costs and avoid holding illiquid stocks.

The EMH justifies the move to using index funds. These aim to duplicate the performance of selected market indices at the lowest possible research and trading cost.

6 Limitations of the EMH

The analysis above only relates to the links between information and security prices. This says nothing about whether the market is 'efficient' in the sense normally used in economics, that is, assisting the most advantageous deployment of capital in the economy. Clearly when markets are in the grip of bubbles and panics, which cause too much and too little investment respectively, they are inefficient in this wider sense.

Appendix 2 The time value of money

1 Interest rate and risk

An interest rate is simply the rate of return that links cash flows paid or received on different dates, or the required rate of return if a sum of money is received in one year's time rather than today. It is the opportunity cost of money since it is the interest lost if money is spent today rather than saved for a year. The interest rate is often referred to as the discount rate.

The interest rate, denoted by r, is made up of a real risk-free rate plus four risk premiums that compensate for risk.

r = Real risk-free rate + Inflation premium + Default risk premium + Liquidity premium + Maturity premium

The **real risk-free rate** is the interest rate for a totally risk-free security assuming expectations of zero inflation. It reflects the underlying preference of individuals to consume today rather than tomorrow.

The **inflation premium** reflects the average inflation rate expected by investors and the inflation premium compensates for the erosion of purchasing power due to inflation. The nominal risk-free rate is approximately the sum of the real risk-free rate and the inflation rate (strictly the product of 1 plus the real risk-free rate and 1 plus the inflation rate). In the US, for example, the nominal risk-free rate is quoted as the Treasury bill rate over the appropriate time horizon.

A **default risk premium** is the compensation for the risk that the borrower will fail to make a payment that is contractually agreed.

The **liquidity premium** reflects the time or the cost involved in converting the asset to cash. A Treasury bill does not pay a liquidity premium but for a bond which is illiquid and/or is a long time way from maturity there might well be a liquidity premium.

A **maturity premium** reflects the increased sensitivity of long-term debt to a change in market interest rates. The difference in interest rates on long-term debt versus short-term debt will partly be explained by a maturity premium.

Inflation erodes the purchasing power of money, so one dollar tomorrow will buy fewer goods and services than one dollar today. We now need to answer the question: "what is a dollar to be received sometime in the future worth *today?*"

2 Future value of a single sum of money

Starting with a known value today (present value), equation 2.1 below finds the future value (FV) for a single sum of money paid over a number of discrete periods:

Equation 2.1

To calculate the future value (FV) and present value (PV) of a single sum of money use:

$$FV_N = PV(1 + r)^N$$

where:

FV_N=future value, N periods from today

N=number of periods from today

PV=present value today

r=rate of interest, or required rate of return, per period

If interest rates are assumed to be positive, then FV_N will always be greater than PV.

The raising of the term in brackets by the exponent N is called compounding. As interest is calculated in the first period, it is added to the initial amount to yield the closing balance for the first period. Interest is calculated on this higher closing value, therefore, the second interest payment will be higher than in the first period. This process continues each and every period.

Example 2.1: Future value of a single sum of money

A lump-sum of $1,000 is deposited today into an account that will pay interest at a rate of 10% annually for three years. What will be the value of the deposit at the end of three years?

$$PV = \$1,000$$
$$r = 10\% = 0.10$$
$$N = 3$$

$$\begin{aligned}
FV_N &= PV(1 + r)^N \\
&= \$1,000(1 + 0.1)^3 \\
&= \$1,000 \times 1.10^3 \\
&= \$1,000 \times 1.331 \\
&= \$1,331.00
\end{aligned}$$

A time line can also be used to show the relationship between present values and future values. In a time line the index t represents a point in time a stated number of periods from today, so for a time N periods from today t = N. A time line is shown below.

3 Present value of a single sum of money

Starting with a known future value, equation 2.1 can be rearranged for present value (PV) for a single sum of money:

Equation 2.2

$$PV = \frac{FV_N}{(1 + r)^N}$$

where:

FV$_N$=future value, N periods from today

N=number of periods from today

PV=present value today

r=rate of interest, or required rate of return, per period

The process of bringing distant cash flows to today is called discounting, which is the fundamental quantitative technique of investment analysis.

Assuming that the rate of interest (r) is positive, the denominator in the above equation will be greater than 1.0, and dividing FV by a number greater than 1.0 will always make PV < FV.

Note that PV does not have the subscript N. Unlike FV$_N$, PV can only be at one time: today.

Example 2.2: Present value of a single sum of money

An investment will be worth $7,000 in five years' time, and the opportunity cost rate (the best rate of return available on investments of similar risk) over the next five years will be 3%. What is the fair value of the investment today?

$$FV = \$7,000$$
$$r = 3\% = 0.03$$
$$N = 5$$

$$PV = \frac{FV_N}{(1 + r)^N}$$

$$= \frac{\$7,000}{(1 + 0.03)^5}$$

$$= \frac{\$7,000}{1.15927}$$

$$= \$6,038.26$$

4 Stated and effective annual interest rates

In all of the previous examples, we have assumed that interest payments are made once a year. In many cases, however, interest is paid more frequently than once a year, even though the interest rate is quoted in annual terms. The stated annual interest rate excludes the reinvestment of interest; whereas, the effective annual rate (EAR) includes the reinvestment of interest. The EAR for m compounding periods per year is given by equation 2.3 below.

Equation 2.3

$$EAR = \left(1 + \frac{r_s}{m}\right)^m - 1$$

where:

m=number of compounding periods per year

r_s stated annual interest rate

If interest were paid continuously, then the EAR is given by equation 2.4 below:

Equation 2.4

$$EAR = e^{r_s} - 1$$

If interest is compounded more frequently than once a year (m > 1), than the EAR will be higher than the stated rate. If interest is paid annually (m = 1), then the EAR will equal the stated annual rate.

Example 2.3: Computing effective annual rates

An investment product offers a stated annual interest rate of 6%, and interest will be reinvested at the same rate. What is the effective annual rate if interest is paid:

- annually?

- quarterly?

- monthly?

- continuously?

If interest is paid **annually**, then m = 1, and we use equation 2.3 to solve for EAR:

$$EAR = \left(1 + \frac{r_s}{m}\right)^m - 1 = \left(1 + \frac{0.06}{1}\right)^1 - 1 = 1 + 0.06 - 1 = 6\%$$

If interest is paid **quarterly**, then m = 4, and we use equation 2.3 to solve for EAR:

$$EAR = \left(1 + \frac{r_s}{m}\right)^m - 1 = \left(1 + \frac{0.06}{4}\right)^4 - 1 = (1 + 0.015)^4 - 1$$
$$= 0.0614, \text{ or } 6.14\%$$

If interest is paid **monthly**, then m = 12, and we use equation 2.3 to solve for EAR:

$$EAR = \left(1 + \frac{r_s}{m}\right)^m - 1 = \left(1 + \frac{0.06}{12}\right)^{12} - 1 = (1 + 0.005)^{12} - 1$$
$$= 0.0617, \text{ or } 6.17\%$$

If interest is paid **continuously**, and we use equation 2.4 to solve for EAR:

$$EAR = e^{r_s} - 1 = e^{0.06} - 1 = 1.0618 - 1 = 0.0618, \text{ or } 6.18\%$$

Note that the EAR becomes higher as the compounding frequency increases.

---

5 Value of money for periods other than annual

If payments are made more frequently than once a year we also need to adjust the FV formula. Equation 2.5 is the adjusted FV formula.

Equation 2.5

$$FV_N = PV\left(1 + \frac{r_s}{m}\right)^{m \times N}$$

where:

m=number of compounding periods per year

r_s=stated annual interest rate

N=number of years

As the compounding frequency increases, FV increases. If taken to the limit, interest can be compounded over an infinite number of periods (m approaches ∞). This leads to the continuous compounding formula, shown below:

Equation 2.6

$$FV_N = PVe^{r_s \times N}$$

where:

e is the natural exponent whose value is approximately 2.7183

Example 2.4: Comparing FV for different compounding periods

An investment product offers a stated annual interest rate of 6%, with a three-year maturity. Interest will be reinvested at the same rate. If an investor buys $1,000 of the product, how much money will he receive in three years' time, assuming that interest is paid:

- annually?
- quarterly?
- monthly?
- continuously?

Write down the known variables:

$$PV = \$1,000$$
$$r_s = 6\% \text{ , or } 0.06$$
$$N = 3$$

If interest is paid **annually**, then m = 1, and we use equation 2.1 to solve for FV:

$FV_N = \$\,1{,}000(1 + 0.06)^3 = \$1{,}000 \times 1.191016 = \$1{,}191.02$

If interest is paid **quarterly**, then m = 4, and we use equation 2.5 to solve for FV:

$$FV_N = \$1{,}000\left(1 + \frac{0.06}{4}\right)^{4\,\times\,3} = \$1{,}000(1 + 0.015)^{12}$$
$$= \$1{,}000 \times 1.195618$$
$$= \$1{,}195.62$$

If interest is paid **monthly**, then m = 12, and we use equation 2.5 to solve for FV:

$$FV_N = \$1{,}000\left(1 + \frac{0.06}{12}\right)^{12\,\times\,3} = \$1{,}000(1 + 0.005)^{36}$$
$$= \$1{,}000 \times 1.196681$$
$$= \$1{,}196.68$$

If interest is paid **continuously**, and we use equation 2.6 to solve for FV:

$$FV_N = PVe^{r_s\times\,N} = \$1{,}000e^{0.6\,\times\,3} = \$1{,}000e^{0.18} = \$1{,}000 \times 1.197217$$
$$= \$1{,}197.22$$

Note that the FV becomes higher as the compounding frequency (m) increases.

Example 2.5: FV and PV of a series of uneven cash flows

An investment will pay $5,000 at the end of the first year, $4,000 at the end of the second year, and $3,000 at the end of the third year. If the required rate of return is 12%, what will be the value of these payments at the end of three years?

Calculate the FV of each cash flow separately by compounding, and add them together:

Year 1: FV of $5,000 =	$5,000 × (1.12)^2 =	$6,272.00
Year 2: FV of $4,000 =	$4,000 × (1.12)^1 =	$4,480.00
Year 3: FV of $3,000 =	$3,000 × (1.12)^0 =	$3,000.00
	Sum =	$13,752.00

If the cash flows were paid at the beginning of each year, then all of the cash flows would have been compounded by an extra period.

Calculate the PV of each cash flow separately by discounting, and add them together:

$$PV = \frac{\$5,000}{(1.12)^1} + \frac{\$4,000}{(1.12)^2} + \frac{\$3,000}{(1.12)^3}$$

$$= \$4,464.29 + \$3,188.78 + \$2,135.34$$

$$= \$9,788.41$$

We could have obtained the same answer by discounting $13,752 for three years:

$$PV = \frac{FV}{(1 + r)^N}$$

$$= \frac{\$13,752}{(1 + 0.12)^3}$$

$$= \frac{\$13,752}{1.404928}$$

$$= \$9,788.40$$

You can also use the cash-flow worksheet embedded in your CFA Institute-approved financial calculator to solve for PV (but not FV) of a series of uneven cash flows.

6 Timelines

A time line illustrates cash inflows and outflows for any given financial problem. A **time index** is a scale used on the time line to distinguish between PF, FV, and the intermediate cash flows. By visualizing the problem, a time line can help solve any financial problem.

Consider the time line containing information about a single cash deposit:

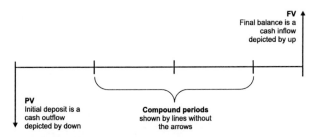

For a mortgage, the borrower receives an initial cash inflow (positive PV) and makes a series of payments (negative outflow) over the life of the mortgage.

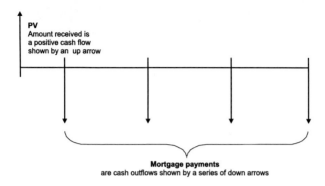

Mortgage payments
are cash outflows shown by a series of down arrows

Part 3: Investment products

Introduction

The UK has a wide variety of collective investment structures, each of which may have advantages for individuals having different needs and circumstances. Advisers need to have a detailed understanding of the differences between the OEIC/unit trust, ISAs, life assurance and pension structures and particularly their tax implications, all of which are covered in chapter 12.

The methods and styles of management within equity, bond, property, hedge and absolute return funds are dealt with in chapter 13, chapter 14 and chapter 15. There are those who advocate exclusive use of active or passive investment strategies, but advisers are increasingly likely to apply both within client portfolios, for reasons of efficiency and cost. The very low expense ratios of exchange traded funds (ETFs) are likely to lead to their domination of the 'index tracker' sector.

Structured products (chapter 16) have demonstrated both good and bad features in recent years, with counterparty risk (for example with Lehman-backed products) offsetting the ability to limit risk for cautious clients.

Methods of analysing and selecting funds have grown more sophisticated in recent years. The tools and rating systems available to advisers are covered in chapter 17.

The investment adviser needs to harness investment skills and methods into solutions for clients (chapter 18). Such solutions are advisory or discretionary services applying active or passive strategies using open or closed-end funds and structured products.

Chapter 12
Structures, tax and costs

1 Fund management business

The UK is one of the largest markets in the world for fund management, along with the US and Japan.

The latest figures from the Investment Management Association show that the UK fund management industry was responsible for £3.4tn of funds. Of this, funds managed on behalf of insurance companies and pension funds account for around three-quarters, with retail investment funds and private clients accounting for the remainder. Some 28% of assets were held in pension funds and a further 23% was managed by or on behalf of insurance companies. The vast majority of investment funds relate to long-term insurance policies, in which premiums paid over many years are invested by insurance institutions in order to meet the liability at maturity. Retail clients held close to £800bn in investment funds, with an increasing number of these funds being domiciled outside of the UK in centres such as Luxembourg and Dublin, although they remain largely managed in the UK.

The UK is also Europe's leading centre for managers of hedge funds, with the assets of over three-quarters of European hedge funds managed from London, as well as being the leading centre for managers of private equity funds.

Private clients remain a significant part of the UK market, with assets managed by stockbrokers, private client investment managers and financial advisers.

The scale of this fund management business means there is a wide range of investment products available to investors. In this chapter, we will look at their structures, costs and tax treatment.

2 The relative advantages of investing collectives and purchasing portfolios of securities direct

Investors can choose to invest in collectives or they can invest directly in portfolios of securities. Collectives include OEICs and unit trusts, but in this context they can also mean funds held through life assurance policies, pensions as well as investment trusts and ETFs.

There are several issues to take into account in deciding which route to take: diversification, management, tax and cost.

Diversification

One of the most important issues facing investors is the need to diversify over a range of different asset classes, companies and markets. With collectives, adequate diversification can usually be achieved for quite small amounts of capital – perhaps as little as a few hundred pounds. This can be especially important for a client who is saving a few pounds a month.

A portfolio of individual securities needs to have roughly 20 to 30 different stocks to eliminate unsystematic risk. There is room for disagreement about the minimum level of investment that it is economic to hold in an individual stock, and much depends on the dealing charges that investors incur. If the minimum economic holding is about £5,000 and a portfolio should not hold less than about 30 stocks, this would suggest that the minimum diversified portfolio of individual stocks would be about £150,000. However, other factors (such as management issues) could lead investors to consider investing rather less than this amount into directly held securities – probably rather more.

Many portfolios of direct holdings of securities also include collectives. This may be to provide a client with a relatively small exposure to a particular market with an adequate level of diversification.

Management

Collectives can provide a wide variety of management styles, ranging from passive to a range of active approaches to managing portfolios. An investor who buys several collectives can benefit (or otherwise) from a variety of different managers and management styles. In contrast, a wealth manager will generally apply a single approach to investment management within a portfolio of directly held securities.

Investors usually have difficulty accessing high quality professional management for comparatively small portfolios of directly held securities. Professional expertise is available from the thousands of collective funds available in the market, although it has to be admitted that relatively few active investment fund managers consistently beat the index against which they benchmark their performance. Moreover, it is particularly difficult to predict which investment managers are likely to outperform the benchmark.

One of the advantages of collectives is the very inexpensive passive fund management offered by some institutions. Cost effective passive fund management is not available to people who invest directly in securities.

Tax

The income from direct and collective investments is broadly taxed in the same way, although there are minor differences with respect to certain offshore funds. However, the taxation of capital gains generally favours collectives. Collectives pay no CGT on disposals of stocks within the fund and the CGT is only payable when the owner disposes of their units. In contrast, the holder of securities is potentially liable for CGT on all disposals of individual shares. Fund managers should be able to accumulate gains within a collective without a leakage of up to 28% tax on realised profits and build a larger capital amount, all things being equal.

Costs

The costs of investing using either approach can vary considerably according to the way in which the investments are managed. Key costs are dealing and annual management charges. A stock broker or other wealth manager who looks after portfolios of individual shares may charge 0.5% to 1.0% a year, and dealing costs will depend on the extent to which the portfolio is turned over each year. The costs of managing a portfolio of collectives might be similar, but the holdings of collectives should generally be more stable. However, there will be additional charges made by the collectives themselves.

The costs of investing collectives varies very widely from 5% initial charge and annual management charge of up to 1.5% down to passive investments where there is no initial charge and the annual charge may be as low as 10 or 15 basis points, or even lower than that.

Conclusion

Clients with reasonably large portfolios who want active investment management from specific managers should consider buying individual investments, and even they would consider using collectives for parts of their portfolios. Otherwise, most investors are likely to purchase collectives.

3 Collective investment schemes

Unit trusts, open-ended investment companies (OEICs) and investment companies are all collective investment schemes, designed to allow a large group of investors to participate in a broad portfolio of bonds, shares and other instruments.

A collective investment fund is a way for a large number of investors to pool their funds to purchase shares or other securities and investments. By investing in this way, investors can participate indirectly in a pool of investments that would be more difficult to own directly as individuals. Because of this, collective investments are also known as 'pooled investments'.

Collective investments are widely used by individual investors and investment institutions for the following reasons:

- They provide an effective way to invest relatively small sums of money, because the investor's capital is pooled in a much larger fund.

- They offer access to professional investment management, where the fund managers make the initial and ongoing investment decisions.

- Investors can gain access to geographical markets, asset classes or investment strategies which might otherwise be difficult to achieve.

- The individual investor's risk is reduced by the wide spread of investments in the underlying portfolio.

- The pooling of resources can enable investment in a wide spread of investments at a lower cost than could have been achieved by investors acting on their own.

Authorisation of funds

In the UK, authorisation of collective investment schemes is undertaken by the Financial Services Authority (FSA). Collective investment schemes that have been authorised by the FSA can be freely marketed in the UK.

In general terms, the FSA will only authorise those schemes that are sufficiently diversified and that invest in a range of permitted assets. The restrictions include limitations on:

- The types of underlying asset which such vehicles may invest in.

- Asset and sector concentrations.

- The levels of gearing.

- The use of derivatives.

In addition, schemes are also required to ensure adequate liquidity to enable them to fulfil redemption requests.

While some collective investment schemes are authorised, others are unauthorised or unregulated funds. Funds that have not been authorised by the FSA cannot be marketed to the general public. These may take the form of non-UCITS retail schemes and qualifying investor schemes, which offer a different degree of regulatory restrictions in return for greater or fewer restrictions on marketing. These unauthorised vehicles are perfectly legal, but their marketing must be carried out subject to certain rules and in some cases only to certain types of investor.

UCITS

UCITS stands for Undertakings for Collective Investment in Transferable Securities and refers to a series of EU regulations that were originally designed to facilitate the promotion of funds to retail investors across Europe Union (EU) and the European Economic Area (EEA).

The aim of the directives was to create a framework for cross-border sales of investment funds throughout the EU that would allow an investment fund to be sold throughout the EU subject to regulation by its home country regulator.

The rationale was that allowing funds to be sold across borders would reduce the costs involved and improve customer choice.

The original directive was issued in 1985 and established a set of EU-wide rules governing collective investment schemes. Funds set up in accordance with these rules could then be sold across the EU, subject to local tax and marketing laws. This means that a fund established in, say, Luxembourg which is authorised as a UCITS fund can be freely sold in the UK.

Since then, two further directives have been issued which broadened the range of assets a fund can invest in, in particular allowing managers to use derivatives more freely, and introduced a common marketing document, the 'simplified prospectus'. These are usually referred to as UCITS111.

A UCITS fund, therefore, complies with the requirements of these directives, no matter which EU country it is established in.

While UCITS regulations are not directly applicable outside the EU, other jurisdictions, such as Switzerland and Hong Kong, recognise UCITS when funds are applying for registration to sell into those countries. Internationally, compliance with UCITS rules is seen as a sign of sound investor protection and has enabled the large fund management groups to establish funds in, say, Luxembourg and then market them not only across Europe but internationally as well.

Characteristics of collective investment schemes

A wide range of collective investment schemes is available to investors.

In the UK, the most well-known types are unit trusts and OEICs. There are other types as well which are listed and traded on stock exchanges, such as investment trusts, real estate investment trusts (REITs) and ETFs. European versions of collective investment schemes are also now seen more often as fund management groups seek to exploit economies of scale by maintaining funds they can distribute across the whole of Europe and beyond.

In continental Europe, the equivalent of the OEIC is known as a SICAV (*société d'investissement à capital variable*), but there are a variety of other structures in use.

Each of these products has a different structure and characteristics. The key features are whether they are open ended or closed ended, the legal structure and how dealings are undertaken.

Open-ended and closed-ended funds

A key characteristic of the various types of collective investment scheme is that they are open ended or closed ended.

An open-ended fund is one for which new units or shares can be created, to meet investor demand, and shares or units can be cancelled when investors sell. This means their capital base can expand or contract, hence the term 'open ended'. Unit trusts and OEICs are types of open-ended fund.

A closed-ended fund is one where the capital base is fixed. If investors want to buy shares in a closed-ended fund, they will buy these from other investors on the stock market in the same way they might buy equities. Investment trusts and REITs are examples of closed-ended funds.

As you will see from the above, the key difference is in the fund's share capital. Open-ended funds can expand and contract to meet investor demand whereas closed-ended funds have a fixed capital so that investors need to trade with other investors to buy and sell shares.

Another term that is encountered in relation to collective investment schemes is an 'investment company with variable capital' (ICVC). As the name suggests, an ICVC is a company whose capital base can change and this is the legal basis for open-ended funds that are created as a company. An OEIC is a UK example of an ICVC and a SICAV is the European version.

A hybrid of the two types, a semi-open fund, has been developed over the last few years. As the name suggests, creation and redemption of units or shares can take place but these tend to occur at long intervals.

Closed-ended funds can be set up to invest in private equity or property and may require investors to commit their money for long periods of time so that the planned investments have time to deliver their expected returns. They may not be traded on a stock market and so periodic redemptions offer investors a way to realise all or part of their investment.

This approach has also been seen in open-ended funds, particularly those that invest in property. The downturn in property prices in 2007 led many investors to realise their holdings of property unit trusts, causing liquidity issues for the funds as the underlying properties could not be quickly sold to meet the payments which were due to outgoing investors. This led to the development of the semi-open model in order to protect the funds and the remaining investors in the funds against extensive cash outflows. The mechanisms used include setting minimum investment terms known as 'lock-up periods' and setting notice periods or maximum redemption rates per year.

Legal structure

Collective investment schemes can be created using a variety of different legal structures.

The earliest collective investments were investment trusts. These first appeared in the 1860s following the passing of the first Companies Act, which allowed the creation of companies with limited liability. An investment trust is like any other company except that its purpose is to pool investor funds. It is closed ended so that when a fund group wants to bring in new investors it has to create a new trust and promote it to potential investors.

In the US, the open-ended mutual fund was developed as an alternative to closed-ended funds. There were early concerns about what would happen in the event of a major sell-off by investors, but these were dispelled by the aftermath of the 1929 Wall Street crash. The UK soon started to use the same model and the first unit trusts were set up in the 1930s. The unit trust became the dominant model from the 1950s until recently.

In Europe, collective investment schemes developed along different lines. The concept of a trust is not recognised in civil law jurisdictions and funds were instead set up using contract law. Changes to company legislation later allowed the creation of companies with variable capital and the SICAV quickly grew to be one of the major legal structures in use. The flexibility of the SICAV model was followed in the late 1990s in the UK, when the creation of open-ended investment companies was permitted.

Other models are in use, such as limited partnerships, but the majority of funds that are encountered have either a corporate or trust structure.

Dealing

Another major difference between funds is how dealings in the units or shares of the fund take place.

Some funds are dealt directly with the fund group, while others are dealt on a stock exchange. Open-ended funds, such as unit trusts, OEICs and SICAVs, are dealt directly with the fund management group. Instructions from investors to buy or sell are given directly to the fund and the fund manager either creates new shares or units when investors want to buy, or cancels them when they want to sell. The price that investors will pay or receive will usually be set daily and be based on the underlying net asset value of the fund's portfolio.

Closed-ended funds, such as investment trusts and REITs, are different. Their share capital is fixed unless they go through a capital-raising process. When a new fund is launched, the fund group will seek subscriptions from investors. Once the company is created, it will seek a stock exchange listing and all subsequent dealing in the shares of the company will take place there. A stock exchange brings together buyers and sellers in an organised marketplace and so sellers of investment trust shares will sell their shares to new investors in the company. The price that the investor will pay or receive depends upon the demand and supply rather than purely on the underlying net asset value (NAV) of the fund's portfolio.

The advantage that funds traded on stock exchanges have over conventional unit trusts and OEICs is that they can be traded whenever the stock exchange is open and can be traded and settled in exactly the same way as equities. For investment firms, this means they can use the same systems that are used for bonds and equities, whereas dealing and settling unit trusts and OEICs requires a separate administration process to be created.

The most recent development in the structure of collective investment schemes has been the creation of ETFs. The structure of ETFs combines the advantages of an open-ended capital structure with the efficiencies that can be gained from exchange-traded instruments.

Types of collective investment scheme

The structure of the main types of collective investment scheme is set out below.

Unit trusts

When a unit trust is created, its legal structure is as a trust in which the trustee is the legal owner of the underlying assets and the unit holders are the beneficial owners.

A trust deed is executed to form the trust, with the parties being the manager and the trustee. The trust deed is required to clearly state the investment objectives of the unit trust along with what are allowable investments and any limits on the amounts that can be invested in any one instrument or asset class.

The role of the unit trust manager is to decide, within the rules of the trust and the various regulations, which investments are included within the unit trust. This will include deciding what to buy and when to buy it, as well as what to sell and when to sell it. The unit trust manager may outsource this decision making to a separate investment manager in some cases.

The trustee is the legal owner of the assets in the trust, holding the assets for the benefit of the underlying unit holders. The trustee also protects the interests of the investors by, among other things, monitoring the actions of the unit trust manager. Whenever new units are created for the trust, they are created by the trustee. The trustees are organisations that the unit holders can trust with their assets, normally large banks or insurance companies.

A unit trust can be a UCITS fund so it can be marketed throughout the European Economic Area. Trusts are, however, not recognised in many European countries, limiting the value of a unit trust being registered as a UCITS fund.

The unit trust manager provides a market for the units by dealing with investors who want to buy or sell them. It carries out the daily pricing of units, based on the NAV of the underlying constituents. Most funds are valued on a daily basis. The time at which the fund is valued and the price is determined is known as the 'valuation point'.

The pricing of the units can be on either a single-priced or dual-priced basis. Most unit trusts are dual priced, which involves using the bid and offer prices of the underlying assets to produce separate prices for buying and selling units in the fund, the offer price and the bid price.

The calculation of the maximum offer price starts with the lowest quoted offer prices of the underlying investments, to which are added brokers' commission and stamp duty and any accrued income. This gives the NAV, to which is added any initial charge. The minimum bid price, also known as the 'cancellation price', is calculated by taking the highest quoted bid prices for the investments, deducting brokers' commission, and adding any accrued income. The NAV of the fund is then divided by the number of units in existence to produce the separate buying and selling prices that the fund will use.

These represent the maximum and minimum prices that the fund can use but it is industry practice to switch between these bid and offer prices depending on whether there are more buyers (in which case the 'offer basis' is used) or more sellers (the 'bid basis') of a fund at any one time.

A fund is likely to use the offer basis when a fund is expanding or the market is moving upwards and the manager is a net seller of shares or units. The fund manager will set the buying price at the maximum that is permitted and the selling price will be set at a level greater than the minimum. This means that investors who buy units will pay a price for new shares or units that corresponds to the actual costs involved in purchasing the underlying investments. The bid price will be set at a level around 5%–6% below the offer price. This means that investors who sell units benefit because the selling price will be higher than the cancellation price.

A fund is likely to use the bid basis when it is contracting and the manager is a net repurchaser of shares and units. In such circumstances, the fund manager will set the selling or bid price at the minimum permitted, the cancellation price, which represents the actual amounts that would be received in cash if the portfolio was liquidated. The price for buying the shares or units, the offer price, will be calculated by adding a spread of 5%–6% to the cancellation price. This means that investors who sell receive the minimum price allowed and buyers benefit from being able to buy at less than the maximum offer price.

Units can be either income units, where the income from the portfolio is paid to the unit holders by way of a distribution, or accumulation units, where the income is accumulated and reinvested.

Open-ended investment companies

An OEIC is a type of collective investment scheme whose underlying legal structure is a company.

Although structured as a company, OEICs differ from conventional companies because they are established not under the companies acts but under different legislation. This means that new shares can be created and existing shares redeemed much more easily than for traditional companies. As noted above, because of this ability to expand and contract to meet investor demand OEICs are also referred to as 'investment companies with variable capital' (ICVCs).

When an OEIC scheme is set up, the fund management group that will market the fund to potential investors will create an ICVC. It is a requirement at this stage that an 'authorised corporate director' (ACD) and a depositary are appointed.

The ACD is responsible for the day-to-day management of the fund, including managing the investments, valuing and pricing the fund, dealing with investors and maintaining the register of shareholders. Ultimate responsibility for the investment management of the fund will typically be held by the fund management group which creates the OEIC, which will enter into an investment management agreement appointing the ACD to undertake the role.

The role of the depositary is to safeguard the investments on behalf of the OEIC shareholders and oversee the activities of the ACD. The depositary occupies a similar role to that of the trustee of a unit trust. In some OEICs, some of the ACD's activities may be delegated to specialist third parties and a separate depositary and custodian may be appointed.

When the ACD is valuing and pricing the fund there is a choice of single or dual pricing, although most OEICs use single pricing. This involves valuing the portfolio using the mid-market price of the underlying investments. Cash and any income available for investment are added to the mid-market value of the portfolio to produce the NAV, which is then divided by the number of shares in issue to produce the single price that will be used for dealing.

The initial charge is not included in the calculation of the single price and is instead charged separately. It is important to remember, whenever a comparison is being made, that the initial charge is included in the price of a dual-priced fund and shown separately for single-priced funds.

If a fund persistently expands in size, the single-pricing system collects slightly less from investors who buy than would be needed to purchase the underlying investments. If a fund persistently shrinks in size, the price paid to investors who sell will be slightly greater than the actual liquidation value of the investments. In most cases, due to alternation of expansion and contraction, these effects are minor and often cancel out, but where the depositary has reason to believe that either buyers or sellers may be disadvantaged by such effects, they may require the manager to impose a 'dilution levy'. This small addition to the share price is paid into the fund.

European funds

As a result of the UCITS directives, investment schemes throughout Europe are very similar. The structures encountered in the Channel Islands, Dublin and the Isle of Man are similar to those in the UK and use either a trust, corporate or limited partnership structure.

Luxembourg is the main fund centre in continental Europe, especially for the umbrella funds operated by the big fund management groups who want to market their funds cross-border within Europe and to the Middle East and Far East. Trusts are not generally recognised in continental Europe and investment schemes are therefore structured around a corporate entity or a contract structure.

As noted above, a SICAV is a collective investment scheme that is structured as a company. Like a UK OEIC, it is an ICVC, or investment company with variable capital. A SICAV is a Luxembourg-based company that undertakes the management of the fund. It will appoint a Luxembourg agent to undertake certain administrative functions that the regulator considers to be central to the exercise of effective control over the management and administration of the fund. An approved depositary needs to be appointed to undertake regulatory oversight and safe custody of the assets.

Most SICAVs market their investment funds cross-border. They therefore need to employ a separate transfer agent who deals directly with investors and maintains the share register, and a paying agent to handle distributions of income to investors in different jurisdictions.

The other main type of structure encountered in continental Europe is a *fond commun de placement* (FCP). Its structure is based on a contract between the scheme manager and the investors. It is administered by a management company whose role is to decide on investment policies and manage the fund, and the assets are held in safekeeping by a separate custodian bank. An FCP is not a legal entity and so is treated as tax transparent, so that investors can reclaim withholding tax depending on their domicile.

Exchange-traded funds

An exchange-traded fund (ETF) is a collective investment scheme that is listed and traded on a stock exchange. ETFs are structured as investment companies with variable capital and so are open ended in nature. Many are structured as UCITS III funds and are domiciled in either Dublin or Luxembourg so they can be marketed cross-border.

ETFs are listed and traded on a stock exchange, where market makers quote two-way prices giving investors the ability to trade ETFs at any time the market is open rather than at a set daily price. An ETF trades at prices very close to its

NAV and is not subject to the issue of trading at a discount that is seen with investment trusts.

ETFs have no initial fees and typically have a lower total expense ratio than similar index funds, but it should be remembered that investors will have to pay brokerage charges each time they trade. These features, along with lower costs than traditional investment funds, have made ETFs one of the fastest-growing types of investment fund worldwide.

We look at exchange-traded funds in more detail in chapter 15, together with exchange-traded commodity funds.

Investment companies and trusts

Investment companies and trusts are structured in the same way as normal companies and have a board of directors and shareholders. The board is responsible for the management of the company, which it will often exercise by appointing third parties to undertake the critical activities involved in managing a pooled investment fund.

Investment companies have a fixed capital base that cannot expand and contract in response to investor demand. The only way they can increase their capital base is by the issue of new shares, so they are closed-ended funds.

As well as ordinary shares, an investment company can issue other classes of shares, such as preference shares, zero coupon preference shares and warrants. An investment company can borrow funds on a long-term basis by either borrowing from a bank or issuing bonds. This can enable them to invest the borrowed money in more stocks and shares and so employ leverage or gearing.

Investment companies may be established in the UK or in other jurisdictions, such as the Channel Islands. Investment companies set up in the UK that fulfil certain requirements of UK legislation qualify as investment trusts, which are exempt from tax on their capital gains. They must distribute at least 85% of their income, be UK domiciled, be listed on the London Stock Exchange and not hold more than 15% of the amount in issue of any class of securities they invest in.

Investment companies created in the Channel Islands achieve the same exemption from tax on gains without the other restrictions and most new investment companies and trusts take this form. But many of the largest old-established funds are investment trusts.

In the same way as other listed company shares, shares in investment companies are bought and sold on the London Stock Exchange. An investment company will regularly value its portfolio in order to establish the NAV and the results are communicated to the stock market, but the price at which the shares trade will differ.

Prices are driven by supply and demand and the share price may therefore be above or below the NAV. When the share price of the investment company is above the NAV, it is said to be trading at a premium. When it is below the NAV, it is said to be trading at a discount. Most large companies now have buy-back schemes whereby shares are repurchased by the company if they trade at a certain discount (often 15%) to NAV, thus limiting the extent of the discount that can occur.

Investment trust shares must be listed on the London Stock Exchange. Investment company shares may be listed on the London Stock Exchange or on the Alternative Investment Market, and in recent years more investment companies have chosen lower-cost listings on the latter. These include many specialist funds investing in relatively illiquid markets, in contrast to the old-established investment trusts, which generally hold only liquid marketable securities.

A special class of 'private equity' investment companies invest in private businesses without stock market listings. This topic is covered on page 287.

Real estate investment trusts (REITs)

REITs are a type of investment trust that pools investors' funds to invest in commercial and, possibly, residential property. REITs can provide investors with tax-efficient and diversified exposure to rental properties as they are tax-transparent property investment vehicles.

Provided they distribute at least 90% of their taxable income to investors, they are exempt from capital gains tax (CGT) and from corporation tax. Instead, investors pay tax on the dividends and capital growth at their own marginal tax rates, thus avoiding the double taxation that would otherwise affect investors in UK property companies.

Taxation

The domicile of an investment or the country in which it is incorporated will determine its tax treatment.

Onshore funds

UK-domiciled funds are principally subject to a modified version of the corporation tax regime. Income received by a unit trust or OEIC is subject to corporation tax at a special rate of 20%, while investment trusts are subject to the main corporation tax rate, which for 2009/10 is 28%.

UK dividend income is received by the funds as franked investment income with a 10% tax credit and no further liability arises. The dividends therefore flow through to distributions payable by the fund with no further tax liability, making them transparent for tax purposes.

Where foreign dividends are received they are subject to corporation tax at 20%, but annual management expenses can be offset against non-UK equity income. The fund can also eliminate or reduce the effect of any withholding tax by using double tax treaties.

Authorised funds are exempt from tax on the gains made within their investment portfolios.

For the investor, the tax treatment of distributions from UK-authorised funds is, in general, the same as for directly held bonds and equities, namely:

- Gains are subject to capital gains tax at 18% or 28%.

- Dividends from funds, whether received or accumulated, carry a tax credit which fully covers the tax liability of basic rate taxpayers, and higher rate taxpayers pay a further 22.5% (if their marginal rate is 40%) or 32.5% (if 50%) to bring the liability up to 32.5% or 42.5% of the gross dividend.

- Interest distributions from bond funds are treated in the same way as savings income and are paid subject to a 20% tax deduction.

A new optional tax structure known as the 'tax-elected funds' regime came into effect on 1 September 2009. This allows funds, subject to certain conditions, to elect to divide distributions into two parts, UK dividend and non-dividend income. The effect of electing to use this structure is as follows:

- UK and foreign dividend income will be distributed to the investor as a dividend distribution. The investor will be treated as before and taxed on the basis of receiving dividends.

- Interest income will be distributed to the investor as a non-dividend distribution and will effectively be paid out as interest. The payment will be made subject to deduction of 20% tax and the investor will be taxable as with other savings income. This will allow the tax to be reclaimed by ISAs and pension funds.

In this way, a dividend distribution that would have been made by a fund is split into two separate payments. The tax credit on the dividend distribution cannot be reclaimed but the tax deducted from the interest distribution can be provided that the investor is not liable to tax.

Offshore funds

All the main financial centres are in competition with each other to encourage the establishment of funds within their borders. Economic, regulatory and tax incentives are used to attract funds and this has led to the significant growth of the main fund centres in Europe, such as Luxembourg, Dublin and the Channel Islands.

Many funds are established in an offshore financial centre to take advantage of the favourable tax treatment they can receive in comparison to the tax treatment they would receive if established in the UK.

An offshore-domiciled fund will typically incur little or no tax at the fund level. There may be no VAT on management fees and stamp duty reserve tax on stock market dealing can be avoided. On the negative side, an offshore fund is less able to use double tax treaties to offset withholding tax.

From the investor's point of view, the tax treatment of an offshore fund will depend on how HM Revenue & Customs (HMRC) treats the fund for UK tax purposes. Under the rules, funds are classified as 'reporting funds' or 'non-reporting funds'. They used to be known as 'funds with or without distributor status'.

These rules determine how income and gains arising on offshore funds will be subject to tax. These were introduced to counter what was seen as an unfair competitive advantage for offshore funds over equivalent UK-based products, which in turn could have led to significant loss of tax.

For example, an offshore fund may accumulate income without paying it out. For an investor, this means that when the investment is realised the profit is only chargeable to CGT, which could lead to a lower tax charge for a higher rate taxpayer.

The offshore fund rules counter this by taxing gains on realisations from an offshore fund as income rather than as chargeable gains, unless the offshore fund is certified by HMRC as having reporting fund status throughout the time that the investor held the relevant shares or units. In order to obtain reporting fund status, an offshore fund must apply for approval in advance of the fund's first accounting period and HMRC will be able to give clearance that it meets the conditions for the regime. Reporting fund status will continue until the fund no longer wishes to qualify or no longer meets the conditions. The fund will need to submit its accounts to HMRC annually for auditing.

If an offshore fund has reporting fund status, investors will be within the chargeable gains rules in respect of their disposal of units or shares in the fund. This reflects the fact that the fund's income will have been reported to HMRC and that the fund will therefore have been operating in more or less the same way as a UK-based fund – the major difference being that interest and rental income is distributed gross and the shareholder has to account to HMRC for any tax due.

Where an investor disposes of a holding in an offshore fund, it must have qualified for reporting fund status (or distributor status) throughout the period that the investor held the shares to qualify for this treatment. It is quite possible for different investors to be in a different position in relation to the same fund, or indeed for the same investor to be in a different position in relation to different holdings of shares or units in the same fund.

A fund must apply annually for distributor status and each account period of the fund is considered separately. Separate sub-funds and classes of interest within a fund can qualify separately for distributor status without affecting, or being affected by, other sub-funds or classes of interest.

If the fund does not have reporting status, gains on disposals are charged to tax as income to reflect the fact that the increased value of the holding may derive to a significant extent from accumulated income. Instead of being subject to CGT at 18% on gains, individual UK investors will be subject to income tax and so a higher rate taxpayer could be subject to income tax at 40% or 50% on any gains arising on such disposals.

Costs

Investors in collective investment schemes may incur different types of charges.

Unit trusts and OEICs

An investor in a unit trust or OEIC will face several charges, some of which are explicit (such as the initial charge made for investment) and some that are less so because they are incurred in the necessary management of the fund (such as any audit costs the fund might incur).

The charges that an investor will face are:

- Initial charges.
- Annual management fees.
- Performance fees.
- Exit charges.
- Transaction costs.
- Stamp duty reserve tax.
- Other costs and charges.

An initial charge is made when an investor first invests in a fund. It is usually a percentage of the amount invested and varies depending upon the type of fund invested in. Initial charges on equity funds can be in the range of 3%–6%, while gilt and fixed-interest funds tend to see lower charges in the range of 1%–4%. Other funds, such as index tracker funds and cash funds may have small initial charges or none at all.

Fund managers offer discounts on their initial charges on the basis of how the investment is received. Investment through fund supermarkets and fund platforms will tend to incur significantly lower charges depending upon the amount of discount their buying power allows them to negotiate.

An annual management charge will be made to cover the ongoing costs of the management and administration of the fund, and from this the charges made by the fund manager and the authorised corporate director will be taken. Costs vary from 0.5% to 1.5%, depending upon the level of management required for a fund, and are typically lowest on tracker funds and highest on funds requiring more management such as absolute return funds and offshore funds.

For a small number of funds performance fees have been introduced. These are often encountered with manager of manager funds where subadvisers have been appointed for segregated parts of the portfolio.

Initial charges have been seen as an impediment to sales and so some fund management groups have removed them altogether for certain funds in their range. Where that has been done, they will usually impose an exit charge if the investment is sold within a certain period of time. This can be on a sliding scale over a number of years, at the end of which it disappears.

All funds incur transaction costs when they buy and sell investments. These costs are charged to the fund. The more active the manager in buying and selling the higher these costs will be.

Stamp duty reserve tax is payable on the purchase of UK investments by a UK-domiciled fund. It is either included in or added to the offer price of shares or units.

Managers are entitled under the terms of their management agreements to charge certain other costs to the fund. These include:

- Brokers' commission for trades undertaken.
- Legal and audit fees.
- Fees for specialist taxation advice.

The size of these other charges can have an impact on the performance of the fund and because of the lack of transparency here, funds have to publish a total expense ratio (TER) to provide investors with a clearer picture of the total annual costs involved in running an investment fund.

The TER consists principally of the manager's annual charge, but also includes the costs for other services paid for by the fund, such as the fees paid to the trustee or depositary, custodian, auditors and registrar. Collectively, these fees are known as the 'additional costs'.

TERs are typically between 1% and 2%. It is likely that large funds will have lower TERs than small funds, that funds investing in overseas markets will have higher TERs than UK funds and that new funds will show higher costs than old funds. However, the principal difference in TERs is whether the fund has a higher or lower annual charge.

Note that transaction costs are not included in the TER. The TER is also historical (usually based on the latest annual audited accounts) and if the fund has grown or shrunk substantially since the relevant date the TER may fail to a significant extent to reflect the actual situation.

Exchange-traded funds (ETFs)

One of the main features of ETFs is their low annual fees, especially when compared to traditional funds. ETFs typically have reduced marketing, distribution and accounting costs, which contribute to the lower fees. Annual costs are 0.75% or less.

Investors in ETFs, however, incur charges when they buy or sell shares. These deals will be undertaken through the stock market and so the investor will incur brokers' commission.

Since many funds are registered in Ireland, investors will not be liable to pay stamp duty under current regulations.

Investment companies

As with ETFs, dealing in investment company shares will incur brokers' commission. Apart from that, there are no initial charges or exit charges. The investment company will, however, incur costs for the running of the company and an annual management fee or performance fees for the management of the investment portfolio.

Investment companies, like unit trusts and OEICs, therefore publish total expense ratios (see above). The TER represents the drag on the portfolio performance as a result of all of the annual operating costs of the fund including administration, custody, audit and legal fees.

The TER for investment companies is calculated by Lipper and shown on the Association of Investment Companies website, allowing a comparison of charges to be made with other collective investment vehicles.

4 Life assurance

There are two main types of life assurance contracts: those that provide protection only, such as term assurance, and those that have both a protection and an investment element.

A whole of life policy pays out the sum assured whenever death occurs. By contrast, under a term assurance policy, the sum assured will only be paid if death occurs within the term.

There are three types of whole of life policy:

- Non-profit, that is, for a guaranteed sum only.

- With profits, paying a guaranteed amount plus any profits made during the period between the policy being taken out and death.

- Unit linked, where the return will be directly related to the investment performance of the units in the insurance company's fund.

Some of the key characteristics of life assurance as an investment product are considered below, but it should be remembered that the pure insurance elements are important and should not be overlooked.

With-profits policies

A with-profits policy is an insurance contract under which, in exchange for regular payments by the policyholder, the insurance company guarantees to pay a minimum amount, the sum assured, on a particular date, known as the 'maturity date'.

The sum assured will take into account a conservative assessment of the investment return which the company expects to achieve on the premiums it receives, net of the tax it has to pay on behalf of policyholders.

If the policyholder dies before the maturity date, the sum assured is paid out early. Thus these policies also provide an element of life assurance protection, particularly in their earlier years.

Types of with-profits policy

From an investment point of view there are two main types of with-profits policy:

- **Conventional with-profits policies.** A conventional with-profits policy has an initial sum assured which is increased by the addition of bonuses. Bonuses are usually declared annually in arrears as a percentage of the sum assured. A terminal bonus is added at maturity.

- **Unitised with-profits policies.** A unitised with-profits policy is a unit-linked investment where the premiums are used to buy units in a unitised with-profits fund. The main difference to other unit-linked funds is that the unit price is guaranteed not to fall. Bonuses are declared annually in advance, although they may be amended later in the year, and are usually allocated daily. If the product is a fixed-price policy then extra units are added; if it is a variable policy, the unit price is increased.

Unitised with-profits policies had almost entirely taken over from the conventional ones but there has recently been a resurgence in the sales of traditional policies as nervous investors seek protection from volatile stock markets.

Structurally, with-profits policies come in a variety of types and the main ones are:

- **Whole of life policies.** These policies are open ended with no defined maturity date at which benefits must be taken, other than on death. Premiums may, however, cease at a defined age. Policyholders can choose to take withdrawals or surrender the policy and take the cash sum to obtain the benefits. Alternatively, they may surrender part to achieve a regular income and leave the remainder of the policy to continue in existence with a reduced level of benefit. This type of policy is the basis for with-profits bonds, which are sold as single premium investments.

- **Endowment policies.** These policies have a defined maturity date at which a cash sum will become payable provided that the premiums have been paid and the policyholder has not previously died or surrendered the policy. This type of policy was at the heart of the endowment-misselling scandal. Endowment policies were used extensively for the repayment of mortgages, where a target sum is required on a specific date. For a variety of reasons, many endowment policies taken out in the 1980s and 1990s are unlikely to pay out the amounts originally estimated.

- **Pension policies**. Pension policies purchased to save for retirement usually now take the form of an endowment policy. This is designed to deliver a sum on the date of retirement in a similar way to delivering a sum at maturity but in order to accommodate flexibility over when the policyholder retires a series of maturity dates, or even a range of years, may be defined rather than just one date. The policyholder is provided with a cash sum on the retirement date, which is subject to HMRC rules that require that at least part of the cash sum must be used to purchase an annuity.

- **With-profits annuities.** A policyholder on retirement may choose to purchase a with-profits annuity. This type of product enables holders to remain invested in equities after retirement and benefit from a bonus added each year in the form of a percentage addition to the annuity payment.

With-profit policies are offered by many leading insurance companies and their main advantages are perceived as being that:

- They provide investors who are relatively risk-averse with some exposure to equity markets.

- Bonuses are not directly linked to investment performance in the same way that with unit-linked policies are, because it is possible for a life office to use its reserves. This produces a 'cushioning' effect which irons out the sharp rises and falls that characterise unit-linked investments.

- In some cases, they allow investors to participate in the profits of the insurance company's trading activities.

- Ownership of a mutual life office's with-profit policies represents ownership rights in the life office itself. These should generate either additional profits or shares if the company is demutualised.

A growing number of companies do not offer any with-profit policies and their popularity has declined in relative terms in some areas, particularly for regular savings and mortgage repayments. This is partly because they have the following disadvantages:

- They are difficult to understand and appraise.

- The returns depend to some extent on the insurance company's subjective judgment of long-term returns and their marketing objectives. For example, in the past some companies have increased bonus rates (especially terminal bonus rates) to boost past performance where the underlying investment performance might not have justified that bonus level.

- Since the early 1990s, the trend has been for reversionary bonus rates to fall, and in more recent times terminal bonuses have been significantly reduced as a result of difficult market conditions.

- They may be inflexible and generate poor returns on early surrender, or during periods when the market value reduction (MVR) applies.

- The highly publicised problems of Equitable Life have cast a shadow over with-profits policies, and have underlined their lack of transparency. This prompted a wide-ranging FSA review of with-profits contracts.

- The likely failure of many with-profit endowments to repay the mortgages to which they are linked has also reminded investors of the risks inherent in with-profit investment.

Bonuses

In order comply with FSA rules, a life office has to be able to be able to demonstrate that the bonuses that are allocated are fair. This requires it to:

- Ensure that there is independent input to the bonus-setting process.

- Appoint an actuary allocated specific responsibility by the board to advise it on the fairness implications for policyholders of the bonus decisions it makes.

- Publish details of how it determines its bonus rates and exercises its discretion.

Bonuses take two main forms:

- Regular bonuses, usually called 'annual' or 'reversionary' bonuses. Regular bonuses are usually added once a year, and take the form of an increase to the sum assured. This means that provided policyholders continue to pay their premiums for the full term of the policy, regular bonuses, once added, are guaranteed to be paid at maturity or on earlier death.

- A final bonus, usually called a 'terminal' bonus. Final bonuses are added to a policy only at the maturity date or on earlier death. These bonuses enable the life office to smooth volatility in investment returns by holding back some of the return from good years in order to pay out more than the return achieved in poor years.

The performance of with-profits funds depends upon the performance of the investments. But these investments are also partially determined by the financial strength of the life office, since the larger its free reserves, the greater the proportion of its capital it can invest in riskier, higher-returning assets such as shares and property. Financial strength is measured by the size of the company's reserves and its free asset ratio. The financial strength of most life offices has deteriorated over the last ten years and this has impacted on returns and restricted offices' ability to smooth out poor performance.

Since the 1990s the trend has been for reversionary bonus rates to fall so that a greater proportion of the return is made up of terminal bonuses. Since the late 1990s equity market returns have been such that even the terminal bonuses have been cut. The net effect of this has been that the returns on with-profits policies are largely determined by investment conditions at the time of maturity, thus making them more like unit-linked funds and negating the value of the policy's theoretical smoothing function.

Encashment

Many policyholders choose to surrender their policies before the maturity date.

If this happens, the benefits guaranteed at maturity are irrelevant and the life office will apply a surrender value. Most offices operate surrender values that incorporate a penalty element and can apply a market value reduction (MVR) in times of adverse market conditions.

All offices operate an MVR to protect the interests of investors remaining in the unitised with-profits funds:

- The MVR can be applied at the life office's discretion to reduce the amount payable on surrenders or switches and may operate in times of adverse investment conditions, for example a stock market crash.

- Usually, the MVR does not apply on death or maturity. There may be other points when the MVR does not apply, but changes to valuation rules in 2000 saw many companies abandon fixed-term guarantees.

- The aim of the MVR is to prevent the value leaving the fund from exceeding the value of the underlying assets.

As an alternative to surrender, it may be possible to sell a traditional with-profits policy on the open market and raise a sum greater than the surrender value.

Principles and Practices of Financial Management (PPFM)

The FSA requires life companies that carry on with profits business to publish a document (the PPFM) that sets out how a firm manages its with profits business. Each year the insurance company has to certify to the FSA that the with profits funds have been managed in accordance with the PPFM. With profits companies must also produce a customer-friendly version of the PPFM ('CFPPFM') explaining the main PPFM document in clear and non-technical language.

Regular premiums and qualifying policies

A regular premium policy will usually be structured as a 'qualifying' policy. This status is generally preferred because it means that policyholders can avoid higher rate tax on their policy gains.

To achieve qualifying status, a policy has to satisfy certain rules. For example, an endowment must have a minimum term of ten years and a minimum death benefit related to the total premium due and the policyholder's age. For policyholders under the age of 56 that minimum is 75% of total premiums payable.

Other rules limit the variability of premiums and the way the policy may be altered during its lifetime.

The result is that regular premium qualifying policies have a somewhat rigid structure and as investments are most appropriate for those higher rate taxpayers who are able to stay the course. Investors use qualifying policies as a means of sheltering their investment income from higher rate tax.

The charges inherent in many qualifying policies reinforce the requirement to maintain premiums as there may be significant penalties for stopping premium payment prematurely.

For basic rate taxpayers, the qualifying status is of very little benefit, unless they anticipate that by the maturity date they will be higher rate taxpayers.

All single premium policies, including those that allow for subsequent top-ups, are non-qualifying. As a consequence, higher rate taxpayers face a tax charge on their profits, although this may be deferred.

Unit-linked funds

A unit-linked or investment-linked policy is one in which a proportion of the premium is used to purchase life cover with the balance invested in unit funds. The return on the policy is therefore linked to the performance of the units in the unit funds.

With a unit-linked policy, the premiums are used to buy units in an investment fund managed by the life office or another institution. An investment into a unit-linked fund will incur front-end charges, and after the initial investment is made the value of the policy is dependent on the performance of the fund, measured by the total value of the units allocated to it.

Although premiums are invested in unit funds, the policy wrapper means there is a contractual relationship between the policyholder and the life office. The policyholder's entitlement is governed by the insurance contract and any entitlement is dependent upon the terms of the policy as to when it matures or can be surrendered.

Unit-linked policies include single premium bonds, which are considered later in this section.

The range of unit-linked funds

There are over 8,000 life and pension investment funds available within unit-linked policies, reflecting the diverse range of investment opportunities available today. The Association of British Insurers classifies these funds into seven sectors as follows:

- Mixed-asset funds.
- Distribution funds.
- UK equity funds.
- Overseas equity funds.
- Fixed-interest funds.
- Property funds.
- Other funds.

The mixed-asset sector comprises managed funds which invest in a range of assets. There are four subdivisions:

- Defensive managed, in which the equity content is limited to 35% of the fund.

- Cautious managed, in which the equity content is limited to 60% of the fund.

- Balanced managed, in which the equity content is limited to 85% of the fund.

- Flexible managed, in which the equity content is at the discretion of the fund manager.

Balanced managed is by far the largest sector.

Investment returns

The returns on unit-linked funds differ markedly from with-profits policies. With unit-linked funds, the returns depend entirely on the investment performance of the underlying fund and the timing of investment and encashment.

The fund with the best performance will clearly vary over time. This has led to the concept of the managed fund, where the fund managers invest in whichever of their funds they feel is best at any particular time.

Recognising the fact that the performance of each of the funds will vary from time to time, life offices offer a switching facility. This gives policyholders the option to switch their investment from one fund to another. A small charge may be levied for this service, but it does allow the investor to control which funds are used.

Obviously, the value of units can fall as well as rise and therefore it is possible for the policy to fall in value, unlike a conventional policy. As a result, while the potential annual return of a unit-linked policy may be higher than that of a non-linked contract, the risks will usually be greater.

Pricing and charges

The pricing of units in a linked fund operates in a similar fashion to the way that unit trusts are priced. Most unit-linked funds have a dual-price structure so that for each fund two prices are quoted, the offer price and the bid price.

The offer price is the price used to allocate units to a policy when premiums are paid. If the offer price is £1 and the whole of a £100 premium is to be applied to buy units, it will buy 100 units. The bid price is the price policyholders will receive if they wish to cash in or claim under the policy. This is always lower than the offer price.

There is commonly a difference of around 5% between offer and bid prices. This is known as the bid-offer spread. For example, the bid-offer spread may be 0.95−1.00, which means the 100 units that had been bought could be sold at 95p each to give total proceeds of £95. The bid-offer spread is, in effect, a charge made to cover the expenses incurred in setting up the policy.

There is also usually an annual management charge, typically 0.75%−1%, which is deducted from the fund monthly before the prices of the units are calculated.

With some single premium policies, there is no bid-offer spread and instead penalties are charged for early surrender to recoup the expenses incurred in the early years of the contract. Such policies often also levy a 'set-up' charge of around 1% a year for an initial period of five years. These products may prove more beneficial for clients who hold their policies to the expected maturity date.

Unit-linked funds may comprise two types of units, initial units and accumulation units. Initial units are used for the early years of regular premium unit-linked policies and for these there is a higher monthly management charge to enable the life office to recoup the initial expenses associated with the policy.

Encashment

As with with-profits policies, there are various charges for early encashment, and unit-linked regular savings policies frequently have no surrender value in the first year.

With lump sum or 'single premium' policies, investors can opt to receive regular payments. This can be seen as an income but for tax purposes it is treated as a return of the original capital investment.

Under current legislation, it is possible to take as income an amount equal to the original capital invested while deferring any possible income tax liability. The maximum annual income is 5%, so a tax-deferred income of 5% of the original capital subscribed could be taken for 20 years. If not used in one year, the unused allowance can be carried forward to the next year. This income can be taken yearly, quarterly or monthly and, provided the total withdrawn does not exceed 5% of the original investment each policy year, then there is no liability to income tax until the policy is encashed. When the policy is encashed, a 'chargeable event' calculation is made to establish the exact tax position and whether or not further income tax is payable.

Unit-linked policies are usually written as a cluster of identical policies, a practice known as 'segmentation'. This allows individual policies to be surrendered, which means the policyholder can take advantage of different tax regimes that apply to full and part surrenders. This may result in a lower overall tax charge.

Unit-linked bonds

A unit-linked investment bond is a non-qualifying single premium life assurance policy used for lump sum investments.

These products are usually written as whole of life policies with no fixed maturity date and no obligation to pay any more contributions during the duration of the plan. They are structured primarily for investment and so there is only a small amount of life cover built into the policy, typically just in excess of the value of the fund on death, usually a payment of 101% of the bid value.

On investment, the single premium is used to buy units in one or more of the underlying funds. Most funds are dual priced and there is usually around a 5% spread between the bid and offer price. In addition, the underlying funds are subject to an annual management charge, which is typically 1% of the funds under management.

Some investment bonds use a single-pricing system so that there is no explicit initial charge. Instead they will usually have an exit charge for surrenders within the first five years.

Unit-linked bonds can be written on a single or joint life basis and the policy may be written in trust or assigned in a similar way to other life policies.

This product can be best thought of as a tax wrapper in which a series of collective investment funds can be held. Investment choice is now quite wide, with life offices offering selection from their own funds as well as from a wide range of external fund managers. Most allow at least ten underlying funds and permit a number of free switches each year.

Up to 5% withdrawals each year can be taken free of tax (or more accurately on a tax deferred basis), up to a total of 100% of the original capital. Many higher rate taxpayers take an automatic withdrawal of 5% and avoid any immediate payment of tax and this can be continued for up to 20 years until all these allowances have been used up. For 40% taxpayers, this can provide the equivalent of a gross return of 8.33% and provided that the underlying funds grow at more than 5% a year then the capital sum payable on encashment will also be growing.

Basic rate tax is deemed to have been paid on both income and gains within unit-linked bonds and so there is no additional tax liability for a basic rate taxpayer. As before, if the gain pushes a basic rate taxpayer into higher rates, top-slicing relief is available.

If the investor is a higher rate taxpayer, any gain on encashment of the policy will incur an additional tax liability, the difference between the higher rate and the basic rate. From 2010/11 when higher rate tax rises to 50%, the additional tax liability will be 20% or 30%. If the investor is currently a higher rate taxpayer and will be a basic rate taxpayer when the bond matures, they can defer the chargeable event until they become a basic rate taxpayer.

Offshore bonds

Offshore bonds are generally issued by subsidiaries of well-known UK life offices in domiciles such as the Channel Islands, Dublin, the Isle of Man and Luxembourg. They are structured in similar ways to onshore bonds although charges tend to be slightly higher. The policies issued have mainly been investment bonds because it is not possible for offshore companies to provide qualifying policies.

Their main difference is in the tax treatment of the underlying life fund and the investor.

Life offices have set up subsidiaries in offshore centres to take advantage of a more beneficial tax regime in those countries. Offshore life offices are generally subject to little or no tax in their host country. The underlying investment fund will be free of capital gains tax but overseas dividend income will be subject to irrecoverable withholding tax.

For individuals, the same basic tax treatment applies for offshore as onshore policies with two principal differences.

- There is no credit for basic rate tax and so there is a full income tax charge at the taxpayer's marginal rate. So basic rate taxpayers face a 20% basic rate tax charge and higher rate taxpayers will pay the full 40% or 50% rate. Top-slicing relief is always done by reference to the start date of the bond rather than the last chargeable event.

- If the policyholder was non-UK resident for any period during the life of the policy the gain is reduced by a fraction equal to the period of non-residency.

One advantage of an offshore bond is that income can roll up gross and so generate an eventual greater return. Against this must be set the full income tax charge on offshore policies, which represents a higher effective rate of tax than applies to UK policies.

An offshore bond could, however, be advantageous if the investor expects to be non-resident for part of the term of the investment.

Guaranteed income bonds

Guaranteed income bonds are single premium bonds that provide a guaranteed income for terms of one to five years. Income can be paid annually or monthly, and on maturity the investor's capital is returned. The minimum investment is usually £5,000 and the maximum £1m. Charges are built into the product and there can be heavy penalties for early encashment if it is available.

Life offices offer guaranteed income bonds from time to time, depending upon their own internal tax position, and at any one time there are usually only a few life offices in the market offering this product, in limited tranches. The attraction of these bonds is the guaranteed income, but the rates on offer at any particular time vary depending upon market conditions.

Bonds are usually structured to minimise tax liabilities. For basic rate taxpayers, the income from the bond is paid net of basic rate tax, which cannot be reclaimed. Each year, any income from the bond in excess of 5% of the premium paid must be added to investors' other income for that tax year to determine whether they are still basic rate taxpayers. If that pushes investors into the higher rate tax bracket then there may be a further liability to tax.

Top-slicing relief is available for basic rate taxpayers who become higher rate taxpayers purely as a result of policy gains being added to their other income. This involves calculating the chargeable gain, which is the last year's income plus the first 5% of each previous year's income or all of the income if the income yield was below 5%. This gain is then divided by the number of years the bond has been held. The resulting gain is then added as the top slice of the investor's income and that rate of tax then applied to the whole gain.

Guaranteed growth bonds

Guaranteed growth bonds are similar to guaranteed income bonds. In return for payment of a single premium, the investor receives a guaranteed capital sum at the maturity of the bond and there is usually a range of maturity dates available in the market ranging from one up to five years. To achieve the return, the life office invests in gilts and other short- to medium-term instruments and so returns are again dependent upon market conditions.

The tax treatment is the same as for guaranteed income bonds. The bond generates no income and provided that the investor is a basic rate taxpayer at maturity the capital growth is free of any further tax liability. If the gain pushes the investor into higher rate tax then top-slicing relief is again available.

If the investor is a higher rate taxpayer, the value of the guaranteed return is diminished. If the investor is currently a higher rate taxpayer and will be a basic rate taxpayer when the bond matures, then the bond presents a tax planning opportunity.

Distribution bonds

Ordinary unit-linked bonds do not separate income and capital and, as seen above, any withdrawals taken as a form of income are achieved by encashing units. Distribution bonds effectively distinguish between income and capital so that the income paid reflects the income generated by the fund and so leaves the capital intact.

To qualify for inclusion in the Association of British Insurers distribution fund sector, the fund must have a maximum equity content of 60% and a gross yield of at least 125% of the FTSE All-Share gross yield before deduction of management charges. All income must be capable of being paid to the investor.

Although the income of the fund is distributed, it remains as capital for tax purposes and the same tax rules apply for distributions as for ordinary unit-linked bonds.

Guaranteed and protected equity bonds

A number of single premium unit-linked bonds are now available with some form of guarantee or protection. They are fixed-term single premium policies that use a combination of a call option and fixed-term deposits to provide the growth and the guarantee.

Guaranteed equity bonds provide returns based on the performance of a selected index with a guaranteed return of capital at maturity if the index falls in value during the term of the bond. The return may be whatever growth is achieved on the index, but more commonly is a percentage of the index growth. Some guaranteed equity bonds also lock in gains if the index that is selected reaches a certain set point during the policy term, and some mature if certain growth rates are achieved ('kick-outs').

The guarantee is usually arrived at by combining a call option with either a fixed-term deposit or a zero coupon bond. The guarantee usually only applies if the bond is held to maturity and will not apply in the event of an early surrender.

When evaluating the merits of a life office's guaranteed bond, it should be compared against the similar structured products available from asset management houses and the investment notes that are listed on the London Stock Exchange.

Protected equity bonds allow investors to select a quarterly guaranteed level of protection of between 95% and 100% of the capital. They are then protected against any market falls in excess of the selected level.

The capital protection offered is attractive to many investors since it provides a safety net in the event of unexpected market falls during the term of the bond. Although this is an advantage of this type of product, it should be remembered that it comes at a cost. Only a percentage of the growth of an index may be payable and even then, this return will exclude dividends. This, along with the cost of the guarantee, reduces potential returns.

5 Pensions

People are living longer than ever because of medical advances and general improvements in health and as a result planning for retirement is becoming increasingly important. The increasing cost of providing state pensions is forcing governments to reassess how much they pay. Relying on the state to provide a comfortable retirement is clearly not going to provide most people with the lifestyle they would like to enjoy in retirement.

Existing pension plans may also fall short of providing the funds needed in retirement. Defined-benefit pension schemes are being closed to new members and for those still in such a scheme the benefits payable are being reduced and/or the retirement age at which they are payable is being deferred. In their place, defined-contribution schemes have switched the risk and uncertainties of the financing of retirement from employers to individuals, leaving them with no choice but to take their retirement planning into their own hands.

State pensions

The state pension is payable at the official state pension age and is based on your record of national insurance contributions and credits. In some circumstances, the contributions or earnings of a husband, wife or civil partner are used to work out how much state pension you may receive.

To get a state pension, you must have reached your state pension age, which is currently 60 for a woman born before 6 April 1950 and 65 for a man, and meet the contribution qualifying conditions.

The state pension age is changing and the effect of the proposed changes mean that:

- For women, the current state pension age began to rise from 60 to 65 as of April 2010. This affects women born on or after 6 April 1950.

- From December 2018 the state pension age for both men and women will start to increase to reach 66 by April 2020.

- The state pension age will increase further to 67 between 2034 and 2036, and then to 68 between 2044 and 2046.

Currently, there is no set amount of state pension payable.

- Entitlement to the basic state pension is dependent on the number of qualifying years you have earned over your working life and the national insurance contributions you have paid.

- You may also be entitled to an additional state pension, which is changing to become a simple, single rate, weekly top-up to the basic state pension.

- Any benefits built up prior to the change will be protected, for example those from the state earnings-related pension scheme (SERPS) and from the state second pension.

- The Government is also consulting on introducing changes to simplify the state pension system, including proposals for a flat rate state pension of around £140 a week for a single person.

To be eligible for a state pension, you must have reached the state pension age and have paid, been treated as having paid or been credited with enough national insurance contributions for the necessary number of qualifying years in your working life. If you earn less than the threshold at which national insurance is payable but more than the lower earnings limit, you will be treated as having met the conditions even though no payments will have been made. If your earnings are below the limit or you do not work, you can choose to pay voluntary contributions.

If you have not made sufficient contributions, it may be possible for voluntary contributions to be made to effectively backdate contributions in order to either qualify for a basic state pension or increase the rate of pension payable.

The number of years in which you must make contributions is known as the 'working life'. This starts at the start of the tax year in which you become 16 and ends at the end of the tax year before the one in which you reach your state pension age. A working life of 49 years basically covers the potential working years from age 16 to 65. During this period, you must have 30 qualifying years in your working life to qualify for a basic state pension. A qualifying year is a tax year in which you have received qualifying earnings in excess of the lower earnings limit for national insurance.

If you have less than 30 qualifying years you will qualify for a reduced-rate basic state pension. If you have fewer than the 25% qualifying years (in other words less than eight qualifying years), you may not qualify for any basic state pension but may still qualify for an additional state pension.

Most of the amounts that make up the state pension are treated as income for tax purposes and should be included in any tax return. This includes:

- Basic state pension.
- Additional state pension.
- Graduated retirement benefit.
- Long-term incapacity benefit age addition.
- Extra state pension or a lump-sum payment earned by deferring state pension.
- Any increase for adult dependants but not child dependants.

Defined-benefit schemes

Defined-benefit schemes are a form of occupational pension scheme where the pension received is related to the number of years of service and the final salary. They are more commonly known as 'final salary schemes'.

A defined-benefit scheme essentially promises a given level of income at retirement, usually expressed as a proportion of final earnings. Contributions to the fund will normally be made by both the employer and the employee, although who contributes what will vary from scheme to scheme.

These types of scheme vary from company to company but the final pension payable is usually expressed as a fraction of the member's final salary. This is known as an 'accrual rate' and a scheme might provide, for example, one-sixtieth of the member's final salary for each year of service. Over a 40-year working career, the member could build up a pension of two-thirds of final salary. The accrual rate will obviously vary from company to company and some schemes use an average of the salary received over a period of years leading up to retirement.

The point at which the pension or other benefit is payable is known as the 'normal retirement date' or 'normal pension date'.

At retirement, defined-benefit schemes allow part of the member's total benefit to be taken in the form of a lump sum which is tax-free provided it does not exceed 25% of the value of the fund. This tax-free lump sum will often allow the member to fulfil specific plans for retirement, for example a special holiday, or even repaying a mortgage.

The pension may be payable by the pension fund itself from its internal cash flow or may be paid by the provision of a lump sum that is used to purchase an annuity from a life office.

Some defined-benefit schemes provide a guarantee on the minimum period for which the pension is paid, so as to ensure that even if the member concerned dies shortly after retirement, reasonable value will still have been provided by the scheme. Others will have provisions for a reduced pension to be payable to a surviving spouse or dependents.

A death in service benefit is also usually provided in case death should occur before retirement. This is most often expressed as a multiple of pensionable pay and many schemes provide four times pensionable pay. In addition, many schemes also provide income benefits for dependants.

Defined-benefit schemes allow employees to make retirement plans knowing what level of income can be expected in retirement. Their main concerns can be whether this is sufficient, how any annual increases are calculated and the long-term security of the pension fund.

A potential disadvantage of these schemes is that in the final years of working, employees may not be earning as much as when they were at their peak earning power. Also, the final 'pensionable' salary on which the pension will be based may be significantly different from total earnings.

Pension schemes issue annual benefit statements that show the level of pension benefit expected at retirement based on the employee's current earnings. Employees can also request details of the value of their benefits in the form of a transfer value quotation when a transfer to another pension scheme is being considered.

Occupational defined-contribution schemes

A defined-contribution scheme is one where the pension provided is related to the contributions made and investment performance achieved. These schemes are often known as 'money purchase schemes'.

Contributions to the fund will sometimes be made by both the employer and the employee, although who contributes what will vary from scheme to scheme. These contributions are invested to build up a fund that can be used to purchase benefits at retirement. The risk therefore lies with the employee rather than the employer, since the employer has not guaranteed a particular level of pension income.

The money contributed by the employee and employer will be invested either by the pension scheme itself or in the funds managed by a life office. The eventual value of the pension fund will therefore depend upon the investment performance achieved by the fund.

At retirement, a tax-free cash sum can be taken and the balance is used to provide a retirement income by the purchase of an annuity. An open market option allows the member to use the funds to buy an annuity from an alternative provider that is offering the best rates and the mix of benefits most suitable for them.

The amount of pension that the member will be able to generate will therefore depend upon the size of the fund and the prevailing annuity rates at the time of retirement. As an alternative to an annuity, a defined-contribution scheme may permit income withdrawals to be taken instead so that the pension fund remains invested. This can allow flexibility over the timing of when the annuity is eventually purchased, subject to it being no later than the member's 75th birthday.

Most insurance-based defined-contribution pension arrangements allow members to switch between several funds, so they can switch to more cautious funds as retirement approaches.

As the funds will usually be held in a designated account for the member, these schemes provide the security that the funds will be available at retirement. The disadvantage, however, is that the actual income that the member will receive in retirement will not be known until retirement and this makes effective planning significantly more difficult.

Personal pension schemes

Personal pensions are pension arrangements made by an individual in order to provide retirement benefits. An occupational scheme is not available to everyone and personal pensions provide an alternative vehicle for providing retirement benefits that benefit from the same generous tax treatment.

Personal pensions are individual contracts with a pension provider. The provider will usually be a life office but could be a friendly society, a bank, a building society or a unit trust group. Personal pensions will usually be structured as insurance contracts and may be either with profits, unit linked or invested in unit trusts.

These schemes are a form of defined-contribution or money purchase scheme and so the retirement benefits will depend upon the contributions made, the investment performance of the fund and annuity rates at the time of retirement. At retirement a tax-free lump sum can be taken and the balance used to provide retirement income either through the purchase of an annuity, by means of income withdrawals or by an 'alternatively secured pension'.

Personal pensions will tend to have more flexibility and offer more options, especially in relation to investment choices, than many occupational schemes.

Group personal pensions

A number of life offices offer group personal pensions, which allow an employer to facilitate the provision of personal pensions to employees and collect pension contributions through the payroll. A group personal pension is a collection of individual pension contracts for each member. Because of the cost savings, charges can be lower than for normal personal pensions or better benefits can be provided.

Stakeholder pensions

A further alternative is a stakeholder pension. These were introduced in 2001 to provide a relatively simple, low-cost arrangement to encourage more people to save for retirement.

Stakeholder pensions are a type of personal pension and have the same rules for eligibility, transfers, benefits, contributions and taxation. Where they differ from personal pensions is that they have to meet a number of conditions set by the Department for Work and Pensions covering charges, access and terms (CAT).

These CAT standards include the following:

- Initial charges and exit charges are not permitted.
- The annual management charge cannot exceed 1.5% in the first ten years and 1% after that.
- The minimum contribution cannot be set higher than £20.

- The scheme must offer a lifestyle default investment option.
- The scheme must be able to accept transfers from another scheme.

Since 2001, most employers with more than four employees have been required to nominate a stakeholder scheme to which their employees can contribute unless they are exempt.

Self-invested personal pension schemes

Self-invested personal pension schemes (SIPPs), are a type of personal pension plan aimed at investors who wish to have greater control over the investment of the funds within their pension plan. A SIPP is essentially a pension wrapper that can hold investments in a tax-efficient manner. As a type of personal pension scheme it is subject to the same rules on contributions, allowances and benefits.

SIPPs can be established for one individual or for many members and each scheme will have a scheme provider, a scheme administrator and a scheme trustee. SIPPs can be provided by life offices, banks, building societies, unit trusts and friendly societies. The scheme administrator is responsible for ensuring that the scheme is operated in accordance with HMRC rules and the trustee is responsible for holding and safeguarding the fund's assets.

Charges vary significantly from provider to provider and will include an initial set-up fee, annual administration fees and dealing fees. SIPPs are likely to carry higher charges than other personal pensions, which means they are more suitable for large funds and experienced investors.

As well as managing the funds themselves, individuals can use an authorised investment manager to make the decisions for them. The types of investments permitted within a SIPP include:

- Deposit accounts and National Savings and Investments products.
- Government and corporate bonds.
- Shares quoted on a recognised UK or overseas stock exchange.
- Futures and options.
- OEICs, unit trusts and investment trusts.
- Insurance company funds.
- Commercial property.

Small self-administered pension schemes

Small self-administered pension schemes (SSASs) are designed to allow directors of family-owned companies to establish their own pension scheme. They offer a family-operated company an effective pension vehicle for long-term planning and family protection, short-term company planning with respect to flexible investment options and also significant pre-retirement tax planning and savings.

An SSAS is an occupational pension scheme and if it meets certain conditions it can be exempt from some of the provisions of the Pensions Act 1995. Due to the higher investment risks associated with an SSAS, membership is usually restricted to controlling directors and a maximum of 12 members. In most private family-operated companies that opt for an SSAS there are typically only two or three members.

An SSAS must be established under an irrevocable trust with an associated trust deed and rules. It must also appoint a pensioneer trustee, who should be a member of the Association of Pensioneer Trustees. The pensioneer trustee has to be experienced in administering a SASS, a cosignatory on the bank account and a co-owner of any assets, and must ensure the SSAS complies with all rules and regulations.

Permitted investments for an SSAS include cash, shares, futures and options. In addition investment is permitted in certain other assets provided these do not provide a direct or indirect benefit to the members. For example, an SSAS could not buy a residential property to be used by a member and that member's family.

The pension fund can be used to buy the commercial property occupied by the company as the company is considered to be a separate legal entity. It is not possible to purchase property from an SSAS member because the member is a connected person.

The SSAS can also make loans up to a certain size to the company for purposes such as buying commercial property or plant and machinery. This must be for a specified fixed term and at a commercial rate of interest that is at least the base rate plus 3%. The scheme can also borrow money up to set limits to buy an asset for commercial use by the company.

Pension benefits and taxation

Pension funds are given preferential tax treatment as part of the government's drive to encourage individuals to save for retirement.

Major changes were made to pensions legislation in 2006 in order to simplify the rules surrounding pensions, replacing the previous eight tax regimes with one universal regime. These changes were known as 'pension simplification'.

As part of these changes two new controls were introduced, the lifetime allowance and the annual allowance. The other main changes allow all schemes to offer a tax-free cash sum of up to 25%, allow employees the opportunity to continue working for their employer while taking benefits from their occupational pension scheme and allow funds to be placed in all types of investments.

Further changes were made in the 2011 Budget, the most notable of which was the removal of the need for compulsory annuitisation.

The new rules are very detailed and complex but in summary, the tax treatment of pensions is as follows:

- Once a scheme has been authorised by HMRC, any investment income and capital gains arising in the fund are tax-free. As with other investment funds, the tax credit on dividend income cannot be reclaimed.

- There is no limit on the contribution you may pay into a pension. Instead there are limits on what qualifies for tax relief and a tax charge if the annual or lifetime allowances are exceeded.

- The maximum allowable contribution you can make which qualifies for tax relief is the higher of £3,600 gross or 100% of relevant UK earnings in each tax year, subject to a maximum of the annual allowance (see below). Relevant earnings are essentially employment income plus certain other items.

- Any contributions made by a UK resident in excess of 100% of relevant UK earnings, or £3,600 if greater, will not qualify for tax relief.

- If you have earnings in excess of the annual allowance and pay a contribution of 100% of those earnings you may still obtain tax relief on the contribution, but the contribution will give rise to a tax liability under the annual allowance rules.

- Where the contributions are paid under the relief at source rules, tax relief is given by extending the basic rate limit. Any higher rate tax relief needs to be claimed via your self-assessment tax return.

- Tax relief is also given on transfers into a pension scheme of shares acquired under a save-as-you-earn (SAYE) option scheme or share incentive plan provided certain time limits are adhered to.

- Where funds are contributed to a pension in excess of the lifetime allowance a tax charge will arise.

- When benefits are taken either at retirement or death, a check must be made as to whether the lifetime allowance has been exceeded. If it has, the excess funds are subject to a lifetime allowance charge of 25%, but if they are taken from the pension fund as a lump sum the charge is 55%.

The lifetime allowance

The lifetime allowance is the maximum amount of pension savings that can benefit from tax relief before tax penalties apply.

This allowance was initially based on the approximate amount of money that would be needed to buy a pension equal to the maximum HMRC would permit under the tax regime. The initial allowance was broadly the amount required to provide maximum benefits for a 60-year-old with earnings at the earnings cap of £105,600 in 2005/06, and the allowance represented a gross income of £75,000 a year.

The lifetime allowance was initially set at £1.5m and this figure has risen over time, as can be seen in Table 12.1.

Table 12.1 – The lifetime allowance

Tax year	Lifetime allowance
2006/07	£1.50m
2007/08	£1.60m
2008/09	£1.65m
2009/10	£1.75m
2010/11	£1.80m

From 2012/13 onwards, the lifetime allowance for pension savings for individuals will be reduced from the current level of £1.8m to £1.5m.

The allowance limits the amount that can be built up in a pension fund. If a fund exceeds this amount, it is treated as having benefited unduly from pension scheme tax advantages and a tax charge is made.

For the purposes of valuing benefits to measure against the lifetime allowance, all defined contribution benefits are taken at their asset value, while pensions building up in defined benefit schemes are valued at £20 for each £1 of pension, irrespective of the individual's age.

The annual allowance

The annual allowance replaces the previous maximum annual contribution limits for approved pension plans. It was initially set at £215,000 and this figure has risen regularly as shown in Table 12.2.

Table 12.2 – The lifetime allowance

Tax year	Annual allowance
2006/07	£215,000
2007/08	£225,000
2008/09	£235,000
2009/10	£245,000
2010/11	£255,000

On 14 October 2010, the Government announced changes to the annual allowance for tax relief on pensions. From 2011/12 onwards, the annual allowance for tax relief on pension savings for individuals will be reduced from the current level of £255,000 to just £50,000.

If total pension savings are more than the annual allowance for the tax year, you may have to pay the annual allowance charge. You can, however, carry forward any annual allowance that is not used from the previous three tax years to the current tax year. The unused amount is added to this year's annual allowance and only if pension savings exceed this amount is the annual allowance charge payable.

The effect of the annual allowance tax charge is to remove tax relief on any pension savings over the available annual allowance. The amount payable depends on the rate at which tax relief has effectively been given on the excess pension saving. Excess pension savings are added to taxable income and the amount of pension saving:

- Over your higher rate limit will be taxed at 50%;

- Over your basic rate limit, but below your higher rate limit, will be taxed at 40%; and

- Below your basic rate limit will be taxed at 20%.

For defined-benefit schemes, the total amount of pension accrued in a year is limited to the annual allowance. If the annual allowance is exceeded there will be a tax liability.

There is no annual allowance in the year that a pension vests. For the purposes of the annual allowance, contributions to a defined-contribution scheme or increases in the value of a pension in a defined-benefit scheme that take place in the year benefits are vested are ignored. For defined benefit schemes, the increment in annual pension entitlement is multiplied by 16 and if the resultant figure is in excess of the annual allowance a tax charge is payable.

Contributions

The previous limits for contributions have been replaced and there is now no limit on the amount of contributions that can be paid. However, there is a limit on the amount which enjoys tax relief.

Tax relief on contributions is limited to the higher of 100% of relevant earnings or, where tax relief is given at source, £3,600. Where contributions exceed the annual allowance, a charge is levied on the excess.

If you have no earnings it is possible to contribute up to £3,600 a year (£2,880 net of basic rate tax) to a personal pension (which includes a stakeholder pension), where tax relief is received at source. National insurance rebates on contracting out do not count towards the annual limit.

There is no limit at all in the year in which benefits are taken in full.

Retirement age

The minimum age at which pension benefits can be drawn, known as the 'normal minimum pension age', changed to 55 from 6 April 2010. This applies to taking the tax-free lump sum, buying an annuity and income drawdown. The only exceptions whereby pension retirement benefits can be taken early are as follows:

- **People who retire due to ill health.** Benefits can be taken prior to age 55 where a member is in ill health. To pay benefits in these circumstances the pension scheme will need a written opinion from a registered medical practitioner that the member is incapable of continuing his or her current occupation because of physical or mental sickness or disease.

- **Members of occupational pension schemes who already have contractual rights to retire early.** Any member of an occupational pension scheme with contractual rights at 9 December 2003 to take benefits from age 50 can retain this right.

- **People with special occupations with lower retirement ages such as sports people.** For special occupations where individuals have low normal retirement dates and are allowed to retire and take benefits before the minimum pension age, they can continue do so. However, there will be a 2.5% discount deducted from the lifetime allowance for each year before age 55.

The tax-free lump sum — pension commencement lump sum

Pension schemes can pay a tax-free lump sum of up to 25% of the fund value. This is now called the pension commencement lumps sum or PCLS. The value of the fund for the purposes of the PCLS includes the protected rights portion of a pension, additional voluntary contributions, free-standing additional voluntary contributions and transfers received from occupational pension schemes.

For defined-benefit schemes, such as final salary pensions, the scheme must calculate the value of the pension to determine the maximum PCLS. The calculation used by HMRC employs a 20:1 value for converting a defined-benefit scheme to cash, so if you were due to a pension of £25,000 a year, this would represent a cash value of £500,000 and would enable a PCLS of up to £125,000 to be paid.

The PCLS is also limited to a maximum of 25% of the lifetime allowance.

Pension benefits

The balance of the pension fund that is not commuted must be used to provide a pension, which can be provided as a:

- Scheme pension.

- Lifetime annuity.

- Drawdown pension.

The only option available to members of defined-benefit schemes is a scheme pension. A lifetime annuity is an annuity payable by an insurance company. Members can select the best annuity by searching for the highest rates using an open market option.

On 22 June 2010, the Government announced it would end the effective requirement to purchase an annuity by age 75. Following consultation on how to introduce this change, members of a defined contribution or money purchase scheme may also take benefits as a drawdown pension.

The main changes included in the March 2011 Budget are:

- The tax rules for alternatively secured pensions are repealed.

- What are currently unsecured pensions and alternatively secured pensions are amalgamated into one form of pension – called drawdown pension.

- Drawdown pension comes in two forms called 'capped drawdown' and 'flexible drawdown'.

- Capped drawdown works in the same way as income withdrawal before 6 April 2011. There is a maximum amount of pension that can be taken each year, and this amount is regularly recalculated.

- The maximum amount of capped drawdown pension is based around an equivalent annuity – this is called the 'basis amount'. If you are under 75 the maximum amount of drawdown pension is reduced from 120% to 100% of the basis amount. If you are over 75 the maximum amount has increased from 90 per cent to 100% of the basis amount.

- There is no minimum amount of capped drawdown pension that has to be taken when the member or dependant is age 75 or over.

- The period for reviewing the calculation of the amount of capped drawdown pension before age 75 (the reference period) reduces from five years to three years.

- With flexible drawdown there is no minimum or a maximum amount of pension that has to be taken each year. The member or dependant can take as much or as little from their pension fund as they like. There is no need for the scheme administrator to carry out regular calculations of the basis amount.

- To be able to have flexible drawdown the member or dependant must have at least £20,000 of secure pension in payment. This must be derived from the state pension and/or other pensions.

Death benefits

The March 2011 Budget has also changed the rules surrounding payment of death benefits.

Defined benefit scheme:

- A death benefit can now be paid even if the member is over 75.
- If the member died before their 75th birthday, the lump sum death benefit must be paid within two years.
- If the member was under 75 when they died, the lump sum will be tested against the lifetime allowance. If the total benefits taken in respect of the member are less than their lifetime allowance, this lump sum will be tax free. Any excess is liable to the lifetime allowance charge of 55%.
- If the member is over 75, the whole lump sum death benefit is liable to a 55% tax charge.

Money purchase schemes:

- The death benefit payable under a money purchase scheme is referred to as 'an uncrystallised funds lump sum death benefit'.
- If the member dies before they are 75, the lump sum death benefit must be paid within two years.
- If the member was aged under 75 when they died, the lump sum will be tested against the lifetime allowance. If the total benefits taken exceed the lifetime allowance, any excess is liable to the lifetime allowance charge of 55%.
- If the member was aged 75 or older when they died, the lump sum death benefit is not tested against the lifetime allowance. The rate of the special lump sum death benefits charge is 55%.

6 Individual savings accounts

An individual savings account or ISA is a tax-efficient wrapper that can be used to hold investments such as cash deposits, shares and unit trusts. ISAs were launched in April 1999 to replace two other widely used savings vehicles, personal equity plans (PEPs) and tax-exempt special savings accounts (TESSAs).

PEPs were originally introduced in 1986 to encourage direct share ownership and evolved into a vehicle that allowed a tax-efficient way of holding collective investments. In April 2008, all PEPs became stocks and shares ISAs and the PEP legislation was repealed. The TESSA was introduced in 1990 and was effectively a five-year tax-free savings plan linked to bank and building society deposits.

The ISA is a more complex plan than its two predecessors, but it has nevertheless become a popular investment vehicle because of its tax benefits. ISAs have two distinct investment components:

- Cash.

- Stocks and shares.

Although an ISA can be made up of either cash or stocks and shares, different subscription limits apply to each. Transfers can be made from the cash component to the stocks and shares component (but not vice versa) without affecting the annual investment allowance.

Eligibility

To be eligible for an ISA, an investor needs to meet certain age, residency and other conditions. To be able to subscribe to an ISA, the investor must:

- Be an individual aged 16 or over if subscribing to a cash ISA or 18 or over if subscribing to a stocks and shares ISA.

- Be resident and ordinarily resident in the UK unless a crown employee serving overseas.

- Not have subscribed to another ISA of the same type in the relevant tax year and not have exceeded the overall subscription limit.

These conditions are set by HMRC, which lays down the rules by which ISAs are allowed to operate. The rules are complex but some key points are as follows:

- The age conditions are designed to limit access to stocks and shares to those aged 18 and over.

- ISAs are only available to individuals and so accounts in joint names are not permitted.

- ISAs cannot be used by trusts.

- The requirement to be resident in the UK means resident in England, Wales, Scotland or Northern Ireland. It does not include the Channel Islands or the Isle of Man.

- Investors must be 'resident and ordinarily resident' in the UK when they subscribe to an ISA. This means that if existing ISA investors move abroad they will no longer be able to make any further subscriptions to an ISA.

An ISA can remain open but no further contributions can be made until investors can satisfy the residence conditions again.

- An exception is made for crown employees serving overseas who are paid out of the public revenue of the UK and for their spouses or civil partners. Typically, a crown employee is a serving member of the armed forces or a diplomat.

Annual subscriptions

As ISAs benefit from preferential tax treatment, there are limits on the amounts that can be invested. There is an annual maximum overall subscription limit and within that overall limit, no more than 50% may be placed in the cash component.

The annual subscription limit for ISAs is set by the Treasury. So, for example, in the 2011/12 tax year the Treasury allowed all investors to invest in two separate ISAs, with potentially different providers, subject to the maximum limits of £10,680 and £5,340.

From 6 April 2011, the basis of calculating the ISA annual subscription limit changed and any increase is based on the retail prices index (RPI).

- The new limits are calculated by reference to the RPI for the September before the start of the following tax year.

- In the event that the RPI is negative, the ISA limits would remain the same.

- The first of these announcements has now been made. HMRC regularly issues ISA bulletins to keep ISA managers up to date with any new developments affecting ISAs. HMRC used this to announce on 16 October 2010 that the ISA subscription limits for 2011/12 would rise, and that the new overall ISA subscription limit would be £10,680 of which up to £5,340 can be subscribed to a cash ISA.

- A further change to the annual subscription limit was announced in the March 2011 Budget. For 2012/13 and later years, the ISA subscription limits will be increased in line with the consumer prices index (CPI) on an annual basis.

Applications for ISAs may be made in writing, over the telephone or electronically (for example via the internet).

- Applications can allow for subscriptions to be made in the year of application, and in each successive year in which the applicant subscribes to the ISA.

- This allows, for example, a continuous subscription by direct debit, provided at least one payment is made in each tax year.

- Applications cease to be valid at the end of a tax year in which the investor fails to make a subscription. When this happens, the investor must make a fresh application before subscriptions can recommence.

Investment may be by way of cash, including direct debit, credit and debit card and telegraphic transfer. Gifts of cash from third parties are acceptable.

- If an investor subscribes by mistake to a disallowed combination of ISAs (more than one cash ISA and/or more than one stocks and shares ISA) in the same tax year, then the subscriptions to the later ISA are invalid.

- If an investor subscribes to a valid combination of ISAs (one cash and one stocks and shares), but exceeds the overall subscription limit, the excess subscriptions are invalid.

After the end of a tax year, when the ISA managers make their returns, the Savings Scheme Office (SSO) identifies if there has been an invalid subscription. The SSO will notify the ISA manager and the investor of the error and the action that needs to be taken:

- Where an ISA holds cash or stocks and shares, they will arrange with HMRC to repay any tax relief that has been given in error.

- The investor will be given details of any income or gains from the investments, and if the investor is due to pay tax these details must be reported to the investor's tax office.

- Where an ISA holds life assurance, the policy must end if the subscription is invalid – the policy may give rise to a taxable gain if the proceeds are greater than the premiums paid.

- The ISA manager will repay any tax due to HMRC at the basic rate, but the investor must report the gain to their tax office and may have to pay more tax if they are a higher rate taxpayer.

Cash ISAs

Many cash ISAs are structured in exactly the same way as standard deposit accounts and so can be instant access, notice or fixed-term accounts. Any interest arising in a cash ISA is free of tax.

Although cash ISAs are available to individuals aged 16 or over, the tax benefits can be affected if the capital is derived from a parent. If the interest together with any other income from all capital provided by the parent is more than £100 a year, the income will be treated as the parent's until the child reaches age 18. The income must be reported on the tax return of the parent and may not therefore be tax free.

Transfers of an ISA from one provider to another are permitted without affecting the annual subscription allowance. This means that investors can move their money between providers to obtain better rates.

When considering cash ISAs there are a number of factors that need to be taken into account:

- ISA providers pitch their interest rates to take into account the tax advantage of cash ISA accounts.

- The difference between the gross rates on cash ISAs and the net rates available from standard deposit accounts can be minimal for basic rate taxpayers. For higher rate taxpayers, however, the returns can be significantly better.

- Some providers offering high rates will only do so if new funds are introduced for the current year's subscription in the account. Some may also not accept transfers in at all.

- Once a withdrawal has been made it cannot be subsequently redeposited unless investors have not fully used their annual subscription allowance. Cash ISA accounts should not therefore be the first source of funds that are withdrawn for a temporary purpose if there are other liquid funds available.

Stocks and shares ISAs

A stocks and shares ISA can be used to hold a wide range of investments including cash, direct equities and bonds and collective investments. To qualify for inclusion in the ISA, the investment must meet rules set by HMRC. These are complex but the types of investment that can be held include:

- Qualifying shares and certain investment trusts.

- Depositary interests.

- Qualifying securities.

- Government securities.

- UCIT funds and qualifying authorised funds and non-UCITS funds.

- Cash.

Investors can transfer any funds held in cash ISAs into a stocks and shares ISA without affecting the current year's ISA allowance. Investors can also transfer the current year's subscription made to a cash ISA provided that they transfer the whole amount.

Investment in a stocks and shares ISA can be in the form of a CGT-free direct transfer of shares from an approved share incentive plan or a savings-related share option scheme (SAYE). The shares must be transferred within 90 days from the date they emerge from the scheme. The value of shares at the date of transfer counts towards the annual subscription limit.

Investment in a stocks and shares ISA benefits from both income tax and capital gains tax advantages:

- Any interest income received is not liable to income tax.
- The tax credit on a dividend cannot be reclaimed but there is no further liability to income tax for a higher rate taxpayer.
- Any gains on investments are not liable to capital gains tax.

The charges made for stocks and shares ISAs vary from provider to provider. The ISA manager will typically make charges for the operation of the account in order to pay for the administration of the portfolio. Other charges will vary depending upon what investments are held in the account but would typically be the same as if held directly and not in the wrapper.

Investors are also able to transfer stocks and shares ISAs to a different provider altogether or make a partial transfer.

7 Child Trust Funds and Junior ISAs

The Government announced in October 2010 that it intends to create a new tax-free children's savings account to replace the Child Trust Fund (CTF). This section looks at the features of CTFs and then at their replacement, Junior ISAs.

Child Trust Funds (CTFs)

CTFs were first launched on 6 April 2005, following extensive consultation. Around 700,000 children are born in the UK each year and it is estimated that at launch more than 1.5 million children were eligible for the new account.

The Government announced on 24 May 2010 that it intended to reduce and then stop government payments to CTF accounts. The changes required legislation which has now been passed by Parliament.

The effect of these changes is that no further government contributions will be made and HMRC stopped issuing new CTF vouchers from 1 January 2011. Although government contributions have ended, it is still possible to make further contributions to existing CTFs and CTFs will remain part of the investment landscape for some time to come. The following outlines their key features:

- Every child born on or after 1 September 2002 was eligible for the CTF, provided child benefit had been awarded for them by HMRC and the child was living in the UK.
- The CTF is a special form of savings account for children, to which the Government made lump sum payments at specific ages. The CTF is for the

benefit of the child, not the parents and, except in cases of terminal illness, cannot be encashed until the child reaches their 18th birthday.

- There are three basic types of CTF account – savings accounts, share accounts and stakeholder CTFs – all with similar features to ISAs.

- CTFs offer the same benefits as ISAs and these will continue even though Government payments have ceased.

- It is possible to transfer between CTF providers, but partial transfers are not allowed: a child may have only one CTF account. As a general rule, CTF providers must accept transfers.

- When the child reaches 16 they take control of the account and the CTF matures at age 18. At that stage, it will be possible to rollover maturing CTFs into ISAs, thereby maintaining their tax benefits.

CTF accounts may be topped up by parents, relations and friends. The maximum total top up from all sources is £1,200 per year. (The March 2011 Budget proposed that the limit is to be raised to £3,000 to match the subscription limit for new Junior ISAs.)

The top-up subscription year normally runs from the child's previous birthday to the day before their next birthday (for example, 29 January 2011 to 28 January 2012).

Junior ISAs

The Government announced in October 2010 that it intends to create a new tax-free children's savings account to replace the CTF. The new accounts, described as 'Junior ISAs', will offer parents a simple and tax-free way to save for their child's future.

Draft Regulations setting out how the accounts will operate were published as part of the March 2011 Budget. The precise detail of account features are still subject to consultation and further development, however the Government intends that, where possible, account features and reporting requirements will be based on those already in operation for existing ISAs/CTFs so that existing processes can be adapted and used.

The proposed start date for the new Junior ISAs is 1 November 2011 and the planned key features are below.

Eligibility

- All UK resident children (aged under 18) who do not have a CTF will be eligible.

- This includes children who were born before the start of CTF eligibility.

- Children with CTFs will not be eligible for Junior ISAs.

Types of account

- Both cash and stocks and shares Junior ISAs will be available.

- The qualifying investments for each of these will be the same as for existing ISAs.

- Children will be able to hold one cash and one stocks and shares Junior ISA at a time.

- All returns will be tax-free both for the child and their parents.

Annual subscription limit

- Each eligible child will be able to receive contributions of up to £3,000 each year into their Junior ISA(s).

- As with CTFs, any person or organisation will be able to contribute to any child's Junior ISA.

- The contribution limit will operate across both types of account, so a total of £3,000 of contributions each year will be permitted into both accounts combined.

- There will be no rules on how contributions have to be allocated between cash and stocks and shares Junior ISAs, and it will be possible to transfer funds from one type of Junior ISA to another.

Account opening

- Anyone with parental responsibility for an eligible child will be able to open Junior ISAs on their behalf.

- Eligible children over the age of 16 will also be able to open Junior ISAs for themselves.

Account operation

- Until the child reaches 16, accounts will be managed on their behalf by a person who has parental responsibility for that child.

- This will initially be the person who applied for the account for the child, but this responsibility can be transferred to another person with parental responsibility.

- At age 16, the child assumes management responsibility for their account.

- Withdrawals will not be permitted until the child reaches 18, except in cases of terminal illness or death.

Transfers

- It will be possible to transfer accounts between providers, but it will not be possible to hold more than one cash or stocks and shares Junior ISA at any time.

- It will not be possible to transfer CTFs into Junior ISAs or vice versa.

Maturity

- When the child turns 18, the Junior ISA will by default become a normal adult ISA. The funds will then be accessible to the child.

- Having a Junior ISA will not affect an individual's entitlement to adult ISAs. It will be possible for Junior ISA account holders to open adult cash ISAs from the age of 16 and Junior ISA contributions will not affect adult ISA subscription limits.

8 National Savings and Investments

National Savings and Investments (NS&I) is one of the oldest savings institutions in the UK. It was set up over 150 years ago to provide a simple savings scheme aimed at ordinary people. The scheme quickly became very popular and the government used the money deposited to pay for public spending.

NS&I has grown into one of the largest savings institutions in the UK but still retains its two essential characteristics of offering a secure place for people to save and providing the Exchequer with a source of funding.

All NS&I products carry a government guarantee, which means they rank as some of the most secure investments available. There is virtually no risk of default as the government can always raise taxes to repay debts falling due if they cannot simply be refinanced.

The product range includes premium bonds, fixed-rate bonds and variable rate savings accounts. NS&I products have attractions for some taxpayers as some are tax-free and others pay interest without deduction of tax at source, although the income is fully taxable. NS&I admits, however, that the rates on offer are set to reflect the absence of tax.

In 2010 NS&I had over 27 million investors and more than £94bn of investments. During 2010, take up of some of the products offered by NS&I was such that they were able to reach the funding targets set by the Government and many products were removed from sale. A new financing target for 2011/12 has been announced by the Government and so NS&I is to reintroduce the sale of products such as national savings certificates.

Tax-free products

NS&I offers a number of tax-free products including premium bonds, national savings certificates and children's bonus bonds. In addition, it also offers a cash ISA.

Premium bonds

Premium bonds offer purchasers the chance to win a variety of monthly tax-free jackpots. Each bond costs £1 and the minimum purchase that can be made is £100 and the maximum £30,000. Bonds are available to anyone over 16 and can be bought for children under 16 by parents and grandparents. There is no minimum term they need to be held for and they can be encashed at any time.

Instead of paying interest, premium bonds are entered into monthly prize draws once they have been held for one clear month after purchase. Each individual £1 bond is entered into the draw and any winnings are tax-free.

There is a £1m jackpot and over a million other prizes each month. The prize fund is split between three value bands with a percentage share of each month's prize fund allocated to each value band:

- The higher value band is allocated 6% of the prize fund and includes the £1m jackpot.

- The medium value band is allocated 5% of the prize fund and has prizes of £1,000 and £500.

- The lower value band is allocated the bulk of the prize fund, 89%, and has prizes of £25, £50 or £100.

The size of each month's prize fund depends upon the rate of interest earned on all the money invested in premium bonds. The rate normally varies in line with short-term interest rates, and as rates fell, so did the prize fund. With effect from 1 October 2009, the rate was 1.5%.

There is over £41bn invested in premium bonds and at the current interest rate this means that the odds of each £1 bond winning a prize are 24,000 to 1 each month. In theory, holders of a large quantity of bonds should achieve an annual return equivalent to the prize rate, but this annual return may only be achieved as an average over a period of many years, during some of which actual receipts are minimal.

National savings certificates

NS&I makes tranches of national savings certificates available from time to time. There are two forms, fixed rate and index-linked. These are lump sum investments that earn guaranteed returns over the term of the investment that are tax-free. The fixed-rate certificates are typically available for two- and five-year terms.

For higher rate taxpayers it will usually be difficult, but not impossible, to beat the rate on offer by using bank or building society term deposits.

The minimum investment in each issue is £100 and the maximum is £15,000. However, there is no limit on the amount reinvested from previous matured issues.

Certificates can be bought individually, jointly or as a trustee. They are available to anyone over the age of seven and if bought on behalf of a child under seven the child becomes responsible for them on their seventh birthday.

Although certificates can be cashed before maturity, returns will be lower than the figures above. Encashment within the first year earns no interest whatsoever.

At maturity, NS&I writes to holders of national savings certificates to advise them of the options available. If the investor takes no action, the money is automatically reinvested in a new issue of the same duration.

Some investors may still hold 7th–43rd issues of fixed-rate certificates, which matured before 8 October 2001. If these were not encashed or reinvested, they only earn interest at the general extension rate, which is a mere 0.09%.

The index-linked certificates are typically available for three-year and five-year terms. For example, the three-year 19th issue and the five-year 46th issue offered guaranteed compound rates of 1% a year plus index linking. They have the same eligibility criteria and investment limits as above.

NS&I uses the retail prices index to calculate changes in the value of index-linked savings certificates. The inflation uplift is calculated annually and the value at the end of the year cannot be below that at the previous anniversary. As a result, if there is a period of deflation, the only growth would come from the guaranteed 1% a year interest. NS&I has confirmed that a new issue of index-linked savings certificates will retain index-linking against the retail prices index (RPI).

Ultimately the decision between fixed-rate and index-linked certificates is a judgment on whether the rate of inflation will be greater than the difference between the guaranteed rates of both. On that basis, if you expect inflation to be greater over the next five years the index-linked certificates will be the preferred choice. If you believe it is likely to be less, however, you will prefer the fixed-rate certificates.

Children's bonus bonds

The children's bonus bond is a fixed-rate bond with a five-year term. It is designed for investment by parents and others on behalf of children who are under the age of 16.

Up to £3,000 can be invested for a child in each issue of children's bonus bonds. All interest is rolled up until the maturity date, at which stage the bond can be reinvested for another five years, provided the child is still under age 16.

Although designed as a five-year investment, the bond can be cashed at any time. If the bond is cashed in the first year, no interest at all is payable. The tax treatment is important in assessing the attractiveness of this as a product.

The return is tax-free for the child and there is no tax liability for parents if they supply the capital. This is different from other investments. Income from other investments made by parents on behalf of their unmarried minor children is potentially taxable on the parents.

If the investment is made by a parent who is a higher rate taxpayer, it will often be very difficult to match the return available from NS&I. For basic rate taxpayers, better returns are available elsewhere.

Direct ISAs

Like most other savings institutions, NS&I offers a cash ISA. This is a straightforward cash ISA that earns variable rates of interest and can be accessed without notice or penalty. It has the same eligibility criteria, investment limits and tax advantages as other cash ISAs.

Compared to other providers, its variable rate of interest is usually uncompetitive.

Growth products

The growth products offered by NS&I include guaranteed growth bonds and guaranteed equity bonds, although at the moment there are no bonds on sale.

Guaranteed growth bonds

Guaranteed growth bonds are lump sum investments that offer fixed rates for a variety of terms. The minimum investment is £500 and the maximum £1m. There is normally a choice of investment terms from one to five years, with rates rising the longer you are prepared to tie up capital for. Interest is accumulated throughout the term and is paid at maturity. The interest is subject to 20% tax, deducted at source, which is wholly or partly reclaimable by 10% taxpayers and non-taxpayers. Bonds can be encashed before the end of their term, subject to 90 days' loss of interest.

These features demonstrate that it is important to compare what a savings institution is offering within its own range as well as what competitor offerings are.

Guaranteed equity bonds

From time to time, NS&I also offers guaranteed equity bonds for which the return is linked to the performance of the FTSE 100. They are structured products and should be compared against the structures, returns, tax efficiency and costs of products from other providers.

Monthly income products

NS&I offers two products designed to provide monthly income, the NS&I income bond and guaranteed income bonds for a range of terms. The income bond is a variable rate account without any set term, while the guaranteed bonds offer fixed rates over set terms.

Income bonds

The NS&I income bond is a straightforward savings account that can be used by investors who want a monthly income. Interest is paid on the fifth day of each month without deduction of tax, although it is fully taxable. This makes it attractive for non-taxpayers and also for those who pay only a little income tax and so are unable to qualify for gross interest payments from banks and building societies.

The minimum investment is £500 and the maximum £1m. Withdrawals can be made at any time without any loss of interest. Interest rates are variable at six weeks' notice and move broadly in line with bank base rates.

Guaranteed income bonds

Guaranteed income bonds are usually available for terms of one to five years and offer fixed rates, although none are on sale at present. The usual minimum investment is £500 and the maximum £1m. Rates rise the longer you are prepared to tie up capital for. All interest is subject to 20% tax, deducted at source, which is wholly or partly reclaimable by 10% taxpayers and non-taxpayers.

Bonds can be encashed before the end of their term, subject to 90 days' loss of interest.

The rates on guaranteed bonds are typically higher than for the income bond but, when comparing the two, it is important to take into account the future movement of interest rates and whether the payment of gross interest is advantageous.

Savings accounts

NS&I offers two savings accounts, the investment account and the easy access savings account.

The investment account is a deposit account, with variable rate interest paid annually on 31 December. Withdrawals can be made without notice or penalty and all interest is paid gross. It is an old-fashioned passbook account and its rate of interest can be easily beaten by telephone, postal or internet accounts which are offering rates around ten to twelve times as much.

The easy access savings account is a more modern type of account and it replaced the 'ordinary account'. Withdrawals may be made without notice and the account can be operated by phone and cash card, as well as at post offices. All interest is paid gross. Interest rates are tiered and are usually low compared with what is available elsewhere.

9 Private equity

Private equity is the generic name for investment in companies that are not listed on the stock market. Most private equity funds are held by institutions and run by specialist managers and they usually employ high levels of gearing. Individual investors can access a somewhat different form of private equity investment through Venture Capital Trusts (VCTs) and the Enterprise Investment Scheme (EIS), both of which benefit from significant tax concessions (see below). They can also hold shares in specialist investment companies or closed ended funds that are mainly listed.

In contrast to institutional private equity, which often buys listed companies or parts of them, the forms of private equity (sometimes referred to as 'venture capital') available to individual investors involve investing in new or young businesses, with the aim of either obtaining a stock market listing or selling the business to another company. Investment in such young businesses inevitably involves higher risks than investing in listed companies. Partly this is because of the relatively high rate of business failure and partly the absence of liquidity. Where private equity funds use gearing, this adds a further level of risk.

Some private equity managers and funds specialise in particular types of investment, for example technology, alternative energy and entertainment. Confusingly, many companies whose shares are listed on the Alternative Investment Market (AIM) qualify for investment by VCTs and EIS, though only in respect of new share issues, and some VCTs hold a large portion of their assets in AIM-listed stocks.

To qualify for the VCT tax concessions, a VCT's shares must be listed on an EU regulated market. However, because tax relief is granted only on initial subscriptions for VCT shares, the secondary market in VCT shares is generally illiquid, with wide bid-ask spreads. Specialist investment companies that are not eligible for the VCT tax concessions enjoy greater freedoms in selecting and managing investments and their shares may be more easily traded in the secondary market.

Some investment practitioners regard private equity as a separate asset class, but in practice it is a sub-class of 'small-cap' equity investment with poorer liquidity and, especially if there is gearing, significantly higher risk.

Comparison of historic performance is difficult because many funds make substantial dividend distributions, so that conventional 'dividend-reinvested' comparison methods are invalid. The effects of gearing must also be taken into account. The higher levels of gearing of private equity funds may often explain the higher returns they achieve as compared with ungeared funds investing in listed companies.

The management fees and costs of private equity funds are typically much higher than those of funds investing in listed companies.

Enterprise Investment Schemes (EISs)

Tax

Income tax relief is given on qualifying investments up to an annual investment limit.

Income tax relief at 20% is given on qualifying investments up to 5 April 2011, but it was announced in the March 2011 Budget that the rate of relief would increase to 30%. The increase in the rate of EIS income tax relief will have effect for shares issued on or after 6 April 2011, subject to state aid approval for the change from the EU.

Relief is given as a tax credit against an individual's income tax liability, not a reduction in taxable income. Relief is lost if the shares are disposed of within three years of acquisition.

The full amount invested in EIS shares in a year, subject only to the maximum of £500,000, can be carried back into the previous tax year. The March 2011 Budget revealed Government plans to include provisions in the Finance Bill 2012 that will increase the annual amount that an individual can invest under the EIS to £1m.

CGT deferral

An EIS investor can defer all or part of any capital gain chargeable to tax to the extent of their EIS investment (an investment of £100,000 enables the deferment of tax on £100,000 of gains). The EIS investment can be made up to three years after the gain was realised or one year before realisation. The gain deferred is the gross gain, after allowance for any annual exemption.

There is no lower or upper limit to the amount of the gain that can be invested under these rules. CGT deferral relief can be given without income tax relief. On disposal of the EIS shareholding, the deferred gains become taxable. Any gain arising from the EIS investment itself is CGT-free provided income tax relief claimed has not been withdrawn (ie, generally after three years).

Losses

If an EIS disposal creates a loss after allowing for income tax relief, this loss can be offset against either income or capital gains.

IHT relief

EIS shares will generally qualify for 100% IHT business assets relief once they have been held for two years.

Conditions for EIS reliefs

For newly issued shares of a company to qualify for EIS relief, the company must be unlisted and must either carry on a qualifying trade or be a holding company of qualifying subsidiaries. Shares that are listed on the Alternative Investment Market are treated as unlisted.

- The list of qualifying trades excludes most low-risk ventures, such as dealing in land, property development, farming and financial services. The activities of shipbuilding and coal and steel production are also excluded.

- For investors to receive income tax relief, they (or their associates) must neither be a paid employee of the EIS company nor own more than 30% of the company's share capital. These restrictions do not apply to investors seeking only CGT reinvestment relief, who can be 100% shareholders.

- A qualifying EIS company must have gross assets of not more than £7m before the issue of shares and £8m after the issue. Qualifying companies may not employ more than the equivalent of 50 full-time employees at the time shares are issued, nor may they raise more than £2m in total through EIS, VCT and the Corporate Venturing Scheme (CVS) in any 12-month period.

- There were proposals in the March 2011 Budget to change the criteria for a qualifying company from 6 April 2012. The employee limit will rise to fewer than 250 employees and the size threshold to gross assets of no more than £15m before investment. The maximum annual amount that can be invested in an individual company will be increased to £10m.

- For EIS shares issued on or after 22 April 2009, all the funds raised must be employed within two years of the date of the share issue. In general, funds are 'employed' when they are spent for the purpose of the business. However, money which is retained on current account can be treated as being 'employed' if the retention can reasonably be regarded as necessary or advisable for the financing of business requirements.

Venture Capital Trusts (VCTs)

Income tax relief on newly issued VCT shares is available at 30% for investments of up to £200,000 in a tax year. Relief is given as a tax credit against an individual's income tax liability, not a reduction in taxable income. Relief is lost if the shares are disposed of within five years of acquisition (three years for shares issued before 6 April 2006). Dividends are free of income tax, but tax credits cannot be reclaimed.

A VCT's investment holdings are subject to the following restrictions:

- At least 70% of the VCT's investments by value (previously 30% and changed in the 2010 Spring Budget) must be in qualifying newly issued securities in unlisted trading companies (including AIM and PLUS (formerly OFEX) listed companies).

- The provisions for qualifying trades and the gross assets test of company size are the same as for EIS companies.

- No more than 15% of the VCT by value can be invested in any single company or group of companies.

- At least 70% of the VCT's investments must be in new ordinary shares of qualifying companies, with no preferential rights.

- At least 10% of a VCT's investment in any company must be in ordinary, non-preferential shares.

- VCT funds have to be employed within the same timescale as for EIS funds.

Disposals of VCT shares which qualified for income tax relief are CGT-free at any time, but losses are not allowable. Capital gains made within a VCT are tax-free and may be distributed as dividends.

VCT shares acquired without tax relief, eg on the stock market, are also CGT-free provided the total investment did not exceed £200,000 in a tax year. VCT shares, as listed securities, do not qualify for any IHT relief.

10 Stamp duty and SDRT

The scope of stamp duty is now limited to transactions in shares and securities. Transfers of goodwill, debts and other property are now exempt from stamp duty. Stamp duty is a charge on documents or instruments rather than the transactions themselves. Although there is no territorial limit to stamp duty, in practice instruments are chargeable if they are executed in the UK.

A sale of stock or marketable securities in the electronic share transfer system CREST is liable to SDRT at 0.5% of the consideration. Paper transactions are subject to 0.5% stamp duty. It was originally proposed that stamp duty on share sales would be abolished with the advent of paperless trading, such as share sales in CREST, but, perhaps because of the high revenue yield from stamp duty, the government overcame the problem of the lack of documents in CREST by extending SDRT instead. The majority of dealings in listed shares in the UK are now subject to SDRT rather than stamp duty and are accounted for by the financial intermediary. Listed share dealings outside CREST and transfers of shares in an unlisted company are subject to stamp duty.

Stamp duty 'franks' any SDRT due on that transaction, so no double charge should arise. Care is needed to ensure that any reliefs are claimed (for example, for intra-group transfers).

Where a company buys its own shares, this is treated as a share sale liable to stamp duty. Some other securities transactions are subject to SDRT. Bearer instruments are liable to stamp duty or SDRT at 1.5%, as are certain transfers into a clearance system.

Reliefs and exemptions

Certain instruments are not liable to stamp duty. They include:

- A transfer by way of a gift during a person's lifetime.
- Vesting of shares following the retirement or appointment of trustees.
- A transfer of shares following settlement in divorce cases.
- A gift on the transfer of land to a residuary legatee under a will.
- A transfer of property out of a trust fund to a beneficiary under the terms of the trust.
- The transfer of shares to a beneficiary under a will.
- Transfers under a deed of family arrangement.
- Transfers of shares within a group of companies and in certain company reorganisations.
- Sales where the consideration does not exceed £1,000.

Payment of stamp duty

The purchaser of shares is responsible for paying stamp duty. Share transfer documents must be sent to the Stamp Office for stamping. Stamps are impressed on the document to show the duty paid.

- A document must be stamped within 30 days of execution.
- Penalties and interest may be charged where a document is presented for stamping late. Any penalty and interest charges are stamped on the document.
- All conveyances and transfers on sale must be presented to the Stamp Office, whether or not they are subject to duty.
- A company cannot register a share transfer unless the relevant document has been stamped or completed to show no stamp duty is payable.
- No stamp duty is payable where the consideration for the share transfer is £1,000 or less.

Stamping of a document by the Stamp Office does not necessarily signify that it has agreed with the duty charged. An instrument must be 'adjudicated' to obtain formal agreement.

- Adjudication is the process whereby the Stamp Office formally assesses the amount of duty, if any, chargeable on an instrument.

- Instruments that have been adjudicated are marked with a special stamp.

If the payer disputes the duty assessed by the Stamp Office, he or she may appeal within 30 days from the date of the date of notice of the Commissioners' decision being given and after paying the duty assessed plus any penalty and interest. The appeal is to the First-tier Tribunal (Tax).

Summary

- Collective investments are advantageous for most investors because they provide professional investment management, reduce risk through a spread of investments and give access to a wide range of asset classes, markets and strategies.

- Most European funds now conform to the UCITS rules, but of UK funds, only OEICs and ETFs can be freely marketed throughout the EU.

- The majority of retail funds are open-ended, but closed-end funds such as investment companies and REITs are more suitable structures where the underlying assets are illiquid.

- Life assurance companies alone can offer with-profit funds with more or less complex bonus structures, though they also offer open-ended funds similar to OEICs.

- Pension funds fall into three main categories – defined benefit, defined contribution and personal pension – and all benefit from tax concessions and incentives.

- Individual Savings Accounts (ISAs) are a simple tax shelter within which individuals may hold cash, fixed interest investments and shares.

Chapter 13
Active fund choice

The aim of an actively managed fund is to produce a return that is better than a benchmark. A stock selection process is used that identifies the sectors and stocks that are best placed to outperform. A passive investment strategy instead simply aims to replicate the performance of the index which is used as the benchmark.

Advisers may use exclusively active or passive funds to create portfolios, or may combine both in what is termed a 'core-satellite' strategy.

In the following chapters we will look at the differences between active and passive management and some of the more popular investment styles employed by active portfolio managers.

1 Fund categories

There are over 2,000 investment funds available to investors in the UK and a further 8,000 funds that can be accessed through a life assurance policy. Once the range of funds that invest across Europe are included, the choice becomes bewilderingly large.

With such a choice, it is not surprising that industry bodies spend considerable time to allocate funds to different categories to assist investors trying to find suitable funds or wanting to compare the performance of one fund with others.

Three of the main fund classification systems are provided by:

- The Association of British Insurers (ABI) – for life and pension funds.
- The Investment Management Association (IMA) – for UK investment funds.
- The European Fund and Asset Management Association (EFAMA) – for Europe-wide funds.

The main categories of fund correspond with the relevant asset class: cash, bonds, equities and property. In addition, there are multi-manager funds, multi-asset funds, hedge funds and absolute return funds.

2 Money market funds

Money market funds can fulfil a number of roles in investment planning, including:

- A short-term home for cash balances.
- An alternative to bonds and equities.
- Part of the asset allocation strategy.

They can be used as a temporary home for idle cash balances rather than a standard retail bank account. Money market funds can offer higher returns than can be achieved on standard deposits and money market accounts offered by most retail banks.

They also offer a potentially safe haven in times of market falls. When markets have had a long bull market and economic prospects begin to worsen, an investor may want to take profits at the peak of the market cycle and invest the funds raised in the money markets until better investment opportunities arise. The same rationale can be used where the investor does not want to commit new cash at the top of the market cycle. The nature of money market instruments means that they offer an alternative investment that does not give exposure to appreciable market risk.

Within a normal asset allocation, a proportion of funds will be held as cash. Money market funds can therefore be the vehicle for holding such asset allocations.

Money market funds, therefore, have a core role to play in investment planning. It needs to be remembered, however, that they still carry risks. The short-term nature of money market instruments provides some protection, but short-term interest rates fluctuate frequently so these instruments can still be exposed to price volatility.

Money market instruments

The money markets are a major part of the global capital markets.

They are the wholesale or institutional markets for cash and are characterised by the issue, trading and redemption of short-dated negotiable securities, usually with a maturity of up to one year, though three months is more typical.

The minimum investment in a money market instrument can be around £500,000, so direct holdings of these instruments is not generally appropriate for investing a client's cash. Instead they are usually accessed through specialist money market funds.

It is important to recognise that a money market fund is not the same as a cash deposit with a savings institution and carries different risks. Most investors expect the amount invested in a money market fund to remain constant. The money market instruments that they invest in, however, are tradeable instruments and some degree of risk and volatility is therefore inherent in the portfolios of money market funds. This was brought home during the credit crisis when a number of money market funds 'broke the buck': the value of the assets held in the underlying portfolio fell below the value needed to repay investors exactly what they had invested. This happened because money market funds invest in instruments such as commercial paper and asset-backed securities which were hit badly during the credit crisis and the collapse of Lehman Brothers.

An understanding of the structure of the money markets and the instruments that are traded is therefore needed, as advisers will need to be able to assess the risk characteristics of a money market fund to establish if it is suitable for a client's risk profile.

Money market instruments are investments with a lifespan of one year or less that can be sold at very short notice, usually within a day. They are issued by governments and companies, all of which have high creditworthiness. The investors are mainly banks, shuffling reserves around the world and speculating on the direction of interest and exchange rates, so there are high levels of trading.

The short maturity date of money market instruments and the high issuer quality means that they carry low investment risk and as a result they usually offer very low returns. The returns will differ according to the level of creditworthiness of the issuer, with treasury bills at the bottom of the risk/reward curve and one-year commercial paper at the top.

The main types of money market instruments are:

- Cash instruments such as deposits and repos.
- Treasury bills.
- Banker's acceptances.
- Certificates of deposit.
- Commercial paper.

Cash deposits and repos will carry the lowest level of risk because of their inherent nature.

Cash deposits, or money market deposits, are deposits with fixed terms of up to one year with banks and securities houses. They are also known as 'time deposits'. They are not negotiable and so cannot be liquidated before maturity. The interest rate offered will be fixed by reference to the London interbank offered rate (LIBOR) for the same term.

A repo is a transaction where one party borrows cash from another party for a year or less and provides securities as collateral. The collateral provided as security will often be short-term government bonds.

Treasury bills are the largest part of the market. They are issued regularly by central governments and carry a lower yield than the other types of instruments because they carry government backing and so have the lowest default risk. Governments are generally assumed to have a very low risk of defaulting.

Bankers' acceptances are issued as part of a business transaction and payment is guaranteed by both the company and the bank that accepts the risk of providing the guarantee. The acceptance is negotiable and can be sold in the secondary market. The bank will impose charges for the service based on the rate it considers it can sell the acceptance for in the secondary market. The investor who buys the acceptance can collect the loan on the maturity date and in the event of default the bank has ultimate responsibility to repay the loan to its new holder.

Certificates of deposit (CDs) generally trade a few basis points higher than acceptances, with the yield depending upon the credit rating of the issuer. They are receipts from banks for deposits that have been placed with them. The deposits themselves carry a fixed rate of interest usually related to LIBOR and have a fixed term to maturity and so cannot be withdrawn before maturity. The certificates, however, can be traded in the money markets and so are similar to a negotiable money market deposit. The yields on CDs are slightly less than the equivalent money market deposit rate because of the added benefit from being able to trade the CD and so access the capital. Most CDs are issued with maturities of one to three months and interest is paid on maturity. Banks and building societies issue CDs to raise funds to finance their business activities and the yield will depend upon market rates and the credit quality of the issuing bank.

Loans made to companies by banks that are then tradeable are 'commercial paper', which is classified as prime grade or medium grade. Commercial paper will generally trade at a few basis points over CDs, with medium grade commercial paper offering the highest yields to attract investors.

The return on these different types of money market instrument differs and this spread of returns reflects the differing levels of risk attached to each type of instrument.

Types of money market fund

A range of money market funds is available, with many domiciled in Dublin. They can offer some advantages over pure money market accounts. There is the obvious advantage that the pooling of funds with other investors gives investors access to assets they would not otherwise be able to invest in. The returns on money market funds should also be greater than those from a simple money market account offered by a bank.

In the light of 2008's market events, when some funds 'broke the buck', the European Securities and Markets Authority (ESMA) issued guidelines for a common definition of European money market funds. The guidelines set out a two-tiered approach for a definition of European money market funds:

- Short-Term Money Market Funds.
- Money Market Funds.

This distinction recognises the credit risks inherent in the underlying portfolio of a money market fund.

Short-term money market funds must have maintenance of the principal value of the fund as their primary objective and aim to provide a return in line with money market rates. In order to protect capital they can only invest in highly rated securities and must have a weighted average life of no more than 120 days. This is a measure of the average length of time to maturity of all of the underlying securities in the fund and is used to measure the credit risk, as the longer the reimbursement of principal is postponed, the higher is the credit risk. It is also used to limit liquidity risk.

A money market fund, however, must have a fluctuating NAV. In order to protect capital they also must only invest in highly rated securities but can have a portfolio of securities with a longer weighted average life of up to 12 months.

The EFAMA fund classification statistics show over 220 funds from 15 different fund management groups. It is essential therefore to understand the investment strategy and range of instruments held by a money market fund to be able to determine whether the fund is suitable for a specific client. To assess whether a money market fund is suitable, advisers should consider:

- The relative rate of return compared to a money market account or other cash deposit.
- The charges that will be incurred and their effect on returns.
- Speed of access to the funds on withdrawal.
- The underlying assets that comprise the money market fund.
- How the creditworthiness of the underlying assets is assessed.
- The rate of return compared to other money market funds and how that is being generated.
- The experience of the fund management team.
- Any explicit commitments in the fund's prospectus.

3 Bond funds

As bonds have a predictable stream of interest payments and the security of repayment of principal, they can play a large role in the construction of a portfolio to meet the needs of an investor, whether that is providing a secure home for their funds, generating a dependable level of income or providing funds for a known future expense or liability. Their main advantages of bonds are:

- For fixed-interest bonds, a regular and certain flow of income.
- For most bonds, a fixed maturity date.
- A range of income yields to suit different investment and tax situations.

Their main disadvantages of bonds are:

- The erosion of the 'real' value of the income flow by the effects of inflation, except in the case of index-linked bonds.
- Default risk, namely that the issuer will not repay the capital at the maturity date.

Exposure to bonds can be achieved by using a unit trust or open-ended investment company (OEIC) that specialises in investing in bonds. These offer investors a way to invest in the bond markets, diversify risk by investing across a broad range of securities and access professional selection and management of a portfolio.

Advantages and disadvantages of bond funds

A wide range of bond funds is available. Their advantages include:

- **Diversification.** Bond funds will normally hold a range of individual bonds of varying maturities, so the impact of any single bond's performance is lessened if that issuer should fail to pay interest or principal. Since loss of capital in bonds is, unlike equity losses, generally irreversible, avoidance of capital loss is more important in managing bonds than equities.
- **Professional management.** As with other mutual funds, bond funds provide access to professional portfolio managers who are able to analyse individual bonds to determine what to buy and sell and how to achieve sector allocation and yield curve positioning. Certain types of bond funds are also diversified across different bond sectors.
- **Liquidity**. As with other collective investment funds, daily trading allows bond fund holdings to be bought and sold.
- **Income.** Most bond funds pay regular distributions, either half-yearly or monthly, and therefore can provide an investor with a regular income.

Despite these advantages, there are certain factors that need to be borne in mind:

- The investor is buying the shares of a fund which is being actively managed, with bonds being added to and eliminated from the portfolio in response to market conditions and investor demand. As a result, bond funds obviously do not have a specified maturity date and so are less useful where a certain sum is needed at a future date to meet an expected liability. Moreover, whereas an investor who buys a bond will receive a definite amount of income, the income from a bond fund can vary as a result of changes in its portfolio.

- Although bond funds will enable an investor to readily achieve diversification, they are still exposed to credit risk, inflation risk and interest rate risk. The market value of bonds fluctuates daily and so, therefore, will a bond fund's net asset value, meaning that the value of an investor's holding will fluctuate and the price obtained on sale could be higher or lower depending upon how the market and the fund have performed since the shares were bought.

- There is a cost to achieving diversification and professional management. Most funds charge annual management fees averaging 1%, while some also impose initial charges of up to 5% or exit fees for selling shares. The annual management fees charged by the fund will lower returns and so it is important to be aware of the total costs when calculating the overall expected returns.

Bond fund classifications

Bond funds have different investment objectives and use different strategies, so are categorised by the IMA into six sectors to reflect this. These distinctions are often reflected in the title of a fund, so it is important to understand the different classifications.

- UK Gilt Funds – invest a least 95% in sterling denominated triple AAA rated government backed securities, with at least 80% invested in UK Gilts.

- UK Index-Linked Gilt Funds – invest at least 95% of their assets in sterling denominated triple AAA rated government backed index linked securities, with at least 80% invested in UK Index Linked Gilts.

- £ Corporate Bond Funds – invest at least 80% of their assets in sterling denominated BBB minus or above corporate bond securities.

- Strategic Bond Funds – invest at least 80% of their assets in sterling denominated fixed interest securities including convertibles, preference shares and permanent interest bearing shares. These funds can invest across the sterling fixed interest sector, so at any point in time the asset allocation of these funds could, in theory, place the fund in one of the other fixed interest sectors.

- £ High Yield Funds – invest at least 80% of their assets in sterling denominated fixed interest securities including convertibles, preference shares and permanent interest bearing shares. At least 50% of their assets are in below BBB minus fixed interest securities.

- Global Bond Funds — invest at least 80% of their assets in fixed interest securities.

Where the classifications require a percentage to be held in sterling denominated securities, the fund can also hold non-UK securities, provided the currency risk is hedged back into sterling.

Assessing bond funds

Some key factors that should be considered in selecting bond funds include:

- **Investment objectives.** Although bond funds may have similar objectives, such as achieving a high income or preservation of capital, there will be differences in how they go about achieving this. Some may limit their investments to government stocks while others may invest in different bond sectors including government, corporate and asset-backed bonds.

- **Average maturity.** A fund will hold a range of bonds with different maturities and will calculate a weighted average maturity. The longer the maturity, the more sensitive the fund will be to changes in interest rates.

- **Duration.** Duration provides an indication of how much a bond's price will fluctuate with changes in comparable interest rates. If rates rise by 1%, for example, a fund with a five-year duration is likely to lose about 5% of its value. Other factors will, however, also influence a bond fund's performance and share price and so actual performance may differ.

- **Credit quality.** The average credit quality of a bond fund will depend on the credit quality of the underlying securities in the portfolio, so that the greater the exposure to non-investment grade stocks the higher the risk.

- **Performance.** The total return the fund has generated over a period of time needs to be investigated and reviewed in conjunction with the yield it generates to see whether higher yields are being achieved through investments in lower quality securities, which may make the share price of the bond fund investment more volatile.

- **Fees and charges.** The individual and total expenses of the fund need to be established in order that the impact on performance can be assessed and comparisons made with comparable funds.

- **Fund managers.** Bond markets have become increasingly complex and it is therefore important to assess the professional expertise of the fund management team.

Bond exchange-traded funds

An alternative to a bond fund is an exchange-traded fund (ETF) that allows an investor to buy an entire basket of stocks through a single security that tracks the returns of a bond index.

Bond ETFs differ from ETFs that track a stock market index. This is because the bond market is an over-the-counter market and can lack liquidity and price transparency. As bonds are often held until maturity there is not often an active secondary market, which makes it difficult to ensure a bond ETF encompasses enough liquid bonds to track an index.

A bond ETF needs to closely track its respective index in a cost-effective manner despite this lack of liquidity. Clearly, this is a bigger issue for corporate bonds than government bonds. The investment firms offering bond ETFs address this problem by using representative sampling, which simply means tracking only a sufficient number of bonds to represent an index.

There is a wide range of bond ETFs available, covering many of the main global bond markets. As constructing a bond index is considerably different from constructing an equity index, care must be taken in selecting an appropriate index.

4 Equity funds

Equity funds represent the majority of unit trusts and OEICs that are available. They are widely used in investment portfolios by both institutional and retail investors. They offer a number of advantages over direct investment in shares:

- Risk is spread and therefore reduced.
- They provide access to professional, expert and full-time investment management expertise.
- They are cost effective.
- They provide access to markets that could not otherwise be achieved.
- They are heavily regulated and supervised, protecting the investor.

Even where an investor has a direct investment portfolio of equities, it is normal for an investment fund to be used to achieve exposure to certain markets or specialist sectors. There are funds available that provide exposure to global stock markets, to economic regions such as Europe, to the market of just one country and to specialist sectors such as health care. The range can be seen from the IMA's categorisation of equity funds into subsectors:

- UK all companies.
- UK smaller companies.

- Japanese companies.

- Japanese smaller companies.

- Asia Pacific including Japan.

- Asia Pacific excluding Japan.

- North America.

- North American smaller companies.

- Europe excluding the UK.

- Europe including the UK.

- European smaller companies.

- Global growth.

- Global emerging markets.

The wide range of opportunities means that a structured approach is needed to identify what type of fund might be suitable for an investor.

When selecting investment funds for the equity element of a portfolio, an investment adviser might well start by ensuring that they hold funds that will give exposure to stock markets around the world. This may be achieved by a global fund, regional funds or even country-specific funds. In each case, the adviser needs to decide between a fund that targets the market as a whole as its benchmark or funds based on capitalisation or style in the attempt to maximise returns. This could involve adding funds that give exposure to mid-cap and small cap stocks or to areas such as ethical investing, ecological funds or emerging markets.

Advisers should also consider whether a portfolio should be constructed of actively managed funds or passive funds. These aspects are dealt with in chapter 14 and chapter 15.

5 Property funds

The increasing popularity of commercial property investment over the last ten years or so has made this mainstream asset class an essential component of many investment portfolios. As yet, there are no mainstream funds investing in UK residential property.

As an asset class, commercial property has been seen to offer a number of advantages, including:

- Attractive absolute returns over recent years.

- Portfolio diversification.

- Relatively low correlation with bonds and equities.

The period of low interest rates enjoyed until recently led to massive growth in the amount invested in this sector. The end of cheap credit in 2007 has, however, caused this trend to go into reverse and property values fell significantly from 2007 to 2009 in many markets.

There are a number of ways in which individuals can invest in property, including:

- Building a portfolio of directly owned properties.

- Investing in listed property companies or real estate investment trusts.

- Investing in property unit trusts and similar vehicles.

The issues involved in building and maintaining a portfolio of directly owned properties is beyond the scope of this book. Instead, we will look at how this can be achieved through property funds.

Types of property fund

A wide range of property funds is available and they are usually classified as follows:

- Core funds.

- Core plus and value-added funds.

- Opportunistic funds.

Core funds are lower risk and lower return funds that are usually open ended and aim to produce returns benchmarked against an established property index. Core plus and value-added funds use higher gearing and a more active management style to generate higher returns. Opportunistic funds will typically be closed ended and will aim to exploit opportunities to acquire property from distressed sellers, redevelopments and property in emerging markets. They are closer in nature to private equity funds. Property funds can also be differentiated as to whether they are:

- Listed or unlisted funds.

- Invested in real property or in property shares.

- Traded on a stock exchange or direct with the managers of the fund.

- Open ended or closed ended.

- Low risk or high risk.

- Available to private investors or institutional investors.

- Structured as companies, partnerships, trusts or contractual agreements.

Property unit trusts

Property unit trusts can either be authorised by a regulator or unauthorised. Authorised funds are designed primarily for retail investors, while unauthorised funds may only be offered to institutional investors. Authorised funds may invest in real property or in property shares or in a combination. Unauthorised funds usually invest only in real property.

Authorised property unit trusts are exempt from capital gains tax on any gains they make but the income arising in the fund is liable to income tax at 20%. They are designed for the domestic UK market and their unfavourable tax treatment means they are unsuitable for institutional and overseas investors.

Instead, offshore property unit trusts offer greater flexibility, as they are tax effective for a greater range of UK and international investors and are less heavily regulated. These products are structured to be tax transparent and so the fund is not liable to income or capital gains tax, any entitlements being taxable on end investors according to their tax position.

Exchange-traded funds

There is a range of ETFs that track the performance of various European and global real estate indices without the manager selection risk or benefit arising from an investment fund. These indices are all based on listed real estate investment trusts, which are considerably more volatile than real property prices.

iShares, the world's largest provider of ETFs, maintains a range of ETFs that track the FTSE/EPRA indices as follows:

- FTSE/EPRA European Property Yield.
- FTSE/EPRA Asia Property Yield.
- FTSE/EPRA US Property Yield.
- FTSE/EPRA Global Property Yield.
- FTSE/EPRA Macquarie Global Infrastructure.

ETFs can therefore provide investors with exposure to property trends on a global and regional basis. They could be used to complement investment in domestic property markets and bring diversification benefits or provide a mechanism to invest in a particular region which is expected to outperform.

Property ETFs are traded on the stock exchange as other ETFs and so offer the benefits of liquidity, and they should trade close to their net asset value.

Real estate investment trusts

Real estate investment trusts (REITs) are well established in the US, Australia, Canada, Japan, Singapore and Hong Kong. The success of the REIT model in

Japan has led many Asian countries to adopt the same legislative framework, while in Europe the success of the French REIT model has seen similar legislation passed in the UK and Germany.

In simple terms, a REIT is a company that owns and operates income-producing real estate, which can be either commercial or residential. REITs differ from a quoted company that holds a portfolio of property in that the company is not liable to tax on any income or gains made on the property portfolio and instead distributes this as income, with any tax liability falling on the shareholder. This avoids the problem of double taxation, with the company paying tax and then the shareholder also paying tax on any dividends received.

REITs are traded on the stock exchange in the same way as any other shares. This means they are liquid and so easy to buy and sell and readily realised. The price they will trade at will be determined by demand and supply, so they may trade at a premium or discount to the net asset value of the underlying property portfolio.

Limited partnerships

Limited partnerships have been an attractive way of establishing unlisted property vehicles. They are complex structures that are established with a general partner who will be the lead investor and who must have unlimited liability. There can be an unlimited number of partners whose liability is limited.

Some of the key features of limited partnerships are as follows:

- The investment vehicle is tax transparent so any gains or income are taxed on the partners.
- They are usually established for a predetermined number of years, at the end of which the assets are disposed of and the proceeds distributed, unless the partners vote to extend the life of the vehicle.
- The general partner will appoint an operator to oversee the administrative functions.
- Limited partners cannot be involved in decision making, otherwise they will lose their limited liability status.

Jersey and Guernsey are the home for many limited-partnership property funds.

Investing in property funds

The illiquid nature of property makes investment through property funds a practical proposition for investors. Some of the factors an adviser should consider when investing in property funds are:

- Asset price bubbles.
- The relative liquidity of listed vehicles versus investment funds.

- Permitted levels of gearing.
- Redemption charges and notice periods.

Like other asset classes, property is cyclical and vulnerable to asset price bubbles, as has been seen recently in the UK. Property had enjoyed rising prices with no significant falls for around ten years up to 2007 and many investors came to believe that property was a one-way bet which could only go on rising. The recent falls in the property market have reinforced the point that property prices can fall as well as rise.

Funds listed on a stock exchange can be traded easily on a daily basis, and although the pricing is linked to the net asset value of the underlying property portfolio, prices can trade away from this value. By contrast, funds investing in real property will trade at the net asset value but cannot necessarily be traded daily as many funds have monthly or quarterly valuation points.

Listed property funds can have levels of gearing that vary from 0% to 90%, with many funds limited to between 50% and 70%. Gearing can enhance returns but brings risk with it. In considering a property fund an adviser should be aware of the type of fund it is and its gearing, and assess the risk-reward profile against the investor's risk tolerance.

Advisers should be aware of the frequency at which investment funds can be redeemed with the managers, but should also investigate whether the fund manager can impose redemption penalties or notice periods. The fall in property values saw a number of property funds that invested mainly in real property impose redemption penalties to deter investors from realising their investment and forcing the property fund to sell at distressed prices. Others imposed notice periods of 12 months, effectively locking investors into the funds.

6 Funds of funds

Funds of funds (FoFs) are collective investment schemes that invest in other funds.

Instead of employing a professional investment manager to manage a portfolio of securities against an investment mandate, the FoF instead uses skills to assemble a portfolio of funds managed by other fund managers. The performance of these sub-funds will then be monitored, together with the performance of the market as a whole, and component funds changed as necessary in response. In this way, the dilemma is removed that many investors face of which type of fund to invest in and which fund group to buy from. The FoF approach can also allow investors who have only small amounts to invest to access more funds than they might be able to afford on their own.

A FoF will invest in a range of other funds. Sometimes these will be from the same fund management group, sometimes from external firms and often from a mixture of the two. In the retail market, FoFs are often today described as multi-manager funds; however, in institutional markets, a multi-manager fund is one where instead of choosing particular funds, the fund manager chooses individual managers working for different fund management firms, who are each given a part of the portfolio to manage.

The advantages of FoFs include:

- There can be less risk compared to investing in just one or two funds as the FoF will hold a portfolio that is diversified both geographically and among different asset classes.

- The FoF managers will employ screening to eliminate poorer performing funds and those which are closet trackers to identify the funds they consider will perform best.

- The adviser does not need to monitor so many funds.

- FoF managers can make changes in their portfolios more quickly than advisers operating advisory services, who need to obtain client consent for each transaction.

These potential benefits come at a cost. The FoF structure creates a double layer of costs. First, there are the expenses associated with running the FoF itself; management fees, administrative costs and so on. Then there are the management fees and costs associated with the underlying funds. The net result is that total expense ratios for FoFs are usually between 0.75% and 1.5% higher than those of other funds.

In recent years some advisers have created fund structures that enable them to play a part in the investment management of the fund, either through asset allocation or fund selection or both. The regulators describe such funds as Distributor Influenced Funds, and have warned of possible conflicts of interest that could lead to client detriment. The conflict of interest arises because the adviser usually benefits from a share of the fund's annual management charges. Advisers using these funds need to ensure that their recommendations conform to the regulator's suitability guidance (see chapter 18).

7 Hedge funds

Hedge funds are mostly based in offshore tax havens, are largely unregulated and are able to undertake a wider range of deals than would be allowed for a regulated product. As a result, hedge funds have a higher level of risk than traditional assets, but they also have the potential for higher returns. It has been claimed that their performance is largely uncorrelated to other asset classes but recent research has cast doubt on this.

Hedge funds typically make use of gearing (or leverage) to enhance returns and they may also use more sophisticated investment strategies employing derivatives. While onshore UCITS III funds may also use derivatives, they are not permitted to use them to increase leverage, while hedge funds have no such restraints. They are generally used by wealthy individuals or entities such as pension funds or insurance companies. A hedge fund can be a single fund or a fund that invests in other hedge funds — a fund of hedge funds.

Hedge funds are reputed to be high risk. However, this is not true of all hedge funds. In their original form, hedge funds sought to eliminate or reduce market risk and employed 'absolute return' strategies (see below). That said, there are now many different styles of hedge fund — some risk-averse, and some employing highly risky strategies.

The most obvious market risk is the risk that is faced by an investor in shares: as the broad market moves down, the investor's shares also fall in value. Traditional 'absolute return' hedge funds attempt to profit regardless of the general movements of the market by carefully selecting a combination of asset classes, including derivatives, and by holding both long and short positions. A 'short' position may involve the selling of shares which the investor does not at that time own in the hope of buying them back more cheaply if the market falls. Alternatively, it may involve the use of derivatives, as we have already seen. However, innovation has resulted in a wide range of complex hedge fund strategies, some of which place a greater emphasis on producing highly geared returns than controlling market risk.

The types of strategy deployed by hedge funds differ widely and there is no single method of classifying them.

Hedge fund features

The common features of hedge funds are as follows:

- **Structure.** Most hedge funds are established as unauthorised and, therefore, unregulated, collective investment schemes. This means they cannot be generally marketed to private individuals because they are considered too risky for the less financially sophisticated investor.

- **High investment entry levels.** Most hedge funds require minimum investments in excess of £50,000 and some exceed £1m.

- **Investment flexibility.** Because of the lack of regulation, hedge funds are able to invest in whatever assets they wish (subject to the restrictions in their constitutional documents and prospectus). In addition to being able to take long and short positions in securities like shares and bonds, some take positions in commodities and currencies. Their investment style is generally aimed at producing 'absolute' returns — positive returns regardless of the general direction of market movements.

- **Gearing.** Many hedge funds can borrow funds and use derivatives to potentially enhance their returns.

- **Liquidity.** To maximise the hedge fund manager's investment freedom, hedge funds usually impose an initial 'lock in' period of between one and three months before investors can sell their investments on.

- **Cost.** Hedge funds typically levy performance-related fees which the investor pays if certain performance levels are achieved, otherwise paying a fee comparable to that charged by other growth funds. Performance fees can be substantial, with 20% or more of the 'net new highs' being common.

Hedge fund strategies

One of the characteristics of the hedge fund industry is the diversity of strategies, all of which have quite different risk-return profiles. In Figure 13.1 the ranking of the key strategies is summarised on a risk basis. Here we are measuring risk as standard deviation of returns measured over the long term. In the short term the ranking is constantly changing; in the recent financial crisis convertible arbitrage, which was previously perceived as a low volatility strategy, saw the largest falls in value.

The chart categorises strategies as directional or non-directional. A directional strategy is one where the manager is taking a view on market (or currency or commodity price) direction, and can also be taking a view on individual security prices. In a non-directional strategy the manager is not deliberately taking a view on market direction but is looking for mispricing of securities within markets. Directional strategies tend to be riskier because they are picking up market risk; they have betas that are not zero. Non-directional strategies seek to achieve returns from alpha rather than beta exposure; they will be lower risk (most of the time) since they are avoiding or hedging out market risk.

Non-directional strategies

We will now examine some of these non-directional strategies in more detail and look at how they generate alpha and manage risk.

Within the non-directional category we can identify two types of strategy:

- Event driven strategies (or those driven by special situations)
- Relative value strategies.

Event driven strategies

Event-driven strategies include merger arbitrage and distressed-securities funds where the key features of these are as follows:

- **Merger arbitrage funds** typically invest in corporate restructurings, including acquisitions, often establishing a long position in a target

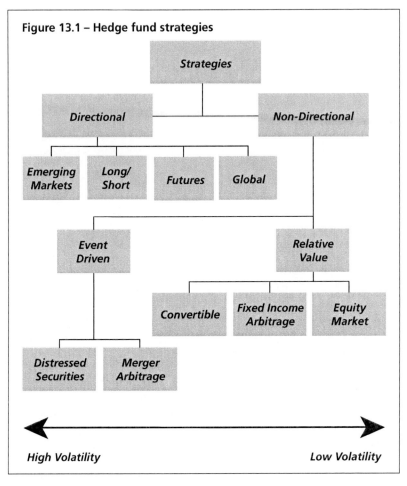

Figure 13.1 – Hedge fund strategies

company and a short position in the acquirer, so their net exposure to the combined company (and market) is close to zero. They are taking a view on the probability of an acquisition being successful, so a major risk is deal risk — the risk that the transaction falls through. The outcome is not directly linked to the performance of the market but these funds tend to do well towards the end of a bull market in equities when there is a lot of merger and acquisition activity. The funds have moderate correlation with global equity markets.

- **Distressed securities funds** invest in companies which are near bankrupt or already in administration. Investment is frequently in debt securities which are bought at deeply discounted prices. These can be longer-term investments and the manager gets involved in the reorganisation. There is an opportunity to generate alpha since many distressed securities are available below their fair value. Traditional investors don't want to hold securities in a company going bankrupt and will often sell at 'any price' because of the following factors:

— They want to get the holdings out of the portfolios. Clients are usually uncomfortable with managers who have invested in companies that have gone bankrupt.

— Distressed securities are usually illiquid.

— They are high risk and may not be permitted holdings in certain funds.

— They require time to analyse because sell-side analysts give them less attention. Analysing distressed companies requires different skills to analysing higher quality investments.

Relative value strategies

Relative value strategies are those which look for mispricing between securities or sectors within a market. These are essentially seeking to generate all the returns from alpha exposure with no beta exposure. But hedging out beta risk can never be perfect, so there is usually some residual beta exposure. Here we look at three of these strategies and how they manage risk:

- **Convertible arbitrage.** These funds were the worst performers in 2008 but among the best in 2009. The fund managers look for mispricing of convertible bonds and convertible preferred shares. A convertible bond is equivalent to a straight bond and a call option on the underlying equity, so mispricing is identified using option pricing models. A typical trade would be to take a long position in a convertible bond (if it was undervalued) and a short position in the related equity in order to hedge out the equity exposure (a delta hedge). But this still leaves several risks:

  — **Interest rate risk.** To make this a non-directional strategy, the duration of the convertible bond could be hedged using interest rate derivatives.

  — **Credit risk.** If the bond is downgraded or a downgrade is anticipated this will hit the value of the long position in the convertible bond but might not affect the price of the shares. Similarly, if credit spreads widened then the convertible bond could lose value while the equity was unaffected, leading to a loss on the arbitrage position. If the bond actually defaulted then the outcome would be uncertain: in the case of bankruptcy, bond holders are more likely to get repaid than equity holders, but if the number of shares shorted was small the profit on the short equity position might not be sufficient to cover a loss on the convertible bonds.

- **Volatility risk.** The embedded option price would be affected by a change in the volatility of the shares. If volatility fell, the option price, other things being equal, would also decline.

- **Financing risk.** Most arbitrage strategies are leveraged, so managers are dependent on financing their position until the convertibles move to fair value. Unfortunately, in any market and certainly in extreme conditions undervalued assets can get cheaper still, and if the cost and availability of financing deteriorates, managers could be forced to liquidate positions at a loss. This was the situation in 2008 and it was compounded by the fact that hedge funds dominated the convertible bond market so managers were competing to sell.

- **Model risk.** This is the risk that the valuation of the convertibles is incorrect, or the hedging techniques fail.

Even though convertible arbitrage strategies would appear to be low-risk alpha-generating strategies it is clear that many risks are being taken. Hedging out all risks is costly and could wipe out a profit from the arbitrage trades.

- **Fixed-income arbitrage.** These strategies are looking for mispricing within fixed-income markets and their derivatives. They take long and short positions in related securities or sectors and hedge out interest rate risk. These arbitrage strategies are still exposed to other risks in order to generate alpha:

  - **Leverage and financing risk.** Fixed-income arbitrage generally produces small profit margins and these are multiplied using leverage. As with convertible arbitrage strategies, leverage can multiply losses as well as profits and involves financing risk – the risk that financing dries up and the manager has to liquidate positions at a loss.

  - **Credit risk.** Many arbitrage strategies are based on exploiting a credit anomaly, or the mispricing of credit risk. For example, a fund takes long positions in corporate bonds and hedges out the credit risk with the purchase of a credit default swap. Such strategies are vulnerable to a change in the pricing of credit risk in the corporate bond or swap market that leaves the arbitrage invalid. With the widening of credit spreads many of the earlier credit arbitrage strategies (for example, to take a long position in low grade bonds, and short positions in high grade bonds) failed.

  - **Model risk.** Fixed-income strategies are usually dependent on sophisticated analytical models. The risk is that these models fail, often because they are based on historic data and market behaviour changes.

- **Equity market-neutral strategies.** These are based on identifying stocks with positive and negative alpha and then buying the stocks with positive alpha and shorting the stocks with negative alpha. Such strategies can be based on fundamental analysis, managers purchasing securities they believe to be undervalued and selling short ones believe to be overvalued (a relative value strategy), or they can use statistical or quantitative models. There are still risks involved:

- **Market risk.** Since this is a market-neutral strategy the manager would normally take equal long and short positions, and aim to have a beta of zero. But hedges will never be 100% accurate as security betas are unstable, leaving the funds with some residual market exposure.

- **Specific risk.** The strategy is based on identifying securities that are mispriced, so in order to generate alpha the managers are taking on stock-specific risk.

- **Model risk.** Funds that have depended on using models have frequently failed to deliver when there were rapid changes in direction in sector or market performance. Momentum-led strategies had a good long-term record but failed to perform in the 2007 market turmoil. Most models are built on similar assumptions using the same historic data, so the situation is compounded by managers trying to buy or sell the same sectors or stocks at the same time.

8 130/30 products

Over recent years 130/30 products have been heavily marketed, as well as 120/20 products and other variants. These are typically equity strategies that involve shorting shares which are overvalued or expected to fall in price and taking long positions in shares that are undervalued or expected to rise in price. The fund manager may employ fundamental analysis (researching a company, making financial forecasts and valuing its shares) or rely on statistical or quantitative methods.

In a 130/30 strategy managers will short up to 30% of the portfolio value and take long positions of up to 130% of the portfolio value. So, for example, if managers raise £100m from investors, they could sell short £30m of shares, giving them £30m proceeds which they can use to buy a total of £130m of shares.

The beta of the combined portfolio will probably be close to one (130% long positions less 30% in short positions) so the market risk will not be dissimilar to that of an index fund or active fund that stays close to the index. However, there is more opportunity to add alpha because:

- The gross investment exposure is 160% or 1.6 times the portfolio value, so the managers have exposure to more stock-specific risk and can potentially earn a significantly higher alpha than if constrained to making a smaller number of bets.

- The managers can take short positions and therefore generate alpha by identifying stocks that will underperform the market on a risk-adjusted basis. They have twice as much opportunity as traditional long-only managers, who can only take advantage of positive alpha.

But there are some drawbacks:

- Short positions are risky. If managers make the wrong judgment and short a stock that rises in value there is an unlimited potential loss (for example, if they shorted Volkswagen shares before the price quadrupled, they faced a loss when buying back the shares of three times the initial amount they shorted). With a long position the most you can lose is the amount invested.

- Although the potential to generate alpha is higher than for a traditional fund, generating alpha consistently is extremely difficult. So managers, once they are given more flexibility, can potentially destroy more value when they make the wrong decisions.

- Managers who have established a reputation as long-only managers may have difficulty applying their skill to make short-selling decisions. Empirically managers add more value from their buy decisions than they do from their sell decisions.

It is worth noting that managers usually collect their management fees on the gross assets of the fund.

9 Absolute return funds

Absolute return funds are onshore UCITS III open-ended funds that aim to deliver a positive return for investors regardless of market conditions. This is an attractive proposition for investors. As a result, absolute return funds are currently being launched at the rate of one a month and there are indications that this trend will continue for some time.

The IMA created an absolute return fund sector in 2008 to house these funds. It should be noted, however, that not all of absolute return funds launched to date have chosen to be listed in this sector. Each of these funds is different and invests in different areas with different targets. When selecting such funds for a particular client it is important to select one that targets an area or investment strategy that is appropriate for them.

Absolute return funds use the wider investment powers under UCITS III, which permit retail investment funds to use financial derivatives. The UCITS regulations require these funds to operate within constraints designed to protect investors. These funds are designed to bring the benefits of hedge funds to the retail investment area. Unlike traditional funds, they are designed to produce positive returns in both rising and falling markets and the funds can take both short and long positions, allowing them to benefit from share price falls as well as rises.

Many funds use 'long-short' strategies, seeking to deliver absolute returns by deploying different tactics at different stages of the economic cycle:

- As an economy starts to turn down, they can use their ability to take short positions to take advantage of a bear market.

- At the end of this stage of the economic cycle, as the market starts to recover, their approach will become similar to traditional long only funds.

- As economic growth picks up and a bull market begins, they will move to an overall long only position and could underperform traditional funds while the managers adjust the portfolio to suit new market conditions.

- In the middle of a bull market, the long only strategy should see them deliver performance that is more in line with long only equity funds.

- As the economy and market start to turn down again, fund performance might once again taper off as the market begins to move into a new cycle before they can deploy their ability to take short positions and start the cycle again.

Funds using long-short strategies are highly dependent on their managers' skills since deciding which stocks to short is even more challenging than deciding which to buy.

Other absolute return funds use 'macro' strategies driven by top-down economic analysis. When the managers identify a trend they expect to continue for some time, they seek to implement as many different ways of exploiting it as possible. For example, an expected rise in the rate of inflation could lead to buying gold, selling conventional bonds and buying index-linked bonds.

Given their different strategies, it is to be expected that the performance of absolute return equity funds will vary over time and this emphasises the importance of taking a long-term approach.

Absolute return funds also differ in other important aspects. One notable difference is that some managers charge a performance fee in addition to the annual management charge, subject to achieving a specified level of performance. Performance fees are typically 15% to 20%, based on a percentage of the growth above a hurdle rate or performance target, which is often undemanding.

Absolute return funds usually express their targeted rate of return as an average annual rate 'over a rolling three-year period'. This in effect means a period of three years to any given end date. It is important to realise that actual returns can be well above or well below the target rate for periods of many months.

Finally, it is important to remember that many regulated absolute return funds have only been in existence since the launch of the absolute return sector in 2008 and so it will take time to see how they perform in markets at different stages of the economic cycle.

10 Multi-asset funds

Multi-asset funds take the concept of multi-manager funds and extend this to incorporate a greater range of investment strategies and a greater range of assets such as commodities, private equity and forestry. The portfolio is invested in assets which tend to have different performance characteristics, which increases the diversification of the fund so that the investor is not exposed to the market gains and losses of a single asset class.

This approach recognises that asset classes tend to perform in a different way over different time periods. By combining several types of assets in one fund, multi-asset managers seek to reduce volatility by offsetting the falls of one asset class with the gains of another.

Fund management groups have designed these funds to take advantage of the wider investment powers available under UCITS III. They are also designed to appeal to investors who appreciate the multi-asset, risk-spreading exposure they funds can provide, particularly in the current investment climate. However, most multi-asset funds still end up with the bulk of their capital in the major asset classes of bonds, property and equities.

Summary

- There are about 10,000 UK funds of various types, most of which fall into four main categories: money market, fixed interest, property and equity, each of which in turn has several subdivisions.

- Risk-profiled (eg Cautious Managed), multi-asset, Fund-of-Fund, Hedge and Absolute Return funds invest in multiple asset classes.

- The UCITS3 rules permit funds to use derivatives to take short positions, so 'long-short' and other hedge funds strategies are now permissible for UK authorised funds.

- With the exception of investment companies and ETFs, authorised funds are not permitted to employ leverage.

Chapter 14
Active investment styles

When a fund management group decides to launch a new fund, it will aim to design one around a theme or trend that it thinks will be popular with the investing public. However, whether it is a bond fund or an absolute return fund, how the fund is managed will be determined by the fund manager or fund management team responsible for its investment management.

The investment style that is adopted may make a material difference to the eventual performance and may be critical in assessing the suitability of a fund for a client. With equity funds, the common management styles are 'top down' and 'bottom up'. These two styles are considered below. Active portfolio management, whether top down or bottom up, employs one of a number of more distinctive investment styles when attempting to outperform a predetermined benchmark. Some of these are also considered below.

1 Top-down investment management

Top-down active investment management involves three stages:

- Asset allocation.
- Sector selection.
- Stock selection.

Asset allocation

Asset allocation is the result of top-down fund managers considering the big picture first, by assessing the prospects for each of the main asset classes within each of the world's major investment regions against the backdrop of the world economic, political and social environment. Within fund management organisations, this process is usually carried out on a monthly basis by an asset allocation committee. The committee draws upon forecasts of risk and return for each asset class and correlations between these returns. It is at this stage of the top-down process that quantitative econometric models are often used, in conjunction with more conventional fundamental analysis, to assist in determining which geographical areas and asset classes are most likely to produce the most attractive risk-adjusted returns, taking full account of the client's mandate.

Most asset allocation decisions, whether for institutional or retail portfolios, are made with reference to the peer group median asset allocation. The manager's decision is to be 'over' or 'under' weight in an asset class in relation to this median. This is known as 'asset allocation by consensus' and is undertaken to minimise the risk of underperforming the peer group.

When deciding if and to what extent certain markets and asset classes should be over- or underweighted, most portfolio managers set tracking error parameters, or standard deviation of return parameters, against peer group median asset allocations, such as the CAPS median asset allocation in the case of institutional mandates. This limits the extent of the market or sector 'bets' that may be taken and in theory also limits the maximum volatility of the fund.

Finally, the decision whether to hedge market and/or currency risks must be taken.

Sector selection

Once they have decided on their asset allocation, top-down managers then consider the prospects for those sectors within their favoured equity markets. Sector selection decisions in equity markets are usually made with reference to the weighting each sector assumes within the index against which the performance in that market is to be assessed.

Given the strong interrelationship between economics and investment, the sector selection process is heavily influenced by economic factors, notably where in the economic cycle the economy is currently positioned. This assumes, however, that the portfolio manager knows exactly where in the economic cycle the economy is positioned and the extent to which each market sector is operationally geared to the cycle. Moreover, the assumed timescale of the cycle does not provide any latitude for unanticipated events that may, through a change in the risk appetite of investors, spark a sudden flight from equities to government bond markets, for example, or change the course that the economic cycle takes.

Stock selection

The final stage of the top-down process is deciding upon which stocks should be selected within the favoured sectors. A combination of fundamental and technical analysis will typically be used in arriving at the final decision.

In order to outperform a predetermined benchmark, usually a market index, the active portfolio manager must be prepared to assume an element of tracking error, more commonly known as 'active risk', relative to the benchmark index to be outperformed. Active risk arises from holding securities in the actively managed portfolio in differing proportions to that in which they are weighted within the benchmark index. The higher the level of active risk, the greater the chance of outperformance, though the probability of underperformance is also increased. Top-down active management, as its name suggests, is an ongoing and dynamic process. As economic, political and social factors change so do asset allocation, sector and stock selection.

2 Bottom-up investment management

A bottom-up approach to active management is one that focuses solely on the unique attractions of individual stocks.

Although the health and prospects for the world economy and markets in general are taken into account, these are secondary to factors such as whether a particular company is a possible takeover target or is about to launch an innovative product. A true bottom-up investment fund is characterised by significant tracking error as a result of assuming considerable active risk.

3 Value investing

Value investing is an investment strategy that seeks to identify stocks that are trading at less than their intrinsic value.

Managers who adopt a value-investing strategy actively search for the shares of companies that they believe the market has undervalued. Behind the concept is the belief that markets overreact to good and bad news and this results in share price movements that do not correspond with the long-term fundamentals of the company. These share price movements can provide an opportunity for value funds to buy when the price is deflated and sell when the market correction takes place.

Value funds look to identify shares that have lower than average price/earnings ratios or price to book ratios or high dividend yields. This requires an assessment of what constitutes intrinsic value by undertaking fundamental analysis of the company's published results and estimates of future growth. Essentially, value investing seeks to identify companies that are undervalued and by a sufficient amount to allow some room for error in any estimates of intrinsic value.

Value-investing strategies are based on the work of Benjamin Graham and David Dodd, who were professors at Columbia Business School and published their approach in the text *Security Analysis*. Graham later published *The Intelligent Investor*, which advocated the concept of a margin of safety. This calls for a cautious approach to investing by picking stocks that are trading below their tangible book value as a safeguard against future adverse developments in the stock market.

At the centre of a value-investing strategy is a comparison of the current market value of a company with its intrinsic value. Establishing the current market value is usually straightforward and simply involves multiplying the number of ordinary shares in issue by the current price of each share to arrive at the company's market capitalisation. In doing this, however, attention may also need to be paid to the potential dilution effect of the conversion of convertible stocks or preference shares.

The more difficult issue is to establish what the value of a company should be. Initially, Graham based his stock selection on an analysis of the relationship between a company's net current assets and its share price. His strategy was to buy shares at a price that represented no more than two-thirds of a company's net current assets and then to sell them later once the price had risen and they were no longer undervalued. With the widespread use of value-investing strategies, it is almost impossible to find shares that meet these strict criteria and so value investing has moved on to look at other valuation techniques based on asset value, earnings, cash flows and other financial criteria.

Having established the current market value and the intrinsic value of a company, a value fund will buy when it identifies that the current market value is lower. Later on, when the gap between the two closes, the value fund will close out its position and take the profit.

Graham identified a series of tests that are still widely used in value investing. He recommended seven tests to be carried out when stocks are identified for inclusion in a defensive portfolio:

- **Adequate size.** There can be some risk attributable to the size of a company or enterprise as a smaller company is generally subject to wider fluctuations in earnings. Graham recommended setting minimum size parameters that should be met, such as annual sales.

- **Strong financial condition.** A company should have a current ratio of at least two (cash and near-cash should be twice its near-term liabilities) and long-term debt should not exceed working capital in order to provide a strong buffer against the possibility of bankruptcy or default.

- **Earnings stability.** The company should not have reported a loss over the past ten years, because companies that can maintain at least some level of earnings are, on the whole, more stable.

- **Dividend record.** A company should have a history of paying dividends on its shares for at least the past 20 years in order to provide some assurance that future dividends are likely to be paid.

- **Earnings growth.** To help ensure a company's profits keep pace with inflation, net income should have increased by one-third or greater on a per-share basis over the past ten years, using three-year averages at the beginning and end.

- **Moderate price to earnings ratio.** The current price of a share should not exceed 15 times its average earnings for the past three years to act as a safeguard against overpaying for a security.

- **Moderate ratio of price to assets.** The current price should not be more than one and a half times the book value of assets.

One of the most famous proponents of value investing is the American investor Warren Buffet. He learned value-investing strategies under Graham and Dodd and went on to become what many consider to be the most successful investor in history with his company Berkshire Hathaway.

4 Growth investing

Growth investing is a style of investment management that focuses on identifying companies that exhibit potential for above-average growth even if the share price seems expensive when judged against ratios derived from fundamental analysis. A fund that adopts this investment management style will therefore ignore key data such as price/earnings ratios, price to book ratios or high dividend yields that are so important to funds following a value investment strategy.

Unlike value funds, growth funds focus on the future potential of a company, with much less emphasis on its present price. They may buy shares in companies that are trading higher than their intrinsic value in the belief that the companies' intrinsic worth will grow and therefore exceed their current valuations. A growth strategy is therefore exposed to greater risk than a value fund as it is more dependent on judgments about the business, its markets, its management and its ability to extract future earnings growth from the industry it operates in.

To understand this investment management style it is necessary first to understand what constitutes a growth stock. There are two main factors that qualify a company's shares as a growth stock:

- New technology or research in sectors such as computing, pharmaceuticals, biotechnology or communications can enable a company to enjoy a period of exceptional growth until the next development comes along.

- A company is able to establish a dominant position in a sector of industry where barriers to entry are high and so new entrants find it difficult to enter the market and compete effectively.

One of the UK's most famous growth investors is Jim Slater. In his book *The Zulu Principle* he highlighted 11 criteria that a potential growth stock should be judged against and then classified these as mandatory, important or desirable. He considered that to be considered a growth stock, a company should exhibit the following mandatory features:

- A positive growth rate in earnings per share in at least four of the last five years.

- A low price/earnings ratio relative to the growth rate.

- An optimistic chairman's statement in the report and accounts.

- Strong liquidity, low borrowings and high cash flow.
- Competitive advantage.

While growth investing might originally have meant identifying companies that could grow steadily into successful big businesses, such as Glaxo, Intel or Microsoft, it has since moved on. The bursting of the dotcom bubble revealed as a highly risky strategy the idea that price is irrelevant provided there is the potential for growth. If the growth rate fails to live up to projections then the price of a share will plummet.

Growth-investing funds now tend to seek out stocks with high growth rates that are trading at reasonable valuations. There are many variations on this approach of growth at a reasonable price. 'Growth investing' now refers to any investment style that aims to produce capital growth rather than income. So it also includes investing in recovery shares or in special situations. Many specialist funds, such as those investing in natural resources, technology or infrastructure, are simply specialised growth funds.

5 Blend funds

Although Warren Buffet is regarded as one of the most famous proponents of value investing, he believes that there is little theoretical difference between the two strategies. He is famously quoted as saying "Growth Investing and Value Investing are joined at the hip," which usefully makes the point that a combination of the two strategies is probably a better approach overall. Growth stocks may perform best when the economy is strong, while value stocks have historically tended to perform better when the economy is recovering from a downturn.

Blend investing combines both approaches. Blend managers seek growth stocks, value stocks or stocks that exhibit characteristics of both and so offer the potential benefits and risks of both. Growth stocks may provide the potential for returns that exceed the overall returns of the market, but they can also be more volatile. Value stocks may also outpace the returns of other equity investments in some economic conditions and may also be less volatile.

As growth and value strategies move in and out of favour over time, the advantage of a blend fund is that the fund can emphasise whichever style the manager believes is performing or will perform better. Nevertheless, the manager still needs to make judgments on the economic cycle and on the potential for the relevant style, which is no easier than any other investment decision. A powerful argument against blend funds is that the most successful individual managers of the past half-century have had one personal style that they have stuck to through thick and thin.

6 Income investing

Income investing aims to identify companies that provide a steady stream of income. It may focus on mature companies that have reached a certain size and are no longer able to sustain high levels of growth. Instead of retaining earnings to invest for future growth, mature firms tend to pay out retained earnings as dividends as a way to provide a return to their shareholders. High dividend levels are prominent in certain industries, such as utility companies. The driving principle behind this strategy is to identify good companies with sustainable high dividend yields to generate a steady and predictable stream of income over the long term. Because high yields are only worth something if they are sustainable, income investors will also analyse the fundamentals of a company to ensure that its business model can sustain a rising dividend policy.

'Equity income' funds are largely value driven because their prime requirement is an income higher than the average for shares. This drives them towards shares which are out of favour, often in sectors which are also out of favour, and a relatively long ownership period is often required to reap capital gains on top of the income. Within the equity income sector, there is a distinction between funds that aim for the highest possible income now, and are likely to see relatively slow growth in dividends in the future, and funds that aim for high rates of growth in dividend income, in which case their starting yields may well be only slightly above the market average.

In assessing these funds, total returns are of some use, but it is also instructive to compare the funds' records of actual per share income distributions over a lengthy period.

7 Momentum investing

Momentum investing is an investment strategy that aims to capitalise on the continuance of existing trends in the market. It involves buying shares that have had high returns over the past three to twelve months and selling those that have had poor returns over the same period. The momentum investor essentially believes that it is possible to ride these trends and make profits. This strategy involves taking a long position in an asset which is moving upward and short selling one that has been in a downward trend. The basic idea is that once a trend is established it is more likely to continue in that direction than to move against the trend.

The strategy is credited to the American fund manager Richard Driehaus, who is ranked as one of the most influential people within the mutual fund management industry. His quote sums up the strategy: "Far more money is made buying high and selling at even higher prices."

Momentum investing ignores asset allocation and diversification. The strategy doesn't allow a consideration of these factors because the focus is always on the most popular and fastest-growing investments. Risk is managed instead by moving quickly out of industries and assets that start showing signs of deteriorating performance. It is a research-intensive and time-sensitive strategy that requires a system that can reliably identify stocks that might be on an upward trend and warn when performance begins to deteriorate. Most of the research will be statistical and technical analysis since these are best suited to measuring short-term trends and short-term performance.

As a strategy, momentum investing has the advantage of being able to switch between multiple asset classes and deliver potentially high returns. It is, however, a demanding strategy to implement and the portfolios will be highly volatile.

8 Contrarian investing

Contrarian investing involves going against the conventional wisdom. It is the opposite side of the coin from momentum investing. The contrarian's natural view is that whatever the majority is doing is likely to be wrong. Contrarian managers buy or sell stocks when most investors appear to be doing the opposite. They use fundamental analysis in the same way as value investors to determine whether a stock is underpriced or overpriced, but contrarian managers tend to be more aggressive in backing their judgments. The strategy requires a fairly accurate valuation of a stock.

Contrarian strategy revolves around the concept that crowd behaviour among investors can lead to wrong and exploitable pricing in the securities markets. This can lead to share prices being driven down by widespread pessimism about a company to the point where the share price is so low that the risks are overstated and prospects are understated. Similarly, widespread optimism can result in shares becoming overvalued before an eventual decline in the share price.

Contrarian trading can be applied to individual stocks, an industry or sector or an entire asset class. It can also be applied to the whole market. But while individual investors will usually think of contrarian investing as applying best to situations when the entire market is either rising or falling, successful contrarian managers mostly apply it not to taking market positions but to deciding which stocks to buy or sell heavily.

9 Ethical and socially responsible investing

Ethical and socially responsible investment is an investment strategy whereby companies are selected for inclusion in a fund on the basis of their social, environmental and ethical principles.

Ethical investment strategies typically involve screening out investments in companies involved in specific areas, such as animal testing, armaments manufacture, tobacco and alcohol.

Instead of screening out companies to avoid, socially responsible investing tries to ensure that the investments selected are in areas the investors positively approve of, such as enterprises that exhibit a degree of social responsibility or are proactive in certain desirable activities. Business in the Community is the key example of socially responsible investment in action. It is a charity in which over 800 British companies engage in socially beneficial projects, some on a substantial scale.

However, some believe 'socially responsible investment' is interchangeable with the more common term 'ethical investment'. 'Sustainability' includes elements of both. It is therefore important, when an investor is interested in ethical investment or socially responsible investment, that the product literature is studied carefully to identify the investment approach and restrictions that will be used and that these reflect the investor's concerns.

The risk and return mix of an ethical fund will differ depending upon its ethical stance and the ethical investment strategy it adopts.

Ethical funds

Traditional ethical portfolios are constructed to avoid those areas of investment that are considered to have significant adverse effects on people, animals or the environment.

Fund managers do this by screening potential investments against negative, or avoidance, criteria, using their own research and screening tools developed by Ethical Investment Research Services (EIRIS). Such screening exercises, combined with conventional portfolio management techniques, typically result in a larger than normal percentage of the portfolio being invested in smaller companies.

Traditional ethical investing, because of its negative screening methods, is often perceived as carrying greater risk. These funds tend to exclude many larger companies from their portfolios (in the UK, most large oil, pharmaceutical and banking firms are excluded, for example). Because of this emphasis on small to medium-sized companies, such ethical funds may display more volatile performance than funds investing in larger firms. However, given the criteria and the portfolio, their performance should be measured against more appropriate benchmarks such as the FTSE4Good index rather than the normal indices.

Sustainability funds

Sustainability funds are those that focus on the concept of sustainable development, concentrating on those companies that tackle or pre-empt environmental issues head-on. Unlike ethical investment funds, sustainability funds are flexible in their approach to selecting investments.

Sustainability investors focus on those risks which most mainstream investors ignore. For instance, while most scientists and governments agree that the world's capacity to absorb carbon dioxide is fast reaching critical levels, this risk appears not to have been factored into the share valuations of fossil fuel businesses. Factors such as these are critical in selecting stocks for sustainability funds.

Sustainability fund managers can implement this approach using either positive sector selection or by choosing the best of the sector.

Positive sector selection is selecting those companies that operate in sectors likely to benefit from the global shift to more socially and environmentally sustainable forms of economic activity, such as renewable energy sources. This approach is known as 'investing in industries of the future' and gives a strong bias towards growth-oriented sectors.

Alternatively, fund managers may choose the best of the sector. Companies are often selected for the environmental leadership they demonstrate in their sector, regardless of whether they fail the negative criteria applied by ethical investing funds. For instance, an oil company which is repositioning itself as an energy business focusing on renewable energy opportunities would probably be considered for inclusion in a sustainability fund but would be excluded from an ethical fund.

There is a growing trend among institutional investors of encouraging companies to focus on their social responsibilities. Sustainable investment research teams enter into constructive dialogue with companies to encourage the adoption of social and environmental policies and practices so that they may be considered for inclusion in a sustainable investment portfolio.

Integrating social and environmental analysis into the stock selection process is necessarily more research intensive than that employed by ethical investment funds and requires a substantial research capability.

Summary

- The three main elements in active fund management are asset allocation, sector selection and stock selection. 'Bottom-up' managers focus on stock selection, 'top-down' managers on asset allocation.

- Value investing is one strategy with an academically validated approach: buying out-of-favour stocks. 'Equity income' funds often apply a value investing style.

- Growth investors often follow a GAARP (Growth At A Reasonable Price) methodology. Often this is combined with Momentum, a policy of buying stocks with positive trends in earnings and/or share prices.

- Many successful investors apply contrarian strategies to some extent, though to be truly contrarian an investor must almost always be in disagreement with the majority of investors.

- Using 'ethical' or 'sustainability' criteria in choosing investments is growing in popularity and there are many funds of this type.

Chapter 15
Passive investment

Passive investment management is a method of managing an investment portfolio with the aim of matching the performance of a broad-based market index. It is often referred to as 'indexing' because it entails investing in exactly the same securities, in the same proportions, as an index. It is considered a passive investment style because portfolio managers don't make decisions about which securities to buy and sell. Instead, they simply copy the index by buying the same securities that are included in a particular stock or bond market index.

This method of investment management is based on the belief that it is impossible to consistently beat the average on a risk-adjusted basis. It therefore seeks to hold a portfolio that mirrors the index it is tracking and involves only sufficient trading to ensure that the portfolio's performance is in line with the index.

1 Market indices

Stock market indices act as a barometer of what is happening in the market. They are used to support portfolio management research, asset allocation decisions and the measurement of portfolio performance. They are also used as the basis for index tracker funds, exchange-traded funds (ETFs), index derivatives and other index-related products. There are three main types of market index, price weighted, market value weighted and equal weighted:

- A price-weighted index is constructed on the assumption that an equal number of shares are held in each of the underlying index constituents. The index is calculated by adding together the total of each constituent's share price and comparing this total with that of the base period. The result of this is that those constituents with a high share price have a greater influence on the index value. The Dow Jones industrial average is calculated on this basis.

- A market value-weighted index is constructed by adding together the market capitalisation of each of the constituents. Larger companies therefore account for proportionately more of the index. The FTSE 100 is constructed on a market capitalisation-weighted basis.

- In certain markets, the largest companies can account for a disproportionately large weighting in the index and so an index constructed on a market capitalisation basis can give a misleading impression. Instead, an equal-weighted index is used, which assumes that equal amounts are invested in each share in the index. The Nikkei 225 is an example of an equal-weighted index.

The most widely used methodology is the market value-weighted index, though others such as fundamental-weighted (based on factors such as yield and earnings) and equal-weighted indices are becoming more widely used.

In market capitalisation-weighted indices, the total market capitalisation of a company was formerly included irrespective of who actually held the shares and whether they were freely available for trading. This resulted in distortions, so the constituents of indices are now normally based on the 'free float' – the amount of shares that is in principle available for trading. This excludes, for example, government shareholdings or shares held by founder-controller families. The free float method makes indices more representative of market reality.

2 Bond indices

It is important to note that bond indices are often constructed in an entirely different way from equity indices and this may have an impact on any index tracker products designed to mirror their performance.

Equity indices are based on underlying stocks that are generally highly liquid so that price discovery is relatively transparent. This makes the calculation of an index straightforward: you simply multiply the free float number of shares by the price in order to determine the market capitalisation that will enter the index.

Government bonds are traded heavily each day and so have levels of liquidity and price transparency that allow indices to be calculated in a way that will produce results as robust as those of equity markets. Most bonds, however, are not as liquid. Once you move away from government bonds, liquidity drops dramatically.

To understand this, it is important to recognise that the major investors in bonds are long-term investing institutions such as pension funds and insurance companies. They tend to adopt 'buy and hold' strategies which essentially mean that once they acquire a stock, they will then hold onto it until it matures. Because of this, while the bond markets are significantly larger then the equity markets in terms of capitalisation, the amount of trading that takes place is significantly less. Trading activity is concentrated in a relatively small number of securities (mainly government bonds) that trade very frequently each day, while most other bonds trade only infrequently.

This lack of frequent trading presents issues for the calculation of bond indices. It means that the firms that calculate indices need a method of determining what prices might be and they have no choice but to use price estimates in determining index values. The estimation approach used is matrix pricing. The implication of this is that funds that track bond indices have to use their own valuation models, which can produce results different from those produced by the index providers. Both are attempting to estimate what is happening in the bond markets, but with imperfect information they can end up with different results.

It is essential to understand, therefore that an index-tracking fund that seeks to mirror the performance of a bond index may well produce returns that are at variance with the index.

3 Indexation methodologies

Most index tracker funds are based on market capitalisation-weighted indices, such as the FTSE 100 and S&P 500, where the largest stocks in the index by market value have the biggest influence on the index's value.

Indexed portfolios employ one of three established tracking methods:

- **Full replication.** This method requires each constituent of the index being tracked to be held in accordance with its index weighting. Although full replication is accurate, it is also the most expensive of the three methods so is only really suitable for large portfolios.

- **Stratified sampling.** This requires a representative sample of securities from each sector of the index to be held. Although this method is less expensive, the lack of statistical analysis renders it subjective and potentially encourages biases towards those stocks with the best perceived prospects.

- **Optimisation.** This method costs less than fully replicating the index tracked but is statistically more complex. Optimisation uses a sophisticated computer modelling technique to find a representative sample of those securities that mimic the broad characteristics of the index tracked.

Physical replication is the traditional form of index replication, and it is the form favoured by the largest and longest-established ETF providers. More recently, the synthetic replication method (pioneered by Lyxor ETFs in 2001) has become the fastest growing method of replication in Europe, and it is the one embraced by the vast majority of new entrants.

Synthetic replication involves the fund manager entering into a swap — an OTC derivative — with a market counterparty to exchange the returns on the index for a payment. Sampling will still be used to identify the optimal range of securities to be included.

This approach passes the tracking error and rebalancing risk to the counterparty, while the ETF generates exactly the performance of the index. It is also generally a lower cost method, which is why such funds have been able to lower annual management fees significantly, into the range of 0.15 to 0.85%.

This does, however, introduce counterparty risk, so it is important to understand how the fund will manage this risk. It will usually be managed by ensuring a range of providers are used, credit quality limits are strictly adhered to and collateral management is applied.

4 Tracking error

Tracking error is the difference between a portfolio's return and the return of the benchmark or index it was meant to mimic. A low tracking error means a portfolio is closely following its benchmark. A high tracking error indicates the opposite. As a result, tracking error gives investors a sense of how 'tight' the portfolio in question is being managed around its benchmark.

Tracking error is a reflection of how actively or passively a portfolio is managed and can be an indicator of a manager's skill. Actively managed portfolios seek to provide returns above the benchmark, and to achieve this they must incur extra risk, which shows up in greater deviations of returns from the index. On the other hand, passively managed portfolios seek to replicate index returns and thus minimise tracking error. Several factors determine a portfolio's tracking error:

- The extent to which the portfolio's holdings mirror those of the benchmark.

- Differences in market capitalisation, timing, investment style and other fundamental characteristics of the portfolio and the benchmark.

- Differences in the weighting of assets in the portfolio and in the benchmark.

- Costs, such as management fees, custody fees, brokerage costs and other expenses that affect the portfolio but not the benchmark.

In addition, portfolio managers must accommodate inflows and outflows of cash from investors, which forces them to rebalance their portfolios from time to time. This too involves direct and indirect costs. Index funds are expected to mirror the returns of an index minus the expenses of running the portfolio. These expenses are referred to as the 'management expense ratio'.

There are a number of reasons why tracking error can occur and it is important to be aware of what the deviation is and why it occurs. Tracking error may occur because of the following factors:

- Optimisation can result in tracking error because the portfolio will hold fewer stocks than are contained in the index in order to minimise trading costs.

- The timing of cash dividend payments can create a drag on a portfolio's performance. Most indices assume the receipt and reinvestment of dividends occurs earlier than it actually does.

- Some indices are more difficult to track than others, such as the bond indices mentioned above.

- Index funds that track less liquid markets or securities tend to diverge from the underlying securities because of the difficulty in trading these.

- An index fund may have limits on the maximum allocation that can be made to an individual security. If an index is dominated by a number of large stocks then the fund may be unable to replicate this and may have to adjust for it instead.

Most index fund providers believe that some amount of tracking error is inevitable. Each index fund will have different factors that affect the amount of tracking error that occurs and so it is wise to check reported performance and understand how the portfolio is constructed and how the fund goes about replicating the performance of an index.

5 Index funds

Index funds are collective investment schemes designed to track the performance of an index such as the FTSE 100 or the S&P 500. They have grown in popularity because of their simplicity and lower costs. Another factor is concern over actively managed funds that are nothing more than closet trackers. Many supposedly actively managed funds produce returns that are only in line with the market or worse and yet charge higher fees.

The advantages of index tracking funds include:

- A simple and easy to understand investment objective.

- Returns in line with the index.

- Low costs.

- Lower portfolio turnover.

- No exposure to an active investment management style.

They do have drawbacks, however, including:

- Possible tracking error.

- The fact that they follow markets down as well as up.

Index-tracking funds are offered by many of the large fund management groups and are usually constructed in the form of a unit trust or an open-ended investment company. Dealing in such funds is therefore no different from dealing in actively managed funds.

Increased competition in the traditional index fund market is driving down costs, resulting in much lower annual management fees on index-linked funds. This makes it all the more important that an adviser looks at the costs of various providers. After all, if there are two index funds both tracking the FTSE

100 with minimal tracking error and one is charging an annual management charge of 1% and the other 0.25%, the choice should be obvious.

There is also direct competition for traditional index-tracking funds from exchange-traded funds (ETFs). These do exactly the same thing but in some cases with significantly lower charges. They also offer a wider range of indices that can be tracked, aiding diversification of an investor's portfolio.

The Financial Services Authority (FSA), in its Retail Distribution Review (RDR), made the explicit point that advisers need to familiarise themselves with ETFs because these are not being considered sufficiently when a decision is made on which products are suitable for retail clients.

6 Exchange-traded funds

An exchange-traded fund is a collective investment scheme that is quoted and traded intra-day on a stock exchange. It is a tradable financial instrument that otherwise has the same characteristics as a collective investment vehicle, namely a unit trust or an investment company with variable capital. Its purpose is to pool the savings of investors into one investment vehicle and provide access to an underlying investment portfolio that tracks an index. It is structured as an investment company with variable capital and so is open ended in nature.

Its major differentiating feature is that it is listed and traded on a stock exchange and is cleared and settled as any other equity trade. Market makers quote two-way prices on an ETF, allowing investors to trade the stock at any time the market is open, rather than at a set daily price. An ETF trades at prices very close to its net asset value and is not subject to the trading at a discount that is seen with investment trusts. Clearing and settlement take place using exactly the same market mechanisms as for any other equity trade.

These features, along with lower costs than traditional investment funds, have made ETFs one of the fastest-growing types of investment fund worldwide. Their growth has been explosive and has been at the expense of traditional investment funds.

Structure

The legal structure of an ETF varies between jurisdictions. In the US, many ETFs are structured as unit trust investment funds, while in Ireland they tend to be open-ended investment companies and in Luxembourg *sociétés d'investissement à capital variable* (SICAVs) and *fonds communs de placement* (FCPs). The underlying structures they adopt therefore follow traditional mutual fund lines.

In Europe generally many ETFs are structured as 'UCITS III' funds (under the Undertakings for Collective Investment in Transferable Securities or UCITS directives) and are domiciled in either Dublin or Luxembourg so that they can be marketed cross-border. For example, iShares is established as a Dublin-domiciled open-ended umbrella fund and the FTSEurofirst 100 fund is listed on the London Stock Exchange, Borsa Italiana, Deutsche Borse, Euronext Amsterdam, Euronext Paris and SWX Swiss Exchange.

Processes

Another major differentiating feature is how shares are created and redeemed. In order that they can be dealt on a stock market, ETFs clearly need a different process from that used for unit trusts and OEICs.

While ETFs are structured in the same way as traditional funds, there are significant differences in the creation and redemption process and the way they are traded. Figure 15.1 illustrates how this works.

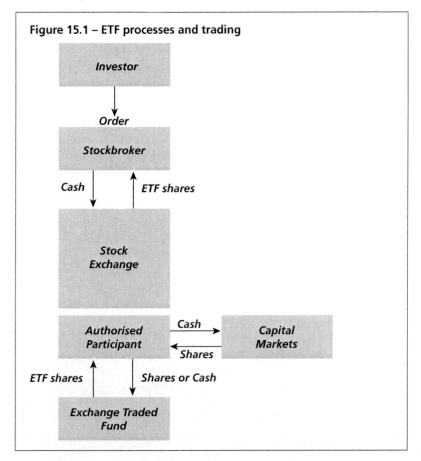

Figure 15.1 – ETF processes and trading

ETF shares are created and redeemed in the primary market, with transactions taking place between financial institutions and the fund.

The only parties who deal directly with the ETF are major financial institutions known as 'authorised participants'. Authorised participants can create new ETF shares in one of two ways:

- They buy a basket of shares in the markets that corresponds exactly with the construction of the underlying index, and then deposit this with the ETF and receive in exchange an institutional block of shares known as 'creation units'.

- They deliver cash to the ETF provider in exchange for a creation unit.

When they wish to redeem units, authorised participants deliver the creation unit back to the ETF provider and receive either the underlying shares or cash. Only market participants can trade in this primary market and each trade has to be made in very large blocks of shares.

These authorised participants will also be market makers on the London Stock Exchange, making a two-way market in the underlying ETF shares during market hours. Trading of the ETF shares therefore takes place on the stock market where the same institutions quote prices at which investors can deal.

Dealing

The ETF provider publishes the content of a basket of shares and the net asset value at the start of each day through Reuters and Bloombergs. During the trading day, intra-day information on the indicative new asset value is published by the relevant stock exchanges, enabling investors to compare this with the bid/offer in the market.

An arbitrage band is created around each ETF's net asset value by arbitrageurs and other traders who can profit from any discrepancy between the ETF price and the price of a stock basket or futures. This ensures that the ETF's price never varies significantly from its net asset value.

Spreads between bid and ask prices on ETFs are normally extremely low. They are in theory constrained by the ability of market participants to exchange listed investments for ETF shares. However, in volatile markets such arbitrage cannot be relied upon and dealing spreads may become as wide as those in other collective funds.

For investors, dealing in ETFs is exactly the same as any other stock market trade. They simply place an order with their broker, who will then execute the order with whichever market maker is offering the best price at that moment in time. The trade will be executed very close to the underlying net asset value of the fund. The broker will charge commission for the execution of the trade but no stamp duty is payable. It will then settle in exactly the same way as for any other trade.

Product development

There is a growing range of indices that can be tracked using ETFs beyond the well-known ones. ETFs are available that track government bonds, corporate bonds, emerging markets, commercial property and specialist areas such as water, power and forestry.

They are also developing beyond simple single index trackers. There are now fundamental-weighted index-tracking ETFs and ETFs following other quantitative strategies. Providers have also launched ETFs that provide geared returns ($2 \times$ the index return) and inverse ETFs (a rise of X% for a fall of X% in the index). These more complex products have caused regulators to warn about possible dangers. Inverse funds, in particular, are often misunderstood by investors; they will not deliver the compound rate of decline in an index over a period of several days because they rebalance daily. Problems of contango with commodity ETFs (see the following section) mean their performance, too, can diverge widely from the instrument they are tracking.

7 Commodity ETFs

Commodities have always had a place in the portfolios of private clients, especially where they are managed by discretionary investment managers.

Within the asset allocation of a portfolio, a percentage is usually allocated to commodity exposure. This exposure has normally been obtained by holding the shares of companies involved in one aspect or another of the commodities world. For example, an investment manager might decide that he wants exposure to gold or other minerals and he therefore includes the shares of companies quoted in the mining sector or an investment fund that specialises in the sector.

Achieving exposure to commodities in this way has never been an optimal solution, as the share price of the company tends to be influenced both by the prospects for the movement of the underlying commodity and by the prospects for the company itself. However, there was no realistic alternative until the advent of exchange-traded commodities.

Exchange-traded commodity funds (ETCs) are investment vehicles that track the performance of an underlying commodity index. There are two main types of ETC: those focusing on a single commodity such as gold or oil and those tracking an index.

ETCs are open to all investors and can be used for a number of purposes where commodity exposure is needed, such as exposure to a single commodity such as gold or as part of an asset allocation strategy. They are an open-ended collective investment vehicles and so additional shares are created to meet demand. They are similar to exchange-traded funds in that they are dealt on the London Stock Exchange in their own dedicated segment. They have market maker support so that there is guaranteed liquidity during market opening hours and are held and settled through Crest in the same way as any other shares.

Some ETCs are similar to ETFs in that they have physical backing. Gold ETCs, for example, issue shares against officially assayed and certificated gold bars held in the vaults of a custodian bank. But the vast majority of ETCs are based on futures contracts. This means they involve counterparty risk on the future settlement of the futures contract. Triple-A ratings are not necessarily adequate, since the formerly triple-A-rated AIG was in fact counterparty to a number of ETCs. A number of measures are being adopted to reduce the element of counterparty risk in ETCs and advisers need to be aware of how ETC managers deal with this issue.

8 Active versus passive management

Active investment management encompasses many different styles and strategies but the essential aim is to manage a portfolio that will produce returns greater than those of the index that the portfolio is benchmarked against. It uses fundamental analysis, technical analysis and macroeconomic analysis to identify future investment trends and pick attractive markets, sectors and stocks to invest in.

By contrast, passive investment management makes no attempt to distinguish between attractive and unattractive securities and makes little or no use of the results of research into which markets, sectors and stocks might perform best. Instead, the assets of the portfolio are allocated across the constituents of an index or in a representative sample of the stock contained in an index. Which performs best? Proponents of each strategy see the investment world in very different ways and deploy powerful arguments in favour of their chosen option.

Passive managers generally believe that it is difficult to beat the market. There is overwhelming academic support for this proposition based on some 40 years of research. Passive managers essentially offer asset class performance that closely matches an index for those investors who are unwilling to assume the risks of active management.

Active managers believe the market can be beaten. While they cannot beat it all the time, many active managers do believe there are certain irregularities in the market that can be taken into consideration to achieve potentially higher returns.

Some of the key advantages and disadvantages of the two approaches are shown in Table 15.1 and Table 15.2.

Research into the relative performance of active and passive funds has shown that only a small percentage of actively managed funds actually beat the index they are tracking with any consistency, and proponents for passive investment

Table 15.1 – Active investment management – advantages and disadvantages

Advantages	Disadvantages
• Informed investment decisions based on experience, judgment and analysis of market trends and prospects.	• Higher fees and operating expenses.
• The possibility of higher returns than the index the portfolio is benchmarked against.	• Market, sector and stock analysis may not produce the right selections and the portfolio could underperform its benchmark index.
• The ability to take defensive measures if managers expect the market to take a downturn by moving into defensive sectors or hedging the portfolio.	• The investment style adopted may adversely impact performance and reduce returns as it may not be in favour with the market.

Table 15.2 – Passive investment management – advantages and disadvantages

Advantages	Disadvantages
• Low operating expenses, because the costs of managing the portfolio are less and there are lower trading costs.	• Performance is dictated by the index and investors must be satisfied with average returns based on the index.
• Returns in line with the index.	• In a downturn, the portfolio will decline in line with the index.
• No reliance on the investment management ability of the fund manager.	• Index fund managers are not able to move out of sectors or stocks that may be about to decline or use hedging.

management use this to strongly argue their case. However, despite their advantages index trackers cannot meet all investor objectives.

Index trackers minimise the risk of underperforming the index and reduce the costs of investing by only transacting when necessary. On the downside, once fees and costs are taken into account a small degree of underperformance against the market often results. Equally, being fully invested in the chosen index means trackers follow the market down as well as up.

Actively managed equity funds address some of these downsides but are plagued by poor performance, compounded by the greater costs and fees associated with running portfolios on an active basis. Many are simply closet trackers that persistently underperform.

Actively managed funds that consistently outperform the market do exist. There are funds that operate unconstrained investment management where truly active managers who have the courage of their convictions implement positions in those stocks they believe to be mispriced. There are also small, nimble funds that are not constrained by holding mainly large, well-researched and well-traded stocks, and funds operating in less well-researched niche areas of world markets. Finally, absolute return funds and hedge funds using a variety of strategies are not subject to the argument that you cannot beat the market, and provided they can in fact deliver positive returns (even if small) throughout a market cycle they can deliver worthwhile results for investors that those investors would be very unlikely to achieve on their own.

9 Core-satellite strategies

Identifying which funds might outperform can be difficult and has led many to believe that a strategy that incorporates both active and passive funds is the best way forward. Index tracking can be combined with active management to varying degrees by adopting strategies such as enhanced indexation and core-satellite portfolios. In each case, the aim is to generate performance in excess of the index and the best features of active and passive management can be combined to work to the investor's advantage

An example of core-satellite management is shown in Figure 15.2.

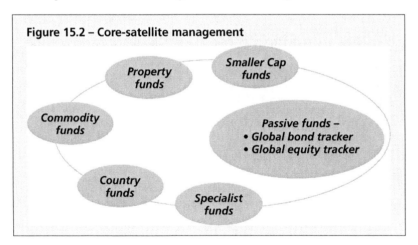

Figure 15.2 – Core-satellite management

By indexing, say, 70% to 80% of the portfolio's value you minimise the risk of underperformance. You then invest the remainder in a number of specialist actively managed funds or individual securities. These are known as the 'satellites'.

The core can also be run on an enhanced index basis, whereby specialist investment management techniques are employed to add value. These include stock lending and anticipating the entry and exit of constituents from the index being tracked.

An alternative would be to create a core from actively managed funds using value-investing methods, since these have the best track record of delivering enhanced returns in the past. Index tracker funds would constitute a frequently changing set of satellites, used opportunistically to enter and exit countries, regions or sectors.

A third possibility is to apply quantitative techniques to create a 'momentum' portfolio of ETFs based on different asset classes as a single satellite to accompany a 'buy and hold' core.

Summary

- The majority of passively managed funds track a well-known index such as the FTSE 100 Index, but an increasing number of 'passive' funds incorporate some element of active selection, though this is usually quantitative and governed by rules.

- Most well-known stock market indices are capitalisation-weighted, but this is not true for most bond indices and funds tracking equal-weighted and fundamental-weighted indices are also available.

- A key metric for passive funds is tracking error, which arises from their fees and costs and from the effectiveness of their chosen method of reproducing the chosen index's return.

- Index tracking funds are normally open-ended in the form of OEICs and ETFs, the latter having the advantage of stock exchange listing and minute-by-minute pricing and dealing.

- Exchange Traded Commodities (also known as Exchange Traded Notes) enable investors to secure returns matching those of precious metals, broad commodity indices and specific commodities such as oil.

- A core-satellite approach to portfolio construction can employ passive and active funds together.

Chapter 16
Structured products

The term 'structured products' describes a range of investment products more commonly known as guaranteed growth bonds, FTSE capital-protected bonds and a whole variety of other marketing names.

A structured product is a fixed-term investment which offers capital growth or income with the benefit of full or partial capital protection. Products are often linked to stock market indices such as the FTSE 100 and offer returns based on their performance. The capital protection feature seeks to preserve investors' original investment in the event of the market falling. Individual products do this to varying degrees. These structured products have been around for some time and their features and terms differ markedly from product to product. Some are designed for the mass retail investment market, others target the high net worth market only, some are for the customers of a single private bank and a few are designed specifically for one wealthy individual.

In its consultation paper on the Retail Distribution Review (RDR) issued in the summer of 2009, the Financial Services Authority (FSA) proposed that if a firm wishes to describe itself as independent it must research the market without restriction or limitation. Within the range of products that must be researched in this way, structured products were expressly mentioned. The FSA has also conducted a review of advice given on those structured products that were backed by the failed investment bank, Lehman Brothers. They found significant levels of unsuitable advice had been given and serious deficiencies in the marketing literature of a number of plan managers.

Following implementation of the RDR proposals and the rule changes arising from the structured products review, advisers will have to ensure they fully understand this range of products so that they can be included within investment recommendations when they are suitable for a client.

1 Key features

Structured products originated in the guaranteed bonds marketed by life offices from the 1970s onwards. They are packaged products based on derivatives which generally feature protection of capital if held to maturity but with a degree of participation in the return from a higher-performing, but riskier, underlying asset. As noted above, they are created to meet the specific needs of high net worth individuals and general retail investors that cannot be met by standardised financial instruments.

These products are created by combining with derivatives underlying assets such as shares, bonds, currencies and commodities. This combination can create structures that have significant risk-return and cost-saving advantages compared to what might otherwise be obtainable in the market. In recent years, the providers of these products have explored ever more innovative combinations of underlying asset mixes which have enabled them to offer a wider range of terms and guarantees.

Structured products have offered a range of benefits to investors and generally have been used either to provide access to stock market growth with capital protection or exposure to an asset, such as gold or currencies, that would not otherwise be achievable from direct investment. The benefits of structured products can include:

- Protection of initial capital investment.

- Tax-efficient access to fully taxable investments.

- Enhanced returns.

- Reduced risk.

- High rates of income.

Interest in these investments has been growing in recent years and high net worth investors now use structured products as a way of achieving portfolio diversification. Structured products are also available at the mass retail level, particularly in Europe, where national post offices, and even supermarkets, sell them to their customers.

2 Characteristics

Structured products are available from a wide range of providers, including banks, building societies, fund management groups and insurance companies. The range of structured products available is wide and growing, as product providers design new structures to meet changing market conditions.

While the type of structured product will change from provider to provider and from time to time, they will generally fall into one of three main structures:

- 100% principal protection — the investor receives the return on the underlying index provided it has risen, and if it has not risen they receive 100% return of the capital invested. This is described as 'hard protection'.

- Partial principal protection — a set return or income level is offered but capital protection is only provided so long as the underlying index does not decline below a set amount. For example, the capital protection might apply, provided that the FTSE 100 does not fall below 40% of its value at the start of the period. This is known as 'soft protection' or 'contingent capital protection'.

- No protection — some structured products provide no capital protection at all, and instead offer exposure to 100% of the movement in the underlying asset or index or a greater leveraged return.

Although it is possible to construct complex forms of structured products, the basic structure is straightforward and all structured products share a number of common characteristics. These include the following:

- Potential growth is based on the performance of an index such as the FTSE 100 or FTSE All-Share.

- Where capital protection is provided in the event that the stock market does not perform as expected then some or all of the initial capital invested is returned.

- The growth is achieved through the purchase of a derivative that tracks the selected index.

- Capital protection is achieved through the investment of part of the cash invested in a secure asset such as a fixed-term deposit or zero coupon bond.

- These products are for fixed terms and withdrawals are not usually permitted, though some products are tradeable.

- Any charges are usually built into the structure of the product rather than being added on.

- The tax treatment will depend upon how the product is structured. It may be structured as a combination of a bond and derivatives in which case any growth is treated as a gain for capital gains tax purposes and any income arising is taxable under the personal income tax rules. Many banks, however, will use a deposit structure so that all returns are taxable as income.

- Structured products can be held in an individual savings account or self-invested personal pension provided they meet the standard criteria for inclusion.

3 Basic structure of a capital-protected structured product

The structure and features of a structured product will clearly differ from provider to provider, but it is possible to identify some basic characteristics. A basic capital growth structured product will provide a return based on an index and provide some form of guarantee of a return of part or all of the initial capital invested at the end of the term.

An example of a common structured product is a five-year growth bond linked to the performance of the UK stock market and an investor places £1,000 into the bond. Charges will be deducted from the amount invested and the remaining amount will typically be split between:

- The purchase of a call option on an index such as the FTSE 100.

- Investment in a zero coupon bond that is due to mature at the end of the term of the structured product.

The issuing company will seek to identify a bond that is due to mature in five years' time, in which it can invest. This may be available in the market or it may be a medium-term note issued by the financial institution itself. The bond will typically be a zero coupon bond and so will be priced at a significant discount to the amount that will be paid at maturity. For example, the bond may be priced at £80 per £100 nominal of the bond.

In this example, £800 of the initial investment is used to buy £1,000 nominal of the bond. This means that in five years' time, £1,000 will be repaid, which is exactly the same as the original amount invested. Essentially, this is how the capital guarantee is provided.

The investor's capital has been secured regardless of what happens to the stock market. This is the initial investment only, however, and in reality the investor has lost out as no interest has been earned and the opportunity has been lost for growth elsewhere.

The balance of the investment, £200, is then used to buy a call option on the FTSE 100 over the five-year period. The financial institution issuing the structured product will enter into a derivatives contract with a counterparty in the market, which will provide a call option of the type it wants and for its preferred period. A call option is an option that gives the buyer the right to buy an underlying asset at an agreed price, in this case the FTSE 100.

The buyer in this case is the financial institution issuing the structured product. The writer of the contract, the counterparty mentioned above, confers the right on the buyer to buy the asset at a pre-specified price in exchange for paying a premium for this right. Assuming that the FTSE was at 5,000 at the time, the buyer has the right to buy the asset at this price and pays a premium, which in this case would be the £200 balance that is being invested. Figure 16.1 illustrates this.

If the FTSE rises over the period the holder can exercise its right to buy the index at 5,000 and take the difference as a profit. If the FTSE is lower, however, the holder can simply walk away from the contract and the loss is limited to the £200 premium that has been paid. The return to the investor is therefore dependent on the performance of the FTSE over the term of the product. The return is referred to as a 'participation rate' and this can vary widely depending upon the amount of protection offered.

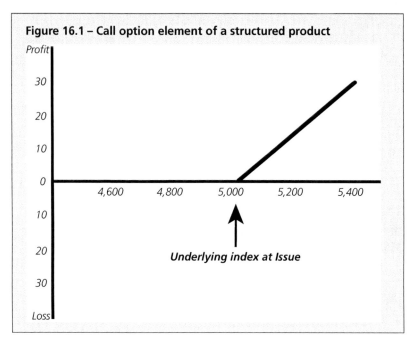

Figure 16.1 – Call option element of a structured product

To keep things simple, let's assume that the participation rate is 100%, which basically means that it provides a standard 1:1 return for any rise in the FTSE. So, if the underlying FTSE 100 index has risen by 50% at maturity, there will be a 50% gain on the maturity of the product. Alternatively, if the index is below 5,000 at maturity, the call option is abandoned and the zero coupon bond repays the original amount invested of £1,000.

The growth on a structured product is therefore contingent on the performance of the option and the underlying asset. The price of the option will be affected by many factors, including:

- **The underlying asset price.** The higher the asset price, the more valuable are call options and the less valuable are put options.

- **The exercise price.** The higher the exercise price, the less valuable are call options and the more valuable are put options.

- **Time to maturity.** The longer the term of the option, the greater the chance of the option expiring 'in the money', and therefore the higher the time value and the higher the premium.

- **Volatility of the underlying asset price.** The more volatile the price of the underlying asset, the greater the chance of the option expiring 'in the money', and therefore the higher the premium.

The result of this is that each tranche of a structured product is unique in that the potential returns will vary depending upon how it is structured and when it is issued.

A basic structured product, therefore, offers exposure to potential growth in the stock market with a guarantee of the return of the initial capital invested. Given the market turmoil of the last few years and the current low level of interest rates, it is unsurprising that structured products are becoming increasingly popular.

There are other types of structured product beyond the guaranteed structure, including trackers that simply maintain a one-for-one relationship with the underlying index, products that offer leveraged performance and reverse trackers that gain if the underlying asset falls.

Another variation on the basic structure is a kick-out plan. These have a basic guarantee structure and a fixed term and offer an annual return. At each anniversary, if the index is higher or at the same level the plan can mature early and deliver the expected return, otherwise it matures at the end of its fixed term.

4 Counterparty risk

The risks associated with a structured product essentially revolve around the creditworthiness of the parties involved in providing the product. These include the product provider, the company issuing the zero coupon bond and the counterparty to the derivatives contract.

The financial institution providing the product in the first place needs to be assessed in terms of its financial soundness, reliability and track record in the issuing of structured products. Some financial institutions may well outsource the administration of the product to a third party, which can present an additional risk. The collapse of Keydata in 2009, with accusations of fraud and loss of client money, shows this to be a real risk.

The creditworthiness of the issuer of the bond also needs to be considered. This involves looking at the credit ratings of the issuer as provided by one of the credit-rating agencies. The three most prominent agencies providing these ratings are Standard & Poor's, Moody's and Fitch. When a bond is first issued, the issuer will provide details of its financial soundness and creditworthiness in a document known as an offering document, prospectus or official statement. But as the bond may not be due for redemption for many years, investors need a method of checking on a regular basis whether the government or company remains capable of meeting its obligations.

Rating agencies assign ratings to many bonds when they are issued and monitor developments during their lifetime. Bond issues subject to credit ratings can be divided into two distinct categories: those accorded an investment grade rating and those categorised as non-investment grade or speculative. The latter are also known as 'high yield' or 'junk' bonds. Investment grade issues offer the greatest liquidity.

The counterparty to the derivatives contract also needs to be considered. Lehman Brothers was the counterparty to many structured products at the time it collapsed in 2008. This prompted an FSA review of the marketing and selling practices associated with structured products, since consumers' money had been placed at risk.

These issues highlight that advisers should ensure they undertake due diligence on the counterparties to a structured product to ensure they are highly rated and regarded. They should keep in mind that better rates can be quoted by providers who use weaker counterparties, and as with any type of investment they should seek to limit their clients' exposure by limiting their reliance on any single provider.

5 Listed structured products

The major disadvantage of many retail structured products issued to date has been that investors have had to hold them to maturity to secure any gains. The gain that an investor would make on, say, a FTSE 100-linked bond would only be determined at maturity, and few bonds offered the option of securing profits earlier. This need for greater flexibility led to the development of listed structured products, and in May 2005 the London Stock Exchange created a new market segment to accommodate both primary and secondary markets in them.

There is a wide range of listed structured products and the terms of each are open to the discretion of the issuing bank. They are known by a variety of names including 'certificates' and 'investment notes'. They are issued directly to investors, and following the closing of the tranche the issuer will arrange for a stock market listing. A market in the structured product is then made by market makers, including the issuing bank. The prices they quote will be derived from the model used to construct the product in the first place.

Despite being traded on the London Stock Exchange, these are not standardised exchange products and the specification will change from issuer to issuer. One key feature they do have, however, is that they are listed, held and settled in Crest. They can be categorised as follows.

Examples of the types of listed structured products are given below. The basic structure is a tracker that replicates an index and the others are variations on this theme.

Trackers

As the name suggests, a tracker replicates the performance of an underlying asset or index. Trackers are usually long-dated instruments and can even be undated so that they have an indefinite life span.

As a tracker replicates the performance of the underlying asset, its price will move in line with it. No dividends are paid on the tracker and instead any income stream is built into the capital value of the tracker over its lifetime. Where the underlying asset is, say, an index on an overseas market such as the Standard & Poor's 500, an investor may be exposed to currency movements. Some trackers will therefore incorporate features that ensure the tracker is constantly fully hedged for currency risk.

An investor can achieve the same performance as a tracker by buying other instruments, such as an exchange-traded fund or a unit trust tracker fund. Where trackers come into their own is in the way they can be used to track other assets such as commodities and currencies or an index representing the same.

Accelerated trackers

With an accelerated tracker, an investor will participate in the growth of the underlying index or asset provided that when it matures its value is greater than the initial value. If the asset or index is valued at less than its initial value, the investor will lose the same amount.

For example, an accelerated tracker might provide for an investor to participate in 200% of the growth of an index. If an investor buys £1,000 of an instrument and the index it is based on rises by 10%, they will receive back their initial investment of £1,000 plus 200% of the growth, which amounts to £200 – that is, £100 growth × 200% = £200.

If the final value of the underlying asset is, say, 10% less than the issue price, the investor will receive back the initial price of £1,000 less the change in the underlying asset – 10% or £100 – which amounts to £900.

The investor will usually surrender any right to the underlying income stream from the asset in exchange for the right to participate in any performance.

Reverse trackers

A reverse tracker is similar to a standard tracker except that, should the underlying asset fall, the value of the tracker will rise. These trackers are also referred to as 'bear certificates'.

Capital-protected trackers

Capital protected trackers, as the name suggests, allow investors to gain some exposure to the growth of an underlying asset or index while providing protection for the capital invested. The amount of participation in any growth and the protection of the capital invested will vary from product to product and are obtained by surrendering any right to income from the underlying asset.

For example, an instrument might be issued to track the performance of the FTSE 100 and provide participation of 140% of any growth but with 100% capital protection. If the FTSE 100 index is at a higher level at maturity, the investor will receive back the initial price plus 140% of the growth over that period. If the index is lower than at the start, the capital protection kicks in and the investor will receive back the initial price.

Trading and settlement

A listed structured product will usually be structured as an instrument such as a zero coupon bond and will be firstly offered in the primary market, where they are made available to investors. These products are treated as derivatives for the purpose of conduct of business rules. A firm distributing these products must give a two-way risk warning, in the form of a generic warrants/derivatives warning notice, and either a tailored risk warning or a copy of the listing particulars.

Once the investment date has passed, the products can be traded in the secondary market. The issuers of the products are obliged to maintain continuous prices throughout the lifetime of the product and to adhere to the standard market maker obligations of minimum size and maximum spread.

On any subsequent dealing in the secondary market, a contract note is issued as normal. This will specify the name of the investment, the nominal amount bought, the price at which it has been dealt and any commission charged. The instruments are issued in uncertificated form and are held in Crest. Settlement takes place as normal within three business days. At the end of the term, the investor will usually sell the investment on the last valuation day, but if it is not traded the instrument representing the structured product will be redeemed using settlement functionality available in Crest.

6 Use of structured products

One of the attractions of structured products is that the client can, and should, know, at the outset how much they can gain or lose, which is quite different to making direct investments in equities or other assets. That being said, there are products which offer contingent capital protection, or barriers, which do introduce further uncertainty into the structured product market.

Some of the benefits of structured products include the following:

- A wide range of underlying asset combinations is available, from single indices to mixes of assets for more complex investment strategies.

- There is no exposure to a particular manager's style or ability.

- The degree of upside participation will be explicitly stated.

- A level of capital protection is generally included.

- The risk and return characteristics are fixed and transparent – although a clear understanding of this can require detailed consideration.

The potential drawbacks of structured products include:

- Caps on participation rates will limit the returns investors could have made in a strongly rising market.

- If the product cannot be sold in the secondary market, maturity could take place during a market fall, meaning that any profits that might have been made will either be reduced or disappear.

- Some products are for fixed terms and early encashment penalties can apply. This means that they are not vehicles to be used to hold funds that might be needed at short notice.

- Falls in equity and other markets could be significant enough for the product to lose its capital protection.

The selection of a suitable structured product needs to be based on the investor's aims and attitude towards risk, in order to identify a product that provides an appropriate mix of capital preservation with the possibility of higher returns from more volatile investment vehicles.

It is important that investors considering structured products, and their financial advisers, thoroughly understand the risks and characteristics of any structured product before they make a purchase. In particular, they should determine the following:

Return	• Precise details of how the return will be calculated;
	• What factors might change the initial estimates;
	• The extent to which the investor will capture any upward movement in the markets;
	• The value of giving up the dividend flow so that the cost of the protection can be judged.
Risk profile	• Assets forming the structure of the product;
	• Risks to the principal amount invested;
	• The extent of any capital guarantees;
	• The provisions relating to limited protection guarantees.
Costs	• Costs and fees associated with buying, holding and selling the structured product;
	• The tax implications for the investor.
Encashment	• Any early encashment penalties;
	• The transparency of pricing if the product can be sold on the stock market;
	• Liquidity in the secondary market;
	• Costs associated with any stock market sale.
Credit risk	• The creditworthiness of the issuer;
	• The creditworthiness of any counterparties involved in the underlying derivatives;
	• The credit rating of any zero coupon bond or other instrument.

Clearly, it is vital that a realistic assessment is made of the risks associated with any structured products. Advisers need to have a full understanding of these so that they can articulate them with clarity, and ensure the client has a clear understanding of the potential risks and rewards.

7 FSA perspective on structured products

Structured products have the potential to do 'exactly what it says on the tin' and can therefore have a role in investment planning. However, the recent controversy surrounding structured products highlights that they can be missold. The FSA is clear that advisers need to fully understand these products and consider them for inclusion in the recommendations they make.

It is therefore worth repeating the considerations that the FSA expects advisers and producers of structured products to bear in mind when assessing the suitability of these products for inclusion in a portfolio. These are set out in Tables 16.1–16.3.

Table 16.1 – Recommending structured products – issues to be considered

When recommending structured investment products, the factors that the FSA expects advisers to consider include, but are not limited to, the following:

- whether the customer has sufficient emergency funds;
- the customer's timescale for investment;
- whether the customer has a potential need for liquid capital during the period of investment and, if so, whether capital has been set aside for this purpose;
- if the investment is designed to provide a set return on a set date to meet a future need for money but the contract has the potential to mature early, what this may mean for re-planning, re-investment, and, hence, potential additional expense for the customer;
- whether the customer has any existing liabilities that may best be repaid before considering investment; and
- the implications of recommending a fixed-term product that cannot be cashed in according to market sentiment.

Source: Financial Services Authority

Table 16.2 – Marketing material for structured products – FSA requirements

Financial promotions for structured investment products must:

- be clear about where customers' money is invested, which may include explaining that it is not invested in an index but is loaned to a single financial company;
- clearly explain any relevant counterparty risk;
- prominently state that capital is at risk (if that is the case);
- use language that the target audience is likely to understand;
- not describe a product as 'protected' or 'guaranteed' if this is an inaccurate or misleading description.

Source: Financial Services Authority

Table 16.3 – Designing structured products – FSA requirements

Firms should:

- state clearly and prominently key product risks, and to assess these against prevailing market conditions;
- assess continually any risks posed to the product before and after the sale, and take action to alert investors if contingency action needs to be taken;
- carry out due diligence in the selection of the securities issuer, using a range of sources; this includes the regulatory regime to which the counterparty is subject;
- ensure all relevant risks – market, liquidity, counterparty – are accurately identified and stress tested during the design process;
- ensure all relevant risks – market, liquidity, counterparty – are accurately identified and stress tested during the design process;
- act with due care and diligence when passing on promotions they have created to distributors;
- ensure systems and controls offer an effective framework for risk management in a range of market conditions; and
- consider the legal characteristics of the product and ensure they comply with all the relevant regulations.

Source: Financial Services Authority

8 Structured funds

The FSA review of structured products led to product providers devising an array of solutions to address the credit risk that comes from linking investment solutions to a single counterparty. Among these is the increasing use of structured funds.

Structured funds are FSA-regulated collective investment schemes that use the wider investment powers available under ICITS 111 regulations. They are equity or fixed income funds that aim to provide investors with a degree of both capital protection and capital appreciation.

The fund structure brings transparency and ease of access, and also helps to avoid timing risk with their flexible holding periods. They can also be held on platforms (like Cofunds), making them more accessible.

9 Structured products and asset allocation

Structured products have been used in the past to meet specific needs only but they can be used as a central part of investment planning by exploiting their potential for diversification within an asset allocation strategy. Structured products can be effective diversification tools because of their combination of guarantees and exposure to markets. There is a weak correlation between structured and traditional management products, which can provide a means of reducing portfolio risk without altering potential gains.

The EDHEC Risk and Asset Management Research Centre has studied the diversification effect of structured products. It concluded that the introduction of structured products into traditional institutional portfolios helped to optimise their risk-return profile by maintaining or raising returns while reducing risk. While the research was from the perspective of institutional investors, these findings are relevant to all investors and suggest that even a modest allocation to structured products can contribute usefully to an investment portfolio.

Structured products can be used to meet an investor's conflicting wishes for both capital protection and equity returns. They can be used to gain exposure to assets which are otherwise difficult to access and to provide tax planning opportunities. They can also be used in situations where there is a requirement for capital at a known future date.

These products can also be deployed, for example, within a core-satellite strategy, either to provide a guaranteed return as part of the core element of the strategy, or as part of the satellite element, where they can provide exposure to different indices or assets or can provide geared exposure.

Summary

- Structured products limit potential capital losses and provide investors with capital protection combined with reduced potential returns from the underlying asset class.

- Most structured products use a combination of put and call options, added to underlying holdings of securities or cash, to generate the promised returns.

- Most structured products have lives of five years or more, but 'kickout' plans can terminate earlier, whenever a specific return target has been reached.

- Some structured products provide 'hard protection' where the investor is guaranteed no capital loss in any circumstances; others only provide 'soft protection', in which case there may be a loss if an index falls below a particular level.

- All structured products involve counterparty risk, since the derivative contract that generates the return is provided by a bank. If the bank fails, the product may fail to deliver, as occurred with many products backed by Lehman Brothers.

- Some UK structured products take the legal form of deposits, while others take the form of funds. Some are also listed on the LSE, though pricing will be determined by the product provider.

Chapter 17
Fund selection

Collective investment schemes pool the resources of a large number of investors, with the aim of pursuing a common investment objective. This pooling of funds brings a number of benefits, including:

- Economies of scale.

- Diversification.

- Access to professional investment management.

- Access to geographical markets, asset classes or investment strategies which might otherwise be inaccessible to the individual investor.

- In many cases, the benefit of regulatory oversight.

- In some cases, deferral of tax.

These advantages come, however, with some drawbacks, including:

- Difficulties in selecting a fund that exactly matches an individual's needs and risk tolerance.

- Investment performance which can vary widely and fail to beat benchmarks.

- Reliance on the investment skill and application of the fund management group.

- An impact on future investment performance when star fund managers switch jobs.

- No influence on the selection of individual investments.

1 Performance measurement

Selecting a fund is usually based primarily on the performance it has achieved. If the performance of an investment fund is to be assessed, the first issue to address is how to measure it.

Investment performance is usually monitored by comparing it to a relevant benchmark. There are three main ways in which portfolio performance is assessed:

- Comparison with a relevant bond or stock market index. An index comparison provides a clear indication of whether the portfolio's returns exceed that of the bond or stock market index being used as the benchmark return. As well as the main stock market indices, many sub-indices have been created over the years which allow a precise comparison to be made.

- Comparison against a custom benchmark. Customised benchmarks are often developed for funds with unique investment objectives or constraints.

- Comparison to similar funds − a 'relevant universe' comparison. Investment returns can be measured against the performance of other fund managers or portfolios which have similar investment objectives and constraints. A group of similar portfolios is referred to as an 'investment universe'.

Most of the major indices used in performance measurement are market value-weighted indices such as the S&P 500 and other S&P indices, the Morgan Stanley Capital International indices, and the FTSE 100 and FTSE All-Share indices.

Where a portfolio spans several asset classes a composite index may need to be constructed by selecting several relevant indices and then multiplying each index by its weighting to arrive at a composite return. An example of such a custom benchmark is the private investor indices produced by FTSE and the Association of Private Client Investment Managers and Stockbrokers (APCIMS). The indices are based on three portfolios which each have different asset allocations to the same set of indices. The current allocations and respective indices are shown in Table 17.1.

Instead of an established index to benchmark portfolio performance, a comparison to a universe of similar funds using a peer group average is sometimes used.

The World Markets Company (WM) is a worldwide independent investment information services company which provides, among other services, performance measurement services to pension funds and other investing institutions. Combined Actuarial Performance Services Ltd (CAPS) is an independent investment performance measurement service for the UK, covering over 1,800 pension funds, and was set up as a joint venture by firms of consulting actuaries. Both WM and CAPS create benchmarks for pension fund portfolios.

Most pension funds adopt cautious investment policies and the guidance and benchmarks they set for fund managers lead to most schemes keeping their asset allocation close to the CAPS or WM averages. Both create universes which are an aggregation of funds or portfolios with similar investment briefs or types of owner, and both are used for peer group comparisons. There are many specialist universe groupings catering for a wide range of fund structures and investment management styles to provide relevant and accurate comparisons.

Table 17.1 – FTSE/APCIMS private investor indices

	Income portfolio %	Growth portfolio %	Balanced portfolio %	Representative index
UK shares	40.0	47.5	42.5	FTSE All-Share Index
International shares	15.0	32.5	25.0	FTSE World Ex-UK Index calculated in sterling
Bonds	35.0	7.5	20.0	FTSE Gilts All-Stocks Index
Cash	5.0	2.5	5.0	Seven-day London interbank offer rate −1%
Commercial property	2.5	2.5	2.5	FTSE UK Commercial Property Index
Hedge funds	2.5	7.5	5.0	FTSE Hedge Index
Total	100.0	100.0	100.0	

Once a suitable benchmark has been selected, the next step is to analyse how the portfolio has actually performed. The method used is performance attribution analysis. Performance attribution analysis attempts to explain why a portfolio had a certain return. It does so by breaking down the performance and attributing the results to the decisions made by the fund manager on asset allocation, sector choice and security selection.

Different types of fund aim to achieve returns in different ways and attribution analysts can show if they are in fact fulfilling their brief. For example, a bottom-up stock-picking fund would be expected to derive most of its returns from specific stock selection decisions. If attribution analysis showed that it was in fact sector selection or asset allocation that was the prime determinant of returns, one might question the managers about their methods.

Almost all investment comparisons are made on a total return basis. This assumes that any income received is immediately reinvested in further shares or units at the price ruling on the date of distribution. While this is a valid means of comparison, advisers may need to assess the income component of returns separately for income-generating investments such as equity income funds.

2 Past performance

One of the most frequently asked questions in the investment world is whether past performance is a reliable guide to future performance. Another way of phrasing this question would be to ask 'what is the probability of a fund that is performing above average this year still being an above-average performer next year'. Investment funds are usually promoted on the basis of their past performance and the level of charges.

One of the greatest myths perpetuated by many product providers is that the better a fund's past performance, the greater its chances of outperforming the peer group in the future. A simple conclusion can be reached: past performance should never be used as the sole basis on which to judge the suitability of a fund or, indeed, be relied upon as a guide to future performance. Moreover, high charges (often justified by managers with reference to past performance) will put an investor at an immediate disadvantage and are likely to be a significant drag on subsequent fund performance.

Although past performance provides initial evidence of a portfolio manager's skill and investment style, against this must be weighed the possibility of:

- Chance: good performance could be the result of luck not skill.

- Change: even if good performance is attributable to skill, very few portfolio managers manage the same portfolio for a considerable length of time. Moreover, manager skill, especially an ability to exploit a particular investment style or rotate between styles, is rarely consistent in changing market conditions.

Unsurprisingly, therefore, a significant amount of research has been undertaken in this area. The vast majority of academic studies of open-ended fund performance have concluded that there is very little persistence of good performance, but some have found a slight tendency for poor performance to persist.

Although there is no failsafe way of ensuring that a particular fund will consistently achieve above-average performance, detailed research and the use of independent fund ratings improve the chances of selecting a fund that produces above-average returns.

3 Independent fund ratings

There are a number of independent ratings agencies that provide ratings for investment funds. Most provide this data free of charge to financial advisers. The majority of these ratings are based on risk-adjusted past performance, though some place considerable weight on qualitative factors such as how portfolio managers run their funds. However, even the evaluation of qualitative factors only provides an indication of how a certain portfolio manager is likely to perform when adopting a particular investment style under specified market conditions.

Although none of these ratings agencies claim to have predictive power, they provide a tool that enables financial advisers to filter out those funds that consistently underperform. Indeed, research tends to suggest that using a fund awarded a top rating by one of these ratings agencies improves upon the 50:50 or coin-toss chance of that fund being an above-average performer in the future.

The main rating agencies use different methodologies and rating systems. The key features are reviewed below.

Lipper

Lipper Leaders is a fund-rating system that provides a simple, clear description of a fund's success in meeting certain investment objectives, such as preserving capital, lowering expenses or building wealth. The Lipper rating system measures a fund's performance against five key criteria:

- Total return relative to a group of similar funds.
- Whether a fund has provided consistent returns compared to a group of similar funds.
- The ability to preserve capital in a variety of market conditions.
- Management of expenses.
- Taxation.

Funds are ranked against each criterion and then compared against their peer group over different time periods, such as three, five and ten years. The results are then displayed in five groups so that for each criterion:

- The top 20% receive a rating of 5 and are named Lipper Leaders.
- The next 20% receive a rating of 4.
- The next 20% receive a rating of 3.
- The next 20% receive a rating of 2.
- The final 20% of funds receive the lowest rating of 1.

The results of each criterion for a given fund can then be analysed and the relative importance considered against the client's investment objectives and risk tolerance.

Morningstar

Morningstar's qualitative rating system gives an assessment of a fund's investment merits. The ratings can be used to narrow down the range of funds which an adviser wants to consider and can then be used in conjunction with Morningstar's fund reports. These provide an insight into current and future drivers of the fund's strategy and its likely performance biases in varying market conditions.

Morningstar's approach uses a combination of past performance and predictions of future performance by looking at five different criteria:

- The quality of the fund management team.

- The quality of the investment firm.

- The investment process used to determine investment strategy and its execution.

- Evaluation of investment performance.

- Analysis of a fund's total expense ratio.

Funds are then allocated a Morningstar qualitative rating against a peer group of pan-European and Asian funds. The ratings are:

- Elite.

- Superior.

- Standard.

- Inferior.

- Impaired.

If a fund is given an elite rating Morningstar believes it is capable of outperforming its peers over the long term. A superior fund rating means that Morningstar believes that the fund is above average and capable of producing peer-beating returns. The rating can be considered in conjunction with a fund report that provides a detailed analysis.

Standard & Poor's

Standard & Poor's uses a quantitative screening approach to identify the range of funds which it will rate. It assesses historical performance to identify the top 20% of funds for further detailed quantitative and qualitative analysis, which includes:

- Analysis of the current portfolio, audited accounts and marketing documents.

- In-depth interviews with the fund management team, covering the fund's investment culture, the investment process, investment disciplines and the experience and skills of the individual fund managers.

- Analysis of the make-up of the fund, including size, turnover, dealing, liquidity, use of derivatives and expenses.

The results of the assessment are then expressed in a rating system:

- AAA rating implies that the fund has demonstrated the highest standards of quality, on the basis of its investment process and the managers' consistency of performance as compared to funds with similar objectives.

- AA rating implies that the fund demonstrates very high standards of quality.

- A rating implies that the fund demonstrates high standards of quality.

4 Fund fact sheets

With so many funds available, the ratings agencies provide a valuable way of filtering them down to a manageable number that an adviser might wish to consider for recommendation to a client. The adviser will then need to drill down into the detail of these particular funds and this can be achieved using the readily available fund fact sheets.

Although fund fact sheets can vary, there are many common formats around as fund management groups often outsource the preparation of the sheets to the ratings agencies which allow their ratings to be added. Figure 17.1 shows the format of a typical fund fact sheet.

Some of the key points to note are as follows.

Investment objective

The fund's investment objective states what it aims to achieve. This could include as in this example to produce reliable growth by tracking the FTSE 100 index or could be more general, such as capital appreciation or income generation. The investment objective may also inform the investor about the investment style of the fund and the kind of risk it is prepared to take in order to achieve its investment objective.

Many equity funds in the past were launched with minimal statements of investment objectives. Today it is more common for them to set out objectives that give the investor a fairly good idea about how the fund will go about its investments. These should also indicate the type of investor for which the fund might be suitable.

Fund profile and portfolio composition

Highlights of the key components of a fund will be given. This information is a snapshot at a particular point in time and so may be well out of date. It is useful, however, as it gives an indication of where the fund is invested and how it is diversified among world markets and sectors. These details should be reviewed to identify areas of concentration and to highlight any issues of potential volatility if it is highly concentrated in certain sectors.

Figure 17.1 – A typical fund fact sheet

ABC Trust

Fund Objective		Fund Profile		
To provide the potential for reliable growth by tracking the performance of the FTSE 100 Index. In order to accurately track this Index, the trust's investments will closely replicate the holdings in that Index.		 UK Equities	Asset Allocation:	
			UK Equities	98.50%
			EU Equities	0.00%
			Bonds	0.00%
			Cash	1.50%

Portfolio Composition

Sector Weighting		Top 10 Holdings		Top 10 Countries	
Information	8.75%	HSBC	9.50%	United Kingdom	99.50%
Software	0.50%	BP	7.50%	Ireland	0.50%
Hardware	0.00%	Vodafone	5.50%		
Media	2.00%	Glaxo Smith Kline	4.75%		
Telecommunication	7.00%	Royal Dutch Shell	4.25%		
Service	38.00%	Royal Dutch Shell PLC B	3.50%	**World Regions**	
Healthcare	9.25%	AstraZeneca	3.00%	Greater Europe	100.00%
Consumer Services	5.35%	Barclays	3.00%	Americas	0.00%
Business Services	2.60%	Rio Tinto	3.00%	Greater Asia	0.00%
Financial Services	22.90%	British American Tobacco	2.95%		
Manufacturing	50.50%				
Consumer Goods	12.70%	Total Stock Holdings	100		
Industrial Materials	13.50%	Total Bond Holdings	0		
Energy	20.50%	Assets in Top 10 Holdings	47.78%		
Utilities	3.70%	Fund Size	£150.00M		

Fund Benchmark	Fund Rating	IMA Sector
FTSE 100		UK All Companies

Standardised Performance		Growth
Year Ended:		– Fund
30 Dec 2005		IMA Sector
30 Dec 2006		
30 Dec 2007		
30Dec 2008		
30 Dec 2009		

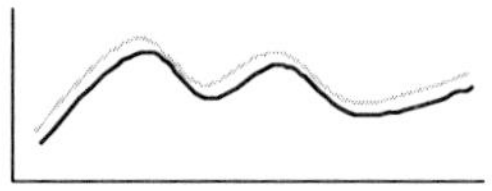

Risk Measures	2004	2005	2006	2007	2008	2009	Performance
R-Squared							Fund
Information Ratio							+/–IMA
Tracking Error							Percentile Ranking
Sharpe Ratio							
Std Dev							

General Information

Fund Launch	Domicile	Minimum Initial Investment
Fund Manager	Currency	Minimum Top Up
Latest Distribution Date	UCITS	Minimum Monthly Investment
Latest Ex-Dividend	ISA	Initial Charge
Historic Yield	IMA Sector	Annual Management Fee
Distribution Yield	ISIN	Extra Expenses
Underlying Yield	SEDOL	Performance Fee

The fact sheet should also provide details of the fund's top 10 holdings, which should be viewed in the context of the total number of holdings in the portfolio and the percentage this top 10 represents. If there is a high level of concentration, this should raise questions about the volatility of the fund as it may well generate good returns during market upturns but suffer in downturns.

Fund performance

The fund fact sheet should provide details of the index that the portfolio is benchmarked against and the IMA sector it is included in, together with the rating provided by one of the fund-rating agencies.

Discrete portfolio performance figures should be provided showing the actual returns achieved over a series of five years. These are one way of making a quick initial assessment of the consistency of returns in previous years. The returns should also be presented in graphic format and a comparison against a benchmark given along with how the fund ranks in percentile terms for its sector.

The performance figures need to be reviewed for the absolute returns they have generated and also compared to the benchmark and IMA sector to gain an understanding of the relative performance. The graphic presentation in particular should be checked to see what the fund is being compared against and whether other comparisons should be sought.

The fund fact sheet will identify what percentile ranking the fund has against its IMA sector, and its relative position should be investigated to identify whether there are other areas that should be investigated.

Turnover

Turnover is not given on all fund fact sheets but it is a key indicator in fund management and in the selection of funds. The turnover ratio is the percentage of a fund's holdings that are sold every year. Turnover is calculated by dividing the value of both the purchase and sale transactions for the period by two and dividing that figure by the total holdings of the fund. The ratio is used to measure trading activity, with higher ratios usually indicating higher associated expenses.

Growth funds tend to have high turnover ratios as managers of those funds seek companies and industries that demonstrate the promise of growth. The challenge for growth fund managers, and managers of any high turnover funds, is in achieving performance that compensates for the cost consequences associated with high turnover. Value funds, on the other hand, offer an example of a type of fund that typically has low turnover as managers of these funds tend to buy and hold stocks they believe to be undervalued.

Trading by a fund will incur brokers' commission and other charges and so higher levels of trading will incur significantly greater expenses that will detract from investment returns. These costs are not separately disclosed and instead it is necessary to draw conclusions from the level of turnover that takes place. This needs to be compared to the stated investment objective and investment approach of the fund. Where high levels of trading take place the fund manager needs to justify how this contributes to returns.

Research has shown that a turnover level of 100% in a year is the equivalent of an addition to the total expenses ratio of approximately 1%.

Risk measures

The section on risk measures assesses the fund using a variety of industry-standard measures, with a history of at least three years. These measures assess a fund's volatility as well as looking at its risk against a given benchmark.

Standard deviation measures the dispersion of the fund's returns over three years. Funds with a higher standard deviation are generally considered to be riskier. Standard deviation is the conventional measure of volatility. Other risk measures are based on this.

R-squared measures the degree to which the fund's performance can be attributed to the index against which it is benchmarked. For example, if a fund is benchmarked against the FTSE 100 and has an R-squared of 80%, this would indicate that 80% of its returns can be attributed to movements in the index itself.

The **information ratio** is a measure of the risk-adjusted return achieved by a fund. It takes the excess return over a benchmark achieved by the fund and divides this by the standard deviation of this excess return. A high information ratio indicates that when the fund takes on higher risks (so that its standard deviation rises) it increases the amount by which its returns exceed those of the benchmark index. It is therefore a sign of a successful fund manager.

The **Sharpe ratio** is simpler and measures the fund's return over and above the risk-free rate. The higher the Sharpe ratio, the better the risk-adjusted performance of the portfolio and the greater the implied level of active management skill. But the Sharpe ratio makes no allowance for the extra risk incurred in achieving those higher returns.

5 Rating agency reports

A fund fact sheet can only provide a snapshot of a fund. An adviser should see this therefore as part of a filtering exercise. Fund ratings help to reduce the universe of funds to be considered to a more manageable number and a review of the fund fact sheets allows this number to be reduced further.

The next stage is to review in detail the ratings agency report on the funds that have been short-listed and assess their suitability in meeting the client's investment objectives and their attitude to risk.

6 Fund manager ratings

As well as assessing the fund itself, many advisers believe it is important to consider individual fund manager ratings as well.

The fund management group designs the product but it is the skill of the individuals in the fund management team that delivers the performance. While the ratings agencies will include an assessment of the skill and experience of the fund management team in their rating, many consider that it is also worth looking at how highly rated or otherwise an individual fund manager is. Fund managers regularly switch funds and jobs, so the top-performing funds are not necessarily being run by the managers who were responsible for their high performance levels.

Citywire produces fund manager ratings to identify the individual managers who have the best risk-adjusted personal performance track records over three years. Its website also shows the funds these individuals are currently managing. Citywire's rating approach uses a version of the information ratio to identify which fund managers are adding value to their funds in terms of outperformance against their benchmark.

A figure of more than 1 is regarded as unusual and impressive as it indicates the fund manager delivers more than 1% outperformance of the index for each 1% deviation from the index. A figure of 0.5 is impressive. A positive figure is good; negative is not good.

The rating system covers fund managers from across Europe and the approach followed is as follows:

- The adjusted information ratio is established over a 36-month period.
- The first filter is then applied, which excludes any fund manager with an information ratio below 0.25.
- The information ratios of the remainder are then averaged to produce two pools.
- The top pool is then grouped into three classifications rated AAA, AA or A.

Within each country, less than 1% of managers receive an AAA rating and less than 10% receive any rating at all.

7 Other information available

As well as providing fact sheets, many fund management groups now exploit the internet to provide greater levels of detail about the funds they are managing and prospects for different market sectors. Fund groups now regularly schedule web-based presentations about new funds and markets or arrange online conferences where a fund manager is questioned about his or her investment strategy and plans.

Other resources are available to support fund selection and an understanding of the range and types of funds. An example is Asset TV – Assettvdirect.com – which provides reports on specific funds as well as learning material on topics such as bonds, types of bond funds, derivatives and multi-asset investing.

8 Other factors to consider

As well as considering the data available from fund-rating agencies, there are other factors that an adviser should take into account when comparing funds.

Size

One issue is size. The size of some of the largest fund groups means they have the organisational infrastructure that can support extensive research into the impact of the economic cycle, sector prospects and potentially rewarding new investment themes both in the UK and, in some cases, across the globe. This can give them a competitive edge which can translate into better investment performance.

As an actively managed fund becomes larger, however, its performance may suffer. The larger the fund becomes, the harder it can be to identify investment opportunities or price differences that it can effectively exploit because of the size of the investments it makes.

In fund groups without an effective organisational infrastructure, the manager of a large fund may have less time to conduct in-depth research and monitor each of the fund's holdings. The size of the portfolio may be such that making significant changes in its holdings could move the market against the fund, thus restricting its flexibility.

By contrast, a smaller fund can allow a talented fund manager to demonstrate his or her skills and deliver exceptional returns without the bureaucracy and constraints that might exist in a larger organisation. Many boutique fund management operations have been set up to exploit this very edge. However, these types of fund can present a risk through their dependence on one key individual. The potential for superior investment returns needs to be balanced against the absence of organisational support and the potential impact that can have on the consistency of returns. Whereas a large management group is likely to have several people involved in the management of a fund, so that the departure of one individual will not necessarily have a great impact on performance, boutique funds are often entirely dependent on one individual, and their departure may give advisers little choice but to sell.

Large funds can also spread their costs over a wider base. In particular, size works in favour of passively managed funds, especially those that employ full replication, solely for this reason. Data on fund size is usually contained in fund fact sheets.

In recent years some groups have set maximum figures for the assets they will take under management in a particular fund in order to avoid the risk of diluting performance. Because barring purchases of a UK-authorised open-ended fund is not permitted, managers will usually 'soft close' a fund by applying the full initial charge to all purchases.

Closet trackers

Another issue to consider is the closet tracker. Many supposedly actively managed funds are obsessed with benchmarks and simply aim to ensure that the performance they deliver does not vary significantly from the benchmark they are judged against.

Charges

A further factor to consider is the scale of a fund's charges. Although this is factored into the ratings of the fund agencies it is worth assessing independently as it has such a key impact on the investment performance delivered by the fund. High charges put a fund's potential performance at an immediate disadvantage.

Investment fund charges typically comprise an initial charge and an annual management charge. If an initial charge is not levied, the fund usually makes an exit charge that decreases the longer the fund is held. Increased competition and price transparency in the UK investment fund market has led to initial charges in particular falling quite considerably, though annual management charges have yet to feel the full force of competition.

Redemptions

Yet another issue that has become more significant in recent times is the suspension of redemptions. This has never been applied to funds investing in listed securities, but several UK funds investing in real property suspended redemptions by investors for several months in 2008. Even though these funds had significant liquidity, their problem was that a net asset value could not be determined given the exceptionally volatile and uncertain market conditions. Hence allowing investors to redeem could have resulted in their receiving far more or far less than their entitlement based on the true value of the assets.

This underlines the point that open-ended funds are best suited to holding investments that are listed and liquid. A closed-ended structure is more appropriate for assets that are by their nature illiquid (property) or hard to value (private equity).

Advisers should therefore pay close attention to the terms of real property funds. While most now have bank facilities to facilitate redemptions, they may still suspend redemptions and advisers need to know on what basis and for what periods managers are permitted to do this.

Funds of funds

Funds of funds (FoFs) have substantially increased the size of assets under management in recent years. This raises some issues for advisers. FoFs may become large holders of a particular fund if several FoFs managers – as is often the case – rate a particular manager highly. If all these FoFs then decide to sell at the same time, the fund may have no choice but to liquidate investments, possibly causing prices to fall in response to these sales and thus damaging the interests of ongoing investors. In theory, in these circumstances a 'dilution levy' should be applied, but even if it is, it may be inadequate to make up for the damage caused by large sales.

FoFs managers attempt to deal with this by phasing their purchases and sales, but advisers may consider that knowing the percentage of a fund's assets controlled by FoFs managers is essential, at least in the case of funds where forced sales could have a damaging effect, such as funds investing in stocks with smaller capitalisation or illiquid assets.

Summary

- Academic studies have shown that past performance is not a reliable indicator of manager skill and on its own has no predictive power. Nevertheless, advisers need to consider historic performance and attempt to identify the factors giving rise to above or below average returns.

- The choice of the right benchmark for comparative purposes is important; for example, a UK smallcap fund should not be compared with the FTSE100 Index.

- Fund rating agencies assess both past performance and manager quality. Advisers need to take their conclusions into account.

- Standard deviation is the conventional measure of the riskiness of a fund, but the information ratio, which measures the extra returns gained in relation to the extra risk incurred, is a more appropriate measure of manager skill.

- Advisers can now view manager interviews and presentations on the internet and participate in web conferences where they can put questions to the managers.

Chapter 18
Investment services

When looking at what investment solutions may be appropriate for a client, an adviser will need to consider whether an ongoing investment service should be recommended. There are a range of solutions that can be deployed to meet the client's needs, including the following options:

- Advisers can construct a suitable investment portfolio made up of collective investment schemes or other investment products. They can then arrange the investment and meet regularly with the client to review whether any changes are needed.

- A managed funds service could be provided, whereby advisers themselves undertake the active management of a portfolio of collective investment funds. Advisers normally offer a limited range of portfolios that have objectives that correspond with the main types of investment objectives.

- A Fund of Funds (FoFs) approach could be adopted, using either a single or several FoFs managers.

- Discretionary portfolio management services could be used. These involve the construction and management of a portfolio of direct bonds and equities by an independent investment manager.

1 Retail Distribution Review

The Retail Distribution Review (RDR) will lead to fundamental changes to the landscape in which individual investors buy investment products, as noted in chapter 2. Advisers need to understand how the advice market may change and what effects this may have on the way advice is given and the potential solutions that have to be considered.

The Financial Services Authority (FSA) issued its consultation paper on changes to the way investments are distributed to retail consumers in June 2009. The aim was to address various long-running problems regarding the quality of advice and consumer outcomes, as well as confidence and trust, in the investment market. The proposals will take effect from the end of 2012 and will affect all regulated firms involved in producing or distributing retail investment products and services, including banks, building societies, insurers, wealth managers and financial advisers.

The changes involve:

- Improving the clarity with which firms describe their services to consumers.
- Addressing the potential for adviser remuneration to distort consumer outcomes.
- Increasing the professional standards of advisers.

Investment firms will have to clearly describe their services as 'independent advice' or 'restricted advice'. Firms that describe their advice as 'independent' will have to ensure that they genuinely do make their recommendations based on comprehensive and fair analysis, and provide unbiased, unrestricted advice. Where a firm chooses to give advice only on its own range of products this will have to be made clear.

There will be significant changes to the charges that firms can make for advice, to remove the potential for remuneration bias. The proposals bring to an end the current commission-based system of adviser remuneration, and product providers will be banned from offering commission to secure sales. Instead, all firms that give investment advice will have to set their own charges and agree these with the client, and will also have to meet new standards regarding how they determine and operate these charges.

The minimum level of qualification for investment advisers will be raised. An overarching code of ethics will be introduced and standards for continuing professional development will be enhanced. Maintenance and enforcement of these standards will be achieved through the establishment of a professional standards board.

The proposed changes apply to the delivery of retail investment products, including packaged products, annuities, unregulated collective investment schemes and structured investment products.

Independent and restricted advice

The changes to be introduced from the end of 2012 on how firms describe their services to consumers are designed to achieve greater clarity and involve:

- Defining a wider category of retail investment product to which the standards on independence will apply.

- New standards for firms offering independent services, requiring recommendations to be based on a comprehensive and fair analysis of the relevant market and to provide unbiased and unrestricted advice.

- Requiring firms to make clear to the consumer, before providing advice, whether the services they are offering are independent or restricted.

Description of advice

The FSA policy changes introduce a new standard of independent advice which makes a clear distinction between independent advice and restricted advice:

- Independent advice is unbiased, unrestricted and based on a comprehensive and fair analysis of the relevant market.

- Advice which does not meet these requirements, which may be restricted advice or basic advice.

The intended outcome is that consumers are clear at the outset about which of these services they are being offered. This means that firms providing investment advice on retail investment products will be required to disclose in writing to each client, before providing the service, whether they will provide independent advice or restricted advice.

This will need to be disclosed as part of a firm's initial disclosure information and will have to use the terms 'independent advice' or 'restricted advice'. Firms will have flexibility to explain to clients what restricted advice is with reference to the particular service they are offering, bearing in mind the general requirement that the information should be fair, clear and not misleading.

In addition, firms offering restricted advice will be required to provide oral disclosure using a specific form of words that will include the name of the firm they work for and the range of products they advise on. This is intended to help consumers better understand the nature of the service they are being offered.

Categories of retail investment products

The FSA policy statement has confirmed that the definition of 'retail investment products' is to be widened to incorporate the range of investment products that firms provide recommendations on and on which consumers would expect to receive truly independent advice.

The rules on independent advice bring the following within the scope of retail investment products:

- Packaged products:
  - Regulated collective investment schemes.
  - Investment trust savings schemes.
  - Life assurance policies with an investment component.
  - Certain types of pension product.
- Unregulated collective investment schemes.
- All investments in investment trusts.
- Structured investment products except for structured deposits.
- Other investments which offer exposure to underlying financial assets, but in a packaged form which modifies that exposure compared with a direct holding in the financial asset.

This will mean that firms that provide independent investment advice to retail clients will be expected to have sufficient knowledge of all of the types of products which could be suitable for their clients.

These changes will affect, for example, wealth managers who offer independent advice and recommend their own products, for example structured products.

If they are to hold themselves out as providing independent advice then they cannot limit themselves to providing advice on their own products, and instead will have to consider their products against a wider range of products and solutions in the market and be prepared to recommend these other products.

If a firm decides that it wants to offer only products which give access to that firm's investment strategy, they will be able to do so, but will need to make clear to their clients that they provide restricted advice.

The proposals will also affect advisers who offer funds that they have a degree of influence over, known as 'distributor-influenced funds'. While an adviser will be able to offer these funds will not be able to restrict their advice to these funds alone and will have to rigorously assess whether a product is suitable for the client compared with other products in the market.

An independent adviser will also be expected to consider other solutions when making a recommendation, including cash deposits and National Savings & Investments products, in order to demonstrate that they are providing unbiased and unrestricted advice.

Market analysis and unbiased advice

Under the RDR changes, independent advisers will be required to review the whole market for the field in which they provide advice in order to deliver genuinely independent advice. This requires analysis of all of the retail investment products that are capable of meeting the investment needs and objectives of the client. This means that where a firm specialises in a narrow and distinct field, such as retirement planning or ethical and socially responsible investment, the whole of that specialised market must be considered. Firms will need to make this clear to their clients to ensure that those clients are not left with the impression that they are receiving independent financial advice on all retail investment products.

Where independent advisers are not specialising in a particular market, the relevant market will generally include all retail investment products, so an independent adviser should be considering all retail investment products when making a recommendation.

Where a firm uses product panels, it will need to ensure that any panel is acceptably broad in its composition and is reviewed sufficiently often to ensure that use of the panel does not materially disadvantage clients.

Where a firm uses a third party to conduct a comprehensive and fair analysis of the market, the firm is responsible for ensuring that the criteria used by the third party and the analysis conducted are suitably robust.

The FSA has also made clear that it would not expect independent advisory firms to be unreasonably biased or restricted in the products they offer. This means that firms should not have any kind of contractual agreement, or any other constraint or obligation, with any service or product provider that would restrict their ability to act in their clients' best interests. Anything done by a product provider, for example giving training, should not be allowed to influence the advice given in any way.

Where an independent advisory firm is financed, owned or part-owned by product providers, the firm should take sufficient steps to ensure that any financial interest does not influence it or prevent it in any respect from providing unbiased and unrestricted advice.

Impact on firms

The FSA has highlighted the issues that firms in particular sectors should consider when assessing the practical implications of the RDR proposals. These are shown in Tables 18.1–18.3.

Table 18.1 – Independent advisers – issues to be considered

Typical issues to consider are:

Does the firm satisfy the new independence standards which require the firm to provide advice that is:

- based on a comprehensive and fair analysis of the relevant market; and
- unbiased and unrestricted?

If not, it will not be able to hold itself out as independent and will it need to disclose to clients that it will provide restricted advice.

Does the firm need to modify the way it does business in order to satisfy the new independence standards?

- For the majority of IFAs that are not specialising in a particular market, they should be considering all retail investment products when making a recommendation.
- Some firms may need to consider a wider range of products than they do currently, to reflect the new retail investment product definition such as ETFs and structured investment products.
- Where the firm specialises in a narrow and distinct field such as retirement planning or ethical investments the firm should make this clear to clients and should not hold itself out as independent in a broader sense.
- In order to provide unrestricted advice, the firm should consider financial products such as National Savings & Investments products and cash deposit ISAs where these would meet the needs and objectives of the client.

Firms that use panels and/or third parties should review the use of these to ensure they are in line with the rules. Firms are responsible for ensuring the criteria used by the third party are sufficient to meet the comprehensive and fair analysis requirement.

Source: Financial Services Authority

Table 18.2 – Wealth managers – issues to be considered

Typical issues to consider are:

Does the firm want to describe its advice as independent? If so, it will need to consider – similarly to an IFA – whether it provides advice that is based on a comprehensive and fair analysis of the relevant market; and unbiased and unrestricted.

In practice this might mean the following:

- A wealth manager might need to consider whether, in practice, it is offering a narrow, specialist service (e.g. advice on investing in a particular geographical region) and if so, how to make this clear and avoid holding itself out as independent in a broader sense.
- Some wealth managers may need to check whether they are already considering a full range of solutions for their clients (for example, looking at the suitability of different tax wrappers and products that a client could invest through, or considering insurance-based or structured products).

If a wealth manager does not meet the new independence standards, it will need to disclose to clients that it will provide restricted advice.

Where a wealth manager designs or operates products that invest in a number of underlying investments, such as in house collective investment schemes, basing their advice on such products would not in itself meet the requirements for providing unrestricted advice, even where the products invest in a wide range of underlying investments. Such firms could therefore either:

- disclose to clients that it will provide restricted advice; or
- consider its in-house products impartially, as part of its comprehensive and fair analysis.

Source: Financial Services Authority

Table 18.3 – Banks and other single-tied and multi-tied advisers – issues to be considered

Traditional bank advisers, other single-tied and multi-tied adviser firms do not satisfy the new independence standards.

Firms bound by any form of agreement with a provider that restricts the firm's product range or imposes any obligation that may limit the firm's ability to provide unbiased and unrestricted advice will not satisfy the unbiased and unrestricted requirement.

Firms will need to disclose to clients that they will provide restricted advice.

Source: Financial Services Authority

Adviser remuneration

The changes to incentives and charges are designed to remove the potential for product bias based on the commission payable.

At present, firms that give advice on investments earn different amounts of money depending on which firm and product they recommend, creating a potential conflict of interest that can lead to a breach of their responsibility to act in the client's best interests. The FSA proposes to address this by requiring firms to be paid only for the advice and related services that they provide, through 'adviser charges'.

The charges are to be set out up front and agreed with clients. Whether they are paid directly, or as deductions from their investments, these charges should reflect the services being provided to the client, not the particular product provider, or product, being recommended.

The rules require adviser firms to be paid by adviser charges and do not allow adviser firms to receive commissions set by product providers, even if they intend to rebate these payments to the consumer. Firms will be expected to decide on their own charging structures and to apply these charging structures consistently to consumers. When designing charging structures, firms will be expected to do so responsibly and to meet the following expectations set by the FSA:

- Charges should not vary inappropriately according to the product provider that a firm recommends. The FSA does not expect to see the current variation in commissions replicated in the charging structures.

- Charges should not vary inappropriately according to the type of product offered, where different types are substitutable. Where a firm could recommend a number of competing types of products its charging structure should not incentivise it to recommend a particular type of product, against the interests of the consumer.

- Recommendations should not be influenced by the existence of terms or facilities offered by product providers to collect adviser charges.

Firms will also need to communicate both their overall charging structures and the specific amounts an individual is charged so that consumers are clear about what they will pay.

Under the new rules ongoing charges should only be levied where consumers are paying for an ongoing service such as a regular review of the performance of their investments. This is intended to avoid recreating the difficulty of whether clients are entitled to any services in return for the continuing payment of trail commission out of their investments. There is one important exception to this approach. A firm will be able to levy an ongoing charge, without this necessarily paying for an ongoing service, where a client is buying an investment to which they will contribute over time. This would allow firms to operate a charging structure for services relating to regular contribution products as long as this is made clear to the consumer in advance.

There will also be a ban on product providers offering commission or other benefits and the RDR changes will place new responsibilities on product providers.

As well as tackling the potential for product and provider bias, the changes address other sources of influence − 'inducements' − that have the potential to distort adviser recommendations. On inducements, the rules require that any payments and benefits are designed to enhance the quality of the service to the client.

2 Fund platforms and wraps

Platforms are online services used by intermediaries to view and administer their investment clients' portfolios. They offer a range of tools which allow advisers to see and analyse clients' overall portfolios, and to choose products for them. As well as providing facilities for investments to be bought and sold, platforms generally arrange custody for clients' assets.

The term 'platform' refers to both wraps and fund supermarkets. Wraps and fund supermarkets are similar, but while fund supermarkets tend to offer wide ranges of unit trusts and open-ended investment companies, wraps often also offer greater access to other products such as individual savings accounts, pension plans and insurance bonds.

Wrap accounts enable advisers to take a holistic view of the various assets that a client has in a variety of accounts. Advisers also benefit from using wrap accounts to simplify and bring a degree of automation to their back office using internet technology. The advantage for fund management groups is the ability of the platform to distribute their products to financial advisers.

Platforms earn income by either charging for their services or taking commission from the product provider. After the RDR proposals take effect, it was envisaged that platforms would not be able to take commissions from product providers. The FSA has now issued its proposals for the use of platforms post-RDR covering providing advice through a platform, how platforms are paid, adviser charging, rebating product charges to consumers and requirements for re-registration and provision of fund information. In summary, their proposals are:

- Use of platforms − when an independent firm uses one platform for the majority of its clients it ensures that the platform does not hinder the firm's requirements to meet the independence rules.

- Platform charges − bundled charging, that is product charges and platform charges, need not be separated. Fund managers and other product providers will be allowed to make payments to platforms for the administration services they receive, subject to improved disclosure of the payments to consumers and impartiality in the presentation of products.

- Adviser charging – when payment is facilitated by a platform, the same requirements are placed on the platform as would be placed on a product provider. No method is to be mandated as to how an adviser charge is paid and the FSA expect the adviser to take account of individual client circumstances when agreeing with the client how they will be paid. The FSA make clear that they do not expect advisers to be remunerated by payments or benefits from placing business with a platform in the same way that they should not receive payments or benefits from placing business with a product provider.

- Rebating product charges – product providers will be stopped from offering commission in the form of a cash rebate, which can be used to pay the adviser. As the proposal only prevents cash payments, it would not stop a fund manager from rebating part of their fund charges to customers in the form of additional units.

- Re-registration – rules will be introduced to make it compulsory for platforms to allow assets to be re-registered off their platform.

- Fund information – where investors use platforms to invest in CIS, the platform operator aggregates the holdings and holds them in a nominee account. Investors who access authorised funds in this way are to receive the same information as they would if they had invested directly. This proposal extends to requiring platforms to facilitate the exercising of voting rights on behalf of the end investor.

3 Distributor influenced funds

Distributor influenced funds (DIFs) are funds that individual intermediary firms set up in conjunction with a product or fund provider for the intermediary's exclusive use, and in which the distributor firm takes a more active role than in a wholly independent fund.

They are commonly arranged as OEICs, but can also take other structures, such as insurance funds, all of which enable the intermediary firm to offer their own house range of funds. They can provide investors with the shelter of a fund, if an adviser is to undertake regularly portfolio rebalancing without incurring CGT, and there can be economies of scale.

There are different variations. In some cases, intermediary firms specify a broad asset allocation and the provider firm manages the investments to this brief. In other cases, intermediary firms make individual fund decisions within a fund of funds arrangement.

While the fund administration and management is outsourced to third parties, the distributor has a degree of influence over the fund, with the exception of day-to-day asset selection. This places these funds somewhere on the fund spectrum between broker funds and independent third party funds. DIFs can however, create a conflict of interest between advisers and clients that has to be managed properly.

In addition, the distributor has control of the pricing of the contract and is not dependent on the product provider for remuneration, but this can lead to an increase in the cost, with the potential that a DIF may provide additional remuneration for a firm without providing any additional value for the client.

The specific features of a DIF may make it suitable for some clients, but not necessarily all clients, as the suitability of any fund should depend on the client's specific circumstances and requirements.

The FSA have raised concerns about the use of these funds and state that firms using them should ensure that they are in the best interests of each client and do not simply increase complexity and costs without providing new services that are suitable for the client. Given the potential for conflicts of interest to arise, the FSA expect firms to put in place robust systems and controls to ensure that the use of these products is in the best interests of each client.

4 Managed funds services

The idea behind funds of funds is the recognition that no one fund manager or investment house has expertise in all asset classes, geographic regions and investment styles, so it pays to diversify.

By selecting multiple managers a degree of diversification is obtained and the 'best' managers are selected. The main types of multi-manager fund are fund of funds and manager of managers. These are currently the fastest-growing investment products in the UK. However, the fees associated with these products tend to be higher due to the additional layer of management.

Fund of funds (FoFs)

A FoFs comprises a portfolio of retail collective investment schemes, with the aim of harnessing the best investment management talent available within a diversified portfolio. A FoFs has one overall manager. A FoFs can be either 'fettered' or 'unfettered'. Most FoFs are managed on an unfettered basis, in that the component funds are run by a number of managers external to the fund management group marketing the fund of funds. However, some are managed as fettered products, investing solely in funds run by the same management group as the fund.

The issue of charges needs to be closely looked at. An investor in a FoFs will pay that fund for its investment selection, and will pay the costs of the underlying funds as well. Whether or not this is an issue will depend on the performance that the fund produces compared to alternatives. FoFs is looked at in more detail in chapter 13.

Manager of managers funds

By contrast, a manager of managers funds does not invest in other investment schemes. Instead the fund arranges segregated mandates and appoints managers believed to be the best in their sectors to manage each. One disadvantage is that the initial investment required is usually substantially higher than for a FoFs or other collective investment scheme.

Compared to FoFs, manager of managers funds have the following advantages and drawbacks:

- The fund will have access to institutional managers that a retail investor would not normally be able to gain access to.

- If a portfolio manager fails to perform, the fund simply needs to replace the individual rather than selling the units and buying more and can therefore avoid switching costs.

- They can be cheaper than FoFs because they can access institutional management, where annual charges are usually lower than those in retail management.

- The institutional nature of the segregated mandate can, however, mean that the portfolio is overly diversified, which can turn it into an expensive index tracker.

- The fund may not be able to access the fund managers it wants as it may not be in the interest of another firm to allow a manager to be distracted by managing a portfolio for a third party.

- FoFs can access the investment funds they need because they are investing directly.

- Although a new fund manager can be appointed, there will be delays due to contracts and notice periods whereas the FoFs manager can simply sell and reinvest in another fund.

5 Discretionary investment management

Discretionary investment management is undertaken for wealthy individuals by a range of firms specialising in wealth management. As part of managing the overall wealth of an individual, the firm will construct and manage an investment portfolio that meets the individual investment priorities of the client. Normally this will be done on a discretionary basis, where the client and the investment manager agree on a long-term investment strategy that reflects the client's investment objective and attitude to risk. The investment manager then chooses when to buy and sell investments without obtaining the client's approval.

The construction of the portfolio may be entirely bespoke so that the portfolio is unique to the client. Alternatively, it may conform to one of a number of model investment portfolios that the firm constructs and manages that meet a range of typical private client profiles.

Portfolios will usually contain a mix of fixed income, equities and investment funds and will be managed in accordance with a strict, disciplined approach. An investment policy committee will usually make key asset allocation decisions, which are then implemented by an investment manager across client portfolios in a manner that takes into account individual client objectives and restrictions.

Many firms offering wealth management services are part of larger organisations and leverage their institutional research for the benefit of their private clients.

Wealth managers will usually manage multiple portfolios for clients, including a taxable portfolio and a separate portfolio for individual savings account investments. Asset allocation and investment decisions will take place at a consolidated portfolio level and then be implemented in the appropriate underlying portfolio.

As the investment management is usually undertaken on a discretionary basis, extensive client reporting is normally undertaken to keep clients in touch with how their assets are being managed and the performance that is being achieved.

Not all clients will be prepared to enter into discretionary investment arrangements. Many firms will therefore offer an advisory service to clients who want to maintain an active involvement in the investment management decision-making process.

Many discretionary fund manager services can now be accessed via wrap accounts. Advisers can therefore use several OFMs for clients of different types or with different objectives.

Summary

- Advisers have four principal methods of providing investment services: advisory selection of a set of funds; FoFs; managed fund portfolios; and discretionary management services.

- Under the FSA's RDR proposals, ongoing advisory or discretionary services should all be provided for an annual fee agreed by the client in advance.

- If operating as an IFA, the adviser must research the whole market for products that meet the client's needs, whether these are ETFs, structured products or OEICs.

- Advisers recommending sets of funds will generally use wraps or platforms since holding funds in this way is simpler for the client and facilitates regular reporting.

Part 4: Advising the client

Introduction

The process of advising clients on investment is rarely linear. Often the result of one part of the process is that a previous stage has to be repeated. This is an unavoidable feature of methods that are genuinely personalised and based on interaction with the client. It is possible to design linear processes using simplified model portfolios, but these are unlikely to deliver optimal solutions, especially for wealthy clients with complex affairs.

The initial stages of the process are fact finding and risk assessment, covered in chapter 19. Both are more complex than they appear. In particular, distinguishing between risk perception and risk capacity is an important part of the adviser's role in investigating what is usually described as 'risk tolerance'.

The growing awareness of the biases in human psychology – sometimes incorrectly referred to as 'irrationality' – makes knowledge of these and methods of dealing with them a key skill that advisers need to develop (chapter 20). Dealing with biases such as the endowment effect, framing, anchoring and mental accounting is an important part of the learning process for clients.

Having gathered the relevant information and analysed the client's risk tolerance and circumstances, the adviser needs to apply an asset allocation model as the first step in creating a suitable portfolio (chapter 21). Adviser firms need to develop their own guidelines in order to ensure consistency in the advice given. When asset allocation methods are used, the way reviews and rebalancing are dealt with is a critical feature of an advisory service.

Having determined an appropriate asset allocation, this needs to be implemented through tax wrappers (chapter 22). Normally the client will hold investments within two or more wrappers and advisers need to recommend holdings of the relevant asset types within wrappers so as to minimise tax liabilities while satisfying the client's access needs.

Chapter 19
What clients want

This chapter focuses on the approach a financial planner should adopt when providing investment services to private clients.

1 The planning process

To assist a financial planner in providing investment advice to clients, it is useful to follow a structured process. This should ensure no areas are overlooked and a consistent approach is taken. There are a number of investment process models already in use, each with a varying number of steps. However, they all broadly address the same areas. The following example is based on the model approved by the British Standards Institution in the International Standard ISO 22222:2005 (*Personal Financial Planning: requirements for personal financial planners*).

The objective of this standard is to promote consumer confidence by providing an internationally agreed benchmark for a high level of personal finance service. The standard applies to individuals rather than firms, although individual planners working for a financial planning firm would not be able to achieve the standard without the support of their firm.

The standard specifies requirements and provides a framework that applies to the ethical behaviour, competence and experience of a professional personal financial planner, regardless of employment status. The standard defines six steps in the personal financial planning process:

- Establishing and defining the relationship between the client and the personal financial planner.
- Gathering client data and determining goals and expectations.
- Analysing and evaluating the client's financial status.
- Developing and presenting the financial plan.
- Implementing the financial planning recommendations.
- Monitoring the financial plan and the financial planning relationship.

The standard recommends that a financial planner:

- Is able to deliver, and is competent in, the six stages of the financial planning process as defined.
- Has appropriate academic knowledge (defined in the standard at level 8 of the Scottish Qualifications Authority, which is equivalent to the English QCF level 4 (now the Qualifications and Curriculum Development Framework).

- Has relevant practical experience.

- Carries out relevant continuing professional development.

- Follows a published ethical code.

The standard describes the various methods of assessing conformity with it and specifies requirements applying to each of these. You can self-declare your conformity with the standard or obtain independent third-party certification. The British Standards Institution recommends that those seeking independent third-party certification do so using assessment bodies accredited to the accreditation standard ISO 17024 by the United Kingdom Accreditation Service.

Further information on the personal financial planning standard ISO 22222 can be found at www.cii.co.uk and www.standardsinternational.co.uk.

2 Fact finding

In the first meeting with a new potential client the financial planner should outline the services they can offer, for example:

- Savings and investment services.

- Comprehensive financial planning services.

- Mortgages.

- Pension and retirement planning services.

- Tax planning services.

- Accountancy services.

The financial planner should also provide the client with written confirmation of what they charge for their services, including their regulatory status and professional qualifications. It is a regulatory requirement that a copy of the firm's terms of business and the financial planner's business card are provided at the first opportunity.

In many cases, the initial meeting is offered at no cost and without further obligation to the client. This meeting should enable the client to gather enough information to decide whether to engage the financial planner in the management of their personal financial affairs, and enable the planner to decide if they are able and willing to offer their services to the client.

Once the basis of the ongoing relationship has been established and agreed, the next stage of the investment process involves gathering detailed information on the client's personal and financial circumstances. This data will be used to identify the client's goals, expectations and attitudes.

This is one of the most challenging areas of the financial planner's job, and several meetings, as well as telephone conversations and correspondence, may be needed before the adviser is confident that they know enough to formulate recommendations.

The process of gathering this information is referred to as 'fact finding' and the following paragraphs highlight the key areas that a financial planner should focus on when carrying out this task. Once this process is completed, the adviser should have a sufficient understanding of the client's financial position and investment objectives with which to undertake an analysis and cash flow projections.

Financial planners generally use a range of questionnaires to assist them in gathering the information they need to fully understand a client's financial position, future goals and expectations. It is highly unlikely that a single questionnaire will ever be detailed and flexible enough to capture every piece of information required. However, in addition to purely personal information, the following areas should be considered central to any data-gathering exercise:

- Needs and objectives.

- Assets and liabilities.

- Income and expenditure.

- Priorities.

- Attitude to risk.

Methods of gathering and storing this information vary. Some firms use electronic methods while others continue to use printed questionnaires. Firms may have one 'master' fact-find document and select from this the sections relevant to the client, or have a series of documents, one of which is selected for each client. In some cases, the questionnaires are completed during the course of a meeting with the client, who may then be asked to sign to agree the contents. Other advisers prefer to send a printed form to the client in advance so they can complete most of the routine information before the meeting.

The data-gathering stage is crucial to the rest of the process. The ultimate success of any financial plan developed and implemented by the financial planner relies on a full and frank disclosure by the client. Any events not anticipated or planned for, such as a maturing policy or debt repayment, could affect the client's ability to meet their planned financial objectives. If such a situation occurs this will inevitably lead to some form of financial compromise.

Successful fact finding involves reviewing the answers given in the questionnaire by the client, and then asking supplementary questions in order to fully appreciate their relevance and importance.

The questions contained in the fact find tend to be closed questions, for example:

- What is your date of birth?
- How much do you earn?
- Do you have a pension?
- What income would you like in retirement?
- How much risk are you prepared to take with your investments?

There are of course many facts that cannot be gathered through the use of questionnaires alone and must instead be obtained through a series of discussions with the client. Supplementary questions should be open in nature, because this will enable the financial planner to get a deeper understanding of the client's personal and financial circumstances, needs and aspirations.

Examples of open questions include:

- What kind of lifestyle would you like to have when you retire?
- How would you provide for your family if you were unable to work due to ill health?
- What are your plans for funding your children's future education?
- Tell me about your future financial aspirations and how you plan to afford these.

Facts can be conveniently divided into hard and soft facts. Hard facts are certainties and known quantities:

- Age and marital status.
- Income and employment.
- Assets and liabilities.

Soft facts are preferences, views, opinions and aspirations:

- Tolerance of investment risk (see below).
- Preference for socially responsible investments.
- Desire to have children educated privately.

While it is normal practice to ask the client to sign a completed fact-find document, advisers will base their recommendations on 'soft' facts as well, and these can seldom be fully documented. It is vital that the client also confirms these, and this is usually done by including them in the preamble to the written report.

The facts gathered at the initial stage should be checked from time to time. This is an important part of any subsequent review process. By taking account of any changes in the client's personal circumstances as they happen, the adviser will ensure the investment plan remains current and appropriate. This will also limit the possibility of failing to meet the client's requirements. Some examples of changes that could affect existing plans are:

- Changes to salary and employment.
- Changes to short-term financial objectives, for example funding for holidays or new cars.
- New additions to the family.
- Inheritances.
- Changes to risk tolerance.

It is good practice to review the initial fact find at subsequent meetings, as necessary adding additional notes to the client's file as necessary.

3 Risk assessment

Investment always involves trade-offs between risk and return. For regulatory reasons, assessment of the client's needs and wants in relation to returns and risk are usually referred to as 'risk profiling', but in reality this requires investigation of attitudes to both the risk of loss and the desire for returns, and a more accurate description would be 'risk-return profiling'.

Most clients have little choice about accepting risk, unless they are in the unique position of being able to afford all their current and future financial objectives – in which case they are unlikely to need the services of an adviser. The majority, therefore, need to accept some degree of risk.

The job of the financial planner is to explain to the client the base level of risk required to give them a reasonable chance of achieving their objectives, and to gain their agreement to this. If the client does not agree, or is uncomfortable with the level of risk required, they need to revise their objectives or lower their expectations.

There are three distinct elements the adviser needs to take into account when undertaking the risk assessment process with the client:

- **Risk tolerance** is a personality characteristic best described as a client's willingness to accept a certain level of fluctuation in the value of their investments without feeling an immediate desire to sell.
- **Risk perception** represents the client's personal opinion on the risks associated with making an investment, based on their prior knowledge and experience.

- **Risk capacity** is the client's actual ability to absorb any financial losses that might arise from making a particular investment.

Taken together, these three elements should form the basis for discussions on investment risk. This will assist the financial planner in arriving at a risk classification or profile that is acceptable to the client.

The risk assessment process usually starts with investigation of attitudes; consideration of risk capacity usually follows later, since it requires knowledge of the client's objectives.

The interaction between the three risk elements is also worth considering. For example, tolerance and perception may be less important if the client's capacity for risk is low due to their financial position. As tolerance is based to some extent on the client's personality and shaped by life events, it is likely to vary less than perception and capacity.

Perception may change depending on market conditions; for example, immediately following the market correction of 2008 clients may have perceived greater risk being present. Similarly, a client who is sitting on large losses will have a reduced risk capacity until the value of the portfolio recovers or they come into new money, for example through a bonus or inheritance.

The Financial Services Authority (FSA) has made it clear that it regards assessment of risk capacity as a key factor in giving appropriate advice. Its interpretation of risk capacity is essentially the ability to withstand losses.

Risk tolerance

Assessing a client's tolerance of risk is an important part of the investment process which should always form part of the initial fact find. It is impossible to construct an appropriate investment portfolio and demonstrate that it matches the client's requirements without first quantifying and agreeing the level of risk to be taken.

There are a number of approaches that can be taken to establish the client's attitude to risk, including:

- Printed questionnaires.
- Computer-based assessments.
- Psychometric profiling.
- Numerical scales (1–10).
- Open discussions.
- Graphical representations.

The most effective approach may be one that incorporates some or all of these elements.

Computer-based assessments and psychometric-profiling tools are widely available from a number of different sources, both as stand-alone software packages and online. These offer a more scientific approach to establishing risk and often incorporate some or all of the elements listed above, including graphical representations, numerical scales, direct statements and closed questions.

Question-based assessments are designed to measure a client's emotional response to changes in the value of their investments using both subjective and objective questioning, for example:

Objective questions

- What forms of investment planning have you received advice on?

- What savings and investment products have you purchased in the last ten years?

- Have you taken advice in the past when making investments?

- Which of the following statements best describes your knowledge and experience of investments?

  - I have a very limited knowledge of investments, have made little or no investments in the past and take no interest in following my finances.

  - I have a reasonable to strong knowledge of investments, have previously made investments and take an interest in following the performance of my investments and the progress of my financial plan.

  - I have a very strong knowledge of investments and have previously made a wide range of investments, including sophisticated products. I take an active interest in investments generally and follow the performance of my investments regularly.

Subjective questions

- What is more important for you in the context of investments: the risk or the potential gains?

- What degree of risk would you say you have taken in the past?

- Would you borrow money for the purposes of making an investment?

- If your stocks and shares dropped in value by 20% would you sell them, do nothing or buy more?

Risk perception

Risk perception is a subjective view that clients take on the characteristics and severity of risk. In the present context, this refers to their understanding of the risks involved in making a particular investment, when compared to the alternatives available, based on their own knowledge and experience.

For example, a client may perceive that placing funds in a cash deposit account does not present any risk to the value of their capital. In nominal terms this is true, but once the impact of inflation has been explained and understood, the client will appreciate that the real value of their capital will diminish over time if the rate of interest they receive on their savings does not exceed the current rate of inflation.

Therefore, as the client's practical experience of investing increases, this is likely to shape their perception of risk when they are considering future investment opportunities. Advisers need to be aware that this will happen and, without being patronising, help the client deepen their understanding to whatever extent they wish.

Risk capacity

Risk capacity is the client's ability to absorb any negative financial outcome that may arise from making a particular investment.

Risk tolerance and risk perception are partly subjective, but risk capacity is largely a matter of fact. While most clients have some notion of attitudes to and perception of risk, they are unlikely to have thought precisely about risk capacity, and here the adviser's role is to present the facts as clearly as possible based on their analysis of the client's needs and circumstances. The more detailed the adviser's knowledge of these, the more accurately they can formulate the client's capacity for risk.

In some cases, risk capacity will play the most important role in determining the client's overall risk profile. For example, a client who is retired and drawing an income from their portfolio is likely to have a reduced capacity for risk. Unlike a younger person, they may not be in a position to generate replacement income or new capital to cover any losses made in the portfolio.

By comparison, someone in their mid-30s will have a greater capacity for risk, as they will have the opportunity to replace any portfolio losses through future earnings.

While subjective factors largely determine risk perception and attitude, the key question in assessing risk capacity is a more objective one: what would be the consequences for the client if losses were incurred? Unlike tolerance and perception, this is hard to assess through questionnaires and must be based on the adviser's analysis of the client's circumstances.

The client's capacity for risk will also be affected by the level of investment being considered. If the amount at risk represents a significant portion of the overall portfolio, risk capacity may be diminished. Risk capacity will be greater when the amount at risk is a small fraction of available capital.

Events likely to reduce a client's tolerance of, and capacity for, investment risk include:

- Redundancy.
- Divorce.
- Illness or the death of a close family member.
- Significant losses from other investments.
- Ageing.

Events likely to trigger an increase in the client's capacity for and tolerance of investment risk include:

- Inheritance of a large sum of money.
- An increase in income over expenditure.
- The repayment of debts.
- A pay rise or bonus payment.
- Significant gains on the portfolio.

It is important to note that assessing a client's capacity for risk is regarded by regulators as an essential step in the provision of appropriate advice.

Risk profile

Various classifications of 'risk profiles' are in use today and the following example may be considered as the starting point for most financial planners:

- Cautious.
- Cautious balanced.
- Balanced.
- Balanced aggressive.
- Aggressive.

However, the regulators have raised questions about the use of categories with emotionally loaded descriptive terms. Best practice is to use a series with no such connotations. For example, a series of five profiles could run: minimal, low, moderate, above average, high.

It is possible to break these categories down further, and a series of seven profiles is used by some advisers, but in practice any further differences would be minor. Although it may be obvious to the financial planner, it is often difficult for the clients to understand whether they are at the more cautious end of the balanced class or at the more adventurous end of the cautious class.

A series of five categories is probably sufficient for most clients and financial planners. Subsequent discussions – including risk capacity – where the client uses the appropriate asset allocation model will help the client to arrive at a classification that they feel best reflects their views and their tolerance to investment risk. This should be the basis of future investment decisions.

The outcomes from the initial assessment should correlate with a specific description of the client's risk tolerance. For example:

- A **cautious investor** is not willing to accept any risk to their investment in the short term. They understand that low-risk investments have smaller potential for growth than higher-risk investments do, and that over the long-term inflation will reduce their capital's buying power.

- A **cautious balanced investor** is looking for a higher rate of investment return than those available from a high street deposit account, while accepting that the value of their investment could fall as well as rise. However, they would feel uncomfortable if their investments rose or fell in value very rapidly.

- A **balanced investor** is looking for a balance of risk and reward. Although they are willing to take a level of risk necessary to achieve a potentially higher rate of return, they would not be happy to see their capital eroded or lost completely.

- A **balanced aggressive investor** is willing to accept a higher level of risk on their investment in return for higher returns in the long run. As a result, they are willing to accept fluctuation in the value of their investments.

- An **aggressive investor** is willing to accept a much higher risk on their investments in return for higher returns in the long run. They accept that the value of their investments could fluctuate significantly.

These descriptions should in turn match an appropriate asset allocation model (see chapter 21).

The next step is to consider the client's financial objectives and timescales, and whether the level of risk chosen will be enough to deliver the returns required if a portfolio appropriate to that level of risk is used. If it appears unlikely the objectives will be achieved, the adviser should discuss further with the client to determine whether they are comfortable with taking additional risk to give them a greater chance of achieving their requirements, or whether they are prepared to compromise on their objectives to preserve their capital. This is covered in greater detail later in the chapter.

The adviser should disclose the results of the risk assessment to the client and discuss them before formulating any investment strategy. Once the client has understood and agreed to a particular level of risk to be taken in the management of their portfolio, this should then be documented and the financial planner and the client should signed them off.

When discussing investment strategy with the client, the adviser should point out that the risk profile will apply to the overall portfolio and not necessarily to the individual underlying investments themselves. For example, it is quite possible that a cautious balanced portfolio may include some equity exposure, where the volatility is likely to be higher than that intended for the portfolio as a whole. However, the level of exposure in the context of the overall portfolio will be insignificant and therefore not likely to impact the overall level of risk being taken in the management of the portfolio.

As part of the ongoing review process, the client's risk tolerance should be checked from time to time. Various life events can shape a client's appetite as well as capacity for risk and must be taken into account – see below.

4 Wants and needs

Once the fact-finding process has been completed, the next stage is to identify the client's wants and needs.

Establishing what a client wants is a relatively straightforward process, generally involving questionnaires and straightforward discussions. However, identifying what a client needs usually requires a more in-depth analysis of their financial circumstances.

There is often a conflict between the client's perception of a financial need and the financial planner's perception. This conflict is usually addressed early on in the relationship and involves explaining to the client, through the use of examples, how wants and needs differ from a financial planning perspective.

For example, a financial planner would consider protecting the value of the accumulated portfolio and ensuring the client's continued standard of living as financial needs. In contrast, a client's description of their needs is often centred on current planned or future discretionary expenditure.

Common examples of wants and needs are listed below:

Wants

- A bigger house.
- A new car.
- A new kitchen.
- A round-the-world cruise on retirement.
- Private education for the children.

Needs

- Funds to repay the mortgage on death or illness.

- Funds to pay for future education fees.

- Reducing debts.

- Increasing savings in the short, medium and longer term.

- Retirement planning.

The financial planner has to objectively assess the client's financial position in order to establish what they do in fact need, before comparing this with what they want, and then setting priorities with the client's agreement.

For example, John says he wants to buy a holiday home in France. In discussions with John, the financial planner determines that there is a need to provide funds to cover the cost of his children's education over the next five years. Having reviewed the costs involved, John and the financial planner agree to defer the purchase of the holiday home until after the children's education has been completed.

Most clients are unlikely to be able to afford all their wants and needs, including those identified by the financial planner. Therefore, the next step is to discuss affordability and the realistic possibility of achieving these objectives within the required timescales.

Unrealism

A client's perception of what they can achieve financially is often distorted and it is the financial planner's job to help explain the level of financial commitment required to meet the client's expectations.

Example 19.1: Pension planning

John is 50 years old and earns £50,000 a year. He tells you he would like to retire on a pension of £25,000 a year when he reaches age 55. On further investigation, you discover that his existing pension arrangements have a combined value of £150,000.

You explain to John that, based on current annuity rates, this would be sufficient to provide a pension of around £9,000 a year in today's money. Therefore, assuming annuity rates remain at current levels, John would need a fund of over £400,000 in five years' time to provide the level of income he wants, and this does not even take into account the effects of inflation.

Ignoring investment returns and assuming annuity rates remain unchanged, John would need to commit 100% of his annual income for each of the next five years in order to build a fund large enough to provide the required

---

level of income in retirement. This is unrealistic and, given the short period until retirement, John is unlikely to be prepared to invest his pension fund into more volatile assets, such as equities, in order to provide an opportunity to accelerate growth over the next five years.

In this example John's objective of retirement at age 55 on £25,000 a year is unfeasible, based on the financial provision that he has made so far. You need to explain that his options now include the following:

- Delay his retirement for a few years in order to allow time to increase the value of the pension fund through investment returns and additional contributions.

- Retire on a lower pension income and supplement this by working part time.

Conflicts between objectives

Conflicts can often arise when setting financial objectives. For example, the client wishes to plan for a significant capital outlay in a year when school fees will have to be paid, or when their income is expected to go down because of a planned early retirement.

In setting and agreeing objectives, a financial planner should review the timescale for each and prioritise them with the client's agreement. If circumstances permit, it may also be appropriate to build a contingency into the financial plan to fund unplanned expenditure. This should help to reduce the possibility of any conflict arising, which could otherwise require a compromise or the deferment of planned expenditure.

'What if?' scenarios

'What if?' scenarios can be useful in highlighting the client's needs and often take the form of open questions at the fact-finding stage. Examples might be:

- What if your income was less than expected in retirement?

- What if your income stopped altogether?

- What if you suffered a long-term debilitating illness that prevented you from working again?

- What if the value of your portfolio went down significantly?

- What if some of the assets in your portfolio could not be accessed for an indefinite period of time?

Planning for the most likely outcomes

When setting financial objectives with the client it is important to focus on planning for the most likely outcomes. Agreeing a series of well-defined financial objectives and then designing a plan to achieve these is the most effective route.

However, it is virtually impossible to predict all the future cash inflows and outflows. A sensible approach is one that takes account of known future cash flows and builds a contingency plan to deal with any unexpected cash calls. These can be provided for by additional funds set aside to cover unknown future costs or by financial protection such as:

- Life assurance.
- Critical illness cover.
- Medical expenses cover.
- Mortgage payment protection insurance.
- Redundancy cover.

As the adviser is effectively planning for the unknown it can be difficult to calculate a suitable level of cover or put a value on the size of fund required. Further discussion with the client on the financial implications of an unplanned event, using the 'What if?' scenarios mentioned above, should help the planner and client to arrive at a suitable figure.

5 Accumulation and decumulation

It is possible to consider a client's lifetime cash flow requirements under two distinct headings:

- Accumulation of capital.
- Decumulation of capital.

In the years leading up to retirement, the focus is primarily on the accumulation of capital through saving and investing, with the general aim of increasing the value of the assets in order to fund the client's short-, medium- and longer-term financial objectives.

At retirement and beyond, the focus switches to the 'decumulation' phase, when the value of the portfolio is gradually eroded through expenditure with little or no further new investment.

Life stages

The client's requirements and their ability to fund these will both change as they progress through various life stages. These are shown in Table 19.1.

Table 19.1 – Life stages

Life stage	Client requirements, etc
Single	Recently left university and started first job. Normally renting property, with option to join employer's pension scheme. Disposable income, after payment of rent and student loans, often spent on social life.
Married	Saving towards deposit for joint purchase of home. Starting a family; building up a fund to support couple during maternity leave.
Married with children	Ongoing repayment of mortgage with a view to moving to a larger property to accommodate family. Funding costs of nursery care, private school fees and retirement planning. Concerns on loss of income from illness, death, redundancy, etc.
Middle age	Repaying mortgage and providing financial assistance for children's education.
Retirement	Security of existing capital. Ensuring levels of income are maintained. Provision for long-term care and estate planning.

Accumulation for 40 years to fund decumulation for 40 years

In the UK life expectancy at birth has reached its highest level on record for both sexes. A newborn boy could expect to live 77.2 years and a newborn girl 81.5 years if mortality rates remain the same as they were in 2005–07.

Women continue to live longer than men, but the gap has been closing. Although both sexes have shown annual improvements in life expectancy at birth, over the past 25 years the gap between them has narrowed from 6 years to 4.3 years. Based on mortality rates in 1980–82, 26% of newborn males would die before age 65, but based on 2005–07 rates only 16% would die before 65. The equivalent figures for newborn females were 16% in 1980–82 and 10% in 2005–07.

A similar pattern can be seen for life expectancy at age 65, that is, how many more years someone reaching 65 could expect to live. Based on 2005–07 mortality rates, a man aged 65 could expect to live another 17.2 years, and a woman aged 65 another 19.9 years.

Within the UK, life expectancy varies by country. England has the highest life expectancy at birth (77.5 years for males and 81.7 years for females), while Scotland has the lowest (74.8 years for males and 79.7 years for females). Life expectancy at age 65 is also higher for England than for the other UK countries.

Table 19.2 – Life expectancy, 2005–07

| | Age in years | | | |
| | At birth | | At age 65 | |
	Males	Females	Males	Females
United Kingdom	77.2	81.5	17.2	19.9
England	77.5	81.7	17.3	20.0
Wales	76.7	81.1	16.9	19.6
Scotland	74.8	79.7	16.0	18.7
Northern Ireland	76.2	81.2	16.8	19.7

Source: Interim Life Tables 2005–07, Office for National Statistics

These life expectancy figures make no allowance for future changes in mortality. Taking into account the continued improvements in mortality assumed in the 2006-based principal population projections, life expectancy at birth for those born in 2006 is projected to be 88.1 years for males and 91.5 years for females. Similarly, life expectancy for those aged 65 in 2006 is projected to be 20.6 years for males and 23.1 years for females. It is also projected that a male born in the UK in 2006 would have a 91% chance of reaching age 65, and a female a 94% chance. (All figures from the Office for National Statistics.)

As the data shows, if life expectancy continues to increase at current rates clients will need a much larger fund when they retire to support their income and capital needs for longer. In a few more decades, it is likely that life expectancy will reach, and perhaps even surpass, 100. Even if official retirement age is raised, clients could live for up to 40 years after they cease full-time employment. In other words, they could expect to have 40 years to accumulate the wealth they need to support 40 years of expenditure during retirement.

6 The use of gearing

The use of borrowing to finance an investment, often referred to as 'leverage' or 'gearing', can enhance investment returns, while also increasing the potential capital loss to the client.

Example 19.3: Borrowing to invest

A £10,000 investment generates a total return of 10% or £1,000 over 12 months. Let us suppose the investor borrows £90,000 at an interest rate of 6% a year and invests £100,000 instead of £10,000. This larger investment would generate a return of £10,000 over the same period of time. After the payment of interest costs (£5,400) and principal, the total return is reduced from £10,000 to £4,600. However, this still represents a net return of 46% on the client's own cash investment of £10,000.

However, if the investment returned a loss of 10% over the same period, the situation would be quite different. A 10% loss on the gross investment of £100,000 would be £10,000, leaving £90,000 remaining to repay the £90,000 principal on the loan. The interest payment of £5,400 remains due, so the investor is down by their own cash investment of £10,000 plus the £5,400 interest, making a total loss of £15,400. This equates to a net return of −154% on the original investment of £10,000.

Financing of asset purchase

Financing the purchase of an asset is best illustrated by the purchase of residential or commercial property using a secured loan facility or mortgage. Most lenders require a deposit of at least 10% of the purchase price, with the balance of the purchase cost provided by a loan over an agreed term at a fixed or variable rate of interest. The maximum level of borrowing is usually calculated by reference to the individual's financial circumstances, taking into account their income, other assets and ability to service the repayments.

Mortgage repayment options

There are two distinct options for the repayment of a secured loan or mortgage:

- The payment of both interest and capital in regular amounts over the term of the loan. The outstanding balance goes down over time and is fully repaid by the end of the term.

- The payment of the loan interest only over the term of the mortgage, with the loan capital repaid at the end of the term from the maturing value of an associated savings policy or other assets.

The route chosen depends on the client's financial circumstances and age, the amount borrowed, the term of the loan and the level of interest being charged. Often younger borrowers are not in a position to repay both interest and capital each month, and so opt to pay the interest only, while diverting some of their disposable income into a suitable savings arrangement with a view to using the accumulated sum to repay the capital at the end of the term.

Capital repayment mortgages

The capital repayment route provides greater certainty for the borrower. Payments are calculated to include an element of the loan capital, as well as interest, so that the outstanding balance of the loan is reduced over the course of the term, finally reaching zero at the end.

Interest only mortgages

Combining an interest only mortgage with a regular savings plan is an accepted loan repayment strategy for many homeowners. In addition to regular payments of interest to the lender, additional amounts are invested, usually monthly, in an associated savings plan designed to mature with a capital sum payable to the policyholder at the end of the repayment term.

In the past, with-profits and unit-linked endowments were used as regular savings vehicles to assist with the repayment of the outstanding capital at the end of the term. However, as many policyholders discovered, the maturity values of these policies were often less than expected due in part to poor investment performance. Many policyholders were left still owing capital at the end of the repayment term.

Savings plan requirements

If the borrower is to be reasonably certain of repaying the loan capital on an interest-only mortgage, the total monthly payments made to the interest-only mortgage and the savings vehicle combined should equal those of an equivalent capital and interest repayment mortgage. If the investment returns achieved on the savings vehicle equal the average rate of interest being charged on the loan then the value on maturity will be sufficient to repay the outstanding loan.

Example 19.4: A saving plan to support an interest-only mortgage

John borrows £200,000 for 25 years and pays an average interest rate of 4.5% a year. On an interest-only mortgage his interest payments would be £750 a month, whereas a capital and interest repayment option would cost him £1,111 a month.

John chooses the interest-only option and saves the difference in monthly cost (£1,111 − £750 = £361) in a regular savings policy, which earns an average return of 5% a year over the 25 years.

Year	Year deposits	Total deposits	Year interest	Total interest	Total paid
1	£4,332.00	£4,332.00	£216.60	£216.60	£4,548.60
2	£4,332.00	£8,664.00	£444.03	£660.63	£9,324.63
3	£4,332.00	£12,996.00	£682.83	£1,343.46	£14,339.46
4	£4,332.00	£17,328.00	£933.57	£2,277.03	£19,605.03
5	£4,332.00	£21,660.00	£1,196.85	£3,473.89	£25,133.89
6	£4,332.00	£25,992.00	£1,473.29	£4,947.18	£30,939.18
7	£4,332.00	£30,324.00	£1,763.56	£6,710.74	£37,034.74
8	£4,332.00	£34,656.00	£2,068.34	£8,779.08	£43,435.08
9	£4,332.00	£38,988.0	£2,388.35	£11,167.43	£50,155.43
10	£4,332.00	£43,320.00	£2,724.37	£13,891.80	£57,211.80
11	£4,332.00	£47,652.00	£3,077.19	£16,968.99	£64,620.99
12	£4,332.00	£51,984.00	£3,447.65	£20,416.64	£72,400.64
13	£4,332.00	£56,316.00	£3,836.63	£24,253.27	£80,569.27
14	£4,332.00	£60,648.00	£4,245.06	£28,498.34	£89,146.34
15	£4,332.00	£64,980.00	£4,673.92	£33,172.25	£98,152.25
16	£4,332.00	£69,312.00	£5,124.21	£38,296.47	£107,608.47
17	£4,332.00	£73,644.00	£5,597.02	£43,893.49	£117,537.49
18	£4,332.00	£77,976.00	£6,093.47	£49,986.96	£127,962.96
19	£4,332.00	£82,308.00	£6,614.75	£56,601.71	£138,909.71
20	£4,332.00	£86,640.00	£7,162.09	£63,763.80	£150,403.80
21	£4,332.00	£90,972.00	£7,736.79	£71,500.59	£162,472.59
22	£4,332.00	£95,304.00	£8,340.23	£79,840.82	£175,144.82
23	£4,332.00	£99,636.00	£8,973.84	£88,814.66	£188,450.66
24	£4,332.00	£103,968.00	£9,639.13	£98,453.79	£202,421.79
25	**£4,332.00**	**£108,300.00**	**£10,337.69**	**£108,791.48**	**£217,091.48**

At the end of 25 years John has a total of £217,091 available from the maturing savings plan, which is enough to repay the outstanding loan of £200,000 and leave him with an excess of £17,091 (figures assume that interest is calculated annually and added at the end of each year).

Risks

If John saves less than the combined capital and interest repayment of £1,111 a month he is at risk of not being able to repay the loan unless he achieves a greater return from his investment in the regular savings policy.

For example, if he saves only £300 a month and achieves an average rate of return of 4.5% a year, this will leave him with only £167,654 after 25 years and a shortfall of £64,810 (figures assume that interest is calculated annually and added at the end of each year).

Year	Year deposits	Total deposits	Year interest	Total interest	Total paid
1	£3,600.00	£3,600.00	£162.00	£162.00	£3,762.00
2	£3,600.00	£7,200.00	£331.29	£493.29	£7,693.29
3	£3,600.00	£10,800.00	£508.20	£1,001.49	£11,801.49
4	£3,600.00	£14,400.00	£693.07	£1,694.56	£16,094.56
5	£3,600.00	£18,000.00	£886.25	£2,580.81	£20,580.81
6	£3,600.00	£21,600.00	£1,088.14	£3,668.95	£25,268.95
7	£3,600.00	£25,200.00	£1,299.10	£4,968.05	£30,168.05
8	£3,600.00	£28,800.00	£1,519.56	£6,487.61	£35,287.61
9	£3,600.00	£32,400.00	£1,749.94	£8,237.55	£40,637.55
10	£3,600.00	£36,000.00	£1,990.69	£10,228.24	£46,228.24
11	£3,600.00	£39,600.00	£2,242.27	£12,470.51	£52,070.51
12	£3,600.00	£43,200.00	£2,505.17	£14,975.69	£58,175.69
13	£3,600.00	£46,800.00	£2,779.91	£17,755.59	£64,555.59
14	£3,600.00	£50,400.00	£3,067.00	£20,822.60	£71,222.60
15	£3,600.00	£54,000.00	£3,367.02	£24,189.61	£78,189.61
16	£3,600.00	£57,600.00	£3,680.53	£27,870.14	£85,470.14
17	£3,600.00	£61,200.00	£4,008.16	£31,878.30	£93,078.30
18	£3,600.00	£64,800.00	£4,350.52	£36,228.82	£101,028.82
19	£3,600.00	£68,400.00	£4,708.30	£40,937.12	£109,337.12
20	£3,600.00	£72,000.00	£5,082.17	£46,019.29	£118,019.29
21	£3,600.00	£75,600.00	£5,472.87	£51,492.16	£127,092.16
22	£3,600.00	£79,200.00	£5,881.15	£57,373.31	£136,573.31
23	£3,600.00	£82,800.00	£6,307.80	£63,681.11	£146,481.11
24	£3,600.00	£86,400.00	£6,753.65	£70,434.76	£156,834.76
25	**£3,600.00**	**£90,000.00**	**£7,219.56**	**£77,654.32**	**£167,654.32**

The borrower has to maintain the level of payments to the savings plan and if the current payment level is less than the equivalent capital and interest repayment figure, this should be increased as soon as possible. If a variable rate mortgage is used, the likelihood is that adjustments will not be made as often as they should be; this was a major cause of the shortfalls on endowment mortgages. If a fixed-rate mortgage is used, it is easier to build in a review of the savings plan contributions each time the mortgage interest rate is reset.

One advantage of using a regular savings plan is that clients become used to the fixed and regular nature of the payments. This helps to provide a discipline for those who might find it difficult to put enough aside regularly.

A risk can arise if the client moves house early in the term. The value of the savings plan may be less than the equivalent amount of capital that would have been paid off under a conventional mortgage, leaving less equity available to put towards the next house purchase. Borrowers need to understand that this risk is an inevitable consequence of adopting this type of mortgage repayment plan.

It is also possible to combine both approaches in a part-repayment, part interest-only mortgage.

Offset mortgages

In addition to traditional mortgage arrangements, a further option exists — the 'offset' mortgage. This enables the borrower to add their existing savings to their mortgage account in order to save on interest. Instead of earning interest in a separate account, these savings are 'offset' against the loan balance and interest is charged on the net difference.

For example, a client might have savings of £50,000 with a mortgage of £200,000. If they take out an offset mortgage, instead of paying the interest on the whole £200,000 loan, they pay it on £150,000 only.

With offset mortgages the borrower only pays interest on the actual net debt.

A current account mortgage is a special kind of offset mortgage. This uses a single account with a large overdraft equal to the maximum borrowing limit that the client has requested or been approved for. The client's savings, current accounts, credit cards and loans are all rolled into a single account, with a single interest rate. This means there is only ever one payment to worry about.

In contrast, standard offset mortgages allow the clients to keep their individual accounts separate, but link them together for the purposes of calculating the interest due.

Both current account and standard offset mortgages are tax efficient because no interest is actually paid on the savings and therefore no tax is payable.

With both types of accounts an upper borrowing limit is set and the client can then borrow up to that amount without any penalties. Any capital repayments can in effect be borrowed back again at any stage during the term of the loan.

Clients with large amounts of savings can potentially save a significant amount in interest over the lifetime of the offset mortgage. Clients can also overpay, underpay and take payment holidays depending on the terms of their particular mortgage deal. However, it is important to remember that underpayments and payment holidays will affect the overall rate of repayment.

Offset mortgages may be useful for clients who cannot be sure their income will be the same from month to month, for example:

- Self-employed clients.

- Clients in receipt of annual dividends.

- Employees on bonus schemes.

- Salespeople earning commissions.

Offset mortgages may also be beneficial to higher rate taxpayers, who will be liable to pay higher rate tax on the interest they earn on any deposit savings. If those savings are placed into an offset mortgage account, the amount of interest the client is paying is reduced as well as their overall tax liabilities.

Example 19.5: An offset mortgage for a higher rate taxpayer

Mary is a higher rate taxpayer and has £50,000 in savings, earning gross interest of 4.5% a year. Tax is deducted at source and Mary receives the net interest of 3.6% a year paid into her account each year. At the end of the tax year Mary declares the interest payment on her annual tax return and is required to make a further tax payment of 20%, making her net return 2.7% a year. At the same time, Mary has an outstanding mortgage loan of £100,000, which is currently on a fixed rate of 5% a year for two years.

If Mary remortgages and takes out an offset mortgage instead she will benefit in the following way.

The mortgage interest will now be calculated on the net difference between her accumulated savings of £50,000 and the loan of £100,000. In other words, interest will then be charged on £50,000 instead of £100,000.

As Mary no longer earns interest on the savings balance, her overall financial position is improved as follows:

Old mortgage arrangement

Interest payable at 5% a year on £100,000	£5,000
Interest receivable on £50,000 (2.7% net)	£1,350
Total cost a year	£3,650

New offset mortgage arrangement

Interest payable at 5% a year on £50,000	£2,500
Total cost a year	£2,500

Although Mary is now earning a reduced amount of interest on her savings, she is also paying less interest on the mortgage debt and overall she is £1,150 a year better off in net terms. Another way of expressing this is to say that she would need to earn an interest rate of 8.3% gross on her £50,000 of savings to achieve the same net return as she obtains with the offset mortgage.

Offset mortgages can be arranged on a variety of deals, including base rate trackers.

Mortgage repayment issues

All mortgage holders, and particularly offset mortgage holders, will have to consider how best to use any capital sums they gain access to during the term of the mortgage, for example a maturing investment, bonus or inheritance.

In other words, they need to decide whether to use the capital to repay some of the debt or to invest it with the objective of increasing the value over time to repay the loan capital at the end of the term.

The final decision will be based on a number of factors, including:

- The rate of interest on the loan – the lower this is, the less benefit is secured by paying down the debt.

- The rate of return on the investment – over the very long term, equity returns are sure to be higher than mortgage interest rates, but this may not apply over the term of the client's investment.

- The client's requirements for the capital – if the intention is to release capital from the sale of the property at retirement and invest it, then paying down the debt rather than investing now may not make sense.

- Access – if debt is repaid, the client may no longer have access to the capital if it is needed later.

- Tax position – if the client can obtain tax reliefs on investments such as pension contributions, debt repayment may be less attractive.

- The remaining term to redemption – the longer this is, the greater the likelihood that equity investments will generate a significantly higher return than debt repayment.

With an offset or current account mortgage, the capital placed in the mortgage account immediately reduces the mortgage interest payable. However, the borrower can still at any point take this capital and use it for other purposes.

7 Educated wants

'Educated wants' should emerge from the fact-finding process, discussions with the client and subsequent lifetime cash flow modelling. As we discussed earlier, the purpose of this initial planning stage is to help identify the client's needs and wants, and set timescales for achieving these.

Realism on possible returns

When discussing financial objectives, it is important to be realistic about the returns likely to be achieved from any underlying investment strategy.

Example 19.6: Saving for a deposit

Sarah needs £25,000 in five years' time towards a deposit for house purchase. During the initial fact-find meeting, her adviser determines that Sarah can afford to save a maximum of £200 a month from her income towards the required deposit. This equates to £12,000 saved over the five-year period.

The additional growth required from this investment over the five-year term, in order to achieve the required £25,000, is £13,000 or 26.5% a year compound on £200 invested each month.

Year	Year deposits	Total deposits	Year interest	Total interest	Total paid
1	£2,400.00	£2,400.00	£374.00	£374.00	£2,774.00
2	£2,400.00	£4,800.00	£1,205.30	£1,579.30	£6,379.30
3	£2,400.00	£7,200.00	£2,285.73	£3,865.03	£11,065.03
4	£2,400.00	£9,600.00	£3,689.94	£7,554.98	£17,154.98
5	**£2,400.00**	**£12,000.00**	**£5,514.96**	**£13,069.94**	**£25,069.94**

Achieving a consistent rate of return at this level over five years is certainly unrealistic. Sarah needs to understand that the level of return she is likely to experience may be much less than this. Showing her past performance figures for the various asset classes — cash, fixed interest, property, equities and so on — would enable Sarah to fully appreciate the reality.

Once Sarah's attitude to investment risk is taken into consideration, her ability to achieve the required return may be even less likely. For example, Sarah may prove to be a cautious investor and wish to limit her investment exposure to cash and fixed-interest assets only.

Therefore, some compromise is likely to be required — either extending the time period, increasing the amount saved through reducing expenditure elsewhere or reducing the target fund.

Drawdown

Once a capital sum has been accumulated, the rate at which funds are drawn down to provide income needs to be considered and reviewed. The client needs to understand that if the rate of drawdown exceeds the rate of return, the value of the accumulated fund will be eroded over time.

Example 19.7: Drawing on savings for an early retirement

John is 50 years old and decides to retire early. He has accrued capital in various personal pensions and understands that this will not be accessible until he reaches age 55. His state pension will not be available until he reaches age 65. In the meantime, he plans to use his accrued ISA funds to supplement his cost of living. The current value of his ISA portfolio is £50,000 and it has grown by 5% in the last year.

John has said he will need an income of £15,000 a year to support him in retirement. If he draws funds at this rate and continues to generate a 5% return each year, he can expect to have fully eroded the ISA portfolio after three and a half years.

Year	Starting value	Income taken	Balance remaining	Growth
1	£50,000.00	£15,000.00	£35,000.00	£1,750.00
2	£36,750.00	£15,000.00	£21,750.00	£1,087.50
3	£22,837.50	£15,000.00	£7,837.50	£391.88
4	£8,229.38	£15,000.00	−£6,770.63	−£338.53
5	−£7,109.16	£15,000.00	−£22,109.16	−£1,105.46

John should therefore consider taking less income, delaying his retirement or investing the assets with a view to achieving a return in excess of 5% a year. However, generating improved returns is likely to involve more risk to capital, which John may not be comfortable with. One further alternative is to supplement his income from elsewhere or consider semi-retirement instead.

Timescales

The timescale for achieving each objective is crucial. As you can see from each of the previous examples, adjusting the time period will affect the ability to achieve the objective.

Example 19.8: Changing the timescale

Continuing Example 19.7, if John delays his retirement for another 12 to 18 months, his ISA fund will support him to age 55, assuming the portfolio continues to grow at 5% a year.

Year	Starting value	Income taken	Balance remaining	Growth
1	£50,000.00	£0.00	£50,000.00	£2,500.00
2	£52,500.00	£7,500.00	£45,000.00	£2,250.00
3	£47,250.00	£15,000.00	£32,250.00	£1,612.50
4	£33,862.50	£15,000.00	£18,862.50	£943.13
5	£19,805.63	£15,000.00	£4,805.63	£240.28

Similarly, continuing Example 19.6, if Sarah extends the timescale for saving towards the house deposit from five years to eight, the rate of return required is reduced from 26.5% to 6.5% a year, which is a much more realistic target.

Year	Year deposits	Total deposits	Year interest	Total interest	Total paid
1	£2,400.00	£2,400.00	£86.20	£86.20	£2,486.20
2	£2,400.00	£4,800.00	£252.71	£338.91	£5,138.91
3	£2,400.00	£7,200.00	£430.36	£769.27	£7,969.27
4	£2,400.00	£9,600.00	£619.92	£1,389.19	£10,989.19
5	£2,400.00	£12,000.00	£822.17	£2,211.36	£14,211.36
6	£2,400.00	£14,400.00	£1,037.96	£3,249.32	£17,649.32
7	£2,400.00	£16,800.00	£1,268.21	£4,517.53	£21,317.53
8	**£2,400.00**	**£19,200.00**	**£1,513.88**	**£6,031.40**	**£25,231.40**

8 Prioritising

Once the short-, medium- and long-term financial objectives have been agreed, the next stage is to set a timescale for each objective and decide on the order in which the objectives should be achieved. Assigning a priority to each objective facilitates more accurate planning and should help to ensure all objectives are met within the agreed timescales.

This stage of the process usually involves extensive discussion with the client and negotiating adjustments to timescales and priorities, and possibly risk tolerance. Compromise is often necessary, and some needs or wants may have to be deferred. The client may well 'anchor' on one or more numbers from early discussions (see chapter 20). Because the final plan will probably differ significantly from what the client originally hoped for it is vital that the revised priorities and timescales are clearly set out and that the client confirms their acceptance.

These are the priorities a younger client with a family might consider, in this order:

- Day-to-day living expenses:
    - Prepare a budget.
    - Reduce costs of borrowing and outstanding unsecured debts (for example, expensive credit cards).
    - Establish a short-term savings account to hold funds for one-off discretionary expenses like holidays.
- Financial protection:
    - Build an emergency fund.
    - Ensure funds will be available to support the family if the client dies or has a serious illness.
    - Provide protection in the event the client is unable to work due to long-term illness.
    - Ensure sufficient capital will be available to support the family if the client is made redundant.
- Buying a new family home:
    - Raise a sufficient deposit to provide access to cheaper borrowing.
    - Consider current and future expenditure levels to establish whether a fixed or variable rate is appropriate.
    - Decide between repayment of capital or interest only.
- Saving towards the costs of education in the future.

- Saving for retirement.
- Estate planning.

A middle-aged couple might consider the following priorities, in this order:

- Provide for day-to-day living expenses.
- Repay secured and unsecured debts.
- Provide towards the costs of education.
- Save for retirement.
- Longer-term savings and investment.
- Estate planning.

A couple in their 60s might consider the following order for their financial objectives:

- Provide for current and future living expenses.
- Ensure sufficient funds remain available to cover long-term care costs.
- Assist with grandchildren's education costs.
- Mitigate inheritance tax.

The priorities should be reviewed from time to time, and will change as the client's circumstances change.

9 Cash flow planning

An important aspect of the financial plan is the modelling of expected cash flows into and out of the client's portfolio over time, while taking into account their specific objectives and timescales.

Clients only ever need cash

Clients' financial objectives usually involve gaining access to cash, either as lump sums of capital to meet known future expenses (like school fees or mortgage repayments), or as income to maintain their standard of living on retirement or in the event of illness. The lifetime cash flow model helps to translate the client's objectives into a series of cash flows over time.

Example 19.2: Expected cash outflows in a lifetime cash flow model

£15,000 required in January 2010 to cover known tax liabilities.

£10,000 required in 2010 for a new car.

> £2,500 required in 2011 for a family holiday abroad.
>
> £15,000 required each year from 2012 to 2020 for school fees.
>
> £200,000 required in 20 years' time to repay the mortgage.
>
> £250,000 required at age 55 to provide the required level of income in retirement.

The model should also include the current value of the portfolio and all expected cash inflows or investments into the portfolio such as pension contributions, annual contributions to individual savings accounts (ISAs) and so on. It will then be easier to see whether the client needs to make additional provision now to ensure they meet their cash needs in the short, medium and longer term.

Precision in estimating needs

Forming an accurate picture of what the client's future income and capital needs will be and when they wish to achieve their objectives will help ensure that their expectations are met. The old adage 'Prior planning prevents poor performance' certainly applies in financial planning. If the financial planner has correctly identified the client's financial needs and agreed when and how these should be funded, then predictable or probable events should all be accounted for within the plan.

It is impossible to plan for the unknowns, but if the client's circumstances permit it is often worthwhile building in some additional capacity in the financial model to cover any unexpected cash calls. Any assumptions in terms of amounts and timescales should be agreed with the client and assessed annually as part of the financial review.

Cash flow modelling

Lifetime cash flow planning is increasingly being used by financial planners to forecast a client's income and expenditure over time. A graphical model can show a year-by-year summary of cash inflows and outflows for the portfolio. This can be useful in illustrating the impact of various objectives on the overall value of the portfolio and whether there is a surplus or deficit. The aim is to show the client whether they can maintain their lifestyle and meet their financial goals. The model makes various assumptions in terms of growth and inflation. These variables can be altered to show the outcome based on a variety of scenarios (for example, higher or lower inflation), which can be helpful in 'stress testing' the financial plan.

If the objectives are not affordable, the model will show a progressive decline in the value of the portfolio, with the client running out of money at some point in the future. If the objectives are affordable, the model will show a surplus throughout the period covered.

There are various software packages available to help the planner compile the data and carry out a cash flow analysis. However, it is possible to take the basic principles and carry out the same process using a simple spreadsheet. The main variables to include on a year-by-year basis are:

- Income and capital investment.
- Expenditure.
- Inflation assumptions.
- Interest rate assumptions.
- Growth assumptions for the value of the portfolio.

The information used is taken directly from the fact find and subsequent analysis. All income and expenditure items should be listed individually. The lifetime cash flow is then created from these inflows and outflows using assumptions on the level of growth achieved between now and the relevant payment dates. The cash inputs into the portfolio should be assumed to be net of income tax.

Care must be taken in the assumptions. In particular, clients may optimistically plan for an inheritance or receiving capital from the sale of a property. But if they cannot achieve a particular objective without such a cash inflow, the adviser needs to point this out and encourage the client to be more realistic.

The factors most likely to be varied in a lifetime cash flow model are the timescales set for achieving each financial objective and the level of capital or income required.

The purpose of the initial planning process is to arrive at an agreed series of financial objectives with specific targets in terms of capital and income at set times in the future. The plan should be robust enough to ensure there is a strong possibility of achieving the desired outcome, while allowing sufficient flexibility for adjustment to address changes in the client's personal and financial circumstances.

Timescales

Although the timescales for the objectives will have been agreed at the outset, these are likely to change as the client's circumstances change. Factors that might lead to a change in the timescale and assumptions include:

- Long-term ill health.
- Having children.

- The death of a partner or close family member.
- Redundancy.
- Divorce or remarriage.

Similarly, the client's capital and income requirements will be subject to variation over the course of their life and are also likely to be affected by each of the events listed above.

Sensitivity to variations

It is important to help the client understand how sensitive the outcomes in the cash flow model are to changes in the assumptions used. It is likely that some of the assumptions will ultimately prove to be inaccurate. What is unknown is exactly how inaccurate these will be and what impact that will have on the projected outcomes. Reviewing the assumptions regularly with the client is crucial to the overall success of the plan.

Cash flow models are 'deterministic'. In other words, they simply provide a prediction of what the outcome would be, based on certain assumptions on growth rate, inflation and cash flow. They do not tell us the odds of success or failure for achieving the predictions. This is true of most point of sale illustrations given to clients, for example pension illustrations showing future values based on growth rate assumptions of 5%, 7% and 9% a year.

Stochastic modelling

One way to illustrate the close relationship between the assumptions and the likelihood of achieving the objectives is through the use of stochastic modelling, which involves the use of simulations to estimate probable outcomes for investments based on a series of assumptions. ('Stochastic' means having a chance or random element.)

A stochastic model combines historical economic and market data with current information to simulate future investment returns. Instead of providing one estimate of the possible investment outcome, a stochastic model will estimate the probability of the outcome by calculating thousands of different investment scenarios.

Although both approaches are attempts to project the eventual outcome, there are a number of key differences between deterministic projections (like cash flow models) and stochastic projections:

- A stochastic model will generate thousands of different projections, whereas a deterministic model will normally show a range of between one and three.
- The assumptions used by a stochastic model for each individual projection will be generated by an underlying mathematical formula.

- The stochastic model then analyses a range of outcomes from the series of projections and gives an indication as to the probability of achieving that outcome.

The following elements form a central part of almost all stochastic models, from the very basic to the most complex:

- **Trend variables** refer to the expected returns on the various asset classes, for example equities, fixed interest. They are a very important part of the stochastic model and will determine how the returns from each asset class compare.

- **Range variables** describe the extent to which the returns on each asset class vary from the trend. For example, the range of possible returns on a cash account will be significantly less than the range on an equity fund. More complex models will incorporate the impact and probability of dramatic market events such as market corrections.

- **Relationship variables** explore the connection between events, for example how the price of bonds is affected by changes in the level of the equity market. In other words, they consider how the asset classes may be correlated to each other and to what extent. As the variables may be interconnected, it is important that the model is able to account for the impact a single change has on the estimated probability of achieving the desired outcome.

As well as considering the relationships between asset classes, it is also important to consider how returns from each individual asset class correlate with time (serial correlation). For example, if the bond market sees a decline in one year, what is the probability it will experience a rise the following year?

Stochastic models use the apparatus of portfolio theory, and they are therefore vulnerable to the same criticisms of that theory noted in the introduction to part 2. It is therefore important that the adviser understands the key assumptions in the model and the effect of changing them.

While simpler spreadsheets cannot produce the probabilistic outcome ranges of stochastic models, they can usefully demonstrate to clients the sensitivity of outcomes to changes in assumptions. For example, a 1% increase in average real returns over a 25-year term, or a 1% fall in the average income yield on a portfolio, can produce large variations in the outcome. Because behavioural finance (see chapter 20) has shown how people tend to 'anchor' on single numbers, it is probably a good idea to produce such illustrations and to use outcome ranges, rather than single numbers, in the plans that clients will use as their reference point.

Another criticism of stochastic modelling is that it cannot show the effects of specific future events on the client's financial position. Although useful for broad planning purposes and for illustrating potential outcomes based on known assumptions, stochastic modelling is just another tool in the process and should not be relied upon entirely. In particular, it is well established that most people are not very good at probabilistic reasoning. Their understanding of a stochastic modelling process is also likely to be poor, and if such models are used, the adviser will need to ensure these issues are explained.

10 The investment process

The starting point for any structured investment process should be the establishment of an investment committee within a firm, whose policies and investment selections will provide a framework within which the individual advisers will work.

The investment committee

Each firm should establish an investment committee or similar group (depending on the firm's size) with the objective of creating an investment policy that will be adhered to by all employees when advising clients. It should be formally constituted, preferably with a nominated chairman and a secretary to record the minutes. The committee should:

- Agree the process for establishing the client's risk tolerance.
- Define suitable asset allocation models for each risk profile.
- Agree benchmarks for comparing investment performance.
- Establish a basis for selecting investment funds.
- Publish a list of funds approved by the committee.
- Agree a process for reviewing the approved funds.
- Incorporate an ethical and socially responsible investment policy.

The investment policy should be published, and reviewed regularly to ensure it remains current. The policy should state the committee's overall view on the economic outlook and on markets, in particular categorising markets as undervalued, overvalued or fairly valued and reporting any change in asset allocations.

The next step in the investment process involves the creation of suitable investment strategies for individual clients. Each strategy should be derived from the published investment policy, as agreed by the investment committee. It should also take into account the client's requirements in terms of risk tolerance, timescales and liquidity.

These factors will have been determined earlier during the fact finding and lifetime cash flow analysis. The client's personal tax position and their requirements in terms of income and capital growth should also be considered.

The adviser should:

- Establish the client's objectives.

- Confirm timescale, risk profile and liquidity requirements.

- Choose an appropriate asset allocation model.

- Consider the client's requirements for income or growth and any other considerations (e.g. ethical issues).

- Select a range of investments from the list approved by the investment committee or other agreed source.

- Choose a suitable tax wrapper.

- Review the performance of the investments.

Funding for shorter-term objectives

Shorter-term objectives should be funded out of cash. A variety of cash deposit options are available from banks and building societies, including:

- Instant access accounts.

- Notice accounts.

- Fixed-rate deposit accounts.

These accounts can usually be managed online, by post or over the telephone and the rates of interest on offer will be greater for those accounts with restricted access. The compromise from placing capital into such a highly liquid, low-cost and low-risk environment is the low rate of return received.

In a cash environment greater returns can normally be achieved by giving up access to capital for an agreed period or agreeing to manage the account in line with specific terms and conditions set down by the deposit holder.

Selecting a tax wrapper

Choosing a suitable tax wrapper to hold a client's investment funds is an important part of the investment process. A number of different wrapper options are available, including:

- ISAs.

- Collectives.

- Pensions.

- Investment bonds (onshore and offshore).

In addition, the advisers should consider whether assets should be held within wrap platforms. Where assets are held in trust, the tax rules are different in some respects to the tax rules that apply to individual holdings. The issues involved in the selection of wrap accounts and tax wrappers are dealt with in chapter 22.

11 Review

The final part of the financial planning process is the regular review and monitoring of the portfolio.

Over time clients' circumstances can be expected to change. Life events such as marriage, children and unemployment can all affect the original set of assumptions used in the financial plan. Changes in tax legislation and the economy can affect the outcome of the initial planning exercise and should be assessed regularly.

Frequency of review

The frequency of review should be agreed with the client at the start of the planning process. For some individuals once a year may be sufficient, while others might require a formal valuation and discussion on a quarterly basis. For the majority of clients, six-monthly reporting is probably appropriate. The basis for regular reviews should be documented and agreed at the start of the planning process, and can be altered in the future to suit the needs of the client.

Events not planned for which happen before the next scheduled review date should prompt an interim review — for example, redundancy, an unexpected inheritance or the death of a family member.

It may be appropriate to establish a formal review procedure to ensure a consistent approach is taken with all clients. A review questionnaire could be prepared and sent to clients in advance of the review to collect personal information that may have changed since the last review (for example, salary, employment status or children).

Review considerations

The following points may be useful when reviewing a client's investments:

- The overall returns for the period should be compared with the selected benchmark and any deviations from the benchmark explained.

- The performance of each individual investment should be assessed to ensure it has generated acceptable returns(see chapter 17). Specific comments should be made on any investments that have been removed from the firm's fund list and recommendations made for suitable replacements.

- The allocation should be reviewed. If the current asset allocation has diverged significantly from that agreed, it may be appropriate to rebalance through appropriate sales and purchases, subject to tax and cost implications.

- Where tactical asset allocation methods are being used, specific recommendations should be made for altering allocations.

- If the client is in receipt of income from the portfolio, this should also be reviewed to ensure it is sufficient to meet the client's requirements. The effects of any income withdrawal on the overall value of the portfolio should also be assessed.

- The client's attitude to risk should be reviewed periodically. Discussing the degree of volatility experienced in the portfolio up to the review date and the client's views on this may result in reassessing the client's risk profile.

- The use of the annual tax-free allowances (pensions, capital gains tax, ISAs, inheritance tax) should be considered.

- Any financial commitments agreed with the client should also be reviewed.

The issues in relation to fund selection were covered in chapter 17. But advisers also have to choose products – life assurance bonds, pension plans, SIPPs – in which to hold these funds.

Advisers should have a robust product selection method. For IFAs, this must encompass the whole of the market, so it should start with a long list of all available products, which are progressively whittled down by the use of criteria such as financial strength, administration ability, communications and product features. While many such criteria are generic, the IFA is bound to select products based on individual needs, and the product selection process should enable the application of different criteria depending on the individual client's requirements. Many advisers use independent third party providers of research tools, such as defaqto, for this purpose.

Summary

- In investment planning, fact finding must include realistic estimation of any future capital receipts as well as of future capital and income requirements.

- In order to gain the client's agreement to a statement of their risk tolerance, the adviser needs to investigate their risk perception and assess their risk capacity.

- The adviser must convert the client's statements of wants into an assessment of needs and secure the client's endorsement of this.

- In order to prioritise the client's needs, repeated 'what if?' scenario planning may be required to illustrate the extent of the risks involved in generating the returns that would be needed to achieve all the client's objectives.

- Cash flow planning using stochastic models can help clients understand the possible range of outcomes from investing in different ways.

- Adviser firms need to establish procedures for creating asset allocation models and applying them consistently, and for reviewing client's investments.

Chapter 20
The psychology of investors

1 Types of client

Every client is an individual and different from all other clients in both personality and circumstances. But people do tend to fall into broad categories and it is helpful to consider some of the main types of client that advisers may encounter. It is important not to prejudge people and it is always worth keeping an open mind about how different investors will react to different circumstances and advice. Advisers should aim to recommend investments that will meet their clients' needs and wishes, and avoid suggesting investment strategies that will generate losses the clients cannot tolerate (emotionally or in any other sense).

People have very different attitudes to money: what they want from it, the risks they are prepared to take with it and how they wish to invest it. These views may stay with them all their lives, or they may change radically with age and experience. The feckless young man in his first job with a student loan, no savings and just about making ends meet might be prepared to gamble with a small windfall. A few years later, he might want to invest it securely towards the deposit on a property; at the same time, he might be investing his pension scheme in emerging markets funds that fluctuate wildly in the short run but could provide above-average growth over 30 or 40 years. Then, in middle age with a healthy income and family responsibilities, he may start to build up a diversified portfolio. By the time he reaches retirement, he might have become very conservative in his approach to investing. People change their approach to investing over time.

Many factors affect people's attitudes towards and behaviour with money. Some of them are detailed below.

Personality

There is some evidence for the view that people's basic character traits do not change throughout their lives. Certain individuals are naturally more risk taking and confident than others. But there are many other issues that affect how people think and feel about their investment planning. Upbringing, experience and other influences can change people's views, feelings and habits of thinking and acting in relation to investing — just as they can about many other activities. Investment advisers can be powerful influencers.

Experience

Generally the longer people hold investments, the more confident they become in their decision making about them. Equally, those who have been brought up in families where parents and other relatives have been investors and talked about investments have indirect experiences and memories of how markets behave. Clients who are new to investment often require a lot more work for advisers.

The source of the money

How clients acquired their money can affect their views on how they want to invest it, although not everyone is affected in the same way. Many who have inherited money may feel their investments should not be changed (see under section 3 below on 'endowment bias'). People who accumulated their money themselves are sometimes prepared to take considerable risks with it and may be inclined to invest in new businesses, especially if they are relatively young. Others who have built up their wealth take a very cautious attitude towards it.

Moral or religious outlook

A few people are greatly influenced in their investment decision making by their ethical or religious outlook. They may want to avoid certain types of investment, such as shares in companies manufacturing or selling tobacco or arms. But their beliefs may also lead them to want to invest positively in certain kinds of business activities (such as environmentally friendly firms).

Amount of wealth

Rich people can generally afford to take more risk with their investments than poorer people. The very rich may be able to lose substantial amounts without it affecting their lifestyle. Even if their spendable income is affected, there is generally more scope to adjust their lifestyle without affecting their basic standards of comfort. In contrast, people with fewer reserves of income or capital typically find that losing a substantial proportion of their capital will have a major impact on their lifestyle.

Timescale

People's ability to take on investment risk is great affected by the timescale they have in mind — how soon they need to have access to the investment. If funds are not likely to be needed for some ten or twenty years, an investor can afford to incur much greater losses than someone with a much shorter timescale. It is reasonable for such investors to expect their investments to recover in time, or they could save replacement funds from their excess income. Age is not quite the same as timescale, although for most investors they are obviously related. Older investors generally feel they have a shorter timescale than younger investors.

It may be worth exploring investors' thinking behind these assumptions: in many cases, the timescale may turn out to be longer than they initially estimate.

The relevant timescale for someone in their 50s who is planning their finances for retirement and expects to annuitise their pension fund may be relatively short for an investment in equities. But if they are eventually intending to access their fund through income withdrawal, they may feel that their timescale is rather longer and they can afford to take more risk with the investments.

Subjective and objective factors

The psychological aspects of people's views on investing are just part of the story. Subjective factors like personality traits may be less important than more objective factors like level of wealth and timescale. Where there is a mismatch between a client's attitudes and their objective position, the investment adviser may reasonably try to reconcile them.

For example, a client who is relatively poor with a short timescale but has a rather aggressive high-risk attitude to money – easy come, easy go – would benefit from some words of caution. It might equally be inappropriate for investors with a long timescale and/or substantial wealth to hold the major part of their assets in cash simply because of excessive caution.

2 Risk profiling

There are many methods of risk profiling (see chapter 19). These techniques are increasingly used by investment advisers to help determine the level of risk that clients are prepared to tolerate.

FinaMetrica is widely used internationally for risk profiling, and further discussions with a client may arise within any of the five main areas around which their online process asks questions:

- How clients assess themselves for risk tolerance.
- The history of their behaviour with regard to risk taking.
- Their intended financial behaviour in the future.
- How they might behave in a range of different realistic financial scenarios.
- Their emotional response to various possible financial events and outcomes.

Risk profiling techniques can have a number of advantages for advisers:

- They provide a clear, consistent and verifiable process that ensures advisers have ascertained at least the basics of clients' ability to tolerate investment risk.
- They can be linked to the recommendation of a range of investment portfolios.
- They attach a sense of scientific authority to the provision of investment advice.

But risk-profiling processes that do not also include some discussion around the issues and clients' attitudes could invalidate some of the conclusions and recommendations. Many of the questions are better used as the starting point for a discussion, with further questions and answers, rather than relying on a stand-alone automated process.

As a result of discussions, clients may amend their views about aspects of their risk profile and this could result in a different asset allocation.

An important aspect of the risk profiling process (especially for clients with relatively little direct experience of investments) is describing and discussing the characteristics and behaviour of different asset classes and investment products. Clients' views can change as they learn more about investments and become more accustomed to the fluctuations of investment markets.

In a Guidance Consultation issued in January 2011, the FSA identified shortcomings in the design and use of risk profiling tools. In particular, it found that advisers using risk profiling tools did not properly assess risk capacity, a topic that is hard to assess using questionnaires. These concerns can be overcome by using well-designed tools in conjunction with personal discussions with the client and an assessment of risk capacity.

3 Behavioural finance and advice

A basic knowledge of behavioural finance should be part of every adviser's armoury of skills in advising clients about their investments.

Sooner or later most advisers discover that their clients have a tendency to behave irrationally from time to time. If they are honest with themselves, advisers should also accept that they too can behave illogically in their financial decision making. As we have seen in part 2, chapter 11, behavioural finance can provide valuable insights into client behaviour and can even be used to help clients make more rational decisions about their finances.

It can be helpful if an adviser is able to identify the client's irrational behaviour. The adviser will have a much clearer understanding of what the client is feeling and can steer the conversation towards resolving the problem. Very often the best approach is to describe the feeling to the client, give it a name and reassure the client that everyone has these feelings and that they are genetically hard-wired into human beings. Professional investors have just as much difficulty making rational decisions, which is why they normally have strict in-house oversight on tactics and strategy.

For example, it is common for advisers to find clients who have far too much of their capital tied up in their employer's company. An adviser would generally explain that this investment represents an excessive concentration of risk and that a diversified portfolio would be much safer. But such a rational explanation might not address the problem that the client has a strong emotional attachment to the investment. The client may have strong feelings of security about a company in which they have long invested and that also employs them. The adviser needs to deal with the rational analytical processes separately from the client's irrational feelings. When the client understands the power of 'familiarity effect', knows that their feeling even has a name and that most people also think in much the same way, they are much more likely to consider the issues rationally.

The background to behavioural finance

It is worth knowing a little of the history of behavioural finance when explaining to clients that it constitutes a serious body of knowledge. The pioneers were the American Daniel Kahneman and the Israeli Amos Tversky. They challenged the notion that people always make rational economic decisions (as economists have traditionally assumed) and used the insights of psychology to observe how people really behave. They published work in this area as early as the 1970s and ultimately, such was the importance of their discoveries, Kahneman won the Nobel prize for economics in 2002 (Tversky died in 1996).

The subject has become widely recognised as important and many of its concepts and theories are now widely accepted. It has practical implications for both market behaviour and the most effective ways to advise investors.

General principles

It is also useful if you can outline the basic theory behind behavioural finance. There are essentially two kinds of thinking, arising from two different parts of the brain. The first is intuitive and automatic, while the second is reflective and rational. Automatic thinking is instinctive and involves such emotions as pain, pleasure and fear. It is fast and effortless and associated with gut reactions to things. Reflective thinking is more controlled and deliberate and also much slower. This is the type of thinking people use to plan and analyse.

Much learning consists of training the automatic side of the brain into certain habits of thought by constant practice. Practised car drivers use their many years of driving to react to events very quickly. New car drivers have to use their reflective thinking to react to events and that sometimes means they respond too slowly. When a train starts to shake, the automatic part of a passenger's brain may react with fear of a crash, while it may take a little longer for the reflective side of the brain to override the irrational emotion with the soothing thought that trains are a very safe form of transport.

Most people use their automatic thinking to make quick decisions and estimates, especially about how to act in risky situations. For our remote ancestors, deciding whether a nearby movement in the grass was the next meal or a dangerous predator could have meant the difference between life and death. People still use gut feelings or 'heuristics' (roughly translated as 'short cuts') to make all kinds of decisions just to save time; in many situations these decisions are not only wrong but *predictably* wrong, and they demonstrate some very common biases and mistakes. Advisers need to spot these short cuts in thinking and get clients to re-examine their decisions.

It is often a good idea to discuss with clients very early on in the advice process the possible emotions they might feel as a result of buying and holding investments. They might then find it easier to cope with the feelings when they appear as a result of making losses, for example.

It is possible to change automatic thinking to some extent, mainly by practice and by altering habits. New skills and ways of thinking can be learned. Clients can be helped to overcome their automatic thinking about some aspects of investment and financial planning, but it may take some time. Someone who is fearful of driving a car can get used to it and their reactions on the road can become instinctive, even though they were very tentative when they were first learning to drive. Likewise a person who is fearful of investment risk can become accustomed to taking some risks.

The main behaviour patterns

We have already looked at some of the typical attitudes towards risk identified by behavioural finance (chapter 11). Here we look in more detail at some of the main types of behaviour that clients typically exhibit, and approaches that advisers can take to try and moderate them. In many cases, the most effective approach is to describe the emotion that clients are feeling or the belief that they are expressing and then categorise it as one of the well-known phenomena identified and labelled by the behavioural finance experts. Clients also need reassurance that their feelings and emotions are completely normal, even if they are irrational.

Familiarity bias

A client may hold a high proportion of assets in a single class of investment such as the company that employs them.

This situation usually arises as a result of an employee share scheme. Several heuristics may be present, the most obvious of which is 'familiarity bias'. People tend to underestimate the risks associated with assets they know well, like property or their employer's company shares. Conversely, they tend to overestimate risks associated with the less familiar kinds of assets — foreign investments, for example.

It can be helpful to provide examples of other people who have experienced serious losses as a result of undiversified investment strategies. It is often easier to recognise the mistakes that other people make. For example, many Enron employees held shares personally or through their pension plans and when the company crashed, they lost their jobs, their savings and their pensions. Many employees of UK banks like RBS and Lloyds also held large proportions of their savings in shares in their employers through share-saving schemes.

Status quo bias

Many clients are reluctant to sell investments they have held for many years.

The heuristic here is 'status quo bias', which is close to but not exactly the same as familiarity bias and is often associated with long-term holdings of shares in a client's employer. People tend to overvalue what they already own. It is worth explaining to clients that the primitive urge that inhibits excessive generosity and motivates people to look after their possessions is a powerful feeling, but it is normally not an efficient basis for making investment decisions. The status quo effect leads to inertia in other areas of finance – a reluctance to switch banks, credit cards or even financial advisers.

Part of the appeal of property for many clients is its familiarity, its availability (in its psychological sense, 'availability' means the way property comes easily to mind) and its sheer tangibility. As a result, many investors are committed to property to an excessive extent. The arguments against holding too many investment eggs in the property basket are stronger the nearer in time the discussion takes place to a property downturn, when memories of illiquidity, falling prices and negative equity are still quite fresh in the client's memory.

Endowment bias

Clients are reluctant to sell investments or other assets they have inherited.

This is called 'endowment bias' and it can be even more powerful than status quo bias. Investors tend to value more highly those assets they have inherited or been given. They generally do not like to sell them or even change them in any way.

A good way to help clients understand the power (and illogicality) of endowment bias is to describe the following experiment. The subjects were told they had inherited some investments in the form of cash and up to six mutual funds of varying degrees of riskiness. Half the 'beneficiaries' retained the inheritances in exactly the form they received them, regardless of whether they were 100% invested in the most risky funds or cash and irrespective of their attitude to risk and circumstances. Clearly, this was an irrational response likely to prove damaging to their future wealth.

Regret

Clients are typically very reluctant to sell assets at a loss.

The feelings of regret that investors have when they make a loss are normally much more powerful than the good feelings they have after making a comparable profit. For most people, a profit has to be roughly two and a half times greater than a loss to compensate for the feelings associated with the loss. Faced with having to sell an investment, most clients will prefer to retain a fund that has fallen in value and sell one that is showing a profit, regardless of the respective merits of the funds. Their instinct is to avoid feeling the regret at realising the loss, because as long as they hold the investment there is always hope that it will recover and deliver a profit.

Describing the client's feelings in this way can help to expose how illogical they are, but the language an adviser uses can sometimes also influence their decision. It might be better to talk about 'switching from one investment to another' rather than selling and buying.

Misleading descriptions

The way an adviser describes or frames an investment proposition can make a significant difference to the client's subsequent attitude to the recommendation.

Advisers need to make sure they do not inadvertently give the wrong impression and mislead the client. The following two statements have the same meaning:

- 'Based on past performance there is a 95% chance of making a profit on this investment.'
- 'Based on past performance there is a 5% chance of making a loss on this investment.'

The first statement is likely to have a much more positive impact than the second. But the adviser who wants to communicate the position clearly and fairly should use both formats.

Anchoring

Clients are often unduly influenced by specific numbers.

In the jargon of behavioural finance, clients 'anchor' on specific numbers. The client may have fixed or anchored on the high value an investment achieved and not be prepared to sell it below that point. Likewise, a client may have found an advertisement for an investment especially persuasive even if the fund is unsuitable, simply because of the level of income or growth that is 'guaranteed' (or possibly just indicated) or because of past performance.

The anchoring effect is not widely known outside behavioural finance and clients generally do not recognise the psychological power that numbers have for many people. Anchoring usually comes up as part of a discussion of a wide range of client misconceptions. It is often helpful to describe the phenomenon, put a name to it and analyse the illogicality of some of its effects. To avoid anchoring, it can also be helpful to express projections and illustrations with ranges rather than one specific number.

Availability bias

Some clients react badly if they have invested in an asset and it goes down in price almost immediately.

The pain of losing outweighs other emotions and thoughts and the sensation of loss is the most salient or outstanding feeling. This phenomenon is often called the 'availability bias' (as noted above, in psychological terms 'availability' refers to what is most immediately present in the mind). The most vividly felt and imagined events are the ones that have the biggest mental impact on us. Investors often come to conclusions about the riskiness of actions on the basis of the most recent event, rather than the boring statistics. This 'snake bite' effect (also mentioned in chapter 11) is often best avoided by the adviser warning the client in advance that this might happen. This should make it more likely that the client will be prepared for a possible setback and will be able to rationalise the feeling.

Not looking at the whole picture

Some clients with diversified portfolios find it hard to look at their investment holdings as a whole, and tend to focus on their losses and discount, or even ignore, their profits.

This attitude – very familiar to those who have studied behavioural finance – makes diversified portfolio investment hard to sustain and can lead to chronic underperformance as a result of long-term investment in very low-risk investments. It is often helpful to talk through the logic of diversification and appeal to the rational side of clients' brains. It takes self-discipline, practice and time for some investors to try to suppress feelings of regret and promote feelings of satisfaction that their overall position has improved, even if parts of the portfolio have declined in value. Clients who cannot make the adjustment may have to invest within their narrow comfort zone and live with the consequences.

Magical thinking

Some clients who have a bad early experience with an investment – especially those who bought into the market just before a crash – may feel they are particularly unlucky and in some way jinxed or especially marked out for failure with investment.

This is an extreme example of the way in which people try to make sense of the world even when events are random. The term for this in the vocabulary of behavioural finance is 'magical thinking', and it is surprisingly common. It is characterised by the confusion of correlation with causation and the attribution of meaning to random events or coincidences. Its most frequent manifestation is the construction of narratives that justify the most recent trend in markets.

Many investors buy at the top of the market and sell at the bottom. They extrapolate trends from the most recent events, so if the market is going up, they tend to think it will continue to do so, and if it is declining, they typically believe that it will continue to go down. The most recent and salient events have the biggest impact. So in 2008, it was hard to persuade investors of the truth of the old Rothschild adage, 'Buy on the declaration of war and sell on the outbreak of peace.'

This is exactly contrary to most people's natural feelings. The evidence of long-term performance statistics – especially in pictorial form – might have a corrective impact. One approach to a client who is determined to sell at the bottom or buy at the top is to suggest not selling completely out of the market or making one purchase, but instead to make periodic investments (or disinvestments) in regular tranches.

Herding

Many investors like to copy the investment decisions of their colleagues or neighbours or other benchmark figures.

Investors often want to behave like other investors: the instinct to conform and follow the herd is very strong. In some cases, 'herding' behaviour might turn out to be a good choice, if the resulting portfolio of investments happens to conform to the individual's risk profile based on objective grounds, such as their timescale and level of wealth. But if the wisdom of the crowd turns out to be inappropriate for the individual because the chosen investment is too risky (for example, shares in the client's employer) or too low (deposit accounts for long-term investment growth), it may turn out to be hard for an adviser to persuade the investor to break away from the group view.

Aside from making the logical case, it is worth questioning whether the expertise of the group is really as great as the knowledge, skills and experience of the adviser and the adviser's team of investment specialists. It can also be helpful to distinguish between the client's particular circumstances and those of other members of the group.

The framing effect

Clients naturally choose what they perceive to be the average risk profile.

If a client is offered a choice from, say, five portfolio descriptions, ranging from 'no risk' to 'very aggressive', the chances are the majority of choices will cluster around the middle. Advisers should be on their guard against this 'framing effect'. The choice of risk profile may reflect the client's wish to avoid apparent extremes rather than their genuine approach to investments, hence the need for discussion with the client and questions that do not directly lend themselves to framing.

Money illusion

Most clients focus on nominal investment returns and ignore the impact of inflation in their estimates of their future needs.

Most clients suffer from what the behavioural economists call 'money illusion'. This can lead them to favour fixed-interest funds or cash (in the past) with high immediate yields, and to make no allowance for the likely long-term decline in the purchasing power of money. One way to help clients understand the impact of inflation is to look at history. Many advisers simply describe inflation rates as annual percentage figures, but it is more effective to state the amount by which a pound needed to be revalued in order to keep its purchasing power.

For example, most investors could have difficulty relating to the statement that between January 1999 and January 2009, the retail prices index rose by an average of 2.6% a year. It is much more effective to point out that £1 would have needed to increase to £1.29 in nominal terms just to maintain its buying power during this decade of relatively low inflation.

As discussed in chapter 1, it is also possible to educate clients to think 'in real terms' by consistently presenting information in this form.

Hyperbolic discounting

Most clients tend to save too little or want to have a high income now at the expense of long-term future income.

Short-termism can distort investment decisions very seriously. It is very common for clients to underestimate the importance of having access to capital and income in the future rather than having them now. The technical term for this 'take no care for the morrow' approach is 'hyperbolic discounting'. When comparing cash now with a greater amount of cash at some point in the future, we tend to overvalue the benefit of the cash now and over-discount the value of the future benefit. The present is inevitably much more salient than the unknown future.

Appealing to reason will probably be only partly successful in counteracting this effect. A more effective approach might be to try to make the future as real as possible. The future seems very distant and uncertain to most people. Ten years ahead is almost inconceivably remote; but looking backwards could help clients realise that ten years is a short period, and even 20 years is not in fact so distant. While people tend to imagine that most things will be different in ten years' time, the truth is that most things will probably be the same, and for most people aged over 45, for whom today is not so different from ten years ago, reference to this experience can help them to be more realistic about their future needs.

Money and its future value may seem abstract and hard to think about. So there may also be a case for helping the client to envisage what their life will be like in the future, for example after they retire. The adviser can facilitate this by helping the client budget for expenditure to make the need for income at that time much more real.

Mental accounting

Clients often do conflicting things with different pockets of money.

For example, a client may have a short-term savings account for holidays or Christmas while still paying interest on a balance on a credit card. The client could use the short-term savings to pay off the credit card bill and save much more interest than they would forgo from closing the savings account. Behavioural finance describes this kind of behaviour as 'mental accounting'. Clients use mental accounting ('this is for that') because it seems to simplify life and is good for financial discipline. Investment advisers tend to discourage it because it can lead to a duplication of investments, potentially higher costs — because of the fragmentation of bank accounts and investment portfolios — and a loss of control over strategy.

In many cases, advisers should aim to reduce the investment costs and drawbacks of mental accounting while helping clients to retain control over their financial lives by using this approach. An ability to view all your investments in one account, a theoretical benefit offered by wrap accounts, may in fact engender uncertainty and doubt unless the adviser reminds the client about their objectives and progress made towards them.

Overconfidence

Clients can be excessively optimistic about investment returns, especially where they have some actual or apparent control over the situation.

The decisions and views reached by the automatic parts of the brain are not only fast, they are also generally very firm and confident. In many cases investors are excessively confident about their ability to achieve good outcomes. Business owners are notorious for overestimating the likely future value of their business and the ease with which they can sell it. Investors who manage their own investments frequently overestimate their past investment returns. Investors expect to be able to retire comfortably without having to save much.

This tendency to over-optimism is exacerbated by 'attribution bias'. Most people tend to look for patterns in events that confirm what they already believe and ignore inconvenient facts that do not fit their view of the world. Kahneman said that the most robust finding of behavioural finance was the over-confidence of investors.

'Hindsight bias' is another behavioural pattern that tends to confirm over-confidence: when they look back, people tend to think that past events could have been easily predicted and that they would have forecast them.

Dealing with excessive optimism and over-confidence is especially difficult for investment advisers. Being well prepared with the facts is essential, but it is not usually sufficient to overcome strongly held but wrong opinions about investment. Also helpful are tact and the use of descriptions and anecdotes about the behaviours in question. Documenting the clients' own views about the future and then playing them back much later can reduce excessive confidence.

4 Changing views

Over time, advisers are likely to influence their clients' attitudes to and perception of risk as the messages become clearer and the clients gain experience of the world of investment. But advisers should not anticipate their clients' changing views and should always give investment advice that keeps their clients inside their comfort zones. Discussions with clients and their developing attitudes to investments should always be well documented and advisers should be absolutely clear whether or not clients have really changed their views. Some clients do not change and many adapt very slowly. All clients are different.

Summary

- Advisers should take account of general influences on people's attitudes to money such as personality, upbringing, religion and the source of their capital.

- Behavioural finance provides useful descriptions of many psychological biases that can cause people to behave in ways that damage their wealth.

- Advisers should be familiar with the main biases such as the endowment effect, mental accounting, herding, anchoring and regret and be capable of explaining them.

- Though many of the effects described by behavioural finance are often termed 'irrational', this is only from the perspective of economic theory, and advisers need to reassure clients that most psychological biases are in fact not unusual but normal.

- Herding and magical thinking are biases that can result in genuinely irrational behaviour and where they are present the adviser has a duty to encourage the client to recognise them.

Chapter 21
Applying asset allocation

1 Asset allocation models

The purpose of an asset allocation model is to set out the proportion of capital the adviser recommends the client to invest in each asset class. The amount allocated to each class is determined by the client's risk profile and overall financial objectives. The decision on how much to invest in each class is the most important investment decision and the adviser needs to ensure that clients understand this, since they often tend to focus on the specific investments within the asset classes. Accordingly, some advisers present the investment solution in two parts, the first being simply the proposed asset allocation linked to objectives and risk profile, and the second the actual investments within the asset classes.

Where assets are being divided among several wrappers, it is important to establish the overall allocation for the portfolio before discussing the wrappers and the assets to be held within them.

In presenting investment recommendations, advisers should ensure they link the client's objectives and their risk tolerance to the proposed asset allocation. If the client questions the allocation, they can be referred to their agreement with the set of prioritised objectives and the risk tolerance rating the adviser has used.

The asset classes and their classification were discussed in part 1, chapter 5. A basic model may use only four classes:

- Cash.
- Fixed interest.
- Property.
- Equities.

These can be broken down into various subclasses, for example:

- Cash:
  - Instant access.
  - Fixed-rate deposit.
  - Notice accounts.

- Fixed interest:
  - Corporate bonds.
  - Government bonds.
- Property:
  - Residential.
  - Commercial.
- Equities:
  - Developed markets.
  - Emerging markets.
  - Unlisted.

In addition, each individual asset class can be further subdivided according to its geographical sector, for example Asia-Pacific equities, euro-denominated corporate bonds, global property.

The asset allocation model used by advisers should be approved by the firm's investment committee. It can either be outsourced or developed in-house. If a particular asset allocation tool is used, it should be used consistently by all the advisers within the firm.

A simple model

An example of a simple asset allocation model is shown in Table 21.1.

Table 21.1 – A simple asset allocation model

Asset class	Target portfolio weightings
Cash	10–20%
Fixed interest	20–30%
Equity	30–40%
Property	20–30%

Advisers may use more complex models that incorporate alternative investments, commodities and absolute return funds. While general asset allocation models (as above) will often have a range of values for each asset class, more specific risk-profiled allocations normally have a single target number.

Care must be taken with the categorisation of assets. Some forms of investment, such as infrastructure, timber or water, are sometimes referred to as alternative investments. However, if the asset class is accessed via listed equity (as it will be through most collective investment funds), then evidence shows that returns are very likely to correlate positively with other forms of equity investment. Only if these asset classes are accessed directly – which is normally possible only for institutional investors – can significant diversification benefits be obtained.

A range of asset allocation models is normally created for each risk profile. The risk-rated portfolios need to be aligned with the methods used to classify clients' risk tolerance levels in the fact-finding process (see chapter 19).

Risk-rated portfolios

A set of risk-rated portfolios could comprise:

- Cautious.

- Cautious balanced.

- Balanced.

- Balanced aggressive.

- Aggressive.

The proportions held in each asset class will vary between each model. For example, the equity content would be expected to increase as you move from the cautious model to the aggressive model. Possible allocations for three profiles are shown in Table 21.2.

Table 21.2 – Possible allocations for three risk-rated portfolios

| | *Percentage of total capital allocated to asset class* | | |
	Cautious	Balanced	Aggressive
Cash	20%	10%	5%
Fixed interest	30%	15%	7.5%
Absolute return	20%	15%	7.5%
Property	10%	15%	5%
Equity	20%	45%	75%

Firms may create model portfolios that include specific funds within each asset class, or they may leave the selection of specific funds to the adviser. Where the adviser chooses specific funds, it is desirable for the firm to have in place a review procedure to ensure recommendations are consistent with the policy of the investment committee.

Firms may create separate model portfolios conforming to ethical requirements, or simply create these as and when they are required.

Static and dynamic asset allocation

Many advisers use static asset allocation models. In this case the amounts invested in each asset class remain fixed until the next formal review. The client agreement should specify that no interim advice will be given until such a review takes place.

Over time, the individual investments within each asset class will perform differently, and as a result the proportions of capital held in the asset classes can change and affect the overall risk profile of the portfolio. To take account of this, a dynamic asset allocation model will rebalance the portfolio at regular intervals to ensure the proportion in each asset class, and thus the level of risk, remains broadly the same.

For example, an asset allocation model might say a client should have 35% of their portfolio invested in equities. At the first annual review, suppose the value of the equities has risen to 45% of the total portfolio value because of some exceptional returns on the underlying investment funds. As a result, the portfolio has a greater exposure to the equity asset class and may now be considered a higher-risk profile. To bring the portfolio back into balance with the original model, part of the equity holdings should be sold and the capital reallocated across the other asset classes.

If a dynamic asset allocation method is used, rebalancing should occur at least annually and preferably every six months or even more frequently. The optimal portfolios derived from portfolio theory are rebalanced monthly, but the evidence suggests that the costs of rebalancing outweigh the advantages of rebalancing more than twice a year.

Tactical asset allocation

Some advisers incorporate a tactical element into their asset allocation models. This permits the adviser to vary the proportion of capital in any asset class by a pre-set percentage. Advisers using this system believe it can generate superior returns, but as this is in essence a form of market timing, considerable skill will be required to produce consistently positive returns.

If such methods are used, it falls to the investment committee to set the appropriate rules and to ensure that they are consistently applied across all client portfolios.

Asset class models

Some advisers implement asset allocation using only passive (tracker) funds, on the basis that with their lower costs, such funds provide more predictable returns and cannot, unlike actively managed funds, fall significantly short of their benchmark.

The ease and low cost of transaction through some forms of passive fund such as exchange traded funds (ETFs) have led some advisers to use tactical asset allocation methods with these funds. Academic studies have shown that there is a 'momentum' effect in equity markets, though it remains questionable whether the phenomenon is sufficiently reliable to form the sole basis of an investment strategy.

Structured products

Some advisers use structured products to obtain part of the equity exposure for risk-averse clients. In this case, the SPs will need to be 'marked to market' in any portfolio review for the purposes of establishing the asset allocation. In the case of SPs with an exchange listing, this is straightforward, but with unlisted products, the adviser will need to make their own estimate of current value based on the equity participation rate and other relevant product features.

Fund selection factors

Fund selection was covered in chapter 17. The following are aspects of fund selection relevant to portfolio construction.

Exchange traded funds (ETFs)

ETFs are a low-cost way of accessing asset classes. In recent years many more classes have become available in this form, but with proliferation has come complexity and not all ETFs are simple.

- Fixed interest: the construction of corporate bond ETFs using indices presents problems, since historically such indices have often been based on market capitalisation. In 2008, for example, corporate bond indices had as much as 60% of their constituents in the banking sector, with the result that volatility of the ETFs was greater than that of many individual bonds.

- Sectors: some equity ETFs are intended to capture the performance of specific sectors. Examples include water, infrastructure and nuclear energy. However, the index used may be recently created and selection of constituents based on rules ill designed to cope with extreme events.

- Commodities: Exchange Traded Products based on commodity futures are unsuitable for most private investor portfolios. They suffer from a substantial loss of return in relation to the spot commodity price through contango.

- Leverage: leveraged ETFs are highly speculative and because of daily rebalancing do not deliver cumulative market returns.

- Hedge funds: some ETF providers have created ETFs intended to match the performance of proprietary indices, whose composition is often not disclosed.

Absolute return

In recent years many funds have been launched under an 'absolute return' label. However, there is no common definition of what absolute return means and some such funds have shown volatility almost as great as conventional funds. If advisers wish to use funds that limit potential losses, they need to establish clearly the precise mandate of the fund and assess its actual historical volatility carefully. Advisers need to take care to describe these funds' characteristics accurately to clients.

Investment trusts

Investment trusts and investment companies include many old-established reputable funds. These have often been seen as a useful 'core' ingredient for portfolios given their low costs and continuity of management. Advisers need to consider two factors: gearing and liquidity.

- Gearing: most older funds use gearing ratios of up to 20% to enhance returns; they aim to borrow money when markets are low and repay debt when markets are high. It is important to include the effects of gearing in comparative analysis of these trusts. If gearing is 20%, investors should expect a return about 20% above that of the relevant market index and this is not evidence of superior investment management. A similar consideration applies to global property funds investing in REITs. The average gearing ratio of REITs is about 50%, hence investors in funds investing exclusively in REITs should expect a return 50% higher than from real commercial property and with equivalent volatility.

- Liquidity: trusts valued at over about £250m usually have good liquidity and bid-ask spreads are low. There are many trusts with assets of around £50m where bid-ask spreads can be 5% or more, and in difficult market conditions the quantity of shares that can be sold at the normal bid price may be small.

Funds and asset classes

Where model portfolios are based on allocating proportions of capital to asset classes, advisers need to be aware of the degree to which it is possible to add or subtract risk through fund selection. In most sectors, funds can be selected with risk-return significantly higher or lower than that of the asset class. Table 21.3 includes some examples.

Portfolio construction tools use historic data for volatility, but volatility can change dramatically, as witnessed with natural resources after the mid-1990s. Advisers need to form their own views as to the likely future risk-return relationship between actively managed funds and the benchmark for their asset class.

Table 21.3 – Asset classes and funds

Asset class	Index	Lower risk and return	Higher risk and return
UK equities	FTSE 100	Equity Income	Special situations
Corporate bonds		Investment grade	High Yield
Global equities	MSCI World	Multinational blue-chips	Natural resources, smallcap
Global emerging markets	MSCI EM	Fund benchmarked to MSCI	Non-benchmarked, stockpicking

2 Risk, timescale and liquidity

Advisers should take into account risk, timescale and liquidity when creating an investment portfolio for a client. The level of risk a client is prepared to take has a direct influence on the underlying asset allocation. As shown earlier in this chapter, a client with a very cautious profile will have a greater percentage of their assets invested in cash or fixed-interest products. A more aggressive investor is likely to have significant holdings in equities.

Timescale plays an important role in the selection of a suitable asset allocation model. The performance of each asset class will vary over time. As shown in chapter 5, over the long term, an investment in equities will outperform commercial property, fixed interest and cash in that order.

Liquidity is also a very important consideration. The most liquid or readily accessible investment is cash, while an investment in commercial property would be considered illiquid. The level of access the client needs should be established as part of the fact-finding and objective-setting process.

3 Growth and income

The types of investment used within each asset class will depend on whether the client is in the growth (accumulation) or income (decumulation) phase.

Constraints on asset allocation and investment selection

The accumulation pre-retirement phase of a client's life is associated with the saving and investment of capital, and the repayment of debt. The ultimate aim is to establish an asset base to fund the client's financial objectives. In contrast, the post-retirement decumulation phase is characterised by drawing income and capital from wealth that clients have accumulated during their lives to support them when they stop earning.

During the accumulation phase, it is likely that clients will be open to taking more risk with the investment of their capital, in order to accelerate an increase in the value of the portfolio over time through additional investment returns.

In the decumulation phase, most clients are likely to prefer a more conservative approach to the investment of their accrued wealth, in order to protect the accrued capital from any significant falls in value and to protect the level of income being drawn. As such clients are unlikely to be working, they may not be in a position to invest new capital and replace any losses created through exposure to volatile assets.

Risk factors in income generation

When drawing an income from the portfolio the following issues need to be considered:

- Should the level of income drawn be a fixed monetary amount or a percentage of the value of the portfolio?

- Should investment be aimed at generating income, growth or a balance between the two? How frequently are income payments required?

- What will be the client's tax position on receipt of income?

- What is the likely impact of income withdrawal on the value of the accumulated fund?

The risks associated with drawing income include eroding the value of the portfolio because the level of withdrawal exceeds the cumulative returns being generated. A number of US studies have suggested that over the very long term (20–30 years), a client drawing an annual income of over 4% of a portfolio's value risks running out of money.

Clients may feel more comfortable drawing only the 'natural' income from their investments. However, they need to understand that even this can expose them to risks of eventual capital erosion. This is illustrated in example 21.1.

Example 21.1: Capital erosion

Portfolio A has a high equity content. It is necessary to draw some capital as income each year to meet a 4.5% income target, but the higher long-term returns expected from equities should sustain the capital value despite 1.2% a year being drawn from capital.

The higher natural income from portfolio B is derived mainly from bonds, so both income and capital are at risk from inflation, even though the client is not making capital withdrawals.

In nominal terms, portfolio B may appear less risky, but at a historically low 2% inflation rate, it carries more risk of an erosion of income and capital than portfolio A.

	Portfolio A		Portfolio B	
	Capital allocation	Yield	Capital allocation	Yield
Cash	10%	3%	15%	3%
Fixed interest	10%	5%	35%	6%
Property	10%	4%	10%	4%
Equity	70%	3%	40%	4%
Average yield		3.3%		4.5%

Income buffer

To avoid the effects of volatility on income generation, especially in pension portfolios where income drawdown is being used, many advisers establish a 'buffer' of two or more years' worth of income. This sum is held in the client's cash account and is topped up periodically through sales of investments. The prime benefit is that if there is a large decline in values, the sales of investments needed to supplement the natural income can be suspended until markets recover.

Investment selection for income within the asset classes

Within each asset class, investments paying higher or lower rates of income are available. In some cases this will reflect a greater degree of capital risk, in others it will reflect lesser prospects of capital returns.

For example, in corporate bonds, funds investing in investment grade bonds will typically produce an income 200 to 300 basis points lower than funds investing in high yield bonds. High yield bonds involve greater capital risks and funds investing in them are likely to prove more volatile than investment grade funds.

In the case of equities, higher-yielding equity funds usually invest heavily in large, mature blue-chip businesses such as utilities, tobacco, telecoms and oil. The usual presumption is that future growth prospects from such businesses are poorer than average, so that investors will experience slower rates of growth in their capital.

In designing income-oriented portfolios, advisers should ensure clients do not end up taking too much capital risk (in real terms) as a result of attempting to generate too much income.

Investment selection for growth within the asset classes

Within each asset class, there is a wide range of possible investments. In fact the risk/return range within each asset class is so wide that the lowest-risk equities (say, multinational blue chips) may be considered no more risky than many of the highest-risk bonds (high yield or junk bonds). The choice of specific investments within each asset class therefore also plays an important role in achieving the required balance of income, growth and volatility.

For example, within the equity asset class, and restricting the view to funds investing in the UK, the following fund choices are available:

- Index trackers (FTSE 100 index or FTSE All-Share index).
- Large cap growth funds.
- Equity income funds.
- Alpha funds.
- Special situations and recovery funds.
- Small cap funds.

These types of fund have differing risk/return characteristics, which can be identified by looking at the performance of individual funds and of Investment Management Association sector averages, particularly the ratios discussed in chapter 7.

Accordingly, when constructing a cautious portfolio, advisers would usually use the less volatile funds in this range, namely large cap growth funds, equity income funds and index trackers. For clients with higher risk tolerance, portfolios could allocate a significant portion of capital to alpha funds, small cap funds or special situations funds.

However, even for cautious portfolios, there is a case for including a small allocation to more volatile funds provided there is a probability of higher returns. This would apply, on historical evidence, to small cap funds, which have been more volatile than large cap funds but have also delivered higher annualised returns over the long term.

Similar considerations apply to the selection of funds within the other asset classes. These are summarised in Figure 21.1.

Balancing investment styles

In selecting investments within an asset class, the adviser should normally aim to achieve the highest returns possible without taking on more risk than applies to the asset class as a whole. One factor that can assist in achieving this is investment style.

Investment managers use different styles in managing their funds (see chapter 14). The result is that some managers will achieve better results in certain market conditions. The most obvious example is 'value' and 'growth'; over the three years to January 2000, value underperformed growth substantially, but over the following three years the opposite applied. Hence, a

Figure 21.1 – Risk characteristics of fund types
Risk/return spectrum

◄———— Lower   Higher ————►

EQUITIES

Developed market equity income	Emerging market small-cap
Developed market index trackers	Global specialist sectors (eg financials)
Developed market large cap	Emerging markets large cap
Developed markets mid cap	Alpha
	Developed markets small cap
	Special situations
	Unlisted (private equity)

FIXED INTEREST

Developed market government bond	Emerging market government bond
Index linked	High yield
International bond	
Strategic corporate bond	
Developed market corporate bond	
	Distressed debt

PROPERTY

Developed market physical	Emerging market listed
Global mixed funds (physical + listed)	
Developed market listed	
Regional mixed funds (physical + listed)	
	'Vulture' funds

portfolio with a strong bias to one or other of these styles would have shown much greater volatility over the entire period than one incorporating both styles.

Advisers can, therefore, use style as a selection criterion for funds so that portfolios can contain funds using different styles. Where a fund list is constructed using style as a criterion, advisers need to have a good understanding of the likely pattern of behaviour of the various funds.

Multi-manager funds and fund of funds (FoFs) normally use style criteria in their fund selection process.

Number of holdings in a portfolio

The number of holdings in a portfolio of funds should reflect the following:

- Total capital available.
- Risk profile.
- Costs.
- Potential diversification benefits.

Total capital available

When larger capital sums are available, it is possible to add more asset subclasses to the portfolio. In equities, these could include infrastructure funds, specialist sector funds (water, renewable energy, financials etc), small company funds and individual country funds (Russia, China, India etc). In bonds, they could include index-linked, emerging-market debt, high yield and strategic bond funds with different styles.

Risk profile

The more risk averse the client, the more the adviser needs to use all possible means of reducing volatility. Attention should be paid to the use of style factors, and no one fund should constitute a large proportion of the portfolio. For the most risk-averse, structured products may be used to further limit the risk of capital loss.

Costs

Where transaction charges apply to changes in the portfolio, increasing the number of holdings increases the annual costs the investor will incur. This can be avoided by the use of wraps with low transaction costs.

Diversification benefits

The increase in the correlations of equity subclasses in crisis conditions is now well established. Hence an increase in the use of subclasses will deliver diversification benefits only in normal conditions. In general, the use of subclasses should therefore be aimed at enhancing returns, but this requires active monitoring and may require well-timed entry and exit to be successful.

Optimal portfolio size

A realistic minimum to achieve a balanced portfolio in any risk profile is about ten funds. This permits the use of style differences within asset classes as well as avoiding overexposure to any one manager's performance.

Even with substantial capital, about 30 funds is a realistic maximum. This gives scope for exposure to many subclasses and styles. At least ten of these funds would probably be holdings at the 1−3% level (for example, country funds, gold, commodities, specialist sectors).

Where multi-manager funds and FoFs are used, consideration must be given to style risk. While these products achieve diversification through the number of holdings, the asset allocation model of the FoFs manager and the way it selects individual managers and funds will impart a particular style to its funds. Careful comparison of FoFs returns using the ratios outlined in chapter 7 should be undertaken to identify style bias.

Advisers also need to establish clearly the risk constraints on multi-manager funds or FoFs. If they have established a client's risk profile with a specified allocation to the major asset classes, they need to ensure that the funds they use will not transgress these limits.

The same consideration applies where advisers employ discretionary fund managers (DFMs) for all or part of client portfolios. The adviser's risk profiling methods are unlikely to be identical to those of the DFM, so the adviser needs to ensure that portfolios do not incur a risk greater than that agreed with the client.

4 Review and rebalancing issues

Over time, changes in the value of individual holdings within each asset class will create an imbalance. The planner needs to ensure they have a process in place to review and where necessary rebalance the portfolio.

Review factors

As each asset class behaves differently under particular economic conditions, outperformance in one asset class may coincide with underperformance in another. This creates an imbalance that may, if left unchecked, ultimately affect the overall performance of the portfolio and its ability to meet the client's financial objectives. Factors to consider when establishing a review process include:

- Frequency.
- Tax position.
- Transaction costs.
- Discretionary or advisory.

The frequency of review should be discussed and agreed with the client at the outset. It is possible to review the asset allocation against the target allocation fairly regularly, perhaps even monthly, though six-monthly is probably adequate and appropriate for most clients.

Rebalancing method

The initial report and the ongoing review service may be based on rebalancing, so the client understands at the outset that this will be one of the aims of the regular reviews of their portfolio. While half-yearly or quarterly rebalancing will be the optimal solution for many clients, an annual review may be adequate for those with cautious portfolios where few changes are anticipated.

The actual process of rebalancing entails the sale and purchase of individual investments in order to restore the original proportions in each asset class. But if the portfolio is rebalanced too frequently the costs of buying and selling the investments, and any associated tax implications, may reduce the overall rate of return achieved. The evidence from studies of rebalancing is that little advantage is gained from doing this more frequently than six-monthly. However, where tactical asset allocation methods are employed, more frequent rebalancing will probably be necessary.

On the other hand, if rebalancing takes place too infrequently, this may lead to unintended volatility. For example, a significant increase in the equity weighting may lead to a more aggressive asset allocation overall.

Advisory and discretionary

An additional point to consider is how to structure the rebalancing process to reflect the planner's business model, taking account of advisory or discretionary status.

If the service being offered is advisory, a formal recommendation will need to be prepared for each fund switch. The client's agreement will also be required before any sale and purchase of investments can proceed. This can delay the process to some extent and limit the ability of the planner to automate a rebalancing of the asset allocation. But where wrap accounts provide automated rebalancing facilities, one instruction from the client is usually sufficient to authorise all the necessary transactions.

A firm offering a discretionary investment service can rebalance the portfolio under the mandate agreed with the client, and in line with the target asset allocation, without needing to prepare a formal recommendation and gain separate client approval. This means it is possible to design an automatic rebalancing process that is triggered not on a particular date but by changes in values. For example, it could be designed so that if the proportion in any asset class altered by more than 10% from its target percentage (for example, equities rose from 30% to 34% of the portfolio value) then an automatic rebalancing of the portfolio would be triggered.

Rebalancing in practice

Example 21.2: Rebalancing equity holdings

The following portfolio is arranged for a client based on their risk profile and objectives:

Asset class	Proportion	Value
Equities	30%	£30,000
Fixed interest	25%	£25,000
Property	15%	£15,000
Cash	30%	£30,000
Total	100%	£100,000

Three months later the portfolio looks like this:

Asset class	Proportion	Value
Equities	39%	£45,000
Fixed interest	22%	£25,000
Property	13%	£15,000
Cash	26%	£30,000
Total	100%	£115,000

Due to an increase in the value of the equity holding, the portfolio is now out of balance and the proportion invested in equities is actually 30% greater than the target asset allocation.

The equity holdings should be reduced by 9% and the cash generated from these sales should be used to add to holdings within the remaining asset classes in order to return to the proportions shown on the original target allocation.

When an adviser is designing an automatic rebalancing system, a tolerance could be set at 10–15%, for example. Once the holding in any particular asset class exceeds its target by this amount, the portfolio would be automatically rebalanced.

Some firms may charge separately for each purchase and sale transaction when rebalancing the portfolio. Others may see this process as part of the ongoing investment management service, paid for out of an annual management fee.

Some platform and wrap providers offer a facility to automatically rebalance the client's portfolio. The client signs an agreement at the outset effectively giving the provider permission to switch funds and restore the portfolio to the original asset allocation at an agreed frequency.

An important point for anyone seeking to implement regular rebalancing is the cost of switching. If charges are applied to each switch and many switches are carried out each year, this will of course affect the overall return the client achieves. Accordingly, where advisers plan to offer rebalancing services, they should select platform and wrap providers with the lowest possible transaction charges.

Portfolio reviews

Where the adviser is reviewing not just the portfolio but the client's financial affairs in general, it may be useful to send them a brief questionnaire before preparing the review. This way any issues of concern or changes in circumstances can be addressed along with the valuation and portfolio review.

Apart from changes in client circumstances, the adviser also needs to consider if any new products or services would suit the client's needs better than the ones they have. Often, however, costs and tax factors will mean changes would incur costs greater than any potential benefits.

Issues for review

Apart from rebalancing, advisers need to ensure that in reviewing portfolios, they cover the following issues:

- Has the portfolio performed particularly well or badly compared with its benchmark?
- Has any fund performed particularly well or badly?
- Should any funds be recommended for sale or purchase?
- Should any change in the asset allocation be proposed?
- Has the expected level of income been achieved?

In each case, the adviser should provide a clear explanation. Performance may be illustrated by tables showing actual returns, and/or by graphs.

More detailed coverage of investment reviews is in chapter 19.

Generating reports

Some wraps and platforms include tools that enable advisers to generate automated reports for clients. While these may include many useful features, especially graphical representations of performance, advisers need to ensure that the issues likely to be of real concern to the client are addressed.

For this reason advisers should always review the results themselves before generating automated reports, and should add personalised elements as appropriate.

Summary

- Adviser firms need to establish procedures for applying asset allocation models to generate investment recommendations.

- Investment recommendations should be consistent for all clients with similar risk profiles.

- Advisers should take account of clients' risk profiles both in selecting appropriate asset allocation models and recommending investments within asset classes.

- Where clients have specific requirements for income, risks to income should be carefully evaluated independently of risks to capital.

- Clients should have a clear understanding of the process involved in reviewing their investments and advisers' investment reports should cover absolute and relative performance.

Chapter 22
Allocating capital to tax wrappers

After they have decided on an appropriate asset allocation, advisers need to ensure that they recommend the most advantageous deployment of capital across tax wrappers. This is often not a matter of using one but several wrappers and then determining which asset classes should be held in which wrappers.

The main tax wrappers to consider are:

- Individual Savings Accounts (ISAs).

- Pensions.

- Collectives – eg OEICs and unit trusts.

- UK bonds and qualifying policies.

- Offshore bonds.

1 The main characteristics of tax wrappers

Tax wrappers can have four main tax characteristics which can make them more or less attractive to different taxpayers. Different tax wrappers will be attractive to different investors, depending on the combination of characteristics.

Tax position of the input

The investment input may qualify for some kind of tax relief. This can be regarded as either providing an immediate uplift in the value of the investment or it can be considered a reduction in the cost.

Pensions normally qualify for tax relief at the client's marginal tax rate, although the relief is restricted for people with high incomes. Those paying tax at 40% or 50% get the most benefit from pension contributions, especially if they get effective NIC relief as well because their employers make the contributions. Basic rate taxpayers see less benefit, since broadly speaking the income tax paid on income withdrawals balances out the benefit of tax relief on contributions.

Tax on the fund

The invested funds may be taxed at a lower rate than would apply to the income and gains of the investor personally or the funds may be free of tax to a greater or lesser extent. Pension funds, ISAs and offshore bonds are all subject to more or less the same UK tax regime. UK life policies are subject to some tax.

Higher rate taxpayers get more benefit from the differential between the tax rate they pay on their personal income and gains and the tax rate paid on income and gains that accrue within a pension fund or ISA.

The biggest differential between personal and wrapper rates generally arises with respect to interest on deposits and securities. A 40% taxpayer pays 40% tax on personal interest but 0% on interest rolling up in an ISA, pension fund or offshore bond. A basic rate taxpayer will save 20% on the income. In contrast, dividends from equities are not subject to further tax in any of the tax wrappers or in the hands of a basic rate tax payer; so they offer no advantage for a basic rate taxpaying individual with respect to such income. For a 40% taxpayer, the advantage is the saving of just 25% of the dividend.

The capital gains tax advantage offered by most tax wrappers is much less valuable for basic rate taxpayers. Most taxpayers see no benefit, because very few investors pay CGT; the annual exempt amount covers most disposals and CGT is not payable on death.

The lower rate of CGT is currently 18%, and this is very similar to the rate UK life funds pay on their capital gains. Since life funds have no personal allowance, a basic rate taxpayer not making use of their annual exemption is better off in relation to CGT holding collective investments rather than life funds.

The higher rate of CGT is 28%, which is paid not only by higher rate taxpayers but also by basic rate taxpayers whose gain, when added to their taxable income, takes the total above the higher rate income tax threshold. All higher rate taxpayers benefit from a saving of 28% tax on gains on investments within pension funds and ISAs as compared with investments held directly (this applies to all gains in excess of the annual exemption). The benefit with UK life funds may be as high as 10% and with offshore life funds as high as 28%, provided encashments are made at a time when the holder has no personal UK tax liability, but it will usually be lower than this.

Tax on the output

The output from a wrapper could be partly or wholly taxable, or it could be tax free.

The proceeds of a registered pension scheme are partly taxable and partly tax free. The PCLS or tax free lump sum comprising up to 25% of the fund at crystallisation is tax free, but the remainder of the fund is taxable as earned income, although free of NICs. The amount that is tax free therefore grows in line with the overall fund. The impact of tax on the pension will depend on the individual's total income in retirement, including income from the pension scheme.

All proceeds from an ISA are tax-free in the hands of the investor.

With most other wrappers, only the return of the original capital is tax-free and the rest is more or less taxable. The gain on UK and offshore bonds is subject to income tax by being added to the investor's other income and is then taxed at investor's top rate of tax, although this may be reduced by the effects of top-slicing relief.

Collectives such as OEICs and unit trusts normally generate dividends that are taxable on the investor as they arise in the same way as other income. But an individual's capital gains are only taxable when the investment is disposed of. Collectives do not benefit from a particular capital gains tax advantage on disposal, although realised gains on switching investments within the funds are not taxed. But capital gains are generally taxed more advantageously than income because of the annual exemption and the freedom from CGT on death.

Bonds have a tax advantage over collectives if they are the subject of a gift. A gift of a collective to an individual or into trust normally triggers a CGT charge but a similar gift of a bond does not trigger a chargeable event.

The combination of tax characteristics

It is important to look at the tax totality of the tax characteristics of each type of wrapper in the round and in relation to the client's own personal tax position. Some tax wrappers will be attractive for some clients, but not for others.

2 Determining wrapper use

Achieving the right mix of investments across the various tax wrappers is a crucial part of the investment process. The approach taken by the financial planner will depend on a number of factors including:

- The purpose of the investment.
- The client's risk profile.
- The length of time they are prepared to invest for.
- The client's need for access.
- Their current and future tax status.
- The returns likely to be generated by the investments.

Purpose of the investment

Pensions are mainly designed to produce retirement income and unless this forms part of the client's objectives they will not be an appropriate wrapper.

If the client requires access to a large portion of a capital at a specific future date (say, to buy a property or a business or to pay off a loan), then the potential tax liabilities on encashment need to be considered. This may make an investment bond unsuitable for someone who is likely to be a higher rate taxpayer when encashment occurs.

Risk profile

The client's risk tolerance plays a large part in determining the appropriate asset allocation. But it may also influence the choice of wrappers. For example, a low risk investor is unlikely to want to invest in most VCTs and EISs.

Likewise, investments made on the basis of tax savings implicitly assume that current tax rules or exemptions will apply. The more risk averse the client, the less reliance should be placed on this assumption.

Timescale

Pension scheme investments are 'for life' given the limited access to capital (and no access at all before age 55 except on death or serious ill-health).

Where a client needs short-term access to funds, it may not be appropriate to use any tax wrapper if the wrapper involves additional costs, complexity or illiquidity. It is probably not worth investing in most life assurance based wrappers for less than about three years because of the costs and potential tax complications.

Access requirements

It is vital to be clear about these, because a client's change of mind can have damaging tax consequences, especially for higher rate taxpayers withdrawing capital from investment bonds. The possible effects of changes in circumstances should also be investigated with 'what if' scenarios before committing capital for which the client may need access.

Pensions are highly illiquid both before and even after retirement. Maximum investment plans generate returns that are free of personal tax after seven and half years, but the possible higher rate tax charge and cost structure makes them rather illiquid at any earlier date. VCT and EIS investments are likely to trigger tax charges on early encashment and are generally very illiquid because of the underlying investments.

Most ISAs are, strictly speaking, as liquid as the underlying collectives or other investments, but clients may be understandably reluctant to cash their ISAs because of the loss of long term tax benefits.

Current and future tax status

Tax wrappers are of most value to those investors who can take advantage of the tax reliefs and low tax rates on the funds at times when they are paying high rates of tax and can then draw cash from the investments when they pay tax at low rates.

Future tax status is hypothetical on two grounds: the client's projection of their likely future position and the adviser's projection of the likely tax rules applying at that time are both probabilities rather than facts. The more distant in time the projections the less reliance can be placed on them. Hence future tax status should play a smaller part in determining allocation to wrappers than current tax status.

Clients are often motivated by potential tax savings, but when looking more than a few years ahead, such savings must be described as potential and the adviser should ensure the client understands the caveats that apply.

Investment returns

Investment returns (income and gains) bear tax at different rates within different wrappers. Hence which wrapper is most advantageous will depend on the type of investments to be held within it as well as the tax position of the investor.

Collectives are generally most advantageous for growth investments because they are in the capital gains tax regime. Bonds, pensions and ISAs all provide the biggest relative returns from high income investments and in particular cash and fixed interest and some property.

3 Wraps and tax wrappers

Most investment advisers now routinely recommend the use of a wrap account to hold all the client's investments, to simplify the client's affairs and make it possible for the client to access one unified valuation. Wraps have no tax characteristics; they are simply administrative tools.

Wrap accounts

A wrap account provides the client or financial planner with the ability to manage all of their investments through a single administrative platform. This includes providing access to pensions, ISAs, and investment bonds (offshore and onshore) through a single integrated arrangement.

An example of the structure of a wrap account is shown in Figure 22.1.

The wrap account is a useful option for managing a client's portfolio, and facilitates improved administration and reporting.

However, holding investments through a wrap will involve additional costs. Some wraps are wholly transparent in their charging structures and a charge of perhaps 30bps to 50bps is made directly to the client. But the wrap should be able to negotiate lower annual management charges from many of the fund managers.

Other wraps and fund supermarkets are effectively subsidised by the funds and there is little or no charge made to the client. However, the charges made by the funds are generally higher. The trend is to switch to the more transparent business model and this has been encouraged by the FSA's retail distribution review.

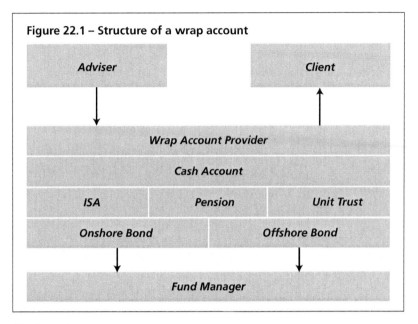

Figure 22.1 – Structure of a wrap account

Choice of tax wrappers

In addition to the client holding investments directly, the financial planner is able to use the following tax wrappers to hold a client's investments. Each has different tax consequences, which need to be understood by both the financial planner and the client.

- Direct holdings.

- ISAs.

- Pensions.

- Onshore investment bonds.

- Offshore investment bonds.

Table 22.1 lists the advantages and disadvantages for each of the main tax wrappers as well as for direct holdings.

Table 22.1. – Advantages and disadvantages of main tax wrappers

Wrapper	Advantages	Disadvantages
Direct holdings	Simplicity	Possible higher rate of income tax on any income
	Availability of personal CGT allowance	Entry of income and gains/losses on tax return

Table 22.1. (cont.) – Advantages and disadvantages of main tax wrappers

Wrapper	Advantages	Disadvantages
		CGT on profits in excess of annual allowance
ISA	Tax-free growth	No tax relief on initial investment
	Tax-free income from deposits and fixed interest	No joint holdings – account must be in individual name
	No higher rate income tax on equity dividends	No income tax benefit on equity dividends for basic rate taxpayers
	Accessible in short term	Withdrawals cannot be replaced in the same tax year
	Flexible	Restricted to holding cash of £5,100
	Can hold cash and/or stocks and shares, funds	Investment limited to £10,200 per tax year
	Wide choice of funds using fund supermarket	
Pension	Tax-free growth and income until benefits are drawn	No access until age 55
	Tax relief on contributions	Income in retirement is taxable
	Tax-free lump sum on retirement	Annuity must be secured by age 75
	Lump sum contributions possible from capital	Restrictions on contributions and tax relief for high earners
	Annuities provide guaranteed income for life	Inflexibility of fixed payments
	Flexible income options with unsecured pension	Complexity and risk of capital loss or income reduction
Onshore and Offshore Investment Bonds	5% of capital can be withdrawn each policy year with tax deferred	Gains chargeable to income tax rather than CGT
	Life assurance cover may protect initial capital on death	Withdrawals in excess of the 5% limit may be subject to income tax
	Free fund switches during the year	May be penalties if all capital is withdrawn in early years
	Can be easily placed into trust	Restrictions on access to trust assets
	Policy segments can be assigned to other family members e.g. children	Restricted list of available funds
	Accessible in short term	Partial surrenders can create complex tax position

Table 22.1. (cont.) – Advantages and disadvantages of main tax wrappers

Wrapper	Advantages	Disadvantages
	Ability to vary income	Danger of capital erosion if a high level of income is withdrawn
Offshore Investment Bonds	Gross roll-up of some types of investment income	Possible withholding tax on some investments
	No need to change investments if owner changes domicile	Higher costs

4 Individual Savings Accounts (ISAs)

ISAs allow clients to shelter up to £10,200 in tax each year (from April 2010), with up to £5,100 in cash or all £10,200 in stocks and shares. ISAs are available through banks, building societies, fund management groups and fund platform providers.

Capital held within ISAs is usually accessible in a matter of days, and without penalty, unless specific conditions apply. Income may be paid out to the client or accumulated within the account, and regular withdrawals of capital can be arranged. Investments can be made as one-off lump sums or by more frequent regular payments (monthly, quarterly etc). ISAs provide the client with the opportunity to invest across a wide range of asset classes with few restrictions, the major exclusion being shares listed on AIM.

The key feature of the ISA is that once capital is invested the tax exemption is permanent, ie for life, which is a unique feature of this vehicle. It is therefore preferable to withdraw capital from direct holdings or investment bonds rather than from an ISA, which is an ideal medium for holding income-generating investments in retirement.

As discussed below, for basic rate taxpayers accumulation of capital in ISAs can be more advantageous than pensions when returns are viewed over the life of the investment.

Table 22.2 – Tax within ISAs

Tax on income from				Tax on gains
Cash	Fixed interest	Property	Shares	
0%	0%	0%	20% (at source)	0%

Advisers today will normally use an ISA linked to a fund supermarket or wrap account that gives access to thousands of funds, enabling any investment objective and asset allocation to be implemented with ease.

5 Pensions

Funds held in pensions grow free of income and capital gains tax, although (as with ISAs) dividend tax credits cannot be reclaimed. Contributions paid into pensions receive a tax credit of up to 50%.

The net returns from pension investments must be compared with those from direct or ISA investments over the entire life of the investment. This is because pensions attract initial tax relief but pension income bears income tax, whereas ISA investments attract no tax relief but generate tax-free income.

In very broad terms, this tax difference between pensions and ISAs results in near-equivalence of net returns for basic rate taxpayers, as shown in the table. The compounding effect of returns means that the pension may deliver a slightly higher overall return (about 6% more). This is a modest reward for the restrictions placed on pension plans.

Table 22.3 – Lifetime returns from ISA and pension investment for a basic rate taxpayer

	ISA	Pension
Net contribution	£800	£800
Tax relief (at 20%)	NIL	£200
Gross investment	£800	£1000
Gross income yield	5%	5%
Gross income	£40	£50
Income tax (20%)	NIL	£10
Net income	£40	£40

Similar considerations apply where the investor is a higher rate taxpayer (at 40%) throughout.

Table 22.4 – Lifetime returns from ISA and pension investment for a higher rate taxpayer

	ISA	Pension
Net contribution	£800	£800
Tax relief (at 20%)	NIL	£533
Gross investment	£800	£1333
Gross income yield	5%	5%
Gross income	£40	£66.70
Income tax (20%)	NIL	£26.70
Net income	£40	£40

As can be seen, whether the individual earns a higher return from a pension investment depends on whether they pay a lower rate of income tax in retirement. An investor who makes contributions to a pension plan while a higher rate taxpayer but pays only basic rate tax on their pension income will secure a high net rate of return on their money. The premium over the ISA return will depend on the term of the investment due to the compounding effect. In the above example, the premium would be 33.4% (on a net income of £53.36) and this would approximately represent the return premium over a one-year term. Since the premium generated by tax relief is greatest over the short term, lump sum pension contributions in the years near to retirement are likely to generate the highest net returns.

From April 2011 individuals earning over £150,000 will have pension tax relief restricted, and for those earning over £180,000 relief will be limited to 20% (between the two income figures a taper will apply). From April 2009, individuals earning over £130,000 have been subject to limits on the maximum contributions they may make to pension schemes.

Funds held in pensions are not accessible until the client reaches age 55 (from April 2010). As a result, the approach taken with asset allocation will vary depending on the individual circumstances of the client. In the years leading up to retirement it is likely that the focus will be on growth, with few restrictions on asset class selection and liquidity.

In the years immediately preceding retirement, the emphasis is likely to shift to capital preservation with a reduction in the percentage of capital held in volatile assets. Greater liquidity will also be necessary as the funds are likely to be required in the near future to provide an income. Once in retirement, investment in asset classes that generate income with reduced volatility and greater overall liquidity should be considered such as fixed interest.

Table 22.5 – Tax within pension funds

Tax on income from				Tax on gains
Cash	Fixed interest	Property	Shares	
0%	0%	0%	20% (at source)	0%

Some group pension funds and personal pension schemes offer access to only a limited range of funds, while others offer a wide range of externally managed funds, making the construction of appropriate portfolios easier.

6 Onshore investment bonds

The tax position for the individual investor depends on their personal circumstances and the structure of the actual investment itself.

Investment bonds are generally offered by insurance companies and provide access to the insurer's own range of funds. In recent years, this has been extended to include funds offered by external fund management groups. A number of wrap platform providers also now have their own investment bond, so that often several hundred funds are available. As a result, there are very few restrictions on the adviser's ability to achieve the target asset allocation. Access is possible within similar timescales to ISAs, albeit subject to the dealing requirements of the underlying fund.

Gains on encashment or withdrawal are chargeable to income tax (at higher rate less basic rate) rather than capital gains tax. This is an important consideration when taking into account the client's need to access capital held within the wrapper in the future. Investment bonds provide the client with the ability to take regular withdrawals of capital each year without a current tax liability. This can be useful in later years when supplementing income in retirement.

To qualify for tax deferral, withdrawals are capped at 5% of the original investment each year and are cumulative. Any withdrawals in excess of 5% are added to the client's income in the year that they are taken and may be subject to a tax charge if the addition of this income takes them into a higher tax bracket. Onshore investment bonds are deemed to have satisfied basic rate tax liabilities as a result of the corporation tax paid on gains generated in the underlying life insurance funds.

Table 22.6 – Tax within onshore investment bonds

Tax on income from				Tax on gains
Cash	Fixed interest	Property	Shares	
20%	20%	20%	20% (at source)	20%*

* After allowance for indexation

UK life assurance funds are liable to tax at 20% on capital gains, but may apply indexation (using the RPI) of cost prices to reduce the chargeable gain. CGT rates paid by UK life offices appear to be about 18%, broadly similar to the lower rate of 18% payable by basic rate taxpayers. Where the individual does not already use their annual CGT allowance, holding investments via an investment bond rather than direct is in principle less efficient. However, this assumes that it is possible to utilise the annual CGT allowance through disposals every year, which may be unrealistic.

On encashment of an onshore investment bond, a basic rate taxpayer incurs no further tax liability. A higher rate taxpayer may be liable to tax at a rate equal to the difference between their marginal rate and the basic rate of 20%. Higher rate taxpayers will therefore incur a tax charge of 20% or 30% as compared with their maximum rate of CGT of 28%.

On substantial investments, advisers can consider a number of ways of reducing a potential higher rate tax bill on encashment or death, such as assignment.

7 Offshore investment bonds

Offshore investment bonds are subject to similar tax rules as onshore bonds with two important exceptions. No tax is levied within the bond, and on encashment a UK resident is liable to their marginal personal rate of income tax on accumulated gains.

As with onshore bonds, the gross roll-up of income is a potential benefit, but the tax position on capital gains may be disadvantageous relative to direct ownership depending on the investor's income tax position.

On substantial investments, advisers can consider a number of ways of reducing a potential higher rate tax bill on encashment or death, such as assignment.

Table 22.7 – Tax within offshore investment bonds

Tax on income from				Tax on gains
Cash	Fixed interest	Property	Shares	
0%	0%	0%*	20% +	0%

* Withholding taxes may apply.
+ For UK shares; different rates of withholding tax apply in other jurisdictions.

8 Allocation in practice

The following paragraphs seek to address the practical allocation across tax wrappers.

Income or capital growth

In addition to the asset allocation model, the client's requirements in terms of income or capital growth are important considerations when selecting wrappers. Obviously, any income requirements should be met from those wrappers that are accessible and offer the most advantageous tax position, normally ISAs and investment bonds. Pensions are unlikely to be suitable unless the client is at least 55 years old.

Cash

Although ISAs offer a tax-efficient home for cash, using such an account to hold short-term access funds would not be the most efficient use of the wrapper. This is because the allowance is available to be used once in each tax year. Any withdrawals taken from ISA funds cannot be replaced in the same tax year.

An instant access bank account may the most appropriate option in this example. The account could be opened in the name of the spouse with the lower tax position or in joint names. Single clients who are higher rate tax payers would have to accept the additional tax liability from any interest being paid on such accounts. However, the level of interest earned on instant access accounts is usually small, leaving a negligible additional liability for the higher rate taxpayer.

Also, most clients' short term access requirements tend to relate to regular expenditure on items such as household, travel costs, utility bills etc. As the funds tend to be withdrawn and replaced regularly, the interest and tax position usually has little bearing on the client's overall financial position.

In practice short term cash is usually excluded from the overall asset allocation as the amounts involved tend to be small.

Certain pension arrangements (Self Invested Personal Pensions or SIPPS) are required to hold a separate bank account with a cash balance to cover the ongoing costs associated with managing the SIPP including administration costs and dealing, management and advisory fees.

Cash holdings in ISAs are restricted to £5,100 per tax year and therefore any balancing allocation will need to be placed elsewhere.

Table 22.8 – Tax on deposit interest

Direct	ISA	Pension	Onshore Bond	Offshore Bond
0%, 20%, 40% or 50%*	0%	0%*	20% +	0% $

Dependent on personal tax position.
+ Possible extra tax on encashment for higher rate taxpayer.
$ Possible 20% tax on encashment for basic rate taxpayer, 40%/50% for higher rate taxpayers.

Fixed interest

Fixed interest assets generate income in the form of a regular interest payment or coupon, which can be paid out to the investor or reinvested to generate growth of the capital. If the client has a need for a certain level of regular income and the adviser determines that this can be best achieved by investing in fixed interest assets, then ISAs will be most advantageous for anyone under the age of 55.

Overall ISAs present the best option because there is no tax at source on the income, no tax liability on withdrawal and there are no restrictions on withdrawals of capital or of income. Interest income within investment bonds bears tax at 20%, and income payments or withdrawals from investment bonds that exceed 5% of the original capital investment in each policy year may create a higher rate income tax liability for the investor. If the client is aged 55 or over and using income drawdown for their pension arrangements, then fixed interest assets may be suitable.

Table 22.9 – Tax on fixed interest income

Direct	ISA	Pension	Onshore Bond	Offshore Bond
0%, 20%, 40%, 50%*	0%	0%*	20% +	0% $

* Dependent on personal tax position.
+ Possible extra tax on encashment for higher rate taxpayer.
$ Possible 20% tax on encashment for basic rate taxpayer, 40%/50% for higher rate taxpayers.

Absolute return

Absolute return funds usually seek to deliver a specified percentage return in excess of a particular benchmark, typically linked to LIBOR. They aim to deliver positive returns in any market and may be used to protect against any significant falls in the market. In many cases, the larger element of returns is capital gains. They are appropriate across all tax wrappers. The tax position will depend on the precise nature of the returns.

Property

Investing into direct commercial property through pensions needs to be carefully considered. Attempting to hold a relatively illiquid asset class within a wrapper that will eventually be used to provide an income in retirement is not an appropriate strategy for most individuals.

Clients who own a business and have a degree of control over how the property is eventually disposed of, or are prepared to continue owning the property while drawing an income from the remainder of their liquid funds, may be comfortable with such ownership, though advisers will need to explain the possible problems on the client's death if residual benefits are to form a significant part of any beneficiary's income.

Direct commercial property investment can only be achieved through SIPPs and SSASs, otherwise investors will need to gain the necessary exposure through collective investments.

Rental income from property is tax-exempt within ISAs and pension funds but bears tax at 20% in life funds. Gains are tax-exempt within ISAs and pension funds but are taxable within life funds at about 20%. Investment bonds are the least advantageous wrapper for property.

Table 22.10 – Tax on income and gains from property

	Direct	ISA	Pension	Onshore Bond	Offshore Bond
Tax on income	0%, 20%, 40%, 50% *	0%	0% *	20% +	0% $
Tax on gains	18%, 28% **	**0%**	**0%**	20% +&	0% $

* Dependent on personal tax position.
** Dependant on personal tax position and after use of annual allowance.
+ Possible extra tax on encashment for higher rate taxpayer.
& After allowance for indexation.
$ Possible 20% tax on encashment for basic rate taxpayer, 40%/50% for higher rate taxpayers.

Equity

Equity gains are tax-exempt within ISA and pension funds but taxable at about 20% in life funds. Dividends incur no extra tax in pensions or ISAs but may bear extra tax when a higher rate taxpayer encashes an investment bond.

Equities are best held in ISAs or pensions, especially if dividend income is required and being paid to a higher-rate taxpaying client. Similar comments apply regarding income drawdown from pensions.

Table 22.11 – Tax on income and gains from equities

	Direct	ISA	Pension	Onshore Bond	Offshore Bond
Tax on income	20%, 32.5%, 42.5% *	0%	20%	20% +&	20% +$
Tax on gains	18%, 28% **	0%	0%	20% ++$	0% $

* Dependent on personal tax position.
** Dependent on personal tax position and after use of annual allowance.
+ Deducted at source from UK dividends
& Possible extra tax on encashment for higher rate taxpayer.
$ Possible 20% tax on encashment for basic rate taxpayer, 40%/50% for higher rate taxpayers.
++ After allowance for indexation

General principles

Taking all the above into account, the following general principles apply to the selection of appropriate tax wrappers:

ISAs

The ISA is the simplest, most flexible and long-lasting tax shelter and for the vast majority of clients, converting income or capital from other sources into an ISA should form part of a long-term investment strategy.

The ISA is the most advantageous vehicle for income withdrawal or decumulation, especially for higher-yielding investments.

The benefits from the freedom of tax on the fund can be the most powerful tax advantage for a pension scheme but only if there is a lot of growth and reinvested income within the fund, usually after many years of holding and the advantages are greater with cash and fixed interest than with equities.

ISAs are attractive for almost any taxpayer. Even if the tax benefit is small because the investor is a non-CGT paying basic rate tax payer, the convenience of not having to report the income and gains to HMRC is in itself useful and there are generally no extra charges associated with an ISA investment.

Pensions

The merits of pension investments depend to a large extent on the current and future tax position; only where a lower future personal tax rate can be predicted with some confidence can superior lifetime returns reasonably be expected.

Given the restrictions on pension funds, advisers should where possible avoid too high a proportion of total capital being deployed in this form.

Life assurance bonds

The tax efficiency of life assurance bonds for UK investors as compared to collectives depends on their effectiveness as tax shelters. In effect they postpone the payment of tax on growth and income. The tax sheltering effect will be worthwhile if the tax rate on the bond during the holding period and then on encashment is lower than the investor's during the holding period.

For example, if the investor is a higher rate taxpayer while holding the bond and then pays basic rate tax on the profit, the tax shelter has been successful. It follows that there is little or no advantage for basic rate taxpayers in holding bonds, especially if there is a danger that they might turn out to be higher rate taxpayers on the encashment.

For basic rate taxpayers and clients whose gains are always likely to remain within the annual exemption, growth oriented investments are generally better held in collectives where gains are subject to capital gains tax rather than income tax. The taxation of gains derived from bonds is marginally disadvantageous to 40% taxpayers and marginally advantageous to 50% taxpayers.

Income oriented funds are typically better held within bonds if the investor is likely to be a higher rate tax payer during the period of ownership when the tax rate in the fund is likely to be lower than the investor's personal rate of tax on income.

Bonds may be useful as tax wrappers for trustee investments because trusts are generally higher rate taxpayers, beneficiaries are often basic rate taxpayers and trustees can make transfers of policy segments to them without triggering a tax charge on the transfer.

Offshore bonds

Offshore bonds are generally less attractive for UK taxpayers, unless they can arrange their income such that they do not pay higher rate tax on the profits of the bond. The more or less nil tax position on the offshore bond fund generates a higher capital value, but the net return from a UK bond will be less on a like-for-like basis than the post tax proceeds from a UK bond. This is because the UK bond gives credit on encashment for the tax deducted from the fund and the gain is not grossed up, so that the effective rate of tax for a 40% taxpayer is nearer 36%. Offshore bonds are useful for people who are likely to be non-taxpayers on encashment, such as non residents and possibly infants, and also for trusts.

Qualifying endowment policies

Qualifying endowment policies are UK life policies where the proceeds are free of personal tax after 10 years of regular investment. In theory therefore they are attractive for higher rate taxpayers, especially those who pay capital gains tax on a regular basis. The drawbacks are the need to make regular investments over the 10 year period, the tax cost of early encashment (although it is often possible to have tax free access within seven and a half years of starting the plan) and the relatively high charges that have been levied on these plans in the past.

Collectives are likely to be the tax wrappers of choice for most investors who want to hold equities because gains fall within the relatively advantageous capital gains tax regime. Offshore funds have some small tax advantages and ETFs generally escape the 0.5% stamp duty that has to be paid on the purchase of most other funds.

Offshore bonds do have 'roll-up' tax advantages as regards income, but since the tax on gains is disadvantageous to UK residents, these bonds should be used with care and generally for income-generating investments.

Since it is now simple and easy to hold collectives directly through fund supermarkets and wraps, the 'convenience' arguments for investment bonds are weak and bonds should generally be used only for specific tax advantages.

Example 22.1: Wrapper allocation

A client has the following portfolio and holds each of the underlying investments in cash.

• Individual Savings Accounts	£100,000
• Personal Pension	£100,000
• Onshore Investment Bond	£100,000

He has asked for an adviser's assistance in managing the portfolio in line with his agreed risk profile, financial objectives and timescales. He is currently single, 35 years old, a basic rate taxpayer and has no immediate income requirements. He is seeking capital growth in the medium to long term.

The adviser has already identified that he is a balanced investor and has agreed to use the following asset allocation model.

Asset allocation model

Cash	10%	£30,000
Fixed interest	15%	£45,000
Absolute return	15%	£45,000
Property	15%	£45,000
Equity	45%	£135,000
Total	100%	£300,000

Taking these circumstances into account the adviser uses the following allocation across all the available tax wrappers, assuming that collective funds will be used for all these investments. Note that access requirements might cause the adviser to adjust these allocations, which are driven primarily by tax factors.

Asset allocation across wrappers

Asset class	Total allocation		ISA	Pension	Onshore Investment Bond
Cash	10%	£30,000	£0	£0	£30,000
Fixed interest	15%	£45,000	£0	£45,000	£0
Absolute return	15%	£45,000	£15,000	£0	£30,000
Property	15%	£45,000	£25,000	£20,000	£0
Equity	45%	£135,000	£60,000	£35,000	£40,000
Total	**100%**	**£300,000**	**£100,000**	**£100,000**	**£100,000**

Tax wrappers for couples

Some married couples prefer to keep their investments in joint names, but in many circumstances holding investments in separate names is more advantageous. This is especially the case when one of the couple pays higher rate tax and the other pays basic rate tax or is a non-taxpayer. In this case, holding any income-generating investments in the name of the basic rate or non-taxpaying partner will avoid a 20%, 40% or 50% tax liability on the interest. While a jointly-owned investment bond might be suitable for a couple where one was a higher rate taxpayer and the other paid basic rate tax, there could be a risk of a higher rate tax charge on encashment, while a bond owned solely by a basic rate taxpayer would avoid this risk.

Where a couple wish to keep their investments separate and have different risk profiles and tax rates, this can result in less than optimal tax efficiency. While the adviser must respect the wishes of the clients, any potential increase in tax liabilities should be brought to their attention.

While there are strategies that can help higher rate taxpayers avoid a tax charge on encashment of an investment bond, the general principle in investment planning should be to use the wrappers that are at least risk of any future changes in tax rules. And as a general rule, keeping clients' affairs as simple as possible is always preferable to making them more complicated.

Summary

- For most clients it will be advantageous to hold some capital within one or more of the ISA, pension and investment bond tax wrappers.

- Advisers should always consider a set of client-specific factors in determining the appropriate allocation of capital to tax wrappers.

- Each tax wrapper has positive and negative features and which is advantageous will depend not only on the client's circumstances and tax position but also on their risk profile and timescale.

- Wrap accounts can simplify the administration of investments and make it easier for clients to understand their portfolios as well as giving them access to current valuations.

- Most clients will hold capital in two or more wrappers and advisers should aim to recommend the most efficient allocation of capital to the different types of investment within each wrapper.

Index